RESPONDING

Ginn Interrelated Sequences in Literature

BASIC SEQUENCE | SIX

WALLACE W. DOUGLAS

with

ALBERT L. LAVIN

Editorial Direction

ALAN C. PURVES

Advisers

ROBERT F. HOGAN

RICHARD OHMANN

WILLIAM E. STAFFORD

GINN AND COMPANY

A XEROX COMPANY

Home Office: Lexington, Massachusetts 02173

~~0-663-23403-4~~

0-663-25052-8

CONTENTS

FOREWORD

Authors, we suspect, have as much aversion to writing "Forewords" as students have to reading them. Yet, "Forewords" do give authors a chance to level with students. So, if you will bear with us briefly, we'll just muse a bit.

This book began as a very disordered collection of miscellaneous writings. As we tried to choose selections and arrange them, we found that two forces were at work. The first, of course, was our own taste. There is nothing in this book that represents an official literary tradition, nothing that illustrates some fact about literary history or literary style or literary convention. All the selections are those that at one time or another interested us and that we have read with some degree of liking. And we hope that you, too, will find them interesting and that you'll like them—most of them, anyway.

The second force at work in our development of the book was our reaction—our response—to the selections. As we began to get the feel of the book, we found selections arranging themselves not only into pairings and sequences of threes and fours but also into larger groups (which we've called "clusters"). There was a good deal of shifting around among these groups, depending upon our reactions to the various selections. The order that you find here is only one of the many that we tried out, but this order seemed to make the most sense to us at the time the book went to press.

You may be interested in the texture, or the personality, of the book. Dialogs follow many of the selections. We think they contribute to the texture of the book because they suggest some responses that you may want to react to. In doing so, they extend the effect of the selections. But they are not to be construed as pathways to wisdom and knowledge, and we certainly don't want them to block or restrict your own personal responses. In other words, just as we changed our responses from time to time, so will you—we hope. Literature exists principally in *that* encounter—in the transaction between readers and what is written or said or sung. That's where the reality of literature is, and that's where the value of literature is created. And if people are different and varied, as they are, so must be their transactions with literature.

With that, we've mused long enough. From here on, we'll try to remain inconspicuous.

W. W. D.

Cluster 1: pp. 1-27
A topical cluster
Focus: the writer's assimilation of his world

1

I, too, dislike it: there are things that are important
beyond all this fiddle.

Reading it, however, with a perfect contempt for it,
one discovers in

it after all, a place for the genuine.

In the meantime, if you demand on the one hand,
the raw material of poetry in
all its rawness and
that which is on the other hand
genuine, you are interested in poetry.

?

—From "Poetry" by Marianne Moore

FIVE MEN

ZBIGNIEW HERBERT

1

They take them out in the morning
to the stone courtyard
and put them against the wall

five men
two of them very young
the others middle-aged

nothing more
can be said about them

2

when the platoon
level their guns
everything suddenly appears
in the garish light
of obviousness

the yellow wall
the cold blue
the black wire on the wall
instead of a horizon

that is the moment
when the five senses rebel
they would gladly escape
like rats from a sinking ship

before the bullet reaches its destination
the eye will perceive the flight of the projectile
the ear record a steely rustle
the nostrils will be filled with biting smoke
a petal of blood will brush the palate
the touch will shrink and then slacken

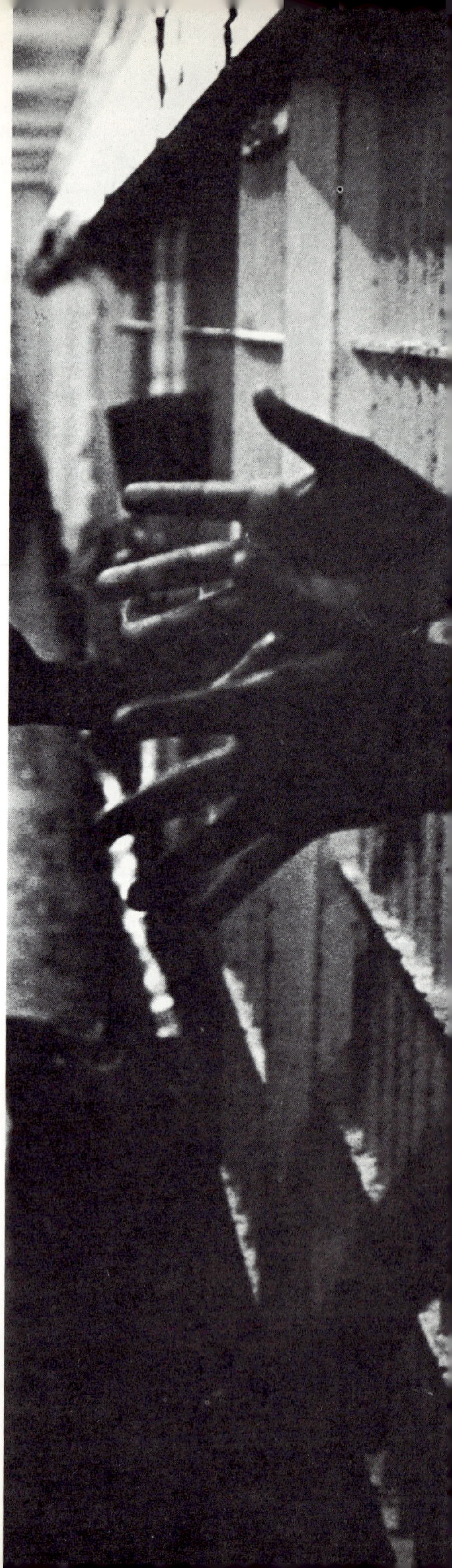

now they lie on the ground
covered up to their eyes with shadow
the platoon walks away
their buttons straps
and steel helmets
are more alive
than those lying beside the wall

3

I did not learn this today
I knew it before yesterday

so why have I been writing
unimportant poems on flowers

See M. Moore's "Poetry," p. 1.

what did the five talk of
the night before the execution

of prophetic dreams
of an escapade in a brothel
of automobile parts
of a sea voyage
of how when he had spades
he ought not to have opened
of how vodka is best
after wine you get a headache
of girls
of fruit
of life

thus one can use in poetry
names of Greek shepherds
one can attempt to catch the color
of morning sky
write of love
and also
once again
in dead earnest
offer to the betrayed world
a rose

—Translated by Czeslaw Milosz and Peter Dale Scott

G. A. Henty: author of boy's books—*By Pyke and Dyke; With Lee in Virginia.*
Rafael Sabatini: author of *Scaramouche* and many other romantic novels.

BATMAN GOT BUSTED IN BROOKLYN

PETE HAMILL

Winter in my old neighborhood was the time of supreme fantasy. When those first harsh winds ripped in off the bay, we locked ourselves in, with the ballbats stashed in the woodbins against that morning when the ground would soften again and the trees would leaf out in Prospect Park. We never played football and we never skied, because both were done by kids whose fathers had gone to college. Instead, we made the tenement hallways our playgrounds, huddling together, it seems now, for something as simple as warmth. We never realized it was a slum until that year after the war when the landlord installed steam heat and we felt suddenly, astonishingly, staggeringly rich.

But there was another richness in that neighborhood in those years, and I don't think much of it is around any more. There was a richness of the imagination that often became truly splendid. This was in the years before TV arrived, discharging its gooey fog into the minds of children and spreading the modern gospel that everything is of equal value. In a slum in those years, some things were more important than others, and one of the most important was the imagination. Because we had to improvise, to create, to make up what we could not buy, I suppose that what we learned in those hallways in the secret afternoons of winter will stay with us forever.

Much of it began with comic books and there is no one I grew up with who is surprised that painters like Larry Rivers and Roy Lichtenstein, and writers like Ken Kesey, Thomas Pynchon, and Tom Wolfe have drawn on them. They were, after all, our myths, just as G. A. Henty was Hemingway's and Hemingway himself served as one for a whole generation of writers. I can understand Norman Mailer when he says that Rafael Sabatini made him want to be a writer. One of the instincts of the writer is toward the creation of heroes.

And the comic books had them all right. The comic strips in the daily papers had gone into their Theodore Dreiser period, led by the realists like Milton Caniff and Frank King. But the books were dazzlingly original, and in the beginning, so were the heroes: Superman, Captain America and Bucky, the Boy Allies, Hawkman, the Green Lantern, the Flash, Sub-Mariner, Captain Marvel, the Human Torch and Toro, Ibia the Invincible, Zatara, the Shining Knight, Plastic Man, Daredevil, Crimebuster and Iron Jaw, The Spirit, Mars God of War, Kaanga, Dollman, Suicide Smith,

"Realists" defines "Theodore Dreiser period"; thus it's not necessary for the class to be able to identify Dreiser. Caniff: originator of "Terry and the Pirates"; now doing "Steve Canyon." Frank King: originator of "Gasoline Alley," popular in the 20's and 30's. Some students might like to compare the political and social milieus in these and other cartoons.

An interesting term but not nearly enough space to explore it here. See *Hamlet,* "To be or not to be," Act III, scene 1, or Dostoevsky's "Notes from the Underground."

The Heap, Bulletman, The Spectre, The Green Arrow, Airboy, and, of course, Batman and Robin.

Poor Batman and Robin, or should I say, poor us. . . . In those years of the war, Batman and Robin grabbed us all. Maybe it was the way they were drawn, with those rich black shadows cast on everything, and with Commissioner Gordon throwing the Batsignal against the sky of Gotham City at night. Maybe it was the villains, because Batman had the best: The Joker, Catwoman, The Penguin. (Neither Superman nor Captain Marvel succeeded in creating first-rate villains. Each had a scientist, Dr. Sivana and Lothar, but the real world soon outstripped them.)

But I think that what probably made us want to be Batman was the fact that he and Robin were mortal. Bullets bounced off Superman. They could kill Batman. Billy Batson could shout Shazam and become Captain Marvel. When we said the word, nothing happened. Batman could not fly, which is why we always saw him swinging on cranes. To be Batman, all you needed was a costume, some agility, and the ability to make an existentialist decision. One became Batman, because one chose to be Batman.

And one winter—it must have been 1944—one of us became Batman for a few glorious weeks. He couldn't have been more than 13, but he was bigger than most of us, and he had a sense of the enemy. So at night he prowled the rooftops, wearing a long black cape and a mask and performing wonders. He dropped bags of water on the cops (knowing that the police in any slum are the enemy); he shot his Red Ryder air rifle through the open doors of the saloons; he missed a loan shark by inches with a brick. We would sit huddled in a doorway, smoking loosies in the evening, and suddenly the cold air would break with a scream and we would look up, and there standing on a rooftop, his cape blowing in the winter wind, was Batman.

But it couldn't last. The loan sharks staked the neighborhood out, and after a week they knew who the kid was. He was arrested by two heroes from the Police Department one evening, and a few weeks later was sent off to Warwick, the place where tough kids had their originality ironed out of them.

Experimental reform school

I don't know when the comics died, but I suspect it was at precisely the moment that the psychiatrists moved in on them. They compared the heroes to Ku Kluxers because of the masks and found erotic moments in everything and deplored their brutality. The kids turned to TV, which was a simpler thing because it did not involve reading, and because the fantasy was acted out by others, and the psychiatrists began looking elsewhere for a fast buck. The other day I picked up a copy of Batman Comics and found that it was the 30th anniversary issue. I read it all the way through. It was the best book I had read in months.

WHERE ARE YOU NOW, SUPERMAN?

Brian Patten

The serials are all wound up now,
Put away in small black boxes
For a decade or so. Superman's asleep
In the sixpenny childhood seats,
Batman and Robin are elsewhere
And can't see the Batsign thrown out
By kids with toffee-smeared mouths.
Captain Marvel's SHAZAM! echoes round the auditorium,
But the magicians don't hear him,
Must all be dead . . .

The Purple Monster who came down from the Purple Planet,
Disguised as a man, is wandering aimlessly about the streets
With no way of getting back.
Sir Galahad's been strangled by the Incredible Living Trees,
Zorro killed by his own sword.
Blackhawk's buried his companions
In the disused hangers of innocence
And Flash Gordon likewise wanders lonely,
Weeping over the girl he loved 7 universes ago.

We killed them all simply because we grew up;
Who made them possible with our uneducated minds
And with our pocket money
And the sixpences we received
For pretending to be Good.
We think we are too old to cheer and boo now,
But let's not kid ourselves,
We still cheer and boo
But do it quietly or at General Elections
Where it's still possible to find a goodie
Now and then.

Clark Kent (alias Superman)
Committed suicide because he failed to find new parts.
The bullets that bounced off him on the screen
Wormed their way in to Real Life.
But who cared then for real life?

We had our own world with our own celluloid imaginations
And now we have a different world,
One that's a little more cynical
And that we are convinced is more real.

Our batsignals now questions flung into space
To attract the attention of passing solutions . . .

Literary Sort: First Batman! Then Superman! When do we get to Shakespeare or Henry Wadsworth Longfellow?

Editor: Please. Try not to be funny; you're not very good at it.

Literary Sort: I am serious.

Editor: You can't be. Why don't you let writers communicate with you instead of always looking for a Famous Name? Those last two pieces were about the past and remembering. . . . They were simple enough, and honest. . . .

Literary Sort: But one wants distinction in a book, doesn't one?

Editor: Oh, I don't know about that. Anyway, why don't you listen—or try to—to the next poem? As you'll see, it sort of touches on your ''Poetry of distinction,'' which is a little different from Marianne Moore's, by the way.

A word we often use loosely in our ritual assignments to students? Do we need to think about its "genuine" meaning? See M. Moore's "Poetry," p. 1.

I Would Like to Describe

Zbigniew Herbert

I would like to describe the simplest emotion
joy or sadness
but not as others do
reaching for shafts of rain or sun

I would like to describe a light
which is being born in me
but I know it does not resemble
any star
for it is not so bright
not so pure
and is uncertain

I would like to describe courage
without dragging behind me a dusty lion
and also anxiety
without shaking a glass full of water

to put it another way
I would give all metaphors
in return for one word
drawn out of my breast like a rib
for one word
contained within the boundaries
of my skin

but apparently this is not possible

and just to say—I love
I run around like mad
picking up handfuls of birds
and my tenderness
which after all is not made of water
asks the water for a face

and anger
different from fire
borrows from it
a loquacious tongue

so is blurred
so is blurred
in me
what white-haired gentlemen
separated once and for all
and said
this is the subject
and this is the object

we fall asleep
with one hand under our head
and with the other in a mound of planets

our feet abandon us
and taste the earth
with their tiny roots
which next morning
we tear out painfully

—Translated by Czeslaw Milosz and Peter Dale Scott

Editor: What did you think of that?

Literary Sort: Beautiful?

Editor: Beautiful! So you didn't listen after all. I wonder what you'll think of the next selection. It's about spring in London. But it's about more than that too.

SOME THOUGHTS ON THE COMMON TOAD

George Orwell

Before the swallow, before the daffodil, and not much later than the snowdrop, the common toad salutes the coming of spring after his own fashion, which is to emerge from a hole in the ground, where he has lain buried since the previous autumn, and crawl as rapidly as possible towards the nearest suitable patch of water. Something—some kind of shudder in the earth, or perhaps merely a rise of a few degrees in the temperature—has told him that it is time to wake up: though a few toads appear to sleep the clock round and miss out a year from time to time—at any rate, I have more than once dug them up, alive and apparently well, in the middle of the summer.

At this period, after his long fast, the toad has a very spiritual look, like a strict Anglo-Catholic towards the end of Lent. His movements are languid but purposeful, his body is shrunken, and by contrast his eyes look abnormally large. This allows one to notice, what one might not at another time, that a toad has about the most beautiful eye of any living creature. It is like gold, or more exactly it is like the golden-colored semiprecious stone which one sometimes sees in signet rings, and which I think is called a chrysoberyl.

For a few days after getting into the water the toad concentrates on building up his strength by eating small insects. Presently he has swollen to his normal size again, and then he goes through a phase of intense sexiness. All he knows, at least if he is a male toad, is that he wants to get his arms round something, and if you offer him a stick, or even your finger, he will cling to it with surprising strength and take a long time to discover that it is not a female toad. Frequently one comes upon shapeless masses of ten or twenty toads rolling over and over in the water, one clinging to another without distinction of sex. By degrees, however, they sort themselves out into couples, with the male duly sitting on the female's back. You can now distinguish males from females, because the male is smaller, darker and sits on top, with his arms tightly clasped round the female's neck. After a day or two the spawn is laid in long strings which wind themselves in and out of the reeds and soon become invisible. A few more weeks, and the water is alive with masses of tiny tadpoles which rapidly grow larger, sprout hind-legs, then forelegs, then shed their tails: and finally, about the middle of the summer, the new generation of toads, smaller than one's thumb-nail but perfect in every particular, crawl out of the water to begin the game anew.

Spring Seeps In

I mention the spawning of the toads because it is one of the phenomena of spring which most deeply appeal to me, and because the toad, unlike the skylark and the primrose, has never had much of a boost from the poets. But I am aware that many people do not like reptiles or amphibians, and I am not suggesting that in order to enjoy the spring you have to take an interest in toads. There are also the crocus, the missel thrush, the cuckoo, the blackthorn, etc. The point is that the pleasures of spring are available to everybody, and cost nothing. Even in the most sordid street the coming of spring will register itself by some sign or other, if it is only a brighter blue between the chimney pots or the vivid green of an elder sprouting on a blitzed site. Indeed it is remarkable how Nature goes on existing unofficially, as it were, in the very heart of London. I have seen a kestrel flying over the Deptford gasworks, and I have heard a first-rate performance by a blackbird in the Euston Road. There must be some hundreds of thousands, if not millions, of birds living inside the four-mile radius, and it is rather a pleasing thought that none of them pays a halfpenny of rent.

One would not expect to see kestrels "flying" or hear blackbirds "performing" in these urban centers of London.

As for spring, not even the narrow and gloomy streets round the Bank of England are quite able to exclude it. It comes seeping in everywhere, like one of those new poison gases which pass through all filters. The spring is commonly referred to as "a miracle," and during the past five or six years this worn-out figure of speech has taken on a new lease of life. After the sort of winters we have had to endure recently, the spring does seem miraculous, because it has become gradually harder and harder to believe that it is actually going to happen. Every February since 1940 I have found myself thinking that this time winter is going to be permanent. But

Persephone,° like the toads, always rises from the dead at about the same moment. Suddenly, towards the end of March, the miracle happens and the decaying slum in which I live is transfigured. Down in the square the sooty privets° have turned bright green, the leaves are thickening on the chestnut trees, the daffodils are out, the wallflowers are budding, the policeman's tunic looks positively a pleasant shade of blue, the fishmonger greets his customers with a smile, and even the sparrows are quite a different color, having felt the balminess of the air and nerved themselves to take a bath, their first since last September.

Urban Foible?

Note the shift from nonconformist "wicked" to labor/ socialist "politically reprehensible."

Is it wicked to take a pleasure in spring, and other seasonal changes? To put it more precisely, is it politically reprehensible, while we are all groaning under the shackles of the capitalist system, to point out that life is frequently more worth living because of a blackbird's song, a yellow elm tree in October, or some other natural phenomenon which does not cost money and does not have what the editors of the Left-wing newspapers call a class angle? There is no doubt that many people think so. I know by experience that a favorable reference to "Nature" in one of my articles is liable to

12

bring me abusive letters, and though the key word in these letters is usually "sentimental," two ideas seem to be mixed up in them. One is that any pleasure in the actual process of life encourages a sort of political quietism. People, so the thought runs, ought to be discontented, and it is our job to multiply our wants and not simply to increase our enjoyment of the things we have already. The other idea is that this is the age of machines and that to dislike the machine, or even to want to limit its domination, is backward-looking, reactionary, and slightly ridiculous. This is often backed up by the statement that a love of Nature is a foible of urbanized people who have no notion what Nature is really like. Those who really have to deal with the soil, so it is argued, do not love the soil, and do not take the faintest interest in birds or flowers, except from a strictly utilitarian point of view. To love the country one must live in the town, merely taking an occasional weekend ramble at the warmer times of year.

Two quite distinct points, which probably ought not to be linked in this fashion, as if discontent is automatically defined in terms of the kinds of wants promoted by advertising.
The whole passage seems an example of rather tricky arguing.

This last idea is demonstrably false. Medieval literature, for instance, including the popular ballads, is full of an almost Georgian°

°PERSEPHONE: the mythical queen of Hades and goddess of spring

°PRIVETS: hedge shrubs

°GEORGIAN: a term for the poets of George V's reign (1910–1936) and an allusion to their personal reverence for nature enthusiasm for Nature, and the art of agricultural peoples such as the Chinese and Japanese centers always round trees, birds, flowers, rivers, mountains. The other idea seems to me to be wrong in a subtler way. Certainly we ought to be discontented, we ought not simply to find out ways of making the best of a bad job, and yet if we kill all pleasure in the actual process of life, what sort of future are we preparing for ourselves? If a man cannot enjoy the return of spring, why should he be happy in a labor-saving Utopia? What will he do with the leisure that the machine will give him? I have always suspected that if our economic and political problems are ever really solved, life will become simpler instead of more complex, and that the sort of pleasure one gets from finding the first primrose will loom larger than the sort of pleasure one gets from eating an ice to the tune of a Wurlitzer. I think that by retaining one's childhood love of such things as trees, fishes, butterflies and—to return to my first instance—toads, one makes a peaceful and decent future a little more probable, and that by preaching the doctrine that nothing is to be admired except steel and concrete, one merely makes it a little surer that human beings will have no outlet for their surplus energy except in hatred and leader-worship.

A jukebox, not an organ

At any rate, spring is here, even in London, N.1, and they can't stop you enjoying it. This is a satisfying reflection. How many a time have I stood watching the toads mating, or a pair of hares having a boxing match in the young corn, and thought of all the important persons who would stop me enjoying this if they could. But luckily they can't. So long as you are not actually ill, hungry, frightened or immured in a prison or a holiday camp, spring is still spring. The atom bombs are piling up in the factories, the police are prowling through the cities, the lies are streaming from the loudspeakers, but the earth is still going round the sun, and neither the dictators nor the bureaucrats, deeply as they disapprove of the process, are able to prevent it.

Postal district

The political, social, economic, and moral implications of these final statements might be amplified by readings of George Orwell's *1984*, Aldous Huxley's *Brave New World,* and Anthony Burgess' *Wanting Seed.*

Capturing

Animals

Ted Hughes

A metal frame in front of a fireplace, to keep coals from rolling into the room.

There are all sorts of ways of capturing animals and birds and fish. I spent most of my time, up to the age of fifteen or so, trying out many of these ways and when my enthusiasm began to wane, as it did gradually, I started to write poems.

You might not think that these two interests, capturing animals and writing poems, have much in common. But the more I think back the more sure I am that with me the two interests have been one interest. My pursuit of mice at threshing time when I was a boy, snatching them from under the sheaves as the sheaves were lifted away out of the stack and popping them into my pocket till I had thirty or forty crawling around in the lining of my coat, that and my present pursuit of poems seem to me to be different stages of the same fever. In a way, I suppose, I think of poems as a sort of animal. They have their own life, like animals, by which I mean that they seem quite separate from any person, even from their author, and nothing can be added to them or taken away without maiming and perhaps even killing them. And they have a certain wisdom. They know something special . . . something perhaps which we are very curious to learn. Maybe my concern has been to capture not animals particularly and not poems, but simply things which have a vivid life of their own, outside mine. However all that may be, my interest in animals began when I began. My memory goes back pretty clearly to my third year, and by then I had so many of the toy lead animals you could buy in shops that they went right round our flat-topped fender, nose to tail, with some over.

A fine statement of the idea central to all modern esthetic theory. This passage is especially important, since it alludes to the notion of a poem (any work of art) as an organic situation: An arm is fully an arm only when attached to a body, though it never loses the appearance of an arm even when removed. See also passage on page 17.

I had a gift for modeling and drawing, so when I discovered plasticine my zoo became infinite, and when an aunt bought me a thick green-backed animal book for my fourth birthday I began to draw the glossy photographs. The animals looked good in the photographs, but they looked even better in my drawings and were mine. I can remember very vividly the excitement with which I used to sit staring at my drawings, and it is a similar thing I feel nowadays with poems.

A nice point for teachers to consider.

My zoo was not entirely an indoors affair. At that time we lived in a valley in the Pennines in West Yorkshire. My brother, who probably had more to do with this passion of mine than anyone else, was a good bit older than I was, and his one interest in life was creeping about on the hillsides with a rifle. He took me along as a retriever and I had to scramble into all kinds of places collecting magpies and owls and rabbits and weasels and rats and curlews that he shot. He could not shoot enough for me. At the same time I used to be fishing daily in the canal, with the long-handled wire-rimmed curtain mesh sort of net.

All that was only the beginning. When I was about eight, we moved to an industrial town in south Yorkshire. Our cat went upstairs and moped in my bedroom for a week, it hated the place so much, and my brother for the same reason left home and became a gamekeeper. But in many ways that move of ours was the best thing that ever happened to me. I soon discovered a farm in the nearby country that supplied all my needs, and soon after, a private estate, with woods and lakes.

My friends were town boys, sons of colliers and railwaymen, and with them I led one life, but all the time I was leading this other life on my own in the country. I never mixed the two lives up, except once or twice disastrously. I still have some diaries that I kept in those years: they record nothing but my catches.

Finally, as I have said, at about fifteen my life grew more complicated and my attitude to animals changed. I accused myself of disturbing their lives. I began to look at them, you see, from their own point of view.

And about the same time I began to write poems. Not animal poems. It was years before I wrote what you could call an animal poem and several more years before it occurred to me that my writing poems might be partly a continuation of my earlier pursuit. Now I have no doubt. The special kind of excitement, the slightly mesmerized and quite involuntary concentration with which you make out the stirrings of a new poem in your mind, then the outline, the mass and color and clean final form of it, the unique living reality of it in the midst of the general lifelessness, all that is too familiar to mistake. This is hunting and the poem is a new species of creature, a new specimen of the life outside your own.

I have now told you very briefly what I believe to be the origins and growth of my interest in writing poetry. I have simplified everything a great deal, but on the whole that is the story. Some of it may seem a bit obscure to you. How can a poem, for instance, about a walk in the rain, be like an animal? Well, perhaps it cannot look much like a giraffe or an emu or an octopus, or anything you might find in a menagerie. It is better to call it an assembly of living parts moved by a single spirit. The living parts are the words, the images, the rhythms. The spirit is the life which inhabits them when they all work together. It is impossible to say which comes first, parts or spirit. But if any of the parts are dead . . . if any of the words, or images or rhythms do not jump to life as you read them . . . then the creature is going to be maimed and the spirit sickly. So, as a poet, you have to make sure that all those parts over which you have control, the words and rhythms and images, are alive. That is where the difficulties begin. Yet the rules, to begin with, are very simple. Words that live are those which we hear, like *click* or *chuckle,* or which we see, like *freckled* or *veined,* or which we taste, like *vinegar* or *sugar,* or touch, like *prickle* or *oily,* or smell, like *tar* or *onion.* Words which belong directly to one of the five senses. Or words which act and seem to use their muscles, like *flick* or *balance.*

An elegant statement of the organic theory of poetry. See page 16.

How many such words does Hughes have in "The Thought-Fox" (p. 18) or in "Pike" (p. 20)?

But immediately things become more difficult. *Click* not only gives you a sound, it gives you the notion of a sharp movement . . . such as your tongue makes in saying "click." It also gives you the feel of something light and brittle, like a snapping twig. Heavy things do not click, nor do soft bendable ones. In the same way, tar not only smells strongly. It is sticky to touch, with a particular thick and choking stickiness. Also it moves, when it is soft, like a black snake, and has a beautiful black gloss. So it is with most words. They belong to several of the senses at once, as if each one had eyes, ears and tongue, or ears and fingers and a body to move with. It is this little goblin in a word which is its life and its poetry, and it is this goblin which the poet has to have under control.

A thin, very sweet syrup or juice

Well, you will say, this is hopeless. How do you control all that? When the words are pouring out, how can you be sure that you do not have one of these side meanings of the word *feathers* getting all stuck up with one of the side meanings of the word *treacle,* a few words later? In bad poetry this is exactly what happens, the words kill each other. Luckily, you do not have to bother about it so long as you do one thing.

That one thing is, imagine what you are writing about. See it and live it. Do not think it up laboriously, as if you were working out mental arithmetic. Just look at it, touch it, smell it, listen to it, turn yourself into it. When you do this, the words look after themselves, like magic. If you do this you do not have to bother about commas or fullstops or that sort of thing. You do not look at the words either. You keep your eyes, your ears, your nose, your taste, your touch, your whole being on the thing you are turning into words. The minute you flinch, and take your mind off this thing, and begin to look at the words and worry about them . . . then your worry goes into them and they set about killing each other. So you keep going as long as you can, then look back and see what you have written. After a bit of practice, and after telling yourself a few times that you do not care how other people have written about this thing, this is the way you find it; and after telling yourself you are going to use any old word that comes into your head so long as it seems right at the moment of writing it down, you will surprise yourself. You will read back through what you have written and you will get a shock. You will have captured a spirit, a creature.

After all that, I ought to give you some examples and show you some of my own more recently acquired specimens.

Foxes destroy chickens and other livestock; Hughes does not blame the farmers for their raids on his foxes. Why, then, did Hughes "capture" foxes?

An animal I never succeeded in keeping alive is the fox. I was always frustrated: twice by a farmer, who killed cubs I had caught before I could get to them, and once by a poultry keeper who freed my cub while his dog waited. Years after those events I was sitting up late one snowy night in dreary lodgings in London. I had written nothing for a year or so but that night I got the idea I might write something and I wrote in a few minutes the following poem: the first "animal" poem I ever wrote. Here it is—*The Thought-Fox.*

I imagine this midnight moment's forest:
Something else is alive
Beside the clock's loneliness
And this blank page where my fingers move,

Through the window I see no star:
Something more near
Though deeper within darkness
Is entering the loneliness:

Cold, delicately as the dark snow,
A fox's nose touches twig, leaf;
Two eyes serve a movement, that now
And again now, and now, and now

Sets neat prints into the snow
Between trees, and warily a lame
Shadow lags by stump and in hollow
Of a body that is bold to come

Across clearings, an eye,
A widening deepening greenness,
Brilliantly, concentratedly,
Coming about its own business

Till, with a sudden sharp hot stink of fox
It enters the dark hole of the head.
The window is starless still; the clock ticks,
The page is printed.

This poem does not have anything you could easily call a meaning. It is about a fox, obviously enough, but a fox that is both a fox and not a fox. What sort of a fox is it that can step right into my head where presumably it still sits . . . smiling to itself when the dogs bark? It is both a fox and a spirit. It is a real fox; as I read the poem I see it move, I see it setting its prints, I see its shadow going over the irregular surface of the snow. The words show me all this, bringing it nearer and nearer. It is very real to me. The words have made a body for it and given it somewhere to walk.

If, at the time of writing this poem, I had found livelier words, words that could give me much more vividly its movements, the twitch and craning of its ears, the slight tremor of its hanging tongue and its breath making little clouds, its teeth bared in the cold, the snow-crumbs dropping from its pads as it lifts each one in turn, if I could have got the words for all this, the fox would probably be even more real and alive to me now, than it is as I read the poem. Still, it is there as it is. If I had not caught the real fox there in the words I would never have saved the poem. I would have thrown it into the wastepaper basket as I have thrown so many other hunts that did not get what I was after. As it is, every time I read

But what would have happened to the poem?

the poem the fox comes up again out of the darkness and steps into my head. And I suppose that long after I am gone, as long as a copy of the poem exists, every time anyone reads it the fox will get up somewhere out in the darkness and come walking towards them.

So, you see, in some ways my fox is better than an ordinary fox. It will live forever, it will never suffer from hunger or hounds. I have it with me wherever I go. And I made it. And all through imagining it clearly enough and finding the living words.

Here, in this next poem, is one of my prize catches. I used to be a very keen angler for pike, as I still am when I get the chance, and I did most of my early fishing in a quite small lake, really a large pond. This pond went down to a great depth in one place. Sometimes, on hot days, we would see something like a railway sleeper lying near the surface, and there certainly were huge pike in that pond. I suppose they are even bigger by now. Recently I felt like doing some pike fishing, but in circumstances where there was no chance of it, and over the days, as I remembered the extreme pleasures of that sport, bits of the following poem began to arrive. As you will see, by looking at the place in my memory very hard and very carefully and by using the words that grew naturally out of the pictures and feelings, I captured not just a pike, I captured the whole pond, including the monsters I never even hooked. Here is the poem, which I called *Pike.*

''tie''

Pike, three inches long, perfect
Pike in all parts, green tigering the gold.
Killers from the egg: the malevolent aged grin.
They dance on the surface among the flies.

Or move, stunned by their own grandeur,
Over a bed of emerald, silhouette
Of submarine delicacy and horror.
A hundred feet long in their world.

In ponds, under the heat-struck lily pads—
Gloom of their stillness:
Logged on last year's black leaves, watching upwards.
Or hung in an amber cavern of weeds

The jaws' hooked clamp and fangs
Not to be changed at this date;
A life subdued to its instrument;
The gills kneading quietly, and the pectorals.

Three we kept behind glass,
Jungled in weed: three inches, four,
And four and a half: fed fry to them—
Suddenly there were two. Finally one

With a sag belly and the grin it was born with.
And indeed they spare nobody.
Two, six pounds each, over two feet long,
High and dry and dead in the willow-herb—

One jammed past its gills down the other's gullet:
The outside eye stared: as a vice locks—
The same iron in this eye
Though its film shrank in death.

A pond I fished, fifty yards across,
Whose lilies and muscular tench
Had outlasted every visible stone
Of the monastery that planted them—

Stilled legendary depth:
It was as deep as England. It held
Pike too immense to stir, so immense and old
That past nightfall I dared not cast

But silently cast and fished
With the hair frozen on my head
For what might move, for what eye might move.
The still splashes on the dark pond,

Owls hushing the floating woods
Frail on my ear against the dream
Darkness beneath night's darkness had freed,
That rose slowly towards me, watching.

Literary Sort: I thought that was very nice—what he said about words, words that live, that we can hear or see or feel. That was *very* nice. And when he spoke about his fox living forever, I *was* impressed.

Editor: Mmmm . . . I was interested in the way the boy Hughes looked at animals "from their own point of view," and I got to wondering how he must have felt when the poultry keeper let his dog get at the fox cub.

TO BILL RUSSELL

I have never seen

an eagle with a beard

but if there is

in some strange

corner of the world

and the Hindu

belief is true

you will return

and beat your wings

violently

over my grave.

—Tom Meschery

Literary Sort: First comics, and now poems about young persons throwing balls through baskets. What next?

Editor: But as has been said by William Wordsworth—it is the poem, not its material, that we should pay attention to.

ELGIN BAYLOR

you had to see it

the leap
sudden
selfgenerated
the moment
bursting
into golden petals
arch
of the neck

ex-
tension of the arm

you just had
to see
the feint
leading
to a takeoff
arms
lifting
the whole flower
glorious
and the great re-
leases
of energy

you had
to see
Baylor
before his knees went

how
he could
dance

—Mark Shechner

Stopping by Woods on a Snowy Evening

Whose woods these are I think I know.
His house is in the village though;
He will not see me stopping here
To watch his woods fill up with snow.

My little horse must think it queer
To stop without a farmhouse near
Between the woods and frozen lake
The darkest evening of the year.

He gives his harness bells a shake
To ask if there is some mistake.
The only other sound's the sweep
Of easy wind and downy flake.

What do you think about as you read these last two lines? Sleep? Is it a comfortable "sleep"? A comforting thought? Or is it disturbing?

The woods are lovely, dark and deep.
But I have promises to keep,
And miles to go before I sleep,
And miles to go before I sleep.

—*ROBERT FROST*

Driving to Town Late to Mail a Letter

It is a cold and snowy night. The main street is deserted.
The only things moving are swirls of snow.
As I lift the mailbox door, I feel its cold iron.
There is a privacy I love in this snowy night.
Driving around, I will waste more time.

—**ROBERT BLY**

My hosts turned out to be very nice and hospitable people. A family worthy of study.

A Young Writer on Vacation

SOUMY
May 30, 1888

I am answering your letter,° which I received only yesterday; the envelope is torn, crumpled, and soiled, and my hosts and family ascribed to this a strong political coloring.

I am staying on the bank of the river Psyol, in the lodge of an old seigniorial estate. I hired the place without seeing it, at random, and have not regretted it so far. The river is wide and deep, abounding in islets, fish, and crayfish. The banks are beautiful with much verdure. Best of all, it is so spacious that I seem to have got for my hundred roubles the right to live on an expanse the bounds of which cannot be seen. Nature and life here are built on a pattern which has become old-fashioned now, and is discarded by editors. Not to speak of nightingales, which sing day and night, the barking of dogs heard in the distance, old neglected orchards, sad and poetical manor houses, nailed up and deserted, where live the souls of beautiful women; not to speak of those survivals of a bygone age, old relics of serfdom, butlers, girls who pine for conventional love—there is, not far from here, such a hackneyed cliché as a water-mill with sixteen wheels, and a miller and his daughter, who always sit at the window and are evidently waiting for something. Everything I see and hear now seems to be long familiar to me from old stories and fairy tales. The one novelty to me is a mysterious bird, the bittern, which sits somewhere in the reeds and day and night utters a cry which sounds partly like a blow on an empty barrel and partly like the bellowing of a cow shut in a shed. Every Ukrainian has seen this bird in his life, but everyone describes it differently, which means that no one has seen it. There is a novelty of another kind, but adventitious, and therefore not quite new . . . .

This passage may contain a germ of *The Cherry Orchard.* At least it is full of details reminiscent of the play.

°Letter to A. S. Souvorin

My hosts turned out to be very nice and hospitable people. A family worthy of study. It consists of six members. An old mother, a very good-hearted, stout woman who has suffered much; she reads Schopenhauer and drives to church to hear the song of praise; she reads conscientiously every number of *Vestnik Europa* and *Severny Vestnik*, and knows novelists of whom I have not even dreamed in my sleep; she attaches great importance to the fact that once the artist Makovsky lived in her lodge, and now a young writer is staying there; talking to Plescheyev she feels a holy thrill in her body, and she rejoices every minute that she "was worthy" to see the great poet.

Her eldest daughter, a woman doctor—the pride of the whole family, and a saint as the peasants call her—is truly extraordinary. She has a tumor on her brain, and in consequence is totally blind; she suffers from epilepsy and constant headaches. She knows what awaits her, and stoically, with amazing coolness, speaks of her death, which is near. In my medical practice I have grown used to seeing people who

are about to die, and I have always felt somehow strange when, in my presence, people whose death was approaching smiled or wept; but here, when I see on the terrace this blind woman, who smiles, jokes, or listens when my "Twilight" is read to her, what seems strange to me is not that she is about to die, but that we do not feel our own death, and write "Twilights" as though we would never die.

The second daughter, also a doctor, is a gentle, shy, and infinitely good-natured creature who loves everyone. Patients are a real torture to her, and she is almost morbidly scrupulous with them. At consultations we always disagree; I bring good tidings where she sees death, and I double the doses which she prescribes. But where death is obvious and inevitable, then my doctor feels in an altogether unprofessional way. Once I was attending patients with her in a certain medical center; a young peasant woman came with a malignant tumor in the glands of her neck and at the back of her head. The tumor had spread so far that a cure was unthinkable. And just because the woman was at present feeling no pain, but would in six months die in agony, my doctor looked at her in a deeply guilty way, as if apologizing for her own health and ashamed that medical science was helpless. She applies herself eagerly to the management of the farm and understands every detail of it. She knows everything about horses. When, for instance, the side horse does not pull or gets restless she knows what to do and instructs the driver. . . . I believe she has never done any wrong to anyone, and it seems to me that she never has been nor ever will be happy a single minute.

The third daughter, who graduated at the Bestoujev University for Women, is a young, strong, sunburned, loud-voiced girl. Her laugh is so loud it could be heard a mile away. A passionate lover of the Ukraine. She has had a school built on the estate at her own expense, and teaches the children of the peasants the fables of Krylov in a Ukrainian translation. She goes to the grave of Shevchenko as a Turk goes to Mecca. She does not cut her hair, wears corsets and a bustle, occupies herself in housework, and loves to sing and laugh. . . .

A poet

As was fashionable with intellectual women at the time

The elder son is a quiet, modest, sensible, hard-working young man, with no special talents and no pretensions, and is evidently satisfied with what life has given him. For his political views he was dismissed from the University the year he should have taken his degree, but of that he does not boast. He talks little, loves his work and the land, and lives harmoniously with the peasants.

The second son is a young man, crazy over Tchaikovsky being a genius. He is a pianist. Dreams of living according to Tolstoy.

A rather ambiguous statement, since Tolstoy's "living" spanned the whole scheme of Russian society, from privileged aristocrat to humble peasant. More than likely Chekhov is here alluding to Tolstoy's later life, a simple peasant's life during which he was content to write children's books and political tracts on universal brotherhood.

—Anton Chekhov

INTERLOCK WITH CLUSTER 2:
An authorial link: Anton Chekhov
A generic link: letters

Cluster 2: pp. 28-37
An author cluster
Focus: Anton Chekhov
A generic cluster
Focus: letters

INTERLOCK WITH CLUSTER 1:
An authorial link: Anton Chekhov
A generic link: letters

2

My holy of holies is the human body, health, intelligence, talent, inspiration, love, and the most absolute freedom—freedom from violence and lying, whatever forms they may take. This is the program that I would follow if I were a great artist.

I have no doubt that the study of medicine has had an important influence on my literary work; it has considerably enlarged the sphere of my observation, has enriched me with knowledge, the true value of which for me as a writer can only be understood by one who is himself a doctor. It has also had a guiding influence, and it is probably due to my close association with medicine that I have succeeded in avoiding many mistakes.

—Anton Chekhov

October 11, 1899

I received the Pushkin Prize. Oh, if only those 500 roubles came to me in the summer time, when it is jolly, but in winter they will be squandered. . . .

—Anton Chekhov

To A. S. Souvorin
MOSCOW. October 27, 1888

. . . You write that the hero of my "Party" is a character worth developing. Good Lord! I am not a senseless brute, you know; I understand that. I understand that I cut the throats of my characters and spoil them, and that I waste good material. . . . On my conscience, I would gladly have spent six months over the "Party"; I like taking things easy, and see no attraction in publishing in white-hot haste. I would willingly, with pleasure, with feeling, in a leisurely way, describe the *whole* of my hero, describe his state of mind while his wife was in labor, his trial, the unpleasant feeling he has after he is acquitted; I would describe the midwife and the doctors having tea in the middle of the night, I would describe the rain. . . . It would give me nothing but pleasure, because I like to take pains and dawdle. But what am I to do? I begin a story on September 10th with the thought that I must finish it by October 5th at the latest. If I don't I shall fail the editor and be left without money. I let myself go at the beginning and write with an easy mind; but by the time I get to the middle I begin to grow timid and to fear that my story will be too long: I have to remember that the *Sieverny Viestnik* has not much money, and that I am one of their expensive contributors. This is why the beginning of my stories is always very promising and looks as though I were starting on a novel, the middle is huddled and timid, and the end is, as in a short sketch, like fireworks. And so in planning a story one is bound to think first about its framework: from a crowd of leading or subordinate characters one selects one person only—wife or husband; one puts him on the canvas and paints him alone, making him prominent, while the others one scatters over the canvas like small coin, and the result is something like the vault of heaven: one big moon and a number of very small stars around it. But the moon is not a success, because it can only be understood if the stars too are intelligible, and the stars are not worked out. And so what I produce is not literature, but something like the patching of Trishka's coat. What am I to do? I don't know, I don't know. I must trust to time which heals all things.

Speaking on my conscience again, I have not yet begun my literary work, though I have received a literary prize. Subjects for five stories and two novels are languishing in my head. One of the novels was thought of long ago, and some of the characters have grown old without managing to get themselves written. In my head there is a whole army of people asking to be let out and waiting for the word of command. All that I have written so far is rubbish in comparison with what I should like to write and should write with rapture. It is all the same to me whether I write "The Party" or "Lights," or a vaudeville or a letter to a friend—it is all dull, spiritless, mechanical, and I get annoyed with critics who attach any importance to "Lights," for instance. I fancy that I deceive them with my work just as I deceive many people with my face, which looks serious or overcheerful. I don't like being successful; the subjects which sit in my head are annoyed, jealous of what has already been written. I am vexed that the rubbish has been done and the good things lie about in the lumber-room like old books. Of course, in thus lamenting I rather exaggerate, and much of what I say is only my fancy, but there is something of the truth in it, a good big part of it. What do I call good? The images which seem best to me, which I love and jealously guard lest I spend and spoil them for the sake of some "Party" written against time. . . . If my love is mistaken, I am wrong, but then it may not be mistaken! I am either a fool and a conceited fellow or I really am an organism capable of being a good writer. All that I now write displeases and bores me, but what sits in my head interests, excites, and moves me—from which I conclude that everybody does the wrong thing and I alone know the secret of doing the right one. Most likely all writers think that. But the devil himself would break his neck at these problems.

Money will not help me to decide what I am to do and how I am to act. An extra thousand roubles will not settle matters, and a hundred thousand is a castle in the air. Besides, when I have money—it may be because I am not accustomed to it, I don't know —I become extremely careless and idle; the sea seems only knee-deep to me then. . . . I need time and solitude.

—Anton Chekhov

To A. S. Souvorin
MOSCOW. May 4, 1889

Nature reconciles man, that is, makes him indifferent. And in this world one must be indifferent. Only those who are unconcerned are able to see things clearly, to be just, and to work. Of course, this includes only thoughtful and noble people; egoists and empty folk are indifferent enough as it is.

You say I have grown lazy. That does not mean that I am now lazier than I used to be. I work nowadays as much as I did three or five years ago. To work, and to look as though I were working constantly from nine in the morning till dinner, and after the evening meal until bedtime, has become a habit with me, and in that respect I am exactly like a government clerk. And if my work does not result in two novels a month or in an income of ten thousand roubles, it is not my laziness that is to blame, but my inborn psychological peculiarities. I do not care enough for money to make a success of medicine, and for literature I have not enough passion, and therefore not enough talent. The fire burns in me slowly and evenly, without sudden spluttering and flaring up. And this is why I cannot cover reams of paper each night, or be so carried away by my work that it keeps me from bed when I am sleepy; this is why I commit no particular follies, or accomplish anything very wise.

I am afraid that in this respect I resemble Goncharov, whom I don't like, who is ten heads taller than I am in talent. I have not enough passion; add to that this sort of lunacy: for the last two years I have for no reason at all ceased to care about seeing my work in print, have become indifferent to reviews, to literary conversations, to gossip, to success and failure, to good pay—in short, I have gone downright silly. There is a sort of stagnation in my soul. I explain it by the stagnation in my personal life. I am not disappointed, I am not tired, I am not depressed, but simply, everything has suddenly become less interesting. I must do something to rouse myself.

—Anton Chekhov

Literary Sort: Chekhov—is that right?—seems somewhat disorganized. One feels him to be not quite aware of the value of being a writer.

Editor: But I think he, too, bathed periodically, ate three meals daily, and performed various duties with a good sense of regularity—much as we all do. Surely, he's aware of the value of being human!

To A. S. Souvorin
MOSCOW. Dec. 23, 1888

I read your play again. There is much that is good and original in it, that dramatic literature has not had before, but there are also things that are not so good, i.e., in the language. Its merits and faults make up wealth that one could dwell upon, if we had critics. But this wealth will lie idle and unproductive until it goes out of date. . . . There are no critics. There are spouters like the trite Tatishchev, the donkey Mikhnevich, and the unconcerned Burenin, —here you have the whole of the Russian critical force. And to write for this force is a thankless job, just as it is to send flowers to one who has a cold in the head.

There are moments when I completely lose heart. For whom and for what do I write? For the public? But I don't see it, and believe in it less than I do in spooks; it is uneducated, badly brought up, and its best elements are unfair and insincere to us. I cannot make out whether this public wants me or not. Burenin says that it does not, and that I waste my time on trifles; the Academy has given me a prize. The devil himself could not make head or tail of it. Write for the sake of money? But I never have any money, and not being used to having it I am almost indifferent to it. For the sake of money I work apathetically. Write for the sake of praise? But praise merely irritates me. Literary society, students, Pleshcheyev, young ladies, etc., were enthusiastic in their praise of my "Nervous Breakdown," but Grigorovich is the only one who has noticed the description of the first snow. And so on, and so on. If we had critics I should know that I provide material, whether good or bad does not matter—that to men who devote themselves to the study of life I am as neccessary as a star is to an astronomer. And then I would take trouble over my work and should know what I was working for. But as it is, you, I, Muravlin, and the rest are like lunatics who write books and plays to please themselves. To please oneself is, of course, an excellent thing; one feels the pleasure while one is writing, but afterwards? In short, I am sorry for Tatyana

Repina° not because she poisoned herself, but because she lived her life, died in agony, and was described absolutely to no purpose, without any good to anyone. A number of tribes, religions, languages, civilizations, have vanished without a trace, vanished because there were no historians or biologists. In the same way a number of lives and works of art disappear before our very eyes owing to the complete absence of criticism. It may be objected that critics would have nothing to do because all modern works are poor and insignificant. But this is a narrow way of looking at things. Life must be studied not from the pluses alone, but from the minuses too. The conviction that the "eighties" have not produced a single writer may in itself provide material for five volumes. . . . I settled down last night to write a tale for the *Novoe Vremya,* but a woman appeared and dragged me to see the poet Palmin who, when he was drunk, had fallen and cut his forehead to the bone. I was busy over the drunken fellow for nearly two hours, was tired out, began to smell of iodoform all over, felt cross, and came home exhausted. . . . Altogether my life is a dreary one, and I begin to get fits of hating people, which used never to happen to me before. Long, stupid conversations, visitors, people asking for help, and helping them to the extent of one or two or three roubles, spending money on cabs for the sake of patients who do not pay me a penny—altogether it is such a hodge-podge that I feel like running away from home. People borrow money from me and don't pay it back, they take my books, they waste my time. . . . Blighted love is the one thing that is missing.

Chekhov was a doctor by profession.

—Anton Chekhov

°TATYANA REPINA: central character in Souvorin's play

To Alex. P. Chekhov
MOSCOW. April, 1883

You underscore trifles in your writings, and yet you are not a subjective writer by nature; it is an acquired trait in you. To give up this acquired subjectivity is as easy as to take a drink. One needs only to be more honest, to throw oneself overboard everywhere, not to obtrude oneself into the hero of one's own novel, to renounce oneself for at least a half hour. You have a story in which a young wedded couple kiss all through dinner, grieve without cause, weep oceans of tears. Not a single sensible word; nothing but *sentimen-*

tality. And you did not write for the reader. You wrote because *you* like that sort of chatter. But suppose you were to describe the dinner, how they ate, what they ate, what the cook was like, how insipid your hero is, how content with his lazy happiness, how insipid your heroine is, how funny is her love for this napkin-bound, sated, overfed goose,—we all like to see happy, contented people, that is true,—but to describe them, what *they* said and how many times they kissed is not enough—you need something else: to free yourself from the personal expression that a placid honey-happiness produces upon everybody. . . . Subjectivity is a terrible thing. It is bad in this alone, that it reveals the author's hands and feet. I'll bet that all priests' daughters and clerks' wives who read your works are in love with you, and if you were a German you would get free beer in all the Bierhalle where the German women serve. If it were not for this subjectivity you would be the best of artists. You know how to laugh, sting, and ridicule, you possess a rounded style, you have experienced much, have seen so much,—alas! The material is all wasted.

Greek and Russian Orthodox priests may marry.

—Anton Chekhov

35

To Alex. P. Chekhov
MOSCOW. April 6, 1886

Respect yourself, for heaven's sake, and don't let your hand grow slack when your brain grows lazy. Write not more than two stories a week, and polish them carefully, so that your work will bear the aspect of work. Do not invent sufferings that you never experienced, and do not paint pictures you never saw, for a lie is even more annoying in a story than in a conversation. . . .

I will conclude this sermon by a quotation from a letter that I recently received from Grigorovich: "Respect your talent, for it is a rare gift; . . . save your impressions for careful, thoughtful work, not written at one sitting. . . . You will at once attract the attention of responsive souls, and before long of the entire reading public."

Another great authority, Souvorin, writes to me, "When one writes a great deal, not everything comes out equally good."

The third great man, our Bilibin, scolds me in his letters for writing too much. . . .

—Anton Chekhov

To Alex. P. Chekhov
BABKIN. May 10, 1886

In my opinion a true description of Nature should be very brief and have a character of relevance. Commonplaces such as, "the setting sun bathing in the waves of the darkening sea, poured its purple gold, etc.,"—"the swallows flying over the surface of the water twittered merrily,"—such commonplaces one ought to abandon. In descriptions of Nature one ought to seize upon the little particulars, grouping them in such a way that, in reading when you shut your eyes, you get a picture.

For instance, you will get the full effect of a moonlight night if you write that on the mill-dam a little glowing star-point flashed from the neck of a broken bottle, and the round, black shadow of a dog, or a wolf, emerged and ran, etc. Nature becomes animated if you are not squeamish about employing comparisons of her phenomena with ordinary human activities, etc.

—Anton Chekhov

To A. N. Pleshcheyev
MOSCOW. Oct., 1889

I am afraid of those who look for a tendency between the lines, and who are determined to regard me either as a liberal or as a conservative. I am not a liberal, not a conservative, not a believer in gradual progress, not a monk, not an indifferentist. I should like to be a free artist and nothing more, and I regret that God has not given me the power to be one. I hate lying and violence in all their forms, and am equally repelled by the secretaries of consistories and by Notovich and Gradovsky. Pharisaism, stupidity, and despotism reign not in merchants' houses and prisons alone. I see them in science, in literature, in the younger generation. . . . That is why I have no preferences either for gendarmes, or for butchers, or for scientists, or for writers, or for the younger generation. . . . I regard trademarks and labels as a superstition. My holy of holies is the human body, health, intelligence, talent, inspiration, love, and the most absolute freedom—freedom from violence and lying, whatever forms they may take. This is the program I would follow if I were a great artist.

—Anton Chekhov

To Mme. L. S. Mizinov
YALTA. March 27, 1894

Not for one moment does the thought leave me that I must, that I am obliged to write. To write, and write, and write. I am of the opinion that inner happiness is impossible without idleness. My ideal: to be idle and love a fat girl. . . .

—Anton Chekhov

INTERLOCK WITH CLUSTER 3:
An affective link: humor

N. B. The excerpt from Chekhov's letter of March 27, 1894 is in a light vein and should provoke at least one chuckle. This light-heartedness carries over into the radio drama that makes up cluster 3.

3

Cluster 3: pp. 38-63
A generic cluster
Focus: drama

INTERLOCK WITH CLUSTER 2:
An affective link: humor

This radio play lends itself to class reading and taping. Problems inherent in the stage directions will be challenges to student ingenuity: How to suggest the bridge, for example, the spacing of four men "vertically"?

ALBERT'S BRIDGE

TOM STOPPARD

Fade up bridge, with painting on mike. Four men are painting a big girdered railway bridge. They are spaced vertically, in ascending order: BOB, CHARLIE, DAD, ALBERT. *To begin with, the mike is at* ALBERT'S *level, the top.*

BOB (*the most distant*): Char-lee!

CHARLIE (*less distant*): Hel-lo!

BOB: Right, Charlie?

CHARLIE: Right! Comin' down! . . . Hey, Dad!

DAD (*an older man, not very distant*): Hel-lo!

CHARLIE: Bob 'n' me is done down here!

DAD: Right!

CHARLIE: Have you done?

DAD: Comin' down! . . . Albert! Al-bert!

CHARLIE (*more distant*): Albert!

BOB (*most distant*): Al-bert!

ALBERT (*very close, crooning softly, tunelessly amid various tunes while painting*):
How high the moon in June?
how blue the moon when it's high noon
and the turtle doves above
croon out of tune in love
saying please above the trees
which when there's thunder you don't run under
—those trees—
'cos there'll be pennies fall on Alabama
and you'll drown in foggy London town
the sun was shi-ning . . . on my Yiddisher Mama.

Lines here refer to titles and lyrics of various songs. Some students might like to get the real songs on tape background--or make a pastiche of their own.

BOB (*most distant*): Albert!

CHARLIE (*less distant*): Albert!

DAD (*off*): Albert!

ALBERT: Hel-lo!

DAD: Bob 'n' me 'n' Charlie's done!

ALBERT: Right!
Dip-brush-slap-slide-slick, and once again, dip, brush, slap—oh, it goes on so nicely . . . tickle it into the corner, there, behind the rivet. . . . No one will see that from the ground; I could cheat up here. But I'd know; so dip, brush, slap, slide and once again from the last time till the next time—every surface sleek, renewed—dip, brush, slap, slick, tickle and wipe—right in there with the old rust-proof rust-brown—all glossed and even, end to end —the last touch—perfection! (*Painting stops.*) Oh my! I could stand back to admire it and fall three hundred feet into the sea. Mind your heads! (*Laughs. Climbing down.*) Mind your head, Dad!

DAD: I'm not your dad. Keep off the wet—work down the slope to the middle—and watch your feet. (*Everyone climbing down, the distance between them closing.*) Going down for good, oh yes, I'm not facing that again. Ten coats I've done, end to end, and now I'm done all right. I had ambitions, you know. . . .

Note variations on theme in Dad's speeches.

CHARLIE (*nearer*): Mind my head, Dad.

DAD: Watch my feet, Charlie—comin' down——

CHARLIE: I'll watch your feet—you mind my head. Watch your head, Bob——

BOB (*nearer*): Watch your feet, Charlie——

CHARLIE: Mind my feet, Bob—watch my head, Dad. . . .

DAD: I'm not your dad, and mind my feet—that's my head, Albert.

ALBERT: Comin' down. . . . Doesn't she look beautiful?

DAD: Looks the same as always. There's no progress. Twenty years, twenty thousand pots of paint . . . yes, I had plans.

CHARLIE: I thought we'd never see the end of it.

BOB: It's not the bleeding end.

CHARLIE: There's no end to it.

DAD: Ten coats non-stop, one after the other, and it's no improvement, no change even, just holding its own against the weather—that's a long time, that's a lot of paint. I could have made my mark.

ALBERT: Continuity—that's hard to come by.

DAD: I've spread my life over those girders, and in five minutes I could scrape down to the iron, I could scratch down to my prime.

ALBERT: Simplicity—so . . . contained; neat; your bargain with the world, your wages, your

Note here and on page 41 the commercial accounting basis of Albert's view of life. What difference between Albert and Dad is established here?

ıy not? (From Albert's point of view, of course.)

time, your energy, your property, everything you took out and everything you put in, the bargain that has carried you this far—all contained there in ten layers of paint, accounted for. Now that's something; to keep track of everything you put into the kitty, to have it lie there, under your eye, fixed and immediate—there are no consequences to a coat of paint. That's more than you can say for a factory man; his bits and pieces scatter, grow wheels, disintegrate, change color, join up in new forms which he doesn't know anything about. In short, he doesn't know what he's done, to whom.

DAD: Watch your feet, Albert. Mind your head, Charlie.

CHARLIE: You mind my head. Take care my feet, Bob——

BOB: Watch your feet, Charlie——

CHARLIE: Mind your feet, Dad——

DAD: That's my head, Albert——

ALBERT: Coming down . . . .
Ah, look at it up there, criss-crossed and infinite, you can't see where it ends—I could take off and swing through its branches screaming like a gibbon!

DAD: Mind where you're putting your feet, Albert.

CHARLIE: Watch my head, Dad.

BOB: Train coming, Charlie. (*Distant train coming.*)

CHARLIE: I've seen it.

BOB (*jumping down on to gravel*): And down.

CHARLIE: Mind where you jump, Dad.

DAD: Seen it.

CHARLIE (*jumping down*): None too soon.

DAD: Train coming, Albert.

ALBERT: I'm with you.

DAD (*jumps down*): Finished.

CHARLIE: Like hell.

BOB: Well, that's another two years behind you.

DAD: A feller once offered me a half share in a very nice trading station in the China Seas. I had it in me.

ALBERT: Mind your toes.
(*He jumps. Climbing down ends. All are now on mike.*)
Now that's a good way to end a day—ending so much else.

CHARLIE: All right for some. Students.

BOB: Slummers.

That is, Albert

CHARLIE: Pocket-money holiday lads, oh yes.

ALBERT: One bridge—freshly painted—a million tons of iron thrown across the bay—rust brown and even to the last lick—spick and span, rust-proofed, weather-resistant—perfect!

DAD: Other end needs painting now. A man could go mad.

Note the visual detail to suggest voice. What is special about "rimless spectacles"?

Implies some sound effect for bridge. (See opening stage direction, p. 39.) Chairman's voice comes on as train fades.

British slang for a coin worth one pound.

(*The train arrives and goes screaming past.*)

(*Set* CHAIRMAN *over end of train, cutting bridge.*)

CHAIRMAN: Let us not forget, gentlemen, that Clufton Bay Bridge is the fourth biggest single-span double-track shore-to-shore railway bridge in the world bar none——

DAVE: Hear, hear, Mr. Chairman——

CHAIRMAN: Thank you, Dave——

GEORGE: I've been studying these figures, Mr. Chairman——

CHAIRMAN: Just a moment, George. We've got an amenity here in Clufton; that bridge stands for the whole town, quite apart from the money earned in railway dues——

DAVE: Hear, hear, Mr. Chairman——

CHAIRMAN: Thank you, Dave.

GEORGE: According to the City Engineer's figures, Mr. Chairman—

CHAIRMAN: Just a moment, George. When my grandfather built this bridge he didn't spare the brass —and I for one, as chairman of the Clufton Bay Bridge Sub-Committee—entrusted as we are with the upkeep and responsibility of what is a symbol of Clufton's prosperity—I for one do not begrudge the spending of a few extra quid on a lick of paint.

DAVE: Hear, hear, Mr. Chairman.

CHAIRMAN: Thank you, Dave.

GEORGE: I know it's a symbol of your prosperity, Mr. Chairman, but——

CHAIRMAN: That's a highly improper remark, George. Clufton's prosperity is what I said.

DAVE: Hear, hear, Mr. Chairman.

CHAIRMAN: Thank you, Dave.

GEORGE: My mistake, Mr. Chairman. But if Mr. Fitch's figures are correct——

FITCH (*distinctive voice; clipped, confident; rimless spectacles*): My figures are always correct, Mr. Chairman.

CHAIRMAN: Hear that, George? The City Engineer's figures are a model of correctitude.

DAVE: Hear, hear, Mr. Chairman.

CHAIRMAN: Thank you, Dave.

GEORGE: Then this new paint he's recommending is going to cost us four times as much as the paint we've been using up to now.

(*Pause.*)

CHAIRMAN: Four times as much? Money?

DAVE: Hear, hear, Mr. Chairman.

CHAIRMAN: Just a moment, Dave. I don't think your figures are correct, George. Mr. Fitch knows his business.

GEORGE: What business is he in—paint?

CHAIRMAN: That's a highly improper remark, George—er, you're not

[N]ote Chairman's dropping of "Mr." Also note the developing arrogance in his speech and the [s]uggestion that Fitch might be involved in corruption. Chairman's character as big chief [b]ureaucrat is interesting, and may give us some idea of Stoppard's concern and focus.

in the paint business, are you, Mr. Fitch?

FITCH: No, Mr. Chairman.

CHAIRMAN: No, no, of course you're not. You should be ashamed, George.

DAVE: Hear, hear, Mr. Chairman.

CHAIRMAN: Shut up, Dave. Now what about it, Mr. Fitch? Is this right what George says?

FITCH: Well, up to a point, Mr. Chairman, yes. But in the long run, no.

CHAIRMAN: Don't fiddle-faddle with me, Fitch. Does this new-fangled paint of yours cost four times as much as the paint we've got, and if so, what's in it for you?

GEORGE: Hear, hear, Mr. Chairman.

CHAIRMAN: Thank you, George.

FITCH: To put the matter at its simplest, Mr. Chairman, the new paint costs four times as much and lasts four times as long.

CHAIRMAN: Well, there's your answer, George. It costs four times as much but it lasts four times as long. Very neat, Fitch. I thought we'd got you there.

GEORGE: What's the point, then?

FITCH: Apart from its silvery color, Mr. Chairman, which would be a pleasanter effect than the present rusty brown, the new paint would also afford a considerable saving, as you can no doubt see.

CHAIRMAN: Everybody see that? Well, I don't.

GEORGE: Nor do I.

DAVE: Hear, hear, George.

GEORGE: Shut up, Dave.

FITCH: If I might explain, gentlemen. As you know, in common with other great bridges of its kind, the painting of Clufton Bay Bridge is a continuous operation. That is to say, by the time the painters have reached the far end, the end they started at needs painting again.

DAVE: I never knew that!

CHAIRMAN AND GEORGE: Shut up, Dave.

FITCH: This cycle is not a fortuitous one. It is contrived by relating the area of the surfaces to be painted—call it A—to the rate of the painting—B—and the durability of the paint—C. The resultant equation determines the variable factor X—i.e., the number of painters required to paint surfaces A at speed B within time C. For example—

CHAIRMAN: E.g.

FITCH: Quite. Er—e.g., with X plus one painters the work would proceed at a higher rate—i.e., B, plus, e.g., Q. However, the factors A and C, the surface area and the lasting quality of the paint remain, of course, constant. The result would be that the painters would be ready to begin painting the bridge

Note Fitch's entire speech here. What language is he speaking? Students might like to see a few "memos" from a large corporation's systems analyst. For more on this theme of linguistic "modification and accomodation" see George Orwell's *1984*.

for the second time strictly speaking before it needed re-painting. This creates the co-efficient—Waste.

CHAIRMAN: W.

FITCH: If you like. This co-efficient belies efficiency, you see.

A pun, but is this possible to render on radio? (tone?)

CHAIRMAN: U.C. You see, George?

GEORGE: OK, I see.

FITCH: To continue. Furthermore, the value of the co-efficient—Waste—is progressive. Let me put it like this, gentlemen. Because the rate of painting is constant—i.e., too fast to allow the paintwork to deteriorate—each bit the men come to requires re-painting even less than the bit before it. You see, they are all the time catching up on themselves progressively, until there'll come a point where they'll be re-painting the bridge, while it's still wet! (*Pause.*) No, that can't be right. . . .

CHAIRMAN: Come to the point, Fitch. Wake up, Dave.

DAVE (*waking up*): Hear, hear, Mr. Chairman.

FITCH: To put it another way, gentlemen, that is to say, conversely. With one too few painters —X minus one—the rate of progress goes down to let us say, B minus Q. So what is the result? By the time the painters are ready to start re-painting, the end they started at has deteriorated into unsightly and damaging rust—a co-efficient representing the converse inefficiency.

CHAIRMAN: Pull yourself together, Fitch. I don't know what you're drivellin' about.

GEORGE: In a nutshell, Fitch, the new paint costs four times as much and lasts four times as long. Where's the money saved?

FITCH: We sack three painters.

(*Pause.*)

CHAIRMAN: Ah. . . .

How would he say this?

FITCH: You see, to date we have achieved your optimum efficiency by employing four men. It takes them two years to paint the bridge, which is the length of time the paint lasts. This new paint will last eight years, so we only need one painter to paint the bridge by himself. After eight years, the end he started at will be just ready for repainting. The saving to the ratepayers would be £3,529 15s.9d. per annum.

GEORGE: Excuse me, Mr. Chairman—

CHAIRMAN: Just a moment, George. I congratulate you, Mr. Fitch. An inspired stroke. We'll put it up to the meeting of the full council.

GEORGE: Excuse me——

CHAIRMAN: Shut up, George.

DAVE: Hear, hear, Mr. Chairman.

FITCH: Thank you, Mr. Chairman.

CHAIRMAN: Thank you, Mr. Fitch.

(*Fade.*)

Local property taxpayers

Note return to "Mr."

How much communication is there between mother and son?

MOTHER: Aren't you getting up, Albert? It's gone eleven. . . . Are you listening to me, Albert?

ALBERT (*in bed*): What?

MOTHER: I'm talking to you, Albert.

ALBERT: Yes?

MOTHER: Yes, what?

ALBERT: Yes, Mother.

MOTHER: That's better. Oh dear, what was I saying?

ALBERT: I don't know, Mother.

MOTHER (*sighs*): I was against that university from the start.

ALBERT: The country needs universities.

MOTHER: I mean it's changed you, Albert. You're thinking all the time. It's not like you, Albert.

ALBERT: Thinking?

MOTHER: You don't talk to me. Or your father. Well, I'm glad it's all behind you, I hope it starts to wear off.

ALBERT: I wanted to stay on after my degree, but they wouldn't have me.

MOTHER: I don't know what you want to know about philosophy for. Your father didn't have to study philosophy, and look where he is, Chairman of Metal Alloys and Allied Metals. It's not as if you were going to be a philosopher or something. . . . Yes, you could have been a trainee executive by now. As it is, you'll have to do your stint on the factory floor, philosophy or no philosophy. That university has held you back.

ALBERT: I'll have to get myself articled to a philosopher. . . . Start at the bottom. Of course, a philosopher's clerk wouldn't get the really interesting work straight off, I know that. It'll be a matter of filing the generalizations, tidying up the paradoxes, laying out the premises before the boss gets in—that kind of thing; but after I've learned the ropes I might get a half share in a dialectic, perhaps, and work up towards a treatise. . . . Yes, I could have my own thriving little philosopher's office in a few years.

"apprenticed"

Is this speech absurd? What might Stoppard be implying about the university? about Albert?

(*Pause.*)

MOTHER: Would you like to have some coffee downstairs?

ALBERT: Yes.

MOTHER: Yes, what?

ALBERT: Yes, please.

(*Pause.*)

MOTHER: I still think it was mean of you not to let us know you had a summer vacation.

ALBERT: I thought you knew. I've had one every year.

MOTHER: You know I've no head for dates. You could have come home to see us.

ALBERT: I'm sorry. There was the temporary job going. . . .

MOTHER: Your father would have given you some money if you'd asked him.

A humorous exchange. But does it also show a serious deficiency in Albert's character?

ALBERT: I thought I'd have a go myself.

MOTHER: You'll have to get up now.

ALBERT: It was fantastic up there. The scale of it. From the ground it looks just like a cat's cradle, from a distance you can take it all in, and then up there in the middle of it the thinnest threads are as thick as your body and you could play tennis on the main girders.

MOTHER: Kate will be up in a minute to make the beds.

ALBERT: It's absurd, really, being up there, looking down on the university lying under you like a couple of bricks, full of dots studying philosophy——

See the way Fraser speaks of "dots," page 58.

MOTHER: I don't want you getting in Kate's way—she's got to clean.

ALBERT: What could they possibly know? I saw more up there in three weeks than those dots did in three years. I saw the context. It reduced philosophy and everything else. I got a perspective. Because that bridge was—separate—complete—removed, defined by principles of engineering which makes it stop at a certain point, which compels a certain shape, certain joints—the whole thing utterly fixed by the rules that make it stay up. It's complete, and a man can give his life to its maintenance, a very fine bargain.

This is probably one of the obligatory speeches in the play. It explains Albert and one of the concerns of the play.

MOTHER: Do you love me, Albert?

ALBERT: Yes.

MOTHER: Yes, what?

ALBERT: Yes, please.

(*Cut to a gavel banged on table.*)

MAYORAL VOICE: Number 43 on the order paper, proposal from Bridge sub-committee. . . .

VOICE 1: Move. . . .

VOICE 2: Second.

MAYORAL VOICE: All in favor. (*Absent-minded murmur of fifty "Ayes."*) Against. (*Pause.*) Carried. Number 44 on the order paper.

(*Fade.*)

(*Fade up knock on door off. Door opens.*)

KATE: Oh, I'm sorry, Mr. Albert.

ALBERT: Hello, I was just thinking of getting up.

(*Cut to.*)

BOB: What—by myself? It would take years.

FITCH: Eight years, yes.

BOB: No. I demand a transfer.

FITCH: I thought I'd give you first refusal.

BOB: I want to go back to painting the Corporation crest on the dustcarts. "trashcarts"

FITCH: I could fit you in on the magenta.

BOB: On the what?

FITCH: It's one man to a color nowadays. Efficiency.

(*Cut.*)

An interesting juxtaposition of term and attitude. We laugh--but at what?

CHARLIE: You must be joking.

FITCH: It's an opportunity for you.

CHARLIE: I'd go mad. What's it all about?

FITCH: Efficiency.

CHARLIE: I'm not doing that bridge on me tod.°

FITCH: It's no more work than before.

CHARLIE: I'd jump off within a month.

FITCH: Oh. Well, we couldn't have that. That would be only one ninety-sixth of it done.

(*Cut.*)

DAD: You mean it's a cheaper way of doing it.

FITCH: More efficient.

DAD: We've been doing a good job.

FITCH: Efficiency isn't a matter of good and bad, entirely. It's a matter of the optimum use of resources—time, money, manpower.

DAD: You mean it's cheaper; I'm an old man.

FITCH: You've got eight years in you.

DAD: It might be my last eight. I haven't done anything yet—I've got a future.

FITCH: Well, I could put you on yellow no-parking lines.

DAD: Yes, all right.

(*Cut.*)

FITCH: . . . But do you have any qualifications?

°ON ME TOD: on my own

ALBERT: I've got a degree in philosophy, Mr. Fitch.

FITCH: That's a little unusual.

ALBERT: I wouldn't say that. There were lots of us doing it.

FITCH: That's all very well if you're going to be a philosopher, but what we're talking about is painting bridges.

ALBERT: Yes, yes, I can see what you're driving at, of course, but I don't suppose it did me any harm. Almost everyone who didn't know what to do did philosophy. Well, that's logical.

Is it "logical"? How does one "do" philosophy? Compare with Albert's "articled to a philosopher" speech, page 45.

FITCH: You're an educated man.

ALBERT: Thank you.

FITCH: What I mean is, you're not the run-of-the-mill bridge painter, not the raw material I'm looking for.

ALBERT: Well, I did it in the vacation.

FITCH: Yes . . . yes, I did have reports of you. But surely. . . .

ALBERT: I know what you mean, but that's what I want to do. I liked it. I don't want to work in a factory or an office.

FITCH: Is it the open-air life that attracts you?

ALBERT: No. It's the work, the whole thing—crawling round that great basket, so high up, being responsible for so much that is so visible. Actually I don't know if that's why I like it. I like it because I was happy up there, doing something simple but so grand, without end. It doesn't get away from you.

Is there a parallel between being a bridge painter and a philosopher?

How many conversations are going on here? To whom are Albert's questions directed?

FITCH: The intellectual rather than the practical—that's it, is it?

ALBERT: Probably.

FITCH: I'm the same. It's poetry to me—a perfect equation of space, time and energy——

ALBERT: Yes——

FITCH: It's not just slapping paint on a girder——

ALBERT: No——

FITCH: It's continuity—control—mathematics.

ALBERT: Poetry.

FITCH: Yes, I should have known it was a job for a university man....

ALBERT: Like me and you—

FITCH: Well, I went to night school myself.

ALBERT: Same thing, different time.

FITCH: That's what I say.

ALBERT: I'm your man, Mr. Fitch.

FITCH: You'll stick to it for eight years, will you?

ALBERT: Oh, I'll paint it more than once.

(*Cut.*)

Sound effects for taping?

(*Breakfast in background.*)

FATHER: Now then, Albert, you've had your fun. When I was your age I'd got six years of work behind me.

ALBERT: Well, I'm starting work now, Father.

FATHER: Quite so, but don't think you're going to start at the top. You'll get there all right in time, but you've got to learn the business first. Is there any more tea, Mother?

MOTHER: Ring for Kate, would you, Albert?

ALBERT (*going*): Yes, Mother.

MOTHER: That reminds me.

FATHER: You'll start where I started. On the shop floor.

ALBERT (*approach*): Well, actually, Father——

MOTHER: I don't want to sound Victorian, but one can't just turn a blind eye.

ALBERT: What?

FATHER: Yes, I never went in for books and philosophy and look at me now.

MOTHER: I suppose that's the penance one pays for having servants nowadays.

ALBERT: What?

FATHER: I started Metal Alloys and Allied Metals—built it up from a biscuit-tin furnace in the back garden, small smelting jobs for the cycle-repair shop.

MOTHER: I've suspected her for some time and now one can't ignore it. Even with her corset.

ALBERT: Who?

FATHER: You can come in on Monday and I'll hand you over to the plant foreman.

ALBERT: I've already got a job. Actually.

FATHER: You haven't got a job till I give you one.

Does Mother's use of this outdated term reveal anything of her character? And, then, of how she might be played?

ALBERT: I'm going to paint Clufton Bay Bridge, starting Monday.

MOTHER: What color?

ALBERT: Silver.

FATHER: Just a minute——

KATE (*off*): You rang, madam?

MOTHER: More tea, Kate, please.

KATE: Yes, madam.

MOTHER: And a word.

KATE: Yes, madam.

MOTHER: Are you ill?

KATE: No, madam.

MOTHER: I believe I heard you being ill in the bathroom this morning.

KATE: Yes, madam.

MOTHER: And yesterday?

KATE: Yes, madam.

ALBERT: What's the matter, Kate?

KATE: Nothing, Mr. Albert.

MOTHER: Leave this to me. Cook tells me you fainted in the kitchen last week.

KATE: I came over funny.

ALBERT: Kate. . . .

MOTHER: Let's not beat about the bush. Is it the gardener's boy?

KATE: No, madam.

MOTHER: Then who is it?

ALBERT: Who's what?

MOTHER: Well, I'm sorry. You can have a month's wages, of course. You'd better make sure that the young man does the right thing by you.

(*Cut.*)

KATE: I never thought you'd do the right thing by me, Albert.

ALBERT: We'll be all right. It's a nice room.

KATE: Your mum didn't like it.

ALBERT: My mother's got no taste. I'll make a fire.

KATE: And wrap up warm when you go out—it'll be freezing up there.

ALBERT: Only a breeze.

KATE: It'll be ice in a month. If you fell I'd die, Albert.

ALBERT: So would I.

KATE: Don't you ever fall. They shouldn't make it a year-round job. It's dangerous.

ALBERT: No—you don't know how big it is—the threads are like ladders and the cross-pieces are like piers into the sky.

KATE: You hold on tight, for the spring, and the baby.

(*Cut in bridge and painting.*)

ALBERT: Slip, slap, brush, dip, slop, slide, slick and wipe. . . . In eight years I'll be pushing thirty, and the Clufton Bay Bridge will be a silver bridge—dip-brush, slick, slide, slap
without end, I'm the bridge man,
web-spinning silver spider-man

The verse here indicates a shift in the play's mode. Hitherto the play has been constructed as a slight exaggeration or skewing of possible situations. Now, it is to be total fantasy for satiric effect. One may well ask how many plays Stoppard has going?

crawling between heaven and
earth on a
cantilevered span,
cat's cradled in the sky . . .
look down at the toy ships
where the sea pounds under
toy trains
to toy towns
under my hand.
Am I the spider or the fly?
I'm the bridge man. . . .

The downstairs maid went upstairs to make a bed that I was in—and suddenly——

(Cut out bridge. Cut in crying baby.)

I name this child Albert.

KATE: You can't.

ALBERT: Very well. I name this child Kate.

KATE: Katherine.

ALBERT: Tomorrow wheel her along to the bridge so I can see you.

KATE: All right. But don't wave, Albert. Don't wave. If you waved and fell——

ALBERT: I shan't wave.

(Cut in bridge and painting.)

Some students might like to work up a musical accompaniment for this and similar passages.

Dip brush, dip brush
without end, come rain or shine;
A fine way to spend my time.
My life is set out for me,
the future traced in brown,
my past measured in silver;
how absurd, how sublime
(don't look down)
to climb and clamber in a giant
frame;

Brand name of British toy trains (A very middle class toy)

British construction toy like Erector in U.S.

dip brush, dip brush, slick, slide
wipe
and again.

(Painting stops.)

I straddle a sort of overflowing gutter on which bathtub boats push up and down. . . . The banks are littered with various bricks, kiddiblocks with windows; dinky toys move through the gaps, dodged by moving dots that have no color; under my feet the Triang train thunders across the Meccano, and the minibrick estates straggle up over the hill in neat rows with paintbox gardens. It's the most expensive toytown in the store—the detail is remarkable. But fragile. I tremble for it, half expecting some petulant pampered child to step over the hill and kick the whole thing to bits with her Startrite sandals.

(Painting.)

Don't look down,
the dots are looking up.
Don't wave, don't fall, tumbling
down a
telescope, diminishing to a dot.
In eight years who will I be?
Not me.
I'll be assimilated then,
the honest working man, father
of three——
you've seen him around,
content in his obscurity, come
to terms with public truths,
digging the garden of a council
house
in what is now my Sunday suit.
I'm okay for fifty years, with
any luck;

Starter shoes for children. At one time, the only brand that middle class mothers would buy.

Public municipal housing

I can see me climb
up a silver bridge to paint it
for the seventh time,
keeping track of my life spent
in painting in the color of my
track:
above it all.
How sublime——
dip brush, dip brush—silvering
the brown.
Which dot is mine?
Don't wave, don't look down.
Don't fall.
(*Cut bridge.*)

KATE: I saw you today.

ALBERT: What was I doing?

KATE: Painting, I suppose. Crawling backwards along a cross-piece.

ALBERT: Pulling silver after me. I didn't see you. Or I didn't see which one was you.

KATE: Coming out of the hairdressers. Six and six, I had it cut.

About 78¢

ALBERT: Just goes to show—if you get far enough away, six and sixpence doesn't show, and nor does anything, at a distance.

KATE: Well, life is all close up, isn't it?

ALBERT: Yes, it hits you when you come back down. How close it all is. You can't stand back to look at it.

KATE: Do you like my hair like this?

ALBERT: Like what? Oh—yes. Do you like mine?

KATE: I got whistled at in the street.

One of the play's numerous "morals." But does it belong to Stoppard or Kate? There is a difference.

ALBERT: It's always happening to me.

KATE: A lorry driver, at the traffic lights.

ALBERT: They're the worst, I find.

KATE: Oh, Albert. I had the pram with me too.

ALBERT: You look too young for it. Big sister.

KATE: And I cook very nice, don't I?

ALBERT: I'd whistle at you.

KATE: I'd come—if you whistled. I'd give you a wink and say, "Cheeky!" "Fresh!"

ALBERT: Oh, yes—you'd get off with me. "pick me up" No trouble at all. I'd take you down by the canal after the pictures.

KATE: What do you know about it—with your education and all?

ALBERT: Me? I'm a working man.

KATE: You don't have regrets, do you, Albert?

ALBERT: No.

KATE: It wasn't a good bargain, on the face of it.

ALBERT: It depends on what you want.

KATE: Me and the baby. Two rooms and a forty-five hour week, hard work and no advancement.

ALBERT: I'm not ambitious.

KATE: You could have had so much—a white wedding, nice house, an office job with real prospects, the country club . . . tennis.

. . . Yes, you could have had Metal Alloys and Allied Metals —the top job, responsibility, your own office with telephones. . . .

ALBERT: Yes, I'm well out of that.

(Cut in bridge and painting.)

Progress. Two lines of silver meeting in an angle bracket—and tickle in there behind the rivet—slip, slop, and wipe, and on we go up the slope. Does the town look up? Do they all gawp and say to each other, Look at him! How ridiculous he looks up there, so small, how laughably inadequate. Or do they say, How brave! One man against the elements! Pitted against so much! The lone explorer feeling his way between the iron crevasses, tacked against the sky by his boots and fingers. Dots, bricks and beetles. I could drown them in my spit.

(Cut bridge, cut in baby's rattle in background.)

KATE: That isn't nice, Albert.

ALBERT: Spitting?

KATE: Talking like that.

ALBERT: It doesn't represent desire. I'll let them live. I'm only trying to tell you what it's like.

KATE: I know what it's like. It's painting a girder. There's other jobs.

ALBERT: It's my bridge—I wish you'd stop her rattling; it's getting on my nerves.

What validates Albert's megalomania and paranoia?

KATE: That's very advanced for six months.

ALBERT: I'm not doubting her progress. If she played the trumpet it would be even more advanced, but it would still be sending me round the twist. Here, give——

"driving me crazy"

(He dispossesses the rattler, who bawls.)

KATE: Now you've set her off. She doesn't *understand.* *(Comforting.)* Come on, then. . . .

ALBERT: Well, see you later.

KATE: Where are you going?

ALBERT: Work.

KATE: It's your Saturday off.

ALBERT: No, it's my Saturday on.

KATE: Last Saturday was your Saturday on.

ALBERT: Well, I'll take two off in a row.

(Cut in bridge.)

Listen . . .
The hot sun makes you think of insects,
but this insect hum is the whole city
caught in a seashell. . . .
All conversation is hidden there,
among motors, coughing fits, applause,
screams, laughter, feet on the stairs,

Clinical sign of madness?

secretaries typing to dictation,
radios delivering the cricket scores,
tapes running, wheels turning, mills grinding,
chips frying, lavatories flushing, lovers sighing,
the mayor blowing his nose.
All audible life in the vibration
of a hairdryer in the room below.

(*Painting.*)

Dip brush, slide, stroke,
it goes on as smooth and shiny
as my sweat. I itch.
Paint on my arm,
silver paint on my brown arm;
it could be part of the bridge.

(*Painting stops.*)

Listen. The note of Clufton is B flat.
The whole world could be the same.
Look down. Is it a fact
that all the dots have names?

(*Cut bridge.*)

KATE: Jack Morris is taking Maureen and little Leslie to Paris.

ALBERT: Who's Jack Morris?

KATE: Next door, Albert.

ALBERT: Oh, yes. Who's Maureen?

KATE: Mrs. Morris.

ALBERT: So little Leslie would be their little girl.

KATE: It's a little boy.

ALBERT: Ah. Why are we talking about them?

KATE: They're going to Paris for a holiday. Where are we going?

ALBERT: When?

KATE: That's what I'd like to know.

ALBERT: What?

KATE: Don't you have a holiday?

ALBERT: Oh. I suppose I must. Everybody does. Yes, I expect Fitch took that into account.

KATE: You're not going to dodge your holiday—I know what you're up to; you're already working full Saturdays; don't think I'm such a fool that I don't know. . . . And you're working till dark.

ALBERT: Overtime. I lose time in the winter.

KATE (*sniffing*): It's because you don't like it here, being at home.

ALBERT: Oh, Kate . . . I've got a schedule, you see.

KATE: You're miles ahead of it.

ALBERT: I've got to have some in hand in case of accidents.

KATE: I told you! You'll fall off, and me and Katherine will be alone.

ALBERT: No, no, no . . . stop crying. We'll have a holiday. I'll take a week.

KATE: A fortnight.

ALBERT: All right, I don't mind.

Where there is a famous bridge.

KATE: Can we go to Paris?

ALBERT: I've been to Paris. There's nothing there, believe me. We could go to Scotland.

KATE: Touring?

ALBERT: Certainly. The Firth of Forth.

KATE: We haven't got a car. Maureen said we could go with them.

ALBERT: But they're going to Paris.

KATE: We could afford it. It wouldn't be hard, it's easier with two children and joined forces. . . . It would be lovely, I've always wanted to see the Champs Elysee and the Ark de Triumph and the Seine and the Eiffel Tower. . . .

Are these misspellings pointless, since as they are written they are not phonetically mispronounced? Or are they supposed to suggest Kate's mispronunciation of the places? If so, are there better phonetic alterations? First you must decide: Does Stoppard want Kate to mispronounce the words? If so, why?

(Cliché French accordion music. Cross-fade to Eiffel Tower. It's the same as Clufton Bridge.)

(*Distant. Shouting up.*) Albert! A-a-albert! (*Repeated, fading, despairing.*) Come down! Please come down!

ALBERT: I thought as much. Dots, bricks, beetles . . . in B flat. Still, I'm glad I came. The pointlessness takes one's breath away—a tower connects nothing, it stands only so that one can go up and look down. Bridge-builders have none of this audacity, compromise themselves with function. Monsieur Eiffel, poet and philosopher, every eight years I'll scratch your name in the silver of Clufton Bay Bridge.

KATE (*distant, despairing*): Al-bert!

ALBERT (*quiet*): Coming down.

(Cut Eiffel Tower.)

(Crockery smashes, flung against wall.)

KATE: What's her name?

ALBERT: Kate. . . .

KATE: What a bloody coincidence!

ALBERT: You've got it all wrong, Kate; there's no woman——

KATE (*crying*): I can smell her on your coat!

ALBERT: It's paint—I tell you I was up on the bridge.

KATE: All night!

ALBERT: I just thought I would. It was nice up there.

KATE: You're barmy if you expect me to believe that, you're round the twist——

ALBERT: It's true——

KATE: And I believe it, I *am* round the twist! I'm as barmy as you are, but I believe it——

ALBERT: That's better.

(*Another cup smashes.*)

KATE: No it isn't—it's worse! A woman would be normal. (*Breaking down.*) You don't talk to me, you don't talk to Katherine, you can't wait to get out of the house and up your favorite girder. (*Quieter, sobbing.*) You don't like me any more—I know you don't—I'm boring for you—I haven't got

Compare with Kate's earlier speech about Albert's many sacrifices, pp. 51-52.

what you want, and you don't want to hear the things I tell you because I've got nothing to tell you—nothing happens. . . .

ALBERT: I like a quiet life, that's all.

KATE: Gutless. You'll spend your whole life painting that bridge.

ALBERT: It's a good job.

KATE: You know damn well it's a stupid job which any thick idiot could do—but you're educated, Albert. You had opportunities. There was Metal Alloys and Allied Metals—you could have gone right up the ladder—we'd have a house and friends, and we'd entertain and Katherine would have nice friends—you could have been an executive!

ALBERT: I was lying in bed one day when the maid came in to make it. . . . She was all starchy. When she moved, her skirt sort of crackled against her nylons. . . . I never had any regrets, but I did want her to be happy too.

KATE (*sobbing*): I've begun talking to myself, over the sink and stove. . . . I talk to myself because nobody else listens, and you won't talk to me, so I talk to the sink and the stove and the baby, and maybe one day one of them will answer me. (*Baby gurgles, almost a word.*)

(*Cut to bridge and painting.*)

ALBERT (*crooning flatly amid and around the tune of "Night and Day"*):

Night and day, I am the one . . .
day and night, I'm really a part of me. . . .
I've got me under my skin.
So why
don't I take all of me. . . .
When I begin the beguine. . . .
I get accustomed to my face.
The thought of me makes me stop
before I begin.
Yes, I've got me under my skin,
and I get a kick out of me. . . .
Day and night, night and day. . . .
Shall I compare me to a summer's day,
'Cos I can't get me out of my mind. . . .
I saw me in Monterey . . .
and I'm all right by me . . .
yes, I'm all right, I'm all right,
I'm all right by me. . . .

(*Applause, two-handed, from quite close. Painting stops.*)

Who's there? Who's that?

FRASER (*applauding*): Very nice, very nice. The egotist school of songwriting.

ALBERT: Who are you?

FRASER: You mean my name?

ALBERT: I suppose so.

FRASER: Fraser.

ALBERT: What are you doing on my bridge?

See annotation on page 52.

FRASER: Yours?

ALBERT: I'm painting it. I'm authorized.

FRASER: You've got a big job ahead of you.

ALBERT: I've got the time.

FRASER: You've got the time perhaps, but I'd say that time is against you. The condition of the paintwork is very shoddy.

ALBERT: Well, it hasn't been done for a fair while.

FRASER: Yes, it's beginning to look definitely tatty.

ALBERT: I'm getting through it bit by bit.

FRASER: Too slow. The old paint isn't lasting. People have noticed, you know. There's been talk.

ALBERT: Look here—are you the bridge inspector or something?

FRASER: What?

ALBERT: Did Mr. Fitch send you?

FRASER: Who?

ALBERT: What's it all about then?

FRASER: Look down there. I came up because up was the only direction left. The rest has been filled up and is still filling. The city is a hold in which blind prisoners are packed wall to wall. Motorcars nose each other down every street, and they are beginning to breed, spread. They press the people to the walls by their knees, pinning them by their knees, and there's no end to it, because if you stopped making them, thousands of people would be thrown out of work, and they'd have no money to spend, the shopkeepers would get caught up in it, and the farms and factories, and all the people dependent on them, with their children and all. There's too much of everything, but the space for it is constant. So the shell of human existence is filling out, expanding, and it's going to go bang.

ALBERT: You're frightened of traffic?

FRASER: We are at the mercy of a vast complex of moving parts, any of which might fail. Civilization is in decline, and the white rhino is being wiped out for the racket in bogus aphrodisiacs.

ALBERT: An animal lover——

FRASER: That was merely a trifle I snatched at in my inability to express the whole. I have never been able to understand, for instance, why anyone should want to be a dentist. I cannot pin down the divinity which ensures that just so many people take up dentistry and just so many agree to milk the cows which would otherwise scream in pain just as children would scream if there were no dentists.

ALBERT: I see. A lunatic, in fact.

FRASER: Not certifiably so. By no means certified. I am simply open, wide open, to certain insights. I do not believe that

Not legally insane by medical standards.

Appropriate usage?
In any way suggestive of Fraser's state of mind?

there is anyone in control. There is the semblance of pattern—supply meeting demand, one-way streets, give and take, the presumption of return tickets, promises to pay the bearer on demand, etcetera—but there's nothing really holding it together. One is forced to recognize the arbitrariness of what we claim to be order. Somewhere there is a lynch pin, which, when removed, will collapse the whole monkey-puzzle. And I'm not staying there till it happens.

ALBERT: I see. Well, we all have our problems, but I don't see how that justifies you climbing about council property. So would you kindly descend——

FRASER: That's what I came up for.

ALBERT: To descend?

FRASER: It never occurred to me to stay.

ALBERT: You came up to go down?

FRASER: To jump.

ALBERT: Jump?

FRASER: Off.

ALBERT: Jump off? You'd kill yourself. Ah.

FRASER: Yes.

ALBERT: I see. All right, then.

FRASER: My mind was made up——

ALBERT: I see your point.

FRASER: It seemed the easiest thing to do.

ALBERT: I agree. Well then, time is hurrying by, waiting for no man. Or is that tide?

FRASER: I see you're trying to humor me. Well, I expected that. You'll be sending for a priest next.

ALBERT: Come, come, don't procrastinate.

FRASER: Me?

ALBERT: You said you were going to jump.

FRASER: Well?

ALBERT: Well, jump.

FRASER: Aren't you going to try to talk me out of it?

ALBERT: You know your own mind. And you're holding me up. I've got to paint where you're standing.

FRASER: You wouldn't just stand there without lifting a finger?

ALBERT: I knew it. You're just a talker. Those ones never do it.

FRASER: I can't believe it. You wouldn't just stand there and watch me kill myself.

ALBERT: I thought that's what you wanted.

FRASER: Well, I did. I couldn't bear the noise and the chaos. I couldn't get free of it, the enormity of that disorder, so dependent on a chance sequence of action and reaction. So I started to climb to get some height, you know, enough

Albert's earlier speeches about the world as seen from a bridge are similiar in thought to this one. (See pp. 46, 47, and 52.) Why, then, doesn't Albert like Fraser?

See beginning of speech and comment on page 57.

height to drop from, to be sure, and the higher I climbed, the more I saw and the less I heard. And look now. I've been up here for hours, looking down and all it is, is dots and bricks, giving out a gentle hum. Quite safe. Quite small after all. Quite ordered, seen from above. Laid out in squares, each square a function, each dot a functionary. I really think it might work. Yes, from a vantage point like this, the idea of society is just about tenable.

ALBERT: Funked it. Well, mind how you go. Don't fall.

(*Cut bridge.*)

CHAIRMAN: Gentlemen, this special emergency meeting of the Clufton Bay Bridge Subcommittee has been called as a result of public representations, both direct and via the press, concerning the unsightly condition of what is the symbol of Clufton's prosperity. My grandfather, who was loved by the public, and owed everything to them, must be turning in his grave. It is a salutary reminder that we are all servants of the public, Mr. Fitch.

DAVE: Hear, hear, Mr. Chairman.

CHAIRMAN: Shut up, Dave. As chairman, I, of course, take full responsibility. That is the duty of the chairman, regardless of where that responsibility actually lies, Mr. Fitch.

GEORGE: Hear, hear, Mr. Chairman.

CHAIRMAN: It is no smiling matter, George. The city publicity officer has been on to me, the Parks and Amenities have been on to me, British Railways have been on to me, and the *Clufton Chronicle* has been doing its damndest to get on to me. This committee is the shame and the laughing stock of the Clufton Council, and as the future—as a possible future Mayor, I am gravely embarrassed by having to carry the can for a lack of foresight and watchfulness on the part of committee members whose names I will not mention, George. I have issued a statement to the effect that the squalid state of disrepair of Clufton's highly-respected bridge is the result of a miscalculation by a senior public official, for which I, as chairman, take full responsibility, Mr. Fitch.

FITCH (*a broken man*): I can only say in mitigation that I have been under pressure—a sick man—domestic and financial worries——

CHAIRMAN: Quite, quite. Let's stick to essentials. Two years ago, at your insistence and against my better judgment, which I left unspoken in deference to your professional capacity, we arranged to switch to improved paint lasting eight years, and through a reasoning which I never pretended to follow, to sack three of the four painters. Today, two years later, we are left with a bridge that is only

Or have we learned (been conditioned?) to accept as our poets, say, a Fitch as against a Wordsworth? Is there a degree of lunacy here?

one quarter painted while the other three-quarters is in a condition ranging from the substandard to the decrepit. Now then—what happened?

FITCH: Mr. Chairman, gentlemen, I have served Clufton man and boy for five years. . . . Clufton is the repository of my dreams and boyhood memories, the temple of my hopes to transform the running of a living community to a thing of precision and efficiency, a cybernetic poem—a programmed machine as perfect as a rose——

which investigates human behavior as a mechanical system or systems. Is a "cybernetic poem," then, a contradiction in terms?

CHAIRMAN: For God's sake, Fitch, pull yourself together.

FITCH: Gentlemen, let us take as our starting point the proposition that X painters painting at the rate of Y would take Z years to paint surface ABC. We found that when X equalled four, Z equalled two, Y and ABC remaining constant. Then along came factor P, a paint lasting eight years——

CHAIRMAN: I can't stand it.

GEORGE: I think what Mr. Fitch is getting at, Mr. Chairman, is that the brown paint on the bridge was only supposed to last two years, the time that it took four painters to finish the job and start again. Well, of course, when we cut down to one painter using eight-year paint, it was obvious that in two years' time he'd only be a quarter of the way along, so the old paint would be ready for another coat.

CHAIRMAN: If it was obvious, why didn't you say so?

GEORGE: I couldn't catch the eye of the chairman. Of course, if we could hang on for another six years, Mr. Fitch would emerge triumphantly vindicated as the poet of precision and efficiency.

CHAIRMAN: I might be dead in six years.

DAVE: Hear, hear, Mr. Chairman.

CHAIRMAN: Thank you, Dave. So what are we going to do about it? Fitch?

FITCH: Er. . . . If we hired extra painters . . . , one to start at the far end, one in the middle going one way, another going the opposite way . . . , no . . . er . . . the progessive element intercedes—— if we have two painters back to back at a point nine-sixteenths from the far end . . . no——

CHAIRMAN: We'd better go back to the old system and hire three more painters. Carry on from there.

FITCH: You can't do that! They wouldn't be quick enough on the one hand . . . and they'd finish too soon on the other . . . you see, the bridge won't need repainting for another six years, . . . and the resultant coefficient—waste and unsightliness—the entire system would disintegrate . . . and cost thousands——

CHAIRMAN: Money? (*Appalled.*) My grandfather—

GEORGE: I think I see a way out, Mr. Chairman. From the points of view of efficiency and expediency, I think we can get the whole thing resolved with just a bit of organization.

FITCH: Every day counts.

GEORGE: One day is all we'll need.

(*Cut.*)

ALBERT: Met a feller up on the bridge the other day.

KATE (*strained*): Oh yes?

ALBERT: Yes. Climbed up to chuck himself off.

KATE: Did he?

ALBERT: No. Once he got up there, the mood passed.

KATE: Albert. . . .

ALBERT (*going*): Just off.

KATE: You used to say good-bye.

(*Cut to bridge.*)

FRASER: Hello.

ALBERT: Who's that?

FRASER: Me again.

ALBERT: Did you forget something?

FRASER: No, it all came back to me. After I went down, it all started again. So I came back up.

ALBERT: To jump?

FRASER: Yes.

ALBERT: Go on then.

FRASER: I'm all right again now. I don't want to.

ALBERT: Now look here, this isn't a public right of way. I'll report you.

FRASER: I can't help it. I'm forced up and coaxed down. I'm a victim of perspective.

ALBERT (*shouts*): Get down!

FRASER: All right, I'm going.

(*Cut bridge.*)

ALBERT: I'm not a complaining man. I let people get on with their own lives, I'm sympathetic to problems, but a line must be drawn. I've found him up there four times now, Mr. Fitch, and each time it's the same story—he doesn't want to jump after all. I've given him every chance.

FITCH: Yes, yes, but that isn't what I've asked to see you about at all. You haven't been listening to me.

ALBERT: It's unnerving me, finding company up there. Well, it's changing the character of the job, and playing hell with my schedule—simply on the level of efficiency I protest.

FITCH: Well, as I say, for the reasons given, the matter is to be resolved. We have to get the bridge finished by the end of the week.

ALBERT: What?

FITCH: We can't allow further deterioration. The public is roused.

ALBERT: Wait a minute—I can't possibly finish by the end of the week.

The beginning of another "cybernetic poem"?

FITCH: I realize, of course, you'll need help. I have made arrangements.

ALBERT: What arrangements?

FITCH: Eighteen hundred painters will report for work at seven o'clock tomorrow morning. By nightfall the job will be done. I have personally worked it out, and my department has taken care of the logistics.

ALBERT: Eighteen hundred?

FITCH: Seventeen hundred and ninety-nine. I kept a place for you. I thought you'd like that.

(*Cut to door slam.*)

ALBERT (*breathless*): They're moving in on me, the dots are ganging up. I'll need food and spare clothes, a couple of blankets. What are you doing?

KATE (*off*): Packing, Albert. I'm going.

ALBERT: Kate, they've got it in for me. They're trying to move me off—and I've earned my position. I've worked for it.

KATE (*approach*): I've got a position—a housemaid, living in. With Katherine. I'll let you know my days off, for visiting. (*Pause*)

ALBERT: Kate . . . I'm sorry. . . . Will you come and see me sometimes . . . ? Will you come along and wave?

(*Cut in bridge and painting.*) (*More rapid than before.*)

Dip brush, dip brush—slap it
on, slide silver
over the iron, glide like mercury—slick, wipe
tickle it wet, swish, slop,
sweep and wipe the
silver slime, it's all I can do—
in eight years I'll be pushing
thirty-two
a manic painter coming
through for the second
time.
Dip brush, dip brush——

FRASER: What's the rush?

(*Painting stops.*)

ALBERT: Fraser.

FRASER: You're going at it.

ALBERT (*shouting*): Get down! Get down!

FRASER: This isn't like you at all.

ALBERT: I'm not having you up here.

FRASER: There's room for both of us.

ALBERT: You're just the first, and I'm not going to have it. If you're going to jump—jump.

FRASER: That's why I came, again.

ALBERT (*closer and quieter*): You're going to jump?

FRASER: No. Not today.

ALBERT (*furious*): Up and down like a yo-yo!

FRASER: I agree that it is ludicrous. Down there I am assailed by the flying splinters of a world breaking up at the speed of procreation without end. The center cannot hold and the outside edge is filling out like a

See Yeats' "The Second Coming." Why does Fraser and not Albert have this line? Or are they one and the same?

balloon, without the assurance of infinity. More men are hungry than honest, and more eat than produce. The apocalypse cannot be long delayed.

ALBERT: You'd be better out of it. I'll tell them why you did it, if that's what's worrying you.

FRASER: . . . So I climb up again and prepare to cast myself off, without faith in angels to catch me —or desire that they should— and lo! I look down at it all and find that the proportions have been re-established. My confidence is restored, by perspective.

ALBERT: But it's my bridge——

FRASER: You think only of yourself —you see yourself as the center, whereas I know that I am not placed at all——

ALBERT: There are other bridges—bigger——

FRASER (*listening*): What's that?

ALBERT: San Francisco—Sydney——

FRASER: Listen.

ALBERT: Brooklyn—there's a place for you——

FRASER: Listen!

ALBERT: —but I was here first—this is mine——

(He tails off as there is the faintest sound of 1,800 men marching, whistling "Colonel Bogey.")

FRASER: There's an army on the march. . . .

ALBERT: So they're coming. . . .

FRASER: A solid phalanx moving squarely up the road, an officer at the head. . . .

ALBERT: Fitch.

FRASER: But they're not soldiers.

ALBERT: He's mad.

FRASER (*appalled*): They're just—people.

ALBERT (*shouts to the people*): Go away!

FRASER: Coming here.

ALBERT: Halt! About turn!

FRASER: They've lined up hundreds and hundreds of ordinary people—the overflow—all the fit men in the prime of life—they're always the ones on the list—preference is given to the old and the sick, the women and children—when it comes to the point, it's the young and able-bodied who go first——

ALBERT: Can't you see—they're taking over!

FRASER: Ten abreast—sixty deep—and another phalanx behind—and another—successive waves—

(The whistling is getting louder.)

—so it has come to this.

ALBERT: They're going to come up!

FRASER: It was the only direction left.

ALBERT: They're going to wheel right——

FITCH (*distant*): Right—wheel!

ALBERT: Off the road and through the gate——

FITCH: Straighten up there!

ALBERT: Up to the end of the bridge, on to the tracks——

FRASER: That's it, then—they have finally run out of space, the edges have all filled out and now there is only up.

ALBERT: Eighteen hundred men—flung against me by a madman! Was I so important? Here they come.

(This is difficult; as the front rank reaches the bridge, the tramp-tramp of the march should start to ring hollow, progressively as more and more leave terra firma and reach the bridge.)

(*From now, approaching tears.*) I could have done it, given time——

FRASER: There will be more behind them—the concrete mixers churn and churn until only a single row of corn grows between two cities, and is finally ground between their walls. . . .

ALBERT: They didn't give me a fair chance—I would have worked nights——

FRASER: They'll all come following—women and children too—and those that are at the top will be pushed off like disgraced legionnaires——

ALBERT: I had it under control—ahead of schedule——

Otherwise the strong cadences will shatter the bridge.

FRASER: Ah well. But they should be breaking step.
(*Tramp tramp.*)
Like soldiers do when they come to a bridge——

ALBERT: I was right—I was doing well——

FRASER: For the very good reason—
(*Tramp tramp.*)
that if they don't——

ALBERT: I was still young—fit——

FRASER: —the pressures cannot bounce—but build and have to break out——
(The rivets are starting to pop.)

ALBERT: —good head for heights——

FRASER: —they don't know, or don't believe it, but the physical laws are inviolable——
(*Cracking and wrenching*)

ALBERT: What's happening?

FRASER: —and if you carry on like that, a bridge will shiver, the girders tensed and trembling for the release of the energy being driven through them——

ALBERT: —it's breaking up!

FRASER: —until the rivets pop——

ALBERT (*screams*): What are they doing to my bridge!

FRASER: —and a forty-foot girder moans like a Jew's harp—
(*Twang.*)
—and one's enough——

ALBERT: To go to such lengths! I didn't do them any harm! What did I have that they wanted?
(*The bridge collapses.*)

Does this complete the "cybernetic poem"? If so, what kind of a poem was it?

INTERLOCK WITH CLUSTER 4: A modal link: irony
A topical link: fantasy and reality

Cluster 4: pp. 64-115
A topical cluster
Focus: Adolescence

INTERLOCK WITH CLUSTER 3:
A modal link: irony
A topical link: fantasy and reality

4

"This is the one thought that has impressed me, Govinda. Wisdom is not communicable. The wisdom which a wise man tries to communicate always sounds foolish."

"Are you jesting?" asked Govinda.

"No, I am telling you what I have discovered. Knowledge can be communicated, but not wisdom. One can find it, live it, be fortified by it, do wonders through it, but one cannot communicate and teach it. I suspected this when I was still a youth and it was this that drove me away from teachers."

—From *Siddhartha* by Herman Hesse

The Pennycandystore Beyond the El

LAWRENCE FERLINGHETTI

The pennycandystore beyond the El
is where I first
                    fell in love
                                  with unreality
Jellybeans glowed in the semi-gloom
of that september afternoon
A cat upon the counter moved among
                                       the licorice sticks
                     and tootsie rolls
              and Oh Boy Gum

Outside the leaves were falling as they died

A wind had blown away the sun

A girl ran in
Her hair was rainy
Her breasts were breathless in the little room

Outside the leaves were falling
                              and they cried
                                             Too soon! too soon!

Jelly beans and Oh Boy Gum and a girl?
Aren't they *very* real? Where is the
"unreality" that Ferlinghetti fell in love with?

Train Whistle Guitar

A boy . . . his dreams . . . his buddy . . . and a hero . . .
And what you learn when you grow up is you can't ever
get long gone from the bad places in the world . . .

albert murray

Lil' Buddy's color was that sky blue in which hens cackled; it was that smoke blue in which dogs barked and mosquito hawks lit on barbed-wire fences. It was the color above meadows. It was my color too because it was a boy's color. It was whistling blue and hunting blue, and it went with baseball, and that was old Lil' Buddy again, and that blue beyond outfields was exactly what we were singing about when we used to sing that old one about it ain't gonna rain no more no more.

Steel blue was a man's color. That was the clean, oil-smelling color of rifle barrels and railroad iron. That was the color that went with Luzana Cholly, and he had a steel-blue 32–20 on a 44 frame. His complexion was not steel blue but leather brown like dark rawhide, but steel blue was the color that went with what he was. His hands were just like rawhide, and when he was not dressed up he smelled like green oak steam. He had on slick starched blue denim overalls then, and when he was dressed up he wore a black broadcloth box-back coat with hickory-striped peg-top pants, and he smelled like the barber shop and new money.

"Louisiana Charlie"

Wide at hips, narrow at cuffs

Luzana Cholly was there in that time and place as far back as I can remember, even before Lil' Buddy was. Because I can remember when I didn't know Lil' Buddy at all. I can remember when that house they moved to was built (Lil' Buddy's papa and mama were still living together when they came to Gasoline Point from Choctaw County, which was near the Mississippi line), and I can also remember when that street (which was called Chattanooga Lookout Street) was pushed all the way through to the AT&N cut. That was before I had ever even heard of Lil' Buddy, and my buddy then was old Willie Marlowe. Lil' Buddy didn't come until after Willie Marlowe had gone to Detroit, Michigan, and that was not until after Mister One-Arm Will had been dead and buried for about nine months.

I can remember him there in that wee time when I couldn't even follow the stories I knew later they were telling about him, when it was only just grown folks talking, and all I could make of it was *Luzana, they are talking something about old Luzana again, and I didn't know what, to say nothing of where Louisiana was.* But old Luze was there even then and I could see him very clearly when they said his name because I had already seen him coming up that road that came by that house with the chinaberry yard, coming from around the bend and down in the railroad bottom; and I had already heard whatever that was he was picking on his guitar and heard that holler too. That was always far away and long coming. It started low like it was going to be a song, and then it jumped all the way to the very top of his voice and broke off, and then it started again, and this time was already at the top, and then it gave some quick jerking squalls and died away in the woods, the water, and the darkness (you always heard it at night), and Mama always said he was whooping and hollering like somebody back in the rosin-woods country, and Papa said it was one of them old Luzana swamp hollers. I myself always thought it was like a train, like a bad train saying look out this is me, and here I come, and I'm coming through.

Yard with chinaberry trees

That was even before I was big enough to climb the chinaberry tree. That was when they used to talk about the war and the Kaiser, and I can remember that there was a war book with Germans in it, and I used to see sure-enough soldiers marching in the Mardi Gras parades. Soldier Boy Crawford was still wearing his Army coat then, and he was the one who used to tell about how Luze used to play his guitar in France, telling about how they would be going through some French town like the ones called Nancy and Saint Die and old Luze would drop out of the company and go and play around in the underground wine shops until he got as much cognac and as many French Frogs as he wanted and then he would turn up in the company again and Capt'n would put him out by himself on the worst outpost he could find in No Man's Land and old Luze would stay out there sometimes for three or four days and nights knocking off patrol after patrol, and one time in another place, which was the Hindenburg Line, old Luze was out there again and there were a few shots late in the afternoon and then it was quiet until about three o'clock the next morning and then all hell broke loose, and the Capt'n thought that a whole German battalion was about to move in, and he sent five patrols out to find out what was happening, but when they got there all they found was old Luze all dug in and bristling with enough ammunition to blow up kingdom come; he had crawled around all during the afternoon collecting hand grenades and a mortar and two machine guns and even a light two-wheel cannon, and when they asked him what was going on he told them that he had fallen off to sleep and when he woke up he didn't know whether or not any Germans had snuck up so he thought he'd better lay himself down a little light barrage. The next morning they found out that old Luze had wiped out a whole German platoon but when the Capt'n sent for him to tell him he was going to give him a medal, old Luze had cut out and was off somewhere picking the guitar and drinking cognac and chasing the mademoiselles again. He went through the whole war like that and he came out of the Army without a single scratch, didn't even get flat feet.

I heard a lot of stories about the war and I used to draw pictures of them fighting with bayonets in the Argonne Forest, and Soldier Boy Crawford used to look at them and shake his head and give me a nickel and say that some day I was going to be a soldier too.

I used to draw automobiles too, especially the Hudson Super-Six, like old Long George Nisby had; he said it would do sixty on a straightaway, and he had a heavy blasting cut-out on it that jarred the ground. Old Man Perc Stranahan had a Studebaker but he was a white man and he didn't have a cut-out, and he drove as slow as a hearse. Old Gander said Old Man Perc always drove like he was trying to sneak up on something but he never was going to catch it like that. The cars I didn't like then were the flat-engine Buick and the old humpbacked Hupmobile. I liked the Maxwell and the Willys Knight and the Pierce Arrow.

I was playing train then too, and the trains were there before the automobiles were (there were many more horses and buggies in that part of town than there were automobiles then). I couldn't sit up in my nest in the chinaberry tree and see the trains yet, because I could not climb it yet, but I saw them when Papa used to take me to the L&N bottom to see them come by and I knew them all, and the Pan American was the fastest and Number Four was the fastest that ran in the daytime. Old Luzana could tell you all about the Southern Pacific and the Santa Fe, but that was later. But I already knew something about the Southern Pacific because Cousin Roberta had already gone all the way to Los Angeles, California, on the Sunset Limited.

Tracks of the Louisville and Nashville Railroad running on bottom land, beside a river

I used to be in bed and hear the night trains coming by. The Crescent came by at nine-thirty and if you woke up way in the middle of the night you could hear Number Two. I was in my warm bed in that house, and I could hear the whistle coming even before it got to Chickasabogue Bridge and it had a bayou sound then, and then I could hear the engine batting it hell-for-leather on down the line bound for Mobile and New Orleans, and the next time the whistle came it was for Three Mile Creek. It was getting on into the beel then. I played train by myself in the daytime then, looking out the window along the side of the house like an engineer looking down along the drivers.

I used to hear old Stagolee playing the piano over in Hot Water Shorty's jook at night too, even then, especially on Saturday night. They rocked all night long, and I was lying in my warm quilted bed by the window. Uncle Jimmy's bed was by the window on the other side of the fireplace. When it was cold, you could wake up way in the night and still see the red embers in the ashes, and hear the wind whining outside, and sometimes you could hear the boat whistles too, and I could lie listening from where I was and tell you when it was a launch pulling a log raft or a tugboat pulling a barge or a riverboat like the *Nettie Queen,* and sometimes it was a big ship like the *Luchenback* called the Looking Back, which was all the way down at the city wharf at the foot of Government Street.

I knew a lot about the big ships because Uncle Jimmy worked on the wharf. That was before the state docks were built and the big Gulf-going and ocean-going ships didn't come on past Mobile then unless they were going up to Chickasaw to be overhauled, but I had already seen them and had been on ships from England and France and Holland and naturally there were always ships from the Caribbean and South America because that was where the fruit boats came from.

All I could do was see old Luzana Cholly and hear him coming. I didn't really know him then, but I knew that he was blue steel and that he was always going and coming and that he had the best walk in the world, because I had learned how to do that walk and was already doing the stew out of it long before Lil' Buddy ever saw it. They were calling me Mister Man, and that was when somebody started calling me The Little Blister, because they said I was calling myself blister trying to say Mister. Aun Tee called me My Mister and Mama called me My Little Man, but she had to drop the little part off when Lil' Buddy came, and that was how everybody started calling me The Man, although I was still nothing but a boy, and I said to myself Old Luzana is the man, Old Luzana is the one I want to be like.

Then I was getting to be big enough to go everywhere by myself and I was going to school. That was when I knew about Dunkin's Hill and going up through Egerton Lane. That was the short way to school, because that was the way the bell sound came. Buddy Babe and Sister Babe and old double-jointed, ox-jawed Jack Johnson all went that way too, but when it rained you couldn't get across the bottom, and that was when everybody went the Shelton way, going through behind Stranahan's store and Good Hope Baptist to the old car line and then along that red clay road by the Hillside store.

Then Lil' Buddy was there and it was sky blue and we were blue hunters and every day was for whistling and going somewhere to do something you had to be rawhide to do, and some day we were going to live in times and places that were blue steel too. We found out a lot about old Luzana then, and then we not only knew him we knew how to talk to him.

The best time (except when he was just sitting somewhere strumming on his guitar) was when he was on his way to the Gambling Woods. (So far as anybody knew, gambling and guitar picking and grabbing freight trains were the only steady jobs he ever had or ever would have, except during the time he was in the Army and the times he was in jail—and he not only had been in jail, he had been in the penitentiary!) We were his good luck when he was headed for a skin game, and we always used to catch him late Saturday afternoon right out there where Gins Alley came into the oil-tank road, because he would be coming from Miss Pauline's cookshop then. The Gambling Woods trail started right out across from Sargin' Jeff's. Sometimes old Luze would have the guitar slung across his back even then, and naturally he had his famous 32-20 in the holster under his right arm.

"gambling"

"Say now, hey, Mister Luzana," I would holler at him.

"Mister Luzana Cholly one-time," Lil' Buddy always said, and he said that was what old Luze's swamp holler said too.

"Mister Luzana Cholly all night long," I would say then.

"Nobody else!" he would holler back at us then, "nobody else but."

"The one and only Mister Luzana Cholly from Booze Ana Bolly come Solly go Molly hit 'em with the fun folly."

"Talk to me, little ziggy, talk to me."

"Got the world in a jug," I might say then.

"And the stopper in your hand," old Lil' Buddy would say.

"You tell 'em, little crust busters, 'cause I ain't got the heart."

"He's a man among men."

"And Lord God among women!"

"Well tell the dy ya," old Luze would say then, standing wide-legged, laughing, holding a wad of Brown's Mule chewing tobacco in with his tongue at the same time. Then he would skeet a stream of amber juice to one side like a batter does when he steps up to the plate and then he would wipe the back of his leathery hand across his mouth and squint his eyes.

"Tell the dy-damn-ya!"

"Cain't tell no more," Lil' Buddy would say then, and old Luze would frown and wink at me.

"How come, little sooner, how goddam come?"

"Cause money talks."

"Well shut my mouth and call me suitcase."

"Ain't nobody can do that."

"I knowed you could tell 'em, little ziggabo, I knowed good and damn well you could tell 'em."

"But we ain't gonna tell 'em no more."

"We sure ain't."

"Talk ain't no good if you ain't got nothing to back it up with."

Old Luze would laugh again and we would stand waiting and then he would run his hands deep down into his pockets and come out with two quarters between his fingers. He would throw them into the air and catch them again, one in each hand, and then he would cross his hands and flip one to me and one to Lil' Buddy.

"Now talk," he would say then. "Now talk, but don't say too

much and don't talk too loud, and handle your money like the white folks does."

We were going to be like him even before we were going to be like cowboys. And we knew that blue steel was also root hog or die poor, which was what we were going to have to do whether we liked it or not. Lil' Buddy said it was not just how rough-and-ready old hard-cutting Luze was and how nobody, black or white, was going to do him any dirt and get away with it, and all that. It was that too, but it was also something else. It was also the way he could do whatever he was doing and make it look so easy that he didn't even seem to have to think about it, and once he did it, that seemed to be just about the only real way to do it.

Satchel Paige, one of baseball's greatest black pitchers, who—for many years—was not allowed to play in the segregated major leagues.

Old Luze did everything his own way just like old Satch played baseball his way. But we knew that we wanted to be like him for more reasons than that too. Somehow or other just as he always seemed to be thirty-five years old and blue steel because he had already been so many places and done so many things you'd never heard of before, he also always seemed to be absolutely alone and not needing anybody else, self-sufficient, independent, dead sure, and at the same time so unconcerned.

Mama said he was don't-carified, and that was it too (if you know the full meaning of the Negro meaning of that expression). He was living in blue steel and his way was don't-carified, because he was blue steel too. Lil' Buddy said hellfied, and he didn't mean hell-defying either, you couldn't say he was hell-defying all the time, and you couldn't say he went for bad either, not even when he was doing that holler he was so notorious for. That *was* hell-defying in a way, but it was really I don't give a damn if I *am* hell-defying, and he was not going for bad because he didn't need to, since everybody, black and white, who knew anything about him at all already knew that when he made a promise it meant if it's the last thing I do, if it's the last thing I do on this earth—and they knew that could mean I'll kill you and pay for you as much as it meant anything else. Because the idea of going to jail didn't scare him at all, and the idea of getting shot at didn't seem to scare him either. *Because all he ever said about that was if they shoot at me they sure better not miss me, they sure better get me the first time.*

He was a Negro who was an out and out Nigger in the very best meaning of the word as Negroes use it among themselves (who are the only ones who can), and nobody in that time and that place seemed to know what to make of him. White folks said he was crazy, but what they really meant or should have meant was that he was confusing to them, because if they knew him well enough to say he was crazy they also had to know enough about him to know that he wasn't even fool-hardy, not even careless, not even what they wanted to mean by biggity. The funny thing, as I remember it now, was how their confusion made them respect him in spite of themselves. Somehow or other it was as if they respected him precisely because he didn't care anything about them one way or the other. They certainly respected the fact that he wasn't going to take any foolishness off of them.

Negroes said he was crazy too, but they meant their own meaning. They did not know what to make of him, but when they said he was crazy they almost did, because when they said it they really meant something else. They were not talking so much about what he did, but how he was doing it. They were talking about something like poetic madness, and that was the way they had of saying that he was doing something unheard of, doing the hell out of it, and getting away with whatever it was. You could tell that was what they meant by the very way they said it, by the sound of it, and by the way they were shaking their heads and laughing when they said it.

The way he always operated as a lone wolf and the unconcerned, "-ness" not the Negro-ness as such, were the main things then. (Naturally Lil' Buddy and I knew about Negroes and white folks, and we knew that there was something generally wrong with white folks, but it didn't seem so very important then. We knew that if you hit a white boy he would turn red and call you nigger that did not sound like the Nigger the Negroes said and he would run and get as many other white boys as he could and come back at you, and we knew that a full-grown white had to get somebody to back him up too, but we didn't really think about it much, because there were so many other things we were doing then.)

Nobody ever said anything about old Luzana's papa and mama, and when you suddenly wondered about them you realized that he didn't seem to have or need any family at all, it really was as if he had come full-grown out of the swamp somewhere. And he didn't seem to need a wife either. But that was because he was not going to settle down yet. Because he had lived with more women from time to time and place to place than the average man could even shake a stick at.

We knew somehow or other that the Negro-ness had something to do with the way we felt about him too, but except for cowboys and the New York Yankees and one or two other things, almost everything was Negro then; that is, everything that mattered was. So the Negro part was only natural, although I can see something special about it too now.

When you boil it all down, I guess the main thing was how when you no more than just said his name, *Louisiana Charlie, old Luzana Cholly, old Luze,* that was enough to make you know not only him and how he looked and talked and walked that sporty limp walk, but his whole way of being, and how you knew right off the bat that he all alone and unconcerned in his sharp-edged and rough-backed steel had made it what it was himself.

That was what old Lil' Buddy and I were going to do too, make a name for ourselves. Because we knew even then (and I already knew it before he came) that doing that was exactly what made you the kind of man we wanted to be. Mama said I was her little man, and Aun

Tee always called me her little mister, but I wasn't anybody's man and mister yet and I knew it, and when I heard the sound of the name that Mama taught me how to write I always felt funny, and I always jumped even when I didn't move. That was in school, and I wanted to hide, and I always said *they are looking for me, they are trying to see who I am,* and I had to answer because it would be the teacher calling the roll, and I said Present, and it sounded like somebody else.

And when I found out what I found out about me and Aun Tee and knew that she was my flesh and blood mama, I also found out that I didn't know my real name at all, because I didn't know who my true father was. So I said *My name is Reynard the Fox,* and Lil' Buddy said *My name is Jack the Rabbit and my home is in the briar patch.* That was old Luzana too, and when you heard that holler coming suddenly out of nowhere just as old Luze himself always seemed to come, it was just like it was coming from the briar patch.

So when Mama said what she said about me and Aun Tee at that wake that time and I heard it and had to believe it, I wished that old Luzana had been my real papa, but I didn't tell anybody that, not even Lil' Buddy although Lil' Buddy was almost in the same fix because he didn't have a mama any more and he didn't really love his papa because it was his papa that ran his mama away.

But we were buddies and we both did old Luzana's famous walk and we were going to be like him, and the big thing that you had to do to really get like him was to grab yourself a fast armful of fast freight train and get long gone from here. That was the real way to learn about the world, and we wanted to learn everything about it that we could. That was when we started practicing on the switch engine. That was down in the oilyards. You had to be slick to do even that because naturally your folks didn't want you doing stuff like that, because there was old Peg Leg Nat. Old Peg Leg butt-headed Nat could hop a freight almost as good as old Luzana could. . . . He spent most of his time fishing and sometimes he would come around pushing a wheel-barrow selling fresh fish, shrimps, and crabs, but every now and then he would strike out for somewhere on a freight just like old Luze did. Mama used to try to scare us with old Nat, telling us that a peg leg was just what messing around with freight trains would get you, and for a while she did scare us, but not for long, because then we found out that it never would have happened to old Nat if he hadn't been drunk and showing off. And anybody could see that getting his leg cut off hadn't stopped old Nat himself anyway since he could still beat any two-legged man we knew doing it except old Luze himself. Naturally we had to think about it, and naturally it did slow us up for a while, but it didn't really stop us. Because there was still old Luze, and that was who we were anyway, not old Peg Leg Nat.

Then that time when I found out all about me and Aun Tee, I was going to run away, and Lil' Buddy was ready too. Then old Lil' Buddy found out that old Luze was getting ready to get moving again and we were all set and just waiting and then it was the day itself.

I will always remember that one.

I had on my brogan shoes and I had on my corduroy pants under my overalls with my jumper tucked in. I had on my blue baseball cap too and my rawhide wristband and I had my pitching glove folded in my hip pocket. Lil' Buddy had on just about the same thing except that he was carrying his first-base pad instead of his catcher's mitt. We had our other things and something to eat rolled up in our blanket rolls so that we could sling them over our shoulders and have our arms free.

That is, he had on his heavy shoes (and clothes) because he was preparing to jump the freight train to run away.

Lil' Buddy had gotten his papa's pearl-handled .38 Smith & Wesson, and we both had good jackknives. We had some hooks and twine to fish with too, just in case, and of course we had our trusty old slingshots for birds.

It was May and school was not out yet, and so not only were we running away, we were playing hooky too. It was hot, and with that many clothes on we were sweating, but you had to have them, and that was the best way to carry them.

There was a thin breeze that came across the railroad from the river, the marsh, and Pole Cat Bay, but the sun was hot and bright, and you could see the rails downright shimmering under the high and wide open sky. We had always said that we were going to wait until school was out, but this was our chance now, and we didn't care about school much any more anyhow. This was going to be school now anyway, except it was going to be much better.

We were waiting in the thicket under the hill. That was between where the Dodge mill road came down and where the oil spur started, and from where we were, we could see up and down the clearing as far as we needed to, to the south all the way across Three Mile Creek bridge to the roundhouse, and where Mobile was, and to the north all the way up past that mill to the Chickasabogue bridge. We knew just about from where old Luzana was going to come running, because we had been watching him do it for a long time now. We had that part down pat.

Side tracks of the railroad

I don't know how long we had been waiting because we didn't have a watch but it had been a long time, and there was nothing to do but wait then.

"I wish it would hurry up and come on," Lil' Buddy said.

"Me too," I said.

"Got to get to splitting."

We were squatting on the blanket rolls, and Lil' Buddy was smoking another Lucky Strike, smoking the way we both used to smoke them in those old days, letting it hang dangling in the corner of your mouth, and tilting your head to one side with one eye squinted up like a gambler.

"Goddam it, watch me nail that sapsucker," he said.

"Man, you watch me."

You could smell the May woods there then, the dogwood, the honeysuckle, and the warm smell of the undergrowth; and you could hear the birds too, the jays, the thrushes, and even a woodpecker somewhere on a dead tree. I felt how moist and cool the soft dark ground was there in the shade, and you could smell that smell too, and smell the river and the marsh too.

Lil' Buddy finished the cigarette and flipped it out into the sunshine, and then sat with his back against a sapling and sucked his teeth. I looked out across the railroad to where the gulls were circling over the marsh and the river.

"Goddam it, when I come back here to this burg, I'm goddam man and a half," Lil' Buddy said all of a sudden.

"And don't care who knows it," I said.

"Boy, Chicago."

"Man, Detroit."

"Man, Philadelphia."

"Man, New York."

"Boy, I kinda wish old Gander was going too."

"I kinda wish so too."

"Old cat-eyed Gander."

"Old big-toed Gander."

"Old Gander is all right."

"Man, who you telling."

"That son of a bitch know his natural stuff."

"That bastard can steal lightning if he have to."

"Boy, how about that time."

"Man, hell yeah."

"Boy, but old Luze though."

"That Luze takes the cake for everything."

"Hot damn, boy, we going!"

"It won't be long now."

"Boy, Los Angeles."

"Boy, St. Louis."

"Man, you know we going."

"Boy, you just watch me swing the sapsucker."

"Boy, snag it."

"Goddam."

"I'm going to natural-born kick that son of a bitch."

"Kick the living guts out of it."

"Boy and when we get back!" I said that and I could see it, coming back on the Pan American I would be carrying two suitcases and have a money belt and an underarm holster, and I would be dressed fit to kill.

"How long you think it will take us to get fixed to come back?" I said.

"Man, I don't know and don't care."

"You coming back when old Luze come back?"

"I don't know."

I didn't say anything else then. Because I was trying to think about how it was really going to be then. Because what I had been thinking about before was how I wanted it to be. I didn't say anything because I was thinking about myself then, thinking: *I always said I was going but I don't really know whether I want to go or not now. I want to go and I don't want to go.* I tried to see what was really going to happen and I couldn't, and I tried to forget it and think about something else, but I couldn't do that either.

I looked over at Lil' Buddy again. Who was lying back against the tree with his hands behind his head and his eyes closed. Whose legs were crossed, and who was resting easy like a ball-player rests before time for the game to start. I wondered what he was really thinking. Did he really mean it when he said he did not know and didn't care? You couldn't tell what he was thinking, but you could tell that he wasn't going to back out now, no matter how he was feeling about it.

So I said to myself goddam it if Lil' Buddy can make it I can too, and I had more reason to be going away than he did anyway. *I had forgotten about that. I had forgotten all about it. And then I knew that I still loved Papa and they had always loved me and they had always known about me and Aun Tee.*

But I couldn't back out then, because what I had found out wasn't the real reason for going anyway. Old Luze was really the reason, old Luze and blue steel, old Luze and rawhide, old Luze and ever-stretching India Rubber.

"Hey, Lebud."

"Hey."

"Going to the big league."

"You said it."

"Skipping city."

"You tell 'em."

"Getting further."

"Ain't no lie."

"Long gone."

"No crap."

That was when Lil' Buddy said my home is in the briar patch. My name is Jack the Rabbit and my natural home is in the briar patch. And I said it too, and I said that was where I was bred and born.

"Goddam it to hell," Lil' Buddy said then, "why don't it come on?"

"Son of a bitch," I said.

Then I was leaning back against my tree looking out across the sandy clearing at the sky and there were clean white pieces of clouds that looked like balled-up sheets in a washtub, and the sky was blue like rinse water with bluing in it, and I was thinking about Mama again, and hoping that it was all a dream.

But then the train was really coming and it wasn't a dream at all, and Lil' Buddy jumped up.

"Come on."

"I'm here."

The engine went by, and we were running across the clearing. My ears were ringing and I was sweating, and my collar was hot and my pants felt as if the seat had been ripped away. There was nothing but the noise and we were running into it, and then we were climbing up the hill and running along the slag and cinders. We were trotting along in reach of it then. We remembered to let an empty boxcar go by, and when the next gondola came, Lil' Buddy grabbed the front end and I got the back. I hit the hotbox with my right foot and stepped onto the step and pulled up. The wind was in my ears then, but I knew about that from practicing. I climbed on up the ladder and got down on the inside, and there was Lil' Buddy coming back toward me.

"Man, what did I tell you!"

"Did you see me lam ino that sucker?"

"Boy, we low more nailed it."

"I bet old Luze will be kicking it any minute now."

"Cool hanging it."

"Boy, yair," I said, but I was thinking I hope old Luze didn't change his mind. I hope we don't miss him. I hope we don't have to start out all by ourselves.

"Going, boy."

"Yeah."

"Going,
don't know where I'm going
but I'm going.
Say now I'm going
don't know when I'm going
but I'm going."

We crawled up into the left front corner out of the wind, and there was nothing to do but wait then. We knew that she was going to have to pull into the hole for Number Four when she got twelve miles out, and that was when we were going to get to the open boxcar.

To pull over to a side track, while waiting for a passenger train to go by

We got the cigarettes out and lit up, and there was nothing but the rumbling noise that the wide-open car made then, and the faraway sound of the engine and the low-rolling smoke coming back. That was just sitting there, and after we got a little more used to the vibration, nothing at all was happening except being there. You couldn't even see the scenery going by.

It was just being there and being in that time, and you never really remember anything about things like that except the sameness and the way you felt, and all I can remember now about that part is the nothingness of doing nothing and the feeling not of going but of being taken.

All I could see after we went through the bridge was the sky and the bare floor and the sides of the gondola, and all I can remember about myself is how I wished that something would happen, because I definitely did not want to be going then, and I was lost even though I knew good and well that I was not even twelve miles from home yet. Because although we certainly had been many times farther away and stayed longer, this already seemed to be farther and longer than all the other times put together.

Then we could tell that it was beginning to slow down, and we stood up and started getting ready. And then it was stopping, and we were ready, and we climbed over and got down and started running for it. That was still in the bayou country and beyond the train smell there was the sour-sweet smell of the swamp. We were running on hard-pounded slag then, and with the train quiet and waiting for Number Four, you could hear the double running of our feet echoing through the cypresses and the marshland.

The wide roadbed was almost half as high as the telegraph wires, and along the low right-of-way where the black creosote poles went along, you could see the blue and white lilies floating on the slimy green water. We came hustling hot to get to where we knew the empty car was, and then there we were.

And there old Luzana himself was.

He stood looking down at us from the door with an unlighted cigarette in his hand. We stopped dead in our tracks. I knew exactly what was going to happen then. It was suddenly so quiet that you could hear your heart pounding inside your head, and I was so embarrassed I didn't know what to do and I thought *now he's going to call us a name. Now he's never going to have anything to do with us any more.*

We were just standing there waiting and he just let us stand there and feel like two puppies with their tails tucked between their legs, and then he started talking.

"It ain't like that. It ain't like that. It just ain't like that, it just ain't."

And he was shaking his head not only as if we couldn't understand him but also as if we couldn't even hear him.

"It ain't. Oh, but it ain't."

We didn't move. Lil' Buddy didn't even dig his toe into the ground.

"So this is what y'all up to. Don't say a word, not a word. Don't open your mouth."

I could have sunk right on down into the ground.

"What the hell y'all think y'all doing? Tell me that. Tell me. Don't say a word. Don't say a goddam mumbling word to me."

We weren't even about to say anything.

"I got a good mind to whale the sawdust out of you both. That's just what I oughta do."

But he didn't move. He just stood looking down.

"Well, I'll be a son of a bitch."

The place where the tracks branch

That was all he said then, and then he jumped down, walked us back to where the switch frog was, and then there was nothing but just shamefaced waiting. Then Number Four came by and then finally we heard the next freight coming south and when it got there and slowed down for the switch he was standing waiting for a gondola and when it came he picked me up and put me on and then he picked Lil' Buddy up and put him on and then he caught the next car and came to where we were.

So we came slowpoking it right on back and got back in Gasoline Point before the whistles even started blowing for one o'clock. Imagine that. All of that had happened and it wasn't really afternoon yet. I could hardly believe it.

We came on until the train all but stopped for Three Mile Creek bridge and then he hopped down and took us off. He led us down the hill and went to a place the hobos used under the bridge. He sat down and lit another cigarette and flipped the match into the water and watched it float away and then he was looking at us and then he motioned for us to sit down too.

That was when he really told us what hitting the road was, and what blue steel was. He was talking evenly then, not scolding, just telling us man to boys, saying he was talking for our own good because doing what we were trying to do was more than a notion. He was talking quietly and evenly but you still couldn't face him, I know I couldn't and Lil' Buddy naturally couldn't because he never looked anybody straight in the eye anyway.

We were back and sitting under Three Mile Creek bridge and he was not really angry and then we were all eating our something-to-eat and then we could talk too, but we didn't have much to say that day. He was doing the talking and all we wanted to do was ask questions and listen.

That was when he told us all about the chain gang and the penitentiary and the white folks, and you could see everything he said and you were there too, but you were not really in it this time because it was happening to him, not you, and it was him and you were not him, you were you. You could be rawhide and you could be blue steel but you couldn't really be Luzana Cholly, because he himself was not going to let you.

Then he was talking about going to school and learning to use your head like the smart white folks. You had to be rawhide but you had to be patent leather too, then you would really be nimble, then you would really be not only a man but a big man. He said we had a lot of spunk and that was good but it wasn't good enough, it wasn't nearly enough.

And then he was talking about Negroes and white folks again, and he said the young generation of Negroes were supposed to be like Negroes and be like white folks too and still be Negroes. He sat looking out across the water then, and then we heard another freight coming and he got up and got ready and he said we could watch him but we'd better not try to follow him.

Then we were back up on the hill again and the train was coming and he stood looking at us with the guitar slung over his shoulder and then he put his hands on our shoulders and looked straight at us, and we had to look at him then, and we knew that we were not to be ashamed in front of him any more.

"Make old Luze proud of you," he said then, and he was almost pleading. "Make old Luze glad to take his hat off to you some of these days. You going further than old Luze ever even dreamed of. Old Luze ain't been nowhere. Old Luze don't know from nothing."

And then the train was there and we watched him snag it and then he was waving good-by.

Editor: A sad story. I keep wondering what will happen to those boys.

Literary Sort: Surely they'll survive.

Editor: Like Old Luze?

10.00
9.10
65.90
47.00
59.30
61.00
56.50
35.00
7.00
160.00
42.40
295.70

869.90

simple arithmetic

Virginia Moriconi

Geneva, January 15

Dear Father:

Well, I am back in School, as you can see, and the place is just as miserable as ever. My only friend, the one I talked to you about, Ronald Fletcher, is not coming back any more because someone persuaded his mother that she was letting him go to waste, since he was extremely photogenic, so now he is going to become a child actor. I was very surprised to hear this, as the one thing Ronnie liked to do was play basketball. He was very shy.

The flight wasn't too bad. I mean nobody had to be carried off the plane. The only thing was, we were six hours late and they forgot to give us anything to eat, so for fourteen hours we had a chance to get quite hungry but, as you say, for the money you save going tourist class, you should be prepared to make a few little sacrifices.

I did what you told me, and when we got to Idlewild I paid the taxi driver his fare and gave him a fifty-cent tip. He was very dissatisfied. In fact he wouldn't give me my suitcase. In fact I don't know what would have happened if a man hadn't come up just while the argument was going on and when he heard what it was all about he gave the taxi driver a dollar and I took my suitcase and got to the plane on time.

During the trip I thought the whole thing over. I did not come to any conclusion. I know I have been very extravagant and unreasonable about money and you have done the best you can to explain this to me. Still, while I was thinking about it, it seemed to me that there were only three possibilities. I could just have given up and let the taxi driver have the suitcase, but when you realize that if we had to buy everything over again that was in the suitcase we would probably have had to spend at least five hundred dollars, it does not seem very economical. Or I could have gone on arguing with him and missed the plane, but then we would have had to pay something like three hundred dollars for another ticket. Or else I

By permission of Virginia Moriconi, from THE BEST SHORT STORIES OF 1964, published by Houghton Mifflin Company. Originally appeared in the *Transatlantic Review*, Vol. XII, Spring 1963.

could have given him an extra twenty-five cents which, as you say, is just throwing money around to create an impression. What would you have done?

Anyway I got here, with the suitcase, which was the main thing. They took two week-end privileges away from me because I was late for the opening of School. I tried to explain to M. Frisch that it had nothing to do with me if the weather was so bad that the plane was delayed for six hours, but he said that prudent persons allow for continjensies of this kind and make earlier reservations. I don't care about this because the next two week-ends are skiing week-ends and I have never seen any point in waking up at six o'clock in the morning just to get frozen stiff and endure terrible pain even if sports are a part of growing up, as you say. Besides, we will save twenty-seven dollars by having me stay in my room.

In closing I want to say that I had a very nice Christmas and I apreciate everything you tried to do for me and I hope I wasn't too much of a bother. (Martha explained to me that you had had to take time off from your honeymoon in order to make Christmas for me and I am very sorry even though I do not think I am to blame if Christmas falls on the twenty-fifth of December, especially since everybody knows that it does. What I mean is, if you had wanted to have a long honeymoon you and Martha could have gotten married earlier, or you could have waited until Christmas was over, or you could just have told me not to come and I would have understood.)

I will try not to spend so much money in the future and I will keep accounts and send them to you. I will also try to remember to do the eye exercises and the exercises for fallen arches that the doctors in New York prescribed.

Love,
STEPHEN

New York, January 19

Dear Stephen:

Thank you very much for the long letter of January fifteenth. I was very glad to know that you had gotten back safely, even though the flight was late. (I do not agree with M. Frisch that prudent persons allow for "continjensies" of this kind, now that air travel is as standard as it is, and the service usually so good, but we must remember that Swiss people are, by and large, the most meticulous in the world and nothing offends them more than other people who are not punctual.)

In the affair of the suitcase, I'm afraid that we were both at fault. I had forgotten that there would be an extra charge for luggage when I suggested that you should tip the driver fifty cents. You, on the other hand, might have inferred from his argument that he was simply asking that the tariff—i.e. the fare, plus the overcharge for the suitcase—should be paid in full, and regulated yourself accordingly. In any event you arrived, and I am only sorry that obviously you had no time to learn the name and address of your benefactor so that we might have paid him back for his kindness.

I will look forward to going over your accounting and I am sure you will find that in keeping a clear record of what you spend you will be able to cut your cloth according to the bolt and that, in turn, will help you to develop a real regard for yourself. It is a common failing, as I told you, to spend too much money in order to compensate oneself for a lack of inner security, but you can easily see that a foolish purchase does not insure stability, and if you are chronically insolvent you can hardly hope for peace of mind. Your allowance is more than adequate and when you learn to make both ends meet you will have taken a decisive step ahead. I have great faith in you and I know you will find your anchor to windward in your studies, in your sports, and in your companions.

As to what you say about Christmas, you are not obliged to "apreciate" what we did for you. The important thing was that you should have had a good time, and I think we had some wonderful fun together, the three of us, don't you? Until your mother decides where she wants to live and settles down, this is your *home* and you must always think of it that way. Even though I have remarried, I am still your father, first and last, and Martha is very fond of you too, and very understanding about your problems. You may not be aware of it but in fact she is one of the best friends you have. New ideas and new stepmothers take a litle getting used to, of course.

Please write me as regularly as you can, since your letters mean a great deal to me. Please try too, at all times, to keep your marks up to scratch, as college entrance is getting harder and harder in this country, and there are thousands of candidates each year for the good universities. Concentrate particularly on spelling. "Contingency" is difficult, I know, but there is no excuse for only one "p" in "appreciate"! And *do* the exercises.

Love,
FATHER

Geneva, January 22

Dear Mummy:

Last Sunday I had to write to Father to thank him for my Christmas vacation and to tell him that I got back all right. This Sunday I thought I would write to you even though you are on a cruze so perhaps you will never get my letter. I must say that if they didn't make us write home once a week I don't believe that I would ever write any letters at all. What I mean is that once you get to a point like this, in a place like this, you see that you are supposed to have your life and your parents are supposed to have their lives, and you have lost the connection.

Anyway I have to tell you that Father was wonderful to me and Martha was very nice too. They had thought it all out, what a child of my age might like to do in his vacation, and sometimes it was pretty strenuous, as you can imagine. At the end the School sent the bill for the first term, where they charge you for the extras which they let you have here and it seems that I had gone way over my allowance and besides I had signed for a whole lot of things I did not deserve. So there was a terrible scene and Father was very angry and Martha cried and said that if Father always made such an effort to consider me as a person I should make an effort to consider him as a person too and wake up to the fact that he was not Rockefeller and that even if he was sacrificing himself so that I could go to one of the most expensive schools in the world it did not mean that I should drag everybody down in the mud by my reckless spending. So now I have to turn over a new leaf and keep accounts of every penny and not buy anything which is out of proportion to our scale of living.

Except for that one time they were very affectionate to me and did everything they could for my happiness. Of course it was awful without you. It was the first time we hadn't been together and I couldn't really believe it was Christmas.

I hope you are having a wonderful time and getting the rest you need and please write me when you can.

All My Love,

Stephen

Geneva, January 29

Dear Father:

Well it is your turn for a letter this week because I wrote to Mummy last Sunday. (I am sure I can say this to you without hurting your feelings because you always said that the one thing you and Mummy wanted was a civilized divorce so we could all be friends.) Anyway Mummy hasn't answered my letter so probably she doesn't aprove of my spelling any more than you do. I am beginning to wonder if maybe it wouldn't be much simpler and much cheaper too if I didn't go to college after all. I really don't know what this education is for in the first place.

There is a terrible scandal here at School which has been very interesting for the rest of us. One of the girls, who is only sixteen, has gotten pregnant and everyone knows that it is all on account of the science instructer, who is a drip. We are waiting to see if he will marry her, but in the meantime she is terrifically upset and she has been expelled from the School. She is going away on Friday.

I always liked her very much and I had a long talk with her last night. I wanted to tell her that maybe it was not the end of the world, that my stepmother was going to have a baby in May, although she never got married until December, and the sky didn't fall in or anything. I thought it might have comforted her to think that grownups make the same mistakes that children do (if you can call her a child) but then I was afraid that it might be disloyal to drag you and Martha into the conversation, so I just let it go.

I'm fine and things are just the same.

Love,
STEPHEN

New York, February 2

Dear Stephen:

It would be a great relief to think that your mother did not "aprove" of your spelling either, but I'm sure that it's not for that reason that you haven't heard from her. She was never any good as a correspondent, and now it is probably more difficult for her than ever. We did indeed try for what you call a "civilized divorce" for all our sakes, but divorce is not any easy thing for any of the persons involved, as you well know, and if you try to put yourself in your mother's place for a moment, you will see that she is in need of time and solitude to work things out for herself. She will certainly write to you as soon as she has found herself again, and meanwhile you must continue to believe in her affection for you and not let impatience get the better of you.

Again, in case you are really in doubt about it, the purpose of your education is to enable you to stand on your own feet when you are a man and make something of yourself. Inaccuracies in spelling will not *simplify* anything.

I can easily see how you might have made a parallel between your friend who has gotten into trouble, and Martha who is expecting the baby in May, but there is only a superficial similarity in the two cases.

Your friend is, or was, still a child, and would have done better to have accepted the limitations of the world of childhood—as you can clearly see for yourself, now that she is in this predicament. Martha, on the other hand, was hardly a child. She was a mature human being, responsible for her own actions and prepared to be responsible for the baby when it came. Moreover I, unlike the science "instructer," am not a drip, I too am responsible for *my* actions, and so Martha and I are married and I will do my best to live up to her and the baby.

Speaking of which, we have just found a new apartment because this one will be too small for us in May. It is right across the street from your old school and we have a kitchen, a dining alcove, a living room, two bedrooms—one for me and Martha, and one for the new baby—and another room which will be for you. Martha felt that it was very important for you to feel that you had a place of your own when you came home to us, and so it is largely thanks to her that we have taken such a big place. The room will double as a study for me when you are not with us, but we will move all my books and papers and paraphernalia whenever you come, and Martha is planning to hang the Japanese silk screen you liked at the foot of the bed.

Please keep in touch, and *please* don't forget the exercises.

Love,
FATHER

Geneva, February 5

Dear Father:

There is one thing which I would like to say to you which is that if it hadn't been for you *I* would never have heard of a "civilized divorce," but that is the way you explained it to me. I always thought it was crazy. What I mean is, wouldn't it have been better if you had said, "I don't like your mother any more and I would rather live with Martha," instead of insisting that you and Mummy were always going to be the greatest friends? Because the way things are now Mummy probably thinks that you still like her very much, and it must be hard for Martha to believe that she was chosen, and I'm pretty much confused myself, although it is really none of my business.

You will be sorry to hear that I am not able to do any of the exercises any longer. I cannot do the eye exercises because my roommate got so fassinated by the stereo gadget that he broke it. (But the School Nurse says she thinks it may be just as well to let the whole thing go since in her opinion there was a good chance that I might have gotten more cross-eyed than ever, fidgeting with the viewer.) And I can not do the exercises for fallen arches, at least for one foot, because when I was decorating the Assembly Hall for the dance last Saturday, I fell off the stepladder and broke my ankle. So now I am in the Infirmary and the School wants to know whether to send the doctor's bill to you or to Mummy, because they had to call in a specialist from outside, since the regular School Doctor only knows how to do a very limited number of things. So I have cost a lot of money again and I am very sorry, but if they were halfway decent in this School they would pay to have proper equipment and not let the students risk their lives on broken stepladders, which is something you could write to the Bookkeeping Department, if you felt like it, because I can't, but you could, and it might do some good in the end.

The girl who got into so much trouble took too many sleeping pills and died. I felt terrible about it, in fact I cried when I heard it. Life is very crewel, isn't it?

I agree with what you said, that she was a child, but I think she knew that, from her point of view. I think she did what she did because she thought of the science instructer as a grownup, so she imagined that she was perfectly safe with him. You may think she was just bad, because she was a child and should have known better, but I think that it was not entirely her fault since here at School we are all encouraged to take the teachers seriously.

I am very glad you have found a new apartment and I hope you won't move all your books and papers when I come home, because that would only make me feel that I was more of a nuisance than ever.

Love,
STEPHEN

New York, February 8

Dear Stephen:

This will have to be a very short letter because we are to move into the new apartment tomorrow and Martha needs my help with the packing.

We were exceedingly shocked by the tragic death of your friend and very sorry that you should have had such a sad experience. Life can be "crewel" indeed to the people who do not learn how to live it.

When I was exactly your age I broke my ankle too—I wasn't on a defective stepladder, I was playing hockey—and it hurt like the devil. I still remember it and you have all my sympathy. (I have written to the School Physician to ask how long you will have to be immobilized, and to urge him to get you back into the athletic program as fast as possible. The specialist's bill should be sent to me.)

I have also ordered another stereo viewer because, in spite of the opinion of the School Nurse, the exercises are most important and you are to do them *religiously.* Please be more careful with this one no matter how much it may "fassinate" your roommate.

Martha sends love and wants to know what you would like for your birthday. Let us know how the ankle is mending.

Love,
FATHER

Geneva, February 12

Dear Father:

I was very surprised by your letter. I was surprised that you said you were helping Martha to pack because when you and Mummy were married I do not ever remember you packing or anything like that so I guess Martha is reforming your charactor. I was also surprised by what you said about the girl who died. What I mean is, if anyone had told me a story like that I think I would have just let myself get a little worked up about the science instructer because it seems to me that he was a villan too. Of course you are much more riserved than I am.

I am out of the Infirmary and they have given me a pair of crutches, but I'm afraid it will be a long time before I can do sports again.

I hope the new apartment is nice and I do not want anything for my birthday because it will seem very funny having a birthday in School so I would rather not be reminded of it.

Love,
STEPHEN

New York, February 15

Dear Stephen:

This is not an answer to your letter of February twelfth, but an attempt to have a serious discussion with you, as if we were face to face.

You are almost fifteen years old. Shortly you will be up against the stiffest competition of your life when you apply for college entrance. No examiner is going to find himself favorably impressed by "charactor" or "instructer" or "villan" or "riserved" or similar errors. You will have to face the fact that in this world we succeed on our merits, and if we are unsuccessful, on account of sloppy habits of mind, we suffer for it. You are still too young to understand me entirely, but you are not too young to recognize the importance of effort. People who do not make the grade are desperately unhappy all their lives because they have no place in society. If you do not pass the college entrance examinations simply because you are unable to spell, it will be nobody's fault but your own, and you will be gravely handicapped for the rest of your life.

Every time you are in doubt about a word you are to look it up in the dictionary and *memorize* the spelling. This is the least you can do to help yourself.

We are still at sixes and sevens in the new apartment but when Martha accomplishes all she has planned it should be very nice indeed and I think you will like it.

Love,
FATHER

Geneva, February 19

Dear Father:

I guess we do not understand each other at all. If you immagine for one minute that just by making a little effort I could imaggine how to spell immaggine without looking it up and finding that actually it is "imagine," then you are all wrong. In other words, if you get a letter from me and there are only two or three mistakes well you just have to take my word for it that I have had to look up practically every single word in the dictionary and that is one reason I hate having to write you these letters because they take so long and in the end they are not at all spontainious, no, just wait a second, here it is, "spontaneous," and believe me only two or three mistakes in a letter from me is one of the seven wonders of the world. What I'm saying is that I am doing the best I can as you would aggree if you could see my dictionary which is falling apart and when you say I should *memmorize* the spelling I can't because it doesn't make any sence to me and never did.

Love,
STEPHEN

New York, February 23

Dear Stephen:

It is probably just as well that you have gotten everything off your chest. We all need to blow up once in a while. It clears the air.

Please don't ever forget that I am aware that spelling is difficult for you. I know you are making a great effort and I am very proud of you. I just want to be sure that you *keep trying.*

I am enclosing a small check for your birthday because even if you do not want to be reminded of it I wouldn't want to forget it and you must know that we are thinking of you.

Love,
FATHER

Geneva, February 26

Dear Father:

We are not allowed to cash personal checks here in the School, but thank you anyway for the money.

I am not able to write any more because we are going to have the exams and I have to study.

Love,
STEPHEN

New York, March 2

NIGHT LETTER

BEST OF LUCK STOP KEEP ME POSTED EXAM RESULTS LOVE

FATHER.

Geneva, March 12

Dear Father:

Well, the exams are over. I got a C in English because aparently I do not know how to spell, which should not come as too much of a surprise to you. In Science, Mathematics, and Latin I got A, and in French and History I got a B plus. This makes me first in the class, which doesn't mean very much since none of the children here have any life of the mind, as you would say. I mean they are all jerks, more or less. What am I supposed to do in the Easter vacation? Do you want me to come to New York, or shall I just stay here and get a rest, which I could use?

Love,
STEPHEN

New York, March 16

Dear Stephen:

I am *immensely* pleased with the examination results. Congratulations. Pull up the spelling and our worries are over.

Just yesterday I had a letter from your mother. She has taken a little house in Majorca, which is an island off the Spanish coast, as you probably know, and she suggests that you should come to her for the Easter holidays. Of course you are always welcome here—and you could rest as much as you wanted—but Majorca is very beautiful and would certainly appeal to the artistic side of your nature. I have written to your mother, urging her to write to you immediately, and I enclose her address in case you should want to write yourself. Let me know what you would like to do.

Love,
FATHER

Geneva, March 19

Dear Mummy:

Father says that you have invited me to come to you in Majorca for the Easter vacation. Is that true? I would be very happy if it were. It has been very hard to be away from you for all this time and if you wanted to see me it would mean a great deal to me. I mean if you are feeling well enough. I could do a lot of things for you so you would not get too tired.

I wonder if you will think that I have changed when you see me. As a matter of fact I have changed a lot because I have become quite bitter. I have become bitter on account of this School.

I know that you and Father wanted me to have some expeari-ence of what the world was like outside of America but what you didn't know is that Geneva is not the world at all. I mean, if you were born here, then perhaps you would have a real life, but I do not know anyone who was born here so all the people I see are just like myself, we are just waiting not to be lost any more. I think it would have been better to have left me in some place where I belonged even if Americans are getting very loud and money con-scious. Because actually most of the children here are Americans, if you come right down to it, only it seems their parents didn't know what to do with them any longer.

Mummy I have written all this because I'm afraid that I have spent too much money all over again, and M. Frisch says that Father will have a crise des nerfs when he sees what I have done, and I thought that maybe you would understand that I only bought these things because there didn't seem to be anything else to do and that you could help me some how or other. Anyway, according to the School, we will have to pay for all these things.

"hysterical fit"

	Concert, Segovia	(Worth it)	16.00	(Swiss Francs)
	School Dance		5.00	
	English Drama	(What do they mean?)	10.00	
"a fee for school guards"	Controle de l'habitant	(?)	9.10	
	Co-op purchases		65.90	
	Ballets Russes	(Disappointing)	47.00	
"Prior's bookstore"	Librairie Prior		59.30	
	Concert piano	(For practicing)	61.00	
"dye shop"	Teinturie	(They ruined everything)	56.50	
	Toilet and Medicine		35.00	
	Escalade Ball		7.00	
	Pocket Money		160.00	
	77 Yoghurts	(Doctor's advice)	42.40	
	Book account		295.70	
		Total	869.90	(Swiss Francs)

Now you see the trouble is that Father told me I was to spend about fifty dollars a month, because that was my allowance, and that I was not to spend anything more. Anyway, fifty dollars a month would be about two hundred and ten Swiss Francs, and then I had fifteen dollars for Christmas from Granny, and when I got back to School I found four Francs in the pocket of my leather jacket and then I had seventy-nine cents left over from New York, but that doesn't help much, and then Father sent me twenty-five dollars for my birthday but I couldn't cash the check because they do not allow that here in School, so what shall I do?

It is a serious situation as you can see, and it is going to get a lot more serious when Father sees the bill. But whatever you do, I imploar you not to write to Father because the trouble seems to be that I never had a balance foreward and I am afraid that it is impossible to keep accounts without a balance foreward, and even more afraid that by this time the accounts have gone a little bizerk.

Do you want me to take a plane when I come to Majorca? Who shall I say is going to pay for the ticket?

Please do write me as soon as you can, because the holidays begin on March 30 and if you don't tell me what to do I will be way out on a lim.

Lots and lots of love,
STEPHEN

Geneva, March 26

Dear Father:

I wrote to Mummy a week ago to say that I would like very much to spend my Easter vacation in Majorca. So far she has not answered my letter, but I guess she will pretty soon. I hope she will because the holidays begin on Thursday.

I am afraid you are going to be upset about the bill all over again, but in the Spring term I will start anew and keep you in touch with what is going on.

Love,
STEPHEN

P.S. If Mummy doesn't write what shall I do?

IN EXILE Philip Roth

This selection is an excerpt from the novel Portnoy's Complaint, *a very funny, also very sad, story about not growing up.*

On Sunday mornings, when the weather is warm enough, twenty of the neighborhood men (this in the days of short center field) play a round of seven-inning softball games, starting at nine in the morning and ending about one in the afternoon, the stakes for each game a dollar a head. The umpire is our dentist, old Dr. Wolfenberg, the neighborhood college graduate—night school on High Street, but as good as Oxford to us. Among the players is our butcher, his twin brother our plumber, the grocer, the owner of the service station where my father buys his gasoline—all of them ranging in age from thirty to fifty, though I think of them not in terms of their years, but only as "the men." In the on-deck circle, even at the plate, they roll their jaws on the stumps of soggy cigars. Not boys, you see, but men. Belly! Muscle! Forearms black with hair! Bald domes! And then the voices they have on them—cannons you can hear go off from as far as our front stoop a block away. I imagine vocal cords inside them thick as clotheslines! lungs the size of zeppelins! Nobody has to tell them to stop mumbling and speak up, never! And the outrageous things they say! The chatter in the infield isn't chatter, it's kibbitzing, and (to this small boy, just beginning to learn the art of ridicule) hilarious, particularly the insults that emanate from the man my father has labeled "The Mad Russian," Biderman, owner of the corner candy store (and bookie joint) who has a "hesitation" side-arm delivery, not only very funny but very effective. "Abracadabra," he says, and pitches his backbreaking drop. And he is always giving it to Dr. Wolfenberg: "A blind ump, okay, but a blind dentist?" The idea causes him to smite his forehead with his glove. "Play ball, comedian," calls Dr. Wolfenberg, very Connie Mack in his perforated two-tone shoes and Panama hat, "start up the game, Biderman, unless you want to get thrown out of here for insults—!" "But how do they teach you in that dental school, Doc, by Braille?"

In Newark, N. J.

Meanwhile, all the way from the outfield comes the badinage of one who in appearance is more cement-mixer than Homo sapiens, the prince of the produce market, Allie Sokolow. The *pisk*° he opens on him! (as my mother would put it). For half an inning the invective flows in toward home plate from his position in deep center field, and then when his team comes to bat, he stations himself in the first-base coaching box

° PISK: "big mouth"

and the invective flows uninterruptedly out in the opposite direction—and none of it has anything to do with any contretemps that may actually be taking place on the field. Quite the opposite. My father, when he is not out working on Sunday mornings, comes by to sit and watch a few innings with me; he knows Allie Sokolow (as he knows many of the players), since they were all boys together in the Central Ward, before he met my mother and moved to Jersey City. He says that Allie has always been like this, "a real showman." When Allie charges in toward second base, screaming his gibberish and double-talk in the direction of home plate (where there isn't even a batter as yet—where Dr. Wolfenberg is merely dusting the plate with the whisk broom he brings to the game), the people in the stands couldn't be more delighted: they laugh, they clap, they call out, "You tell him, Allie! You give it to him, Sokolow!" And invariably Dr. Wolfenberg, who takes himself a little more seriously than your ordinary nonprofessional person (and is a German Jew to boot), holds up his palm, halting an already Sokolow-stopped game, and says to Biderman, "Will you please get that *meshuggener*° back in the outfield?"

And feels himself superior to Jews from Eastern Europe

I tell you, they are an endearing lot! I sit in the wooden stands alongside first base, inhaling that sour springtime bouquet in the pocket of my fielder's mitt—sweat, leather, vaseline—and laughing my head off. I cannot imagine myself living out my life any other place but here. Why leave, why go, when there is everything here that I will ever want? The ridiculing, the joking, the acting-up, the pretending—anything for a laugh! I love it! And yet underneath it all, *they mean it, they are in dead earnest.* You should see them at the end of the seven innings when that dollar has to change hands. Don't tell *me* they don't mean it! Losing and winning is not a joke . . . and yet it is! And that's what charms me most of all. Fierce as the competition is, they cannot resist clowning and kibbitzing around. Putting on a show! How I am going to love growing up to be a Jewish man! Living forever in the Weequahic section, and playing softball on Chancellor Avenue from nine to one on Sundays, a perfect joining of clown and competitor, kibbitzing wiseguy and dangerous long-ball hitter.

I remember all this where? when? While Captain Meyerson is making his last slow turn over the Tel Aviv airport. My face is against the window. *Yes, I could disappear, I think, change my name and never be heard from again*—then Meyerson banks the wing on my side, and I look down for the first time upon the continent of Asia, I look down from two thousand feet in the air upon the Land of Israel, where the Jewish people first came into being, and am impaled upon a memory of Sunday morning softball games in Newark.

°MESHUGGENER: crazy man

A suburb just north of New York City

The elderly couple seated beside me (the Solomons, Edna and Felix), who have told me in an hour's flight time all about their children and grandchildren in Cincinnati (with, of course, a walletful of visual aids), now nudge each other and nod together in silent satisfaction; they even poke some friends across the aisle, a couple from Mount Vernon they've just met (the Perls, Sylvia and Bernie), and these two *kvell*° also to see a tall, good-looking, young Jewish lawyer (and single! a match for somebody's daughter!) suddenly begin to weep upon making contact with a Jewish airstrip. However, what has produced these tears is not, as the Solomons and Perls would have it, a first glimpse of the national homeland, the ingathering of an exile, but the sound in my ear of my own nine-year-old little boy's voice—*my* voice, I mean, at nine. Nine-year-old me! Sure a sourpuss, a face-maker, a little back-talker and *kvetch,*° sure my piping is never without its nice infuriating whiny edge of permanent disgruntlement and grievance ("as though," my mother says, "the world owes him a living—at nine years old"), but a laugher and kidder too, don't forget that, an enthusiast! a romantic! a mimic! a nine-year-old lover of life! fiery with such simple, neighborhoody dreams!—"I'm going up the field," I call into the kitchen, fibers of pink lox lodged like sour dental floss in the gaps between my teeth, "I'm going up the field, Ma," pounding my mitt with my carpy-smelling little fist, "I'll be back around one—" "*Wait* a minute. What time? Where?" "*Up the field,*" I holler —I'm very high on hollering to be heard, it's like being angry, except without the consequences, "*—to watch the men!*"

And that's the phrase that does me in as we touch down upon *Eretz Yisroel:*° to watch the men.

Because I love those men! I want to grow up to *be* one of those men! To be going home to Sunday dinner at one o'clock, sweat socks pungent from twenty-one innings of softball, underwear athletically gamy, and in the muscle of my throwing arm, a faint throbbing from the low and beautiful pegs I have been unleashing all morning long to hold down the opposition on the base paths; yes, hair disheveled, teeth gritty, feet beat and *kishkas*° sore from laughing, in other words, feeling great, a robust Jewish man now gloriously pooped—yes, home I head for resuscitation . . . and to whom? To *my* wife and *my* children, to a family of my own, and right there in the Weequahic section! I shave and shower—rivulets of water stream off my scalp a filthy brown, ah, it's good, ah yes, it's a regular pleasure standing there nearly scalding myself to death with hot water. It strikes me as so *manly,* converting pain to pleasure. Then into a pair of snappy slacks and a freshly dry-cleaned "gaucho"

° KVELL: gush with pleasure
° KVETCH: a person who gripes
° ERETZ YISROEL: The Promised Land; Land of Israel
° KIAHKAS: intestines

shirt—perfecto! I whistle a popular song, I admire my biceps, I shoot a rag across my shoes, making it *pop*, and meanwhile my kids are riffling through the Sunday papers (reading with eyes the exact color of my own), giggling away on the living-room rug; and my wife, Mrs. Alexander Portnoy, is setting the table in the dining room—we will be having my mother and father as guests, they will be walking over any minute, as they do every Sunday. A future, see! A simple and satisfying future! Exhausting, exhilarating softball in which to spend my body's force—that for the morning—then in the afternoon, the brimming, hearty stew of family life, and at night three solid hours of the best line-up of radio entertainment in the world: yes, as I delighted in Jack Benny's trips down to his vault in the company of *my* father, and Fred Allen's conversations with Mrs. Nussbaum, and Phil Harris' with Frankie Remley, also shall my children delight in them with me, and so unto the hundredth generation. And then after Kenny Baker, I double-lock the front and back doors, turn off all the lights (check and—as my father does—double-check the pilot on the gas range so that our lives will not be stolen from us in the night). I kiss good night my pretty sleepy daughter and my clever sleepy son, and in the arms of Mrs. A. Portnoy, that kind and gentle (and in my sugary but modest fantasy, faceless) woman, I bank the fires of my abounding pleasure. In the morning I am off to downtown Newark, to the Essex County Court House, where I spend my workdays seeking justice for the poor and the oppressed.

The references are to radio personalities who were well-known in the 30's and 40's.

Our eighth-grade class visits the courthouse to observe the architecture. Home and in my room that night, I write in my fresh new graduation autograph album, under YOUR FAVORITE MOTTO, "Don't Step on the Underdog." MY FAVORITE PROFESSION? "Lawyer." MY FAVORITE HERO? "Tom Paine and Abraham Lincoln." Lincoln sits outside the courthouse (in Gutzon Borglum's bronze), looking tragic and fatherly: you just know how much he cares. A statue of Washington, standing erect and authoritarian in front of his horse, overlooks Broad Street; it is the work of J. Massey Rhind (we write this second unname-like name of a sculptor in our notebooks); our art teacher says that the two statues are "the city's pride," and we head off in pairs for the paintings at the Newark Museum. Washington, I must confess, leaves me cold. Maybe it's the horse, that he's leaning on a horse. At any rate, he is so obviously a *goy.*° But Lincoln! I could cry. Look at him sitting there, so *oysgemitchet.*° How he labored for the downtrodden—as will I!

A nice little Jewish boy? Please, I am the nicest little Jewish boy who ever lived! Only look at the fantasies, how sweet and savior-like they are! Gratitude to my parents, loyalty to my tribe, devotion to the cause of justice!

° GOY: a Gentile
° OYSGEMITCHET: exhausted

The Carousel

Rainer Maria Rilke

Below the roof, within its shadow whirled,
a train of painted animals careers—
all disenchanted creatures from a world
that lingers long before it disappears.

Used here as a verb; similar to the more popular *careens*

And some are horses, yoked to little carts,
who yet prance proudly on the wooden ground;
sometimes a furious, red lion darts,
and then an elephant rolls slowly round.

A stag leaps with them, arching through the wood,
but carrying a saddle on his back,
to which a tiny, blue-frocked girl sits glued.

Literary Sorts refer to this type of repeated line as a "refrain." That, of course, is quite useless knowledge unless we understand the use of a refrain. Why does Rilke use it here? Does it speed up or slow down the carousel (and the poem)? See dictionary definition for "refrain."

And on the lion rides a wide-eyed boy,
who grips the rein with little, damp, hot hand,
in terror of the lion's teeth and tongue.

And then an elephant rolls slowly round.

And on the horses, gliding gracefully,
are maidens who have long ago outgrown
this make-believing; they swing outward, free,
and glance about them, restless, all alone . . .

And then an elephant rolls slowly round.

And on they grind, and hurtle toward the end,
and whirl and circle, slowing all the while.
Now red, now green, now grey—the colors blend—
and now a small, indefinite profile . . .
And now and then the wheeling figures send
out of their midst a sudden, dazzling smile,
lost in this game so breathless and so blind.

—Translated by William C. Pratt

What does this phrase modify—"game" or "figures"?

THE LONELY DAY

Erskine Caldwell

For a week the wet mid-summer mists had been creeping over Maine from the south, from the coast; sheets of low-hanging gray vapor spread over the country like dirty steam and leveled the foothills into smooth fields, while the mountains had been wrapped in wet gray clouds and put away from sight towards the north, towards Canada. Yesterday the mists had lifted over the housetops, almost over the tops of the elm trees; but today, Sunday, the lower air was so wet that the meshes of the window-screens were filled with panes of opaque water.

Katherine hurried across the wet grass from the garden and went into the house. She opened the kitchen door quietly and closed it slowly as she stood back against it.

The old woman struck at her with the heavy end of the crutch and cursed her.

The girl jumped away and ran to the other side of the kitchen.

The room was wet with the mid-summer mists. There were little balls of water in the dusty spider-web over the stove and a thin stream of water trickled at intervals down the table-legs to the floor.

"Go pick me some berries," the old woman cried at her. "GO PICK ME SOME BERRIES!" she shouted. "Do you hear me? You damned little sneak! Bring me a pail of berries before I take this crutch and kill you!"

"All right," Katherine whimpered. "I'm going."

"Well, why don't you run? I'll break your head if you don't get out of here after those berries!"

Katherine took the berry-pail from the kitchen table and ran outside before the old woman could strike her again. The wet mists clung to her hair as she ran towards the pasture, and tears fell on her dampened cheeks. The berry-field was on the other side of the stream, beyond the sheep pasture. Bordering the field was the State road, running north and south.

She gathered the wet berries as quickly as she could. She knew the old woman was even then waiting at the kitchen door to strike her with the crutch because she had not returned sooner. She tried as hard as she could, but she could not pick them any faster.

Several hundred yards away automobiles passed in both directions, going up into the Provinces, coming back into Maine. All around her was the forest, the deep dark forest where men worked in winter, in the white frozen snow, cutting pulp wood. The men who worked there were French from Canada and she could not understand what they said. Now there was nobody near. The closest settlement was forty miles to the south and the only people who came through the woods were tourists, passing but never stopping. She had never gone so far as the road, but when she picked berries she could hear the roar of the speeding automobiles and occasionally the laughter of men and women. The old woman would not let her go near the road.

While she was gathering the wet berries she thought she heard one of the automobiles stop. As she listened, there came shouts and laughter from the direction of the road, but she was too far away to hear what the people said. She bent over the berry-bushes and tried to fill the pail as quickly as she could.

It was noon before the pail was full. She ran towards the house where the old woman sat waiting for the berries.

While she ran down the hillside toward the stream in the sheep pasture she heard again the shouts and laughter of several persons. When she reached the footbridge she could see them in dim outline through the mists. There were five or six men and girls farther down the stream toward the lower lake.

Katherine crossed the footbridge and went down the stream where the men and girls were. At first she thought they were fishing, but almost before she knew it, she was within a hundred yards of them; and then she saw that they were swimming and diving into the stream. The low-hanging cloud had cleared along the banks of the stream for a few moments and she saw them plainly only a short distance away.

She stared wild-eyed as she saw one of the men and a girl wade out of the water and stand on the bank a moment before diving in again.

She was so confused by what she saw that she could neither cry out nor run away. Her heart was beating madly and her body trembled with excitement.

While she stood in amazement before the scene, one of the girls climbed to the bank of the stream and ran out across the pasture. The girl turned and called to one of the men.

"You can't catch me, Jimmy!"

Laughing, the naked girl ran off and disappeared in the heavy mists.

The other men and girls were laughing and splashing water in the stream.

Katherine stood beside the stream, above them. She had never seen anything such as this happen before in her life, and she could barely believe that men and girls could have such a good time together. It was too incredible to be true, but she could hear everything they said and see everything they did. And still the scene was unreal to her. She had never been with men and girls of her own age, and she was bewildered with the strangeness of their behavior.

Her heart was racing so excitedly that she could stand still no longer. She wanted to run as fast as she could and fall in the midst of those men and girls and laugh with them. Then suddenly she felt the weight of the berry-pail in her hand, and she turned and ran as quickly as she could to the house where the old woman waited.

The old woman snatched the pail of berries from her hands and began eating the fruit. Katherine went to her room and closed the door. She stood beside her bed trembling with excitement, remembering what she had seen and heard down at the stream in the sheep pasture. She ran from window to window trying to see through the wet mists. If only there had been no mists, she knew she could have seen the men and girls in the pasture. But she could see no further than the windows. The mists covered everything outside.

While the old woman sat in the kitchen eating the berries, Katherine slipped quietly from the front of the house and ran towards the stream. As she ran down the hillside she tried to hear the things the men and girls were saying. She wanted to run, just as they were, into their midst and throw herself on the grass beside them. She wanted to laugh and dive into the stream and splash water over everybody.

Running wildly towards the stream, she suddenly saw that the men and girls were not there. They had taken their clothes and gone back to the automobile to dress, and by now they were probably several miles away. Now there was nothing she could do. She did not want to stay at the stream alone. She wanted to be with someone, with men and girls who laughed and splashed water. Alone, she stood crying by the stream.

The wet mists chilled her body and she began to shiver. The warm tears fell cold and hard on her arms and hands.

Slowly she turned and walked up the hillside toward the house. She repeated over and over the words she thought she had heard as she was running so happily to the stream a few minutes before.

The old woman had not missed her. She still sat in the kitchen eating from the pail the berries Katherine had picked that morning.

Katherine sat on the bed in her room crying. She fell backward and crushed the pillow over her face so the old woman could not hear her.

Later in the afternoon she got up. She walked around the room, stopping at a window and trying to penetrate the gray mists that hung over the earth. There was no one to see her, there were no men and girls she could see. It was not what had happened in the sheep pasture that morning, when the gray mists were filled with laughter and the stream with splashing water. It was not the same thing. And she could not laugh aloud.

After supper, when the old woman had gone to bed, Katherine stole out of the house and ran through the wet dark night towards the pasture. When she reached the stream, she could see nothing, not even the grass at her feet. All about her she felt the clinging wet clouds of vapor. The black mists covered everything. Over the hill she thought she heard an automobile speed along the road towards the Provinces. She tried again, but she could not laugh aloud in the wet mists.

She ran across the berry-field until she reached the road where the automobiles passed. When she got there, she stood in the road and waited. It was then after midnight. She waited but no car came from either direction.

While she stood in the center of the road she distinctly heard in the distance the same laughter that had made her so excited that afternoon. Clearly she heard a girl's voice. Someone was calling, "You can't catch me, Jimmy!" Almost immediately the voice of a man could be heard out in the far darkness somewhere. And then, all around her, men and girls were shouting and laughing, just as she had heard them that afternoon in the pasture. From the music of their voices she knew they were splashing water in a stream and lying naked on the grassy banks beside the water. But they were so far away she knew she could never find them while everything was so black and misty.

She waited and listened for an automobile to come up or down the road. But there was none. She wanted to stand in the center of the road and have the men and women see her.

The first light of day broke through the mists and found her lying in the road, her body made lifeless by an automobile that had shot through the darkness an hour before. She was without motion, but she was naked, and a smile that was the beginning of laughter made her the most beautiful woman that tourists speeding to the Provinces had ever seen.

The moral of the story seems to be this: If you are going to pick berries, then, PICK BERRIES. Would you agree? Or are there more important considerations than "morals" and "points" of stories?

A girl . . . prestige in school . . . pep . . . giving kids a sense of caring . . . getting them interested and enthusiastic . . . making school spirit . . . But where does *her* train go?

CHEERLEADER

Margaret English

Jean F., 17, is a senior cheerleader at her Maine high school. She also belongs to the Dramatic Society, International Relations Club, Junior Escorts (graduation ushers), Young Democrats, and a sorority. Her clothes are appropriately pretty, her hair bounces the way it's supposed to. She is the only child of attentive, affectionate, middle-class parents.

Cheerleading is the greatest. When you're cheering, you're really a part of something exciting. You're getting all those people interested and enthusiastic about a thing. It's just kind of inside you that you want your team to win.

You really have to be kind of loud to be a cheerleader. You can't just be a quiet person all the time, and you can't get scared in front of a lot of people. We practice every night in the summer. In the winter, we leave right after school for a wrestling match, get a hamburger someplace, and then rush to the basketball game. You have to be willing to give a lot of time.

Last summer, we all went away to cheerleading school. When we got back, my father had had a brown-and-gold fringe made for our Jeep. Those are our school colors. He lets us use the Jeep to go to games and pull floats and stuff. Once, we were late to a game because it ran out of gas, and we got a standing ovation when we arrived.

Sure, there's a lot of prestige. You're elected by the whole school, and you're a representative of it. If you're a cheerleader, people know who you are. You have to set an example for the other kids. One of the girls was thrown off the team for drinking last year.

"Cheerleader" by Margaret English, from YOUTHQUAKE by the Editors of Cowles and United Press International. Published by permission of Cowles Book Company.

About 60 or 70 kids go out for cheerleading every year. You have to have a 2.6 [B–] average and good citizenship and attendance records. First, you try out in front of the old cheerleaders, three teachers, the sponsor and president of Pep Club, the principal, and the assistant principal. You're judged on pep and enthusiasm, appearance, jumping, accuracy, and coordination. They choose 18 kids to try out in front of the whole school. There are three assemblies. Then six are elected. I have the congratulations notice they sent me hung up on my closet door with all the other things I want to remember.

We have a lot of rallies on Fridays to raise the spirit so we'll be ready to go on Saturday. If the cheerleaders didn't get excited, the crowd never would. Of course, you've got to have a winning team. Last year, our team was City Champion in football. I don't really know what formation they play. I could draw it for you, but I don't know what it's called. Our basketball team was second in the city, and the baseball team won the state championship. So right now the spirit in our school is just great. This is an important thing, because it gives the individual kid a sense of caring about his school aside from just the academic part of it. Without school spirit, kids would just go to school and come home and do nothing but study.

I guess if I spent more time working, I'd probably get better grades. But if I studied all the time, I probably wouldn't have any fun. Besides, you meet so many different people by doing different things. When I go to college, I think it would be just great to room with a Negro girl or a Chinese girl or somebody with a whole different background from mine.

On the whole, I'm a pretty carefree type. My life is generally easy. Our generation has had everything handed to it. Our parents were Depression kids, and they didn't have many things; so now they want us to have them. They value the dollar more than we do. With kids today, if you need money, you get it from your parents; that's all. We may be getting too much too easily, but we have the pressure of learning to accept it all.

I think I have the greatest parents in the world. They were strict with me, and I appreciate this. I was an only child, and they tried not to spoil me. They wouldn't let me date until I was sixteen. Now, it's all new to me, and I'm loving it. I have to be home by one after dances, and I call them if I'm going to be late for some reason. We never disagree on this. I know they love me, and they worry about me. I'm going to be strict with my kids.

When I was in the first grade and I was six years old, I had been a bad girl all that year. I guess I had been just generally sassy and disrespectful. Anyway, I wanted a bicycle for Christmas more than anything. Christmas morning, I ran to the tree to get my bike, and it wasn't there. My father explained that Santa Claus knows everything, and he knew I'd been bad.

Sometimes, parents push their kids too much. Be popular, get good grades, go to college, make money, all that. I don't think anyone should go to college if he doesn't want to. We still need plumbers, you know. As far as I'm concerned, I won't be finished with school until I'm out of law school. But that's just me and what I want to do. The worst thing you can do to a kid is push him into something he doesn't like.

I know there are some kids who have sexual relations before marriage, but I think this is very definitely morally wrong. Marriage is sacred, and you should save it for marriage. If you don't, somehow you'll be punished for it.

I hate missionaries—not doctors and nurses and people who give real help—but people who are always telling you what to do and what to believe. Think about people who worship the sun. Really, in some ways, they get more for their belief than we do. It comes up every morning. It goes down every night. You can understand it. Why should somebody try to sell them something different?

The trouble is that most people don't seem to care about things enough to question them or try to do anything about them. Like Vietnam. People don't pay any attention. They just let it happen. The only ones who do seem to care about it are those beardy people. We saw this movie, *While Brave Men Die,* in school, and it had all these dirty, beatniky types out demonstrating against the war. Yes, they have a right—but I don't know if I would like to call this type of person an American.

A lot of things confuse me, and I think about them a lot, but I'm not really a worrier. I'm not really afraid of the future or death or anything like that. Oh sure, I get panicky for a minute sometimes and worry something's going to happen to my family. But on the whole, I'm not afraid.

Where *does* Jean's train go?

Is it worthwhile for students to compare the loquacious Jean F. with Caldwell's reticent Katherine in "The Lonely Day"?

But He Was Cool or: he even stopped for green lights

super-cool
ultrablack
a tan/purple
had a beautiful shade.

he had a double-natural
that wd put the sisters to shame.
his dashikis were tailor made
& his beads were imported sea shells
(from some blk/country i never heard of)
he was triple-hip.

his tikis were hand carved
out of ivory
& came express from the motherland.
he would greet u in swahili
& say good-by in yoruba.
woooooooooooo-jim he bes so cool & ill tel li gent
cool-cool is so cool he was un-cooled by
other niggers' cool
cool-cool ultracool was bop-cool/ice box
cool so cool cold cool
his wine didn't have to be cooled, him was
air conditioned cool
cool-cool/real cool made me cool—now
ain't that cool
cool-cool so cool him nick-named refrig-
erator.

cool-cool so cool
he didn't know,
after detroit, newark, chicago &c.,
we had to hip
                    cool-cool/ super-cool/ real cool
     that
to be black
is
to be
very-hot.

—Don Lee

WE REAL COOL

The Pool Players.
Seven at the Golden Shovel.

We real cool. We
Left school. We

Lurk late. We
Strike straight. We

Sing sin. We
Thin gin. We

Jazz June. We
Die soon.

—Gwendolyn Brooks

BLACK JACKETS

In the silence that prolongs the span
Rawly of music when the record ends,
The red-haired boy who drove a van
In weekday overalls but, like his friends,

British: "truck"

Wore cycle boots and jacket here
To suit the Sunday hangout he was in,
Heard, as he stretched back from his beer,
Leather creak softly round his neck and chin.

Before him, on a coal-black sleeve
Remote exertion had lined, scratched, and burned
Insignia that could not revive
The heroic fall or climb where they were earned.

In the past

Why not? Has he outgrow
the past, or is he too "tir
to "revive" it?

On the other drinkers bent together,
Concocting selves for their impervious kit,
He saw it as no more than leather
Which, taut across the shoulders grown to it,

Trying to live up to what their jackets suggest about them

"each man's jacket"

An interesting image. Does it imply that the jackets had been bought before the boys could quite fill them out?

How is it possible to account for the almost epic simile here? Would the boy see things this way? Then, who is it that sees the glints of light in that fashion?

Sent through the dimness of a bar
As sudden and anonymous hints of light
As those that shipping give, that are
Now flickers in the Bay, now lost in night.

"ships"

He stretched out like a cat, and rolled
The bitterish taste of beer upon his tongue,
And listened to a joke being told:
The present was the things he stayed among.

If it was only loss he wore,
He wore it to assert, with fierce devotion,
Complicity and nothing more.
He recollected his initiation,

And one especially of the rites.
For on his shoulders they had put tattoos:
The group's name on the left, The Knights,
And on the right the slogan Born To Lose.

—Thom Gunn

MUTINY ON THE BOUNTY
MONSTERS ON THE PROWL
Archie's Joke Book
SPECIAL REPORT
SEPARATISM!
A Hockey Problem?
JANUARY 1971
50 CENTS
WHY JEAN BELIVEAU WON'T QUIT
JERRY WEST—basketball's Mr. Clutch—says:
"I SAW PLAYERS SHAKE WITH FEAR"
Sport Scene
BOBBY ORR
MARCH 1971
75¢
ILLUSTRATED
NEW YORK KNICKS
SPECIAL SECTION
Exclusive Photos
Of The Great Year
"71" SUPER" CAR
ABC's OF
HOW TO
Improve Your
Edge Control;
IT'S WHAT'S OUT FRONT THAT COUNTS!
DRAG RACES
INDIAN SCRAMBLER
Choppers magazine

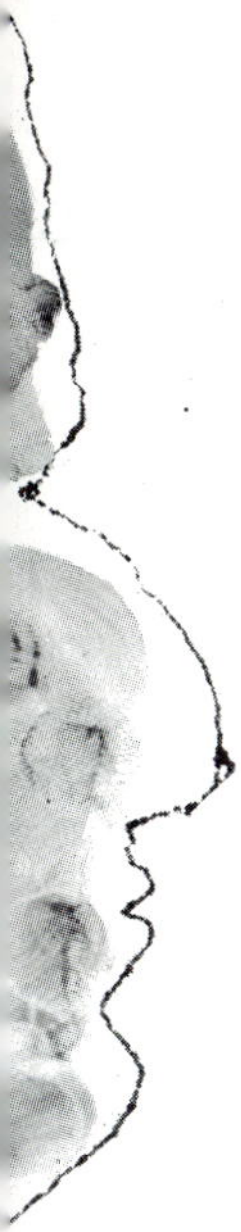

Cluster 5: pp. 116-155
A topical cluster
Focus: life's enigmas

INTERLOCK WITH CLUSTER 4:
A topical link: growth—its enigmatic nature

5

But novelists write for countless different reasons: for money, for fame, for reviewers, for parents, for friends, for loved ones; for vanity, for pride, for curiosity, for amusement: as skilled furniture-makers enjoy making furniture, as drunkards like drinking, as judges like judging, as Sicilians like emptying a shotgun into an enemy's back. I could fill a book with reasons, and they would all be true, though not true of all. Only one same reason is shared by all of us: *we wish to create worlds as real as, but other than the world that is.*

—From *The French Lieutenant's Woman* by John Fowles

The Boy of Winander

William Wordsworth

Some attempts have been made to identify the Boy. There seems to be no reason for looking farther than Wordsworth himself. See *Talks,* p. 38.

There was a Boy; ye knew him well, ye cliffs
And islands of Winander!—many a time,
At evening, when the earliest stars began
To move along the edges of the hills,
Rising or setting, would he stand alone,
Beneath the trees, or by the glimmering lake;
And there, with fingers interwoven, both hands
Pressed closely palm to palm and to his mouth
Uplifted, he, as through an instrument,
Blew mimic hootings to the silent owls,
That they might answer him.—And they would shout
Across the watery vale, and shout again,
Responsive to his call,—with quivering peals,
And long halloos, and screams, and echoes loud
Redoubled and redoubled; concourse wild
Of jocund din! And, when there came a pause
Of silence such as baffled his best skill:
Then, sometimes, in that silence, while he hung
Listening, a gentle shock of mild surprise
Has carried him far into his heart the voice
Of mountain-torrents; or the visible scene
Would enter unawares into his mind
With all its solemn imagery, its rocks,
Its woods, and that uncertain heaven received
Into the bosom of the steady lake.
This boy was taken from his mates, and died
In childhood, ere he was full twelve years old.
Pre-eminent in beauty is the vale
Where he was born and bred: the churchyard hangs
Upon a slope above the village-school;
And through that churchyard when my way has led
On summer-evenings, I believe that there
A long half-hour together I have stood
Mute—looking at the grave in which he lies!

In the earliest version (1798), this and all following pronouns in this section are in the first person.

Coleridge thought these lines particularly "Wordsworthian."

"ten" in the 1805 edition of *The Prelude*

These lines were not in the earliest draft. They first appear in *Lyrical Ballads, 1800.* Afterwards, the whole passage was worked into *The Prelude* (V, lines 389-422).

Literary Sort: I wonder what a girl like Cheerleader would have to say about this poem.

Editor: What do *you* have to say about it?

Timothy Winters

Charles Causley

Timothy Winters comes to school
With eyes as wide as a football-pool,
Ears like bombs and teeth like splinters:
A blitz of a boy is Timothy Winters.

Gambling term; British football is soccer.

His belly is white, his neck is dark,
And his hair is an exclamation-mark.
His clothes are enough to scare a crow
And through his britches the blue winds blow.

When teacher talks he won't hear a word
And he shoots down dead the arithmetic-bird,°
He licks the patterns off his plate
And he's not even heard of the Welfare State.

Timothy Winters has bloody feet
And he lives in a house on Suez Street,
He sleeps in a sack on the kitchen floor
And they say there aren't boys like him any more.

Old Man Winters likes his beer
And his missus ran off with a bombardier,
Grandma sits in the grate with a gin
And Timothy's dosed with an aspirin.

And so there's no legal grounds for interference.

The Welfare Worker lies awake
But the law's as tricky as a ten-foot snake,
So Timothy Winters drinks his cup
And slowly goes on growing up.

Out of concern for Timothy?

At Morning Prayers the Master helves°
For children less fortunate than ourselves,
And the loudest response in the room is when
Timothy Winters roars "Amen!"

So come one angel, come on ten:
Timothy Winters says "Amen
Amen amen amen amen."
Timothy Winters, Lord.

Amen.

Does line 10 have sexual connotations? Or is "arithmetic-bird" merely a way of speaking disparagingly of the subject? or the teacher?

°ARITHMETIC-BIRD: arithmetic teacher?
°HELVES: constantly hammers about the subject

Early Sorrow

Peter Abrahams

This selection is an exerpt from the autobiography *Tell Freedom.*

Wednesday was crackling day. On that day the children of the location made the long trek to Elsburg siding for the squares of pig's rind that passed for our daily meat. We collected a double lot of cow dung the day before; a double lot of moeroga.

I finished my breakfast and washed up. Aunt Liza was at her washtub in the yard. A misty, sickly sun was just showing. And on the open veld the frost lay thick and white on the grass.

Open grass or low brush country in South Africa

"Ready?" Aunt Liza called.

I went out to her. She shook the soapsuds off her swollen hands and wiped them on her apron. She lifted the apron and put her hand through the slits of the many thin cotton dresses she wore. The dress nearest the skin was the one with the pocket. From this she pulled a sixpenny piece. She tied it in a knot in the corner of a bit of colored cloth and handed it to me.

"Take care of that. . . . Take the smaller piece of bread in the bin, but don't eat it till you start back. You can have a small piece of crackling with it. Only a small piece, understand?"

It may be worth noting that Aunt Liza gives him no warning of possible trouble, no suggestion of how to behave or react in the face of the trouble that does come.

"Yes, Aunt Liza."

"All right."

I got the bread and tucked it into the little canvas bag in which I would carry the crackling.

" 'Bye, Aunt Liza." I trotted off, one hand in my pocket, feeling the cloth where the money was. I paused at Andries's home.

"Andries!" I danced up and down while I waited. The cold was not so terrible on bare feet if one did not keep still.

Andries came trotting out of his yard. His mother's voice followed, desperate and plaintive:

"I'll skin you if you lose the money!"

"Women!" Andries said bitterly.

I glimpsed the dark, skinny woman at her washtub as we trotted across the veld. Behind and in front of us, other children trotted in twos and threes.

There was a sharp bite to the morning air I sucked in; it stung my nose so that tears came to my eyes; it went down my throat like an icy draught; my nose ran. I tried breathing through my mouth, but this was worse. The cold went through my shirt and shorts; my skin went pimply and chilled; my fingers went numb and began to ache; my feet felt like frozen lumps that did not belong to me, yet jarred and hurt each time I put them down. I began to feel sick and desperate.

"Jesus God in heaven!" Andries cried suddenly.

I looked at him. His eyes were rimmed in red. Tears ran down his cheeks. His face was drawn and purple, a sick look on it.

"Faster," I said.

"Think it'll help?"

I nodded. We went faster. We passed two children, sobbing and moaning as they ran. We were all in the same desperate situation. We were creatures haunted and hounded by the cold. It was a cruel enemy who gave no quarter. And our means of fighting it were pitifully inadequate. In all the mornings and evenings of the winter months, young and old, big and small, were helpless victims of the bitter cold. Only towards noon and in the early afternoon, when the sun sat high in the sky, was there a brief respite. For us children, the cold, especially the morning cold, assumed an awful and malevolent personality. We talked of "it." "It" was a half-human monster with evil thoughts, evil intentions, bent on destroying us. "It" was happiest when we were most miserable. Andries had told me how "it" had, last winter, caught and killed a boy.

Hunger was an enemy too, but one with whom we could come to terms, who had many virtues and values. Hunger gave our pap, moeroga, and crackling a feast-like quality. When it was not with us, we could think and talk kindly about it. Its memory could even give moments of laughter. But the cold of winter was with us all the time. "It" never really eased up. There were only more bearable degrees of "it" at high noon and on mild days. "It" was the real enemy. And on this Wednesday morning, as we ran across the veld, winter was more bitterly, bitingly, freezingly real than ever.

The sun climbed. The frozen earth thawed, leaving the short grass looking wet and weary. Painfully our feet and legs came alive. The aching numbness slowly left our fingers. We ran more slowly in the more bearable cold.

In climbing, the sun lost some of its damp look and seemed a real, if cold, sun. When it was right overhead, we struck the sandy road, which meant we were nearing the siding. None of the others were in sight. Andries and I were alone on the sandy road on the open veld.

We slowed down to a brisk walk. We were sufficiently thawed to want to talk.

"How far?" I said.

"A few minutes," he said.

"I've got a piece of bread," I said.

"Me too," he said. "Let's eat it now."

"On the way back," I said. "With a bit of crackling."

"Good idea. . . . Race to the fork."

"All right."

"Go!" he said.

We shot off together, legs working like pistons. He soon pulled away from me. He reached the fork in the road some fifty yards ahead.

"I win!" he shouted gleefully, though his teeth still chattered.

We pitched stones down the road, each trying to pitch farther than the other. I won and wanted to go on doing it. But Andries soon grew weary with pitching. We raced again. Again he won. He wanted another race, but I refused. I wanted pitching, but he refused. So, sulking with each other, we reached the pig farm.

We followed a fenced-off pathway round sprawling white buildings. Everywhere about us was the grunt of pigs. As we passed an open doorway, a huge dog came bounding out, snarling and barking at us. In our terror we forgot it was fenced in, and we streaked away. Surprised, I found myself a good distance ahead of Andries. We looked back and saw a young white woman call the dog to heel.

"Damn Boer dog," Andries said.

"Matter with it?" I asked.

"They teach them to go for us. Never get caught by one. My old man's got a hole in his bottom where a Boer dog got him."

I remembered I had outstripped him.

"I won!" I said.

"Only because you were frightened," he said.

"I still won."

"Scare arse," he jeered.

"Scare arse, yourself!"

"I'll knock you!"

"I'll knock you back!"

A couple of white men came down the path and ended our possible fight. We hurried past them to the distant shed where a queue had already formed. There were grown-ups and children. All the grown-ups and some of the children were from places other than our location.

The line moved slowly. The young white man who served us did it in leisurely fashion, with long pauses for a smoke. Occasionally he turned his back.

At last, after what seemed hours, my turn came. Andries was behind me. I took the sixpenny piece from the square of cloth and offered it to the man.

"Well?" he said.

"Sixpence crackling, please."

Andries nudged me in the back. The man's stare suddenly became cold and hard. Andries whispered into my ear.

"Well?" the man repeated coldly.

"Please, *baas,*" I said.

"What d'you want?"

"Sixpence crackling, please."

"What?"

Andries dug me in the ribs.

"Sixpence crackling, please, *baas.*"

"What?"

"Sixpence crackling, please, *baas.*"

"You new here?"

"Yes, *baas.*" I looked at his feet, while he stared at me.

At last he took the sixpenny piece from me. I held my bag open while he filled it with crackling from a huge pile on a large canvas sheet on the ground. Turning away, I stole a fleeting glance at his face. His eyes met mine, and there was amused, challenging mockery in them. I waited for Andries at the back of the queue, out of the reach of the white man's mocking eyes.

The cold day was at its mildest as we walked home along the sandy road. I took out my piece of bread and, with a small piece of greasy crackling, still warm, on it, I munched as we went along. We had not yet made our peace, so Andries munched his bread and crackling on the other side of the road.

"Dumb fool!" he mocked at me for not knowing how to address the white man.

"Scare arse!" I shouted back.

Thus, hurling curses at each other, we reached the fork. Andries saw them first and moved over to my side of the road.

"White boys," he said.

There were three of them, two of about our own size and one slightly bigger. They had school bags and were coming towards us up the road from the siding.

"Better run for it," Andries said.

"Why?"

"No, that'll draw them. Let's just walk along, but quickly."

"Why?" I repeated.

"Shut up," he said.

Some of his anxiety touched me. Our own scrap was forgotten. We marched side by side as fast as we could. The white boys saw us and hurried up the road. We passed the fork. Perhaps they would take the turning away from us. We dared not look back.

"Hear them?" Andries asked.

"No." I looked over my shoulder. "They're coming," I said.

"Walk faster," Andries said. "If they come closer, run."

"Hey, *klipkop!*"

"Don't look back," Andries said.

"Hottentot!"

We walked as fast as we could.

"Bloody Kaffir!"

Ahead was a bend in the road. Behind the bend were bushes. Once there, we could run without them knowing it till it was too late.

"Faster," Andries said.

They began pelting us with stones.

"Run when we get to the bushes," Andries said.

The bend and the bushes were near. We would soon be there.

A clear young voice carried to us: "Your fathers are dirty black bastards of baboons!"

"Run!" Andries called.

A violent, unreasoning anger suddenly possessed me. I stopped and turned.

"You're a liar!" I screamed it.

The foremost boy pointed at me. "An ugly black baboon!"

In a fog of rage I went towards him.

"Liar!" I shouted. "My father was better than your father!"

I neared them. The bigger boy stepped between me and the one I was after.

"My father was better than your father! Liar!"

The big boy struck me a mighty clout on the side of the face. I staggered, righted myself, and leaped at the boy who had insulted my father. I struck him on the face, hard. A heavy blow on the back of my head nearly stunned me. I grabbed at the boy in front of me. We went down together.

"Liar!" I said through clenched teeth, hitting him with all my might.

Blows rained on me—on my head, my neck, the side of my face, my mouth—but my enemy was under me and I pounded him fiercely, all the time repeating:

"Liar! Liar! Liar!"

Suddenly stars exploded in my head. Then there was darkness.

I emerged from the darkness to find Andries kneeling beside me.

"God, man! I thought they'd killed you."

I sat up. The white boys were nowhere to be seen. Like Andries, they'd probably thought me dead and run off in panic. The inside of my mouth felt sore and swollen. My nose was tender to the touch. The back of my head ached. A trickle of blood dripped from my nose. I stemmed it with the square of colored cloth. The greatest damage was to my shirt. It was ripped in many places. I remembered the crackling. I looked anxiously about. It was safe, a little off the road on the grass. I relaxed. I got up and brushed my clothes. I picked up the crackling.

"God, you're dumb!" Andries said. "You're going to get it! Dumb arse!"

I was too depressed to retort. Besides, I knew he was right. I was dumb. I should have run when he told me to.

"Come on," I said.

One of many small groups of children, each child carrying his little bag of crackling, we trod the long road home in the cold winter afternoon.

There was tension in the house that night. When I got back, Aunt Liza had listened to the story in silence. The beating or scolding I expected did not come. But Aunt Liza changed while she listened, became remote and withdrawn. When Uncle Sam came home she told him what had happened. He, too, just looked at me and became more remote and withdrawn than usual. They were waiting for something; their tension reached out to me, and I waited with them, anxious, apprehensive.

The thing we waited for came while we were having our supper. We heard a trap pull up outside.

"a light carriage"

"Here it is," Uncle Sam said, and got up.

Aunt Liza leaned back from the table and put her hands in her lap, fingers intertwined, a cold, unseeing look in her eyes.

Before Uncle Sam reached the door, it burst open. A tall, broad, white man strode in. Behind him came the three boys. The one I had attacked had swollen lips and a puffy left eye.

"Evening, *baas*," Uncle Sam murmured.

"That's him," the bigger boy said, pointing at me.

The white man stared till I lowered my eyes.

"Well?" he said.

"He's sorry, *baas*," Uncle Sam said quickly. "I've given him a hiding he won't forget soon. You know how it is, *baas*. He's new here, the child of a relative in Johannesburg, and they don't all know how to behave there. You know how it is in the big towns, *baas*." The plea in Uncle Sam's voice had grown more pronounced as he went on. He turned to me. "Tell the *baas* and young *basies* how sorry you are, Lee."

I looked at Aunt Liza and something in her lifelessness made me stubborn in spite of my fear.

"He insulted my father," I said.

The white man smiled.

"See, Sam, your hiding couldn't have been good."

There was a flicker of life in Aunt Liza's eyes. For a brief moment she saw me, looked at me, warmly, lovingly; then her eyes went dead again.

"He's only a child, *baas*," Uncle Sam murmured.

"You stubborn too, Sam?"

"No, *baas*."

"Good. Then teach him, Sam. If you and he are to live here, you must teach him. Well—?"

"Yes, *baas*."

Uncle Sam went into the other room and returned with a thick leather thong. He wound it once round his hand and advanced on me. The man and the boys leaned against the door, watching. I looked at Aunt Liza's face. Though there was no sign of life or feeling on it, I knew suddenly, instinctively, that she wanted me not to cry.

Bitterly, Uncle Sam said: "You must never lift your hand to a white person. No matter what happens, you must never lift your hand to a white person. . . ."

He lifted the strap and brought it down on my back. I clenched my teeth and stared at Aunt Liza. I did not cry with the first three strokes. Then, suddenly, Aunt Liza went limp. Tears showed in her eyes. The thong came down on my back again and again. I screamed and begged for mercy. I grovelled at Uncle Sam's feet, begging him to stop, promising never to lift my hand to any white person. . . .

At last the white man's voice said: "All right, Sam."

Uncle Sam stopped. I lay whimpering on the floor. Aunt Liza sat like one in a trance.

"Is he still stubborn, Sam?"

"Tell the *baas* and *basies* you are sorry."

"I'm sorry," I said.

"Bet his father is one of those who believe in equality."

"His father is dead," Aunt Liza said.

"Good night, Sam."

"Good night, *baas*. Sorry about this."

"All right, Sam." He opened the door. The boys went out first, then he followed. "Good night, Liza."

Aunt Liza did not answer. The door shut behind the white folk, and soon we heard their trap moving away. Uncle Sam flung the thong viciously against the door, slumped down on the bench, folded his arms on the table, and buried his head on his arms. Aunt Liza moved away from him, sat down on the floor beside me, and lifted me into her large lap. She sat rocking my body. Uncle Sam began to sob softly. After some time he raised his head and looked at us.

"Explain to the child, Liza," he said.

"You explain," Aunt Liza said bitterly. "You are the man. You did the beating. You are the head of the family. This is a man's world. You do the explaining."

"Please, Liza."

"You should be happy. The whites are satisfied. We can go on now."

"Go on" *where?* Or better yet, *how?*

With me in her arms, Aunt Liza got up. She carried me into the other room. The food on the table remained half-eaten. She laid me on the bed on my stomach, smeared fat on my back, then covered me with the blankets. She undressed and got into bed beside me. She cuddled me close, warmed me with her own body. With her big hand on my cheek, she rocked me, first to silence, then to sleep.

For the only time during my stay there, I slept on a bed in Elsburg.

When I woke next morning, Uncle Sam had gone. Aunt Liza only once referred to the beating he had given me. It was in the late afternoon, when I returned with the day's cow dung.

"It hurt him," she said. "You'll understand one day."

That night Uncle Sam brought me an orange, a bag of boiled sweets, and a dirty old picture book. He smiled as he gave them to me, rather anxiously. When I smiled back at him, he seemed to relax. He put his hand on my head, started to say something, then changed his mind and took his seat by the fire.

Aunt Liza looked up from the floor, where she dished out the food.

"It's all right, old man," she murmured.

"One day . . ." Uncle Sam said.

"It's all right," Aunt Liza repeated insistently.

NIGHTS AWAY FROM HOME

Frank Conroy

This selection comes from Frank Conroy's autobiography, *Stop Time.*

. . . Under the tree on the doctor's lawn, I woke early. Crawling out carefully, I stood up and brushed the pine needles from my clothes and hair. Everything was utterly still—the road, the houses, the damp air itself. I looked around at the town in the colorless dawn light, seeing it for the first time. It was smaller than I'd thought in the darkness. Not even a town, really, just a few houses strung along either side of the highway. I crossed the road and started south. As I approached the police station the red neon sign went out. I went by quickly, without turning my head.

My first ride of the day was a milk truck. The driver, a teen-aged boy, seemed to be standing behind the wheel in the tall, open cab. Then I realized there was a very high seat so he could jump in and out with a minimum of effort. I sat down on the corrugated steel floor and lifted my face to the wind. Behind us the bottles rattled in their wire cages.

"Go ahead, kid," he yelled over the wind and the rattling glass. "Take a quart. I'll chalk it up to breakage."

I opened a bottle and drank in long, deep swallows. The milk was ice cold and delicious. Five or six miles up the road the boy had to turn off to begin his rounds. At the corner I jumped out the open door with a wave, absurdly pleased that he didn't have to stop. The sun was out and I took off my jacket, slinging it over my shoulder as I walked.

It was too early for traffic. When a car passed I'd turn around and walk backward, my thumb in the air, whipping my head as it went by to see the license plate. By never losing my forward momentum I felt less dependent on the cars.

Plowed fields stretched away on either side of the road. I measured my progress by sighting something far ahead—a group of mailboxes, a road sign, or a line of telephone poles—and making it my goal. Passing a huge girl drinking Coca-Cola (the sudden awareness of silence as I walked under her immense eyes, one of them bulging slightly where the paper had blistered), I'd already picked my next target, an isolated gas station on the horizon.

I was sweating as I crossed the asphalt driveway and approached the office. Through the wide plate-glass window I could see an old man sitting with his feet up, staring out at the pumps. His head came around slowly as he caught sight of me. I pushed open the door. Hillbilly music blasted from a radio on the desk beside his feet.

"Can I use the bathroom?"

"What say?"

"Can I use the bathroom, please?"

"Around back." He waved his arm to indicate the direction.

I let the door fall shut and went around the corner of the building. The ground was littered with old oil cans, paper cartons, and fragments of auto bodies. Inside the men's room I looked at myself in the mirror over the washstand, mildly surprised that except for a layer of dirt and messy hair I looked the same as usual. I ran hot water into the basin and pulled my shirt over my head. There wasn't any soap, only a can of Grease-Off, a gray powder that felt like sand between my palms. I scoured myself thoroughly, face, neck, shoulders, and arms, and bent over the small basin to rinse off when the paste began to sting too much.

Back out in front I gathered my courage. I ran my fingers through my hair and went into the office. The old man was cleaning his nails with a penknife.

"Have you got any odd jobs you want done?" I asked, having

rehearsed the question in the bathroom mirror. "Cleaning up or washing windows or something?"

He attacked his index finger with exquisite care. "Nope."

"I could clean up that junk around back."

He answered without raising his head. "This ain't my place. I'm just watching it."

"Will the boss be back soon?"

"Nope." He raised the knife to his mouth and blew something off the tip.

I stood by the door, reluctant to leave. "Well, thanks anyway," I said after a minute, and backed out. I knelt down for a drink from the water tap between the gas pumps, wiping my mouth and glancing back at the office as I finished. The old man hadn't moved. I turned away and crossed the black asphalt back to the highway.

Every hour or so I would take a break. I was resting by the side of the road, my back up against a fence post, when a yellow school bus came around the bend and stopped directly in front of me. The folding doors crashed open and the driver stared down his extended arm at me. "Well, come on," he yelled, his hand opening and closing over the handle of the door lever.

I got up and advanced a step. "I'm not . . ." I began, unsure of how to explain.

"What?" he yelled. He squinted his eyes and, peering down at me, raised his upper lip in an expression of annoyance, exposing a quarter-inch of red gums.

"I don't go to your school," I said, stepping back. "I don't ride the bus."

His mouth fell shut and he pulled the lever to close the doors, his whole body straightening with the effort. "God damn kids."

The children had crowded over to my side to see what was happening. They watched me from behind the glass, their mouths moving silently as they shouted. The bus began to move and they slipped away, pale faces turning into a white blur. I started walking.

As the morning sun rose higher in the sky, traffic picked up, but there were no trucks. It occurred to me that I'd taken a wrong turn somewhere. I was on Route One, but there might have been an alternate, a truck route, that I'd missed. In any event I knew the thing to do was keep heading south. Eventually the roads would rejoin. I wiggled my thumb at a big DeSoto. It went by at a good seventy miles an hour, rocking slightly on the poor road surface. About to turn away, I caught sight of another car in the distance. A flash of sunlight caught something on its roof and I froze in my tracks. A red beacon. The police. It was too late to hide. I turned my back on them and continued walking, my mind spinning in a frantic effort to prepare myself should they stop. Could Jean have notified the police in New York? No, that was out of the question. I realized I should have prepared a story—something from a book I'd read, or a movie. I should have had a false personality and

His stepfather

background at my fingertips so they wouldn't be able to trace me back. No matter what happened, I couldn't let them send me back. Forcing myself not to turn around for a quick glance, I kept walking.

At first a faint sighing, like wind in the tops of distant trees. Then the birth of another sound within the sigh, a sharper sound, very faint but growing steadily, a kind of whine, first heard as a pinpoint in the higher registers, building rapidly to a full hum across the spectrum, growing louder and louder, and then (at the very instant a shock wave of air slammed softly across my shoulders) overtaking the sigh, reversing itself, and plunging down the scale to a steady hum. I watched the black car racing away ahead of me. The taillights came on, a bright, burning red. The entire rear end lifted almost imperceptibly.

After a momentary pause the cruiser began to back up. I stood fascinated, rabbit-like, drinking in the image of the approaching car. When it arrived in front of me, so close I could have touched it, the image was unreal, like something from a dream. The window came down and a pair of blue eyes watched me calmly.

"What you doin' out here, boy?"

"I'm on my way to school. I missed the bus." A certain tranquility spread like oil over the surface of my mind as I plunged into the lie.

"We saw you hitching. Hitching rides is against the law," he said, his voice neither threatening nor reassuring, leaving me plenty of room to answer. He scratched his nose and watched me.

"Well, I'm sorry," I said, looking down. "I was getting awfully late. He turned and stared out the windshield. A speck of shaving soap had dried just under his ear, very white against the red skin. "Where's your books?"

"In my locker," I said. "We didn't have any homework so I left them."

He turned away and spoke to his partner at the wheel. I couldn't hear the short exchange.

"Okay. Get in," he said, staring straight ahead.

"What?" I felt the beginning of panic, like a giant hand squeezing my heart.

"Get in back. We go by the high school."

"Oh, that's great," I said, talking quickly to conceal my relief. "Thanks a lot. I sure appreciate it." I opened the back door and hesitated with one foot inside. The rear of the car was separated from the front by heavy wire mesh and the handles had been stripped off the inside of the doors. I entered after a split second, dazed, overwhelmed by that particular breathless, lightheaded sensation that comes with the sense of having lost control of events, surrendering myself to fate with the same delirious passivity the awkward diver feels as he springs off the board. My body fell back as the car pulled away and I covered my mouth in a convulsive yawn. Through the black mesh I could see the wide bristled necks of the two cops ramrod stiff above their neat gray shirt collars.

"You drive like an old lady, George."

"Uh-huh. Tell the Governor."

"I might do that."

I slid forward on the seat and reached out to hold the wire mesh. Suddenly I wanted to tell them the truth. I opened my mouth to speak but stopped as I felt tears starting in my eyes. My fingers tightened in the mesh and I waited for the emotion to pass.

The radio crackled and the driver reached down for the microphone, pressing it against the side of his mouth. "Twelve. Twelve," he said. "An assist. We got a kid who missed the school bus. It's on our way. Twelve out." A voice responded, talking in numbers. The driver leaned forward and replaced the microphone.

I ran over his words and decided that despite the mysterious word "assist" they were in fact going to do nothing more than drop me off at the local high school.

"I sure appreciate it," I said again. The urge to confess had disappeared. I watched the countryside go by.

That night I came upon a truck depot in Maryland. Hundreds of trucks spaced out in long lines on the hard-packed earth like the vertebrae of some immense animal. A quarter-mile down the line I could see the faint neon haze of the diner. The air was filled with a continuous rumbling as trucks pulled in and out in the distance, air brakes gasping, headlights flashing against the sky. I walked among the tall wheels, staring up at the gargantuan trailers, big as houses, admiring the shiny cabs with their chunky radiator grills and fanciful decorations. Most of the rigs were dark, but every now and then one had been parked with the running lights left burning—small pinpoints of red, green, or amber light describing the huge mass of the trailers high in the air like enlarged examples from a geometry book. I stopped behind each truck to check the banks of license plates. I ran through the eastern seaboard states in my mind, constructing a model of the selection of plates most likely to indicate a truck going to Florida. I found what I was looking for at the edge of the parking area—a sixty-foot semi with plates from Massachusetts to Florida. The barn-sized rear doors were locked. I went around to the front and examined the empty cab. Lettered on the red door were the words "Favario Trucking, North South Express Shipping, Boston Mass.," followed by a series of numbers and specifications. I stepped into the deeper darkness between the cab and trailer, in among the tanks, hoses, and hydraulic lines, and urinated invisibly.

I waited on the running board for an hour or so, dozing off and then waking with a jolt as my back began to slip on the smooth metal of the door. Once I stood up at the approach of voices, but the men passed unseen in the next corridor and continued up the line, their voices dying out after a burst of laughter. I moved away from the truck toward the long grass at the edge of the area. Where the grass began an old cab had been put up

The geography of this trip is a little hard to figure out, inasmuch as the movement zigs and zags. John Updike's *Rabbit Run* covers a similar theme over a similar terrain and pattern. Perhaps students would be interested in comparing *Stop Time* with *Rabbit Run.*

The language here is nothing if not figurative. What do the figures connote? What is to be made of the difference he is alluding to? See his comment below on "the mind of a child."

on blocks, the wheels removed, umbilical cords dangling on the ground. I climbed up on the running board and pulled open the door. It was dark inside, but as my eyes adjusted I could see the cab was empty. Kneeling on the seat I spread the curtain hanging where the rear window should have been and looked into a small compartment. There were two small round windows at each end and a thin mattress to lie on. I climbed in and closed the curtains.

Suddenly it was morning. The porthole at my feet threw a slanting bar of sunlight across my legs. I heard something moving and opened the curtains in time to see a brown cat leap from the seat to the open window of the door and disappear. Climbing down carefully, I rubbed the sleep from my eyes, kicked the door open, and jumped to the ground. The field was empty. I took a few steps, looking around in astonishment. The flat earth spread before me, almost white under the blazing sun, an empty desert the size of a couple of football fields. On the other side I could see the diner, a small square building at the edge of the road. The cat loped toward it, moving in a straight line over the dusty ground, hindquarters jouncing smoothly and head held high. I followed in its tracks.

And it was as I crossed the empty field that something entirely unexpected happened in my head. A sudden switch, a reversal of polarity, overwhelmingly strong and oddly mechanical, as if my brain were one of those old-fashioned treadle machines that start sewing backward if you catch the cycle wrong. I had to return to New York. The decision to go back was as instantaneous as the decision to start in the first place, but while the latter had exploded like some bright, cleansing, beneficent bomb, the former simply held my soul with irrestible firmness, as if God had reached down out of the sky, grabbed my head, and twisted it north.

I remember quite precisely the single fact I allowed myself to believe was the cause of my change of heart —that I would never see the baby again. Jessica was the only complete and uncomplicated love in my life, and once having conjured her up I knew I hadn't the strength to leave her. I followed the cat through the dust and thought of Jessica, relieved to know it was she, and not the others, pulling me back, that it was love, and not lack of courage, forcing me to capitulate. Thus works the mind of a child, always a bit behind the world, swamped with emotion, and innocent of its own cunning. I crossed the road and started hitching North.

His step sister

Will students accept this analysis?

An important rule of hitchhiking is never to let yourself be dropped off in the middle of a city. The reasons are obvious—one can't hitch across and must therefore use public transportation, which takes money and a knowledge of local geography, or walk, which takes time and strength. On the afternoon of my third day on the road I found myself in downtown Wilmington, Delaware, attempting to decide on a course of action. After walking around aimlessly for some time I wound up in front of the railroad station. There would be a waiting room, I suddenly realized, where I could sit down and rest without attracting attention, and perhaps even a newsstand where I could palm a nickel or a dime from the stacks of papers. I moved along the narrow sidewalk to the entrance and slipped inside.

Under the high, vaulted ceiling people walked in all directions, the women's heels clicking against the stone, the men moving with that ghostly, withdrawn air travelers assume everywhere, as if nothing happening were of any importance, as if life itself were in suspension until they reached their destinations. I went to the long benches in the center of the room and sat down. The smell of food from an open lunch counter nearby hung in the air like some exquisite perfume, tickling the underside of my brain and knotting my stomach. I looked around for the newsstand but it was inside a shop, the papers, as I could see through the glass window, well guarded. Next to the shop was a door with the words TRAVELERS AID painted in large letters. My eyes locked on the words. I sat watching for an hour before I made up my mind.

A bell rang somewhere as I entered. It was a small room divided by a wide counter. On my side a small couch with chrome legs, a chair, and a low table covered with magazines, on the other side a couple of desks and a file cabinet. A glass jar filled with white flowers stood on one of the desks, catching sunlight from a rear window. A door opened across the room and a middle-aged woman in a blue suit entered to the distant sound of a toilet flushing. She advanced to the counter, a short woman, just beginning to get heavy, her pleasant, slightly chubby face set in a fixed expression of friendly interest like a mask pulled over her skull. "Yes, young man?" she said. "What can I do for you?"

I folded my hands on the countertop and watched them as I talked. "I was on the train going to New York and I got off to get some comic books and then when I turned around it was pulling out. My ticket and everything was inside so now I'm stuck." It flashed through my mind that I should appear to be more upset, but I was too tired to put it on. "I don't have any money."

"Well, that's not so bad," she said, smiling. "I'm sure we can straighten things out. Now tell me, was anyone with you on the train? We can wire ahead, you see. They'll probably be worried."

I shook my head. "No, I was by myself. I've been visiting my grandfather and I was going home."

"You live in New York?"

"Yes."

"I see." She remained motionless behind the counter. I continued to watch my hands through the long silence. Finally she reached down and brought up a pencil and a pad of paper. "Fine. Now if you'll just give me some information we'll see how we can arrange this. Name?"

"Frank Rawlings."

"All right, Frank. Address?"

"Eighty-one East Eighty-first Street."

"Phone?"

"We don't have one."

"Mother's name?"

"Dagmar, but she's not there. She's away on a trip to Europe."

"Father's name?"

"My father's dead. Look, couldn't you just lend me the money? I'll pay it back. I'll sign whatever you want. Or you could just buy the ticket for me and I'll mail you what it costs when I get home."

"We can't do that, I'm afraid," she said. "Now there must be somebody at home. You can't be staying all by yourself."

"That's the way it is most of the time. There's my stepfather, but he's a truck driver and he's on the road now. He won't be back for days."

"What's his name?"

"Jean."

"Jean what?"

"Jean Florida."

"Jean Florida? That's an odd name," she said, writing it down.

"I don't see why you can't just put me on the train. I give you my word I'll send back the money."

"I know you would," she said. "But we can't do it that way. Now how about your grandfather. Name and address?"

"That won't help. He's an old man, we have to leave him out of it. He's senile."

She looked up from the pad. "I can't do anything unless you cooperate, Frank. You can trust me."

"Suppose you lend me five dollars," I said quickly. "I could get across town to the highway and hitch back."

"You mean hitchhike all the way to New York?" Her eyebrows went up. "A boy your age? All by himself? I couldn't do that. I'd worry about you."

I turned sideways, my arm lying on the counter. "That's what I'm going to do, even without money."

"Why be so hard on yourself?" she said. "We can arrange something. How long since you've had a decent meal?"

I watched the stack of magazines and listened to my insides, to the silent me within me, trying to hear if I should run away before the conversation progressed any further, or stay and tell the truth. I turned the rest of the way, facing the door.

"Now wait a second before you do anything," she said behind me. "Wait just one second and listen to me. When did you eat last?"

I stood quite still, attending myself, but my mind was silent. Very quietly, tentatively, as if the word might destroy me, I answered, "Yesterday." I waited for something to happen inside. I seemed to be floating, everything in perfect balance, all emotion suspended while the logical part of me continued to operate on its own momentum. The sensation was odd, as if I might slowly come apart and go drifting off in all directions.

Her voice was clear. It was pure. "Well, we can fix that right now. You don't have to commit yourself to anything. Sit down and read a magazine and I'll get you some food. You can eat right there at the table."

"No. You'll just get the police."

"I promise I won't do that," she said, and there was something in her voice that made me believe her. "I give you my word. This doesn't have anything to do with the police."

Alone, I sat on the couch, picked up a magazine, and then put it down again. Sunlight was fading through the rear window and I could hear the faint sounds of the station through the closed door. When she came back in with a tray I said, "What happens if I tell you?"

"Unless there's something special," she said as she lowered the tray, "we'll wire home for your fare and you'll be on your way."

The smell of the food made my hands tremble. Franks and beans, thick slices of tomato on a bed of lettuce, bread and butter, two half-pint containers of milk, and a piece of apple pie with a slice of cheese on top. The first mouthful was rapture.

"Don't wolf it down," she said, and sat on the corner of the table. "Try and eat slowly."

I finished one of the hot dogs and most of the beans before I paused. "What does something special mean?"

"If you'd stolen a car, that sort of thing. I can tell you haven't."

I went back to the food. It was amazing how good a simple piece of bread and butter could taste. As the food got into my system the trembling stopped. I could feel a film of sweat on my brow.

"You haven't done anything the police would want to know about, have you?"

I shook my head.

"How long have you been gone?"

"Three days." I wiped up the last of the gravy with the last of the bread. "Excuse my manners." I opened the second container of milk and began on the pie.

"Listen now," she said. "There are some things that are hard to talk about. Things we'd rather forget, or keep to ourselves, but I have to ask, and you have to tell me the truth. It's important. Back home, were you beaten? Were you abused in any way?"

Surprised, I looked up at her, my fork in midair. "Beaten? No. There was never anything like that."

"They fed you and gave you enough clothing?"

"Yes, of course."

She looked me in the eye for a moment and then, apparently satisfied, turned away. "There's no 'of course' about it. We had a boy last year who answered the same as you. It turned out he had scars from his shoulder to the backs of his knees."

"No, really. There wasn't anything like that." I took a sip of milk. "You mean this has happened before? A kid coming in here?"

"Many, many times. Dozens of boys."

I turned the fact over in my mind, examining it from all sides the way a man might study a strange tool to determine its function. She sat silently, watching me while I finished the meal. When the last of the apple pie was gone I leaned back in my chair. "Thank you. You don't know how good that was." We remained motionless, both staring down at the tray. A distant voice was calling out the names of cities over the public address system. "Okay," I said. "Jean Fouchet. Eighty-one East Eighty-sixth Street. Atwater nine, eight-five-nine-nine."

"Why did you run away? Can you tell me?"

I looked away quickly, my face flushing. There was something about the words *run away* that threatened me with loss of control. Hearing them spoken aloud threw my body into a turmoil, as if they were the key phrase in a hypnotic command. I couldn't look at her. "I don't know," I said, shaking my head. "I can't explain it."

She'd been at the desk on the far side of the office for two hours, just out of earshot, picking up the phone every ten minutes. I assumed she was calling New York, and having checked the address and number I'd given her, was trying to get through to Jean. It seemed odd that they were actually going to talk to each other. Suddenly she got up, crossed the office, raised the leaf of the counter, and came and sat beside me on the couch. "I can't get through. He must be out and I'm afraid I can't stay any longer. I have to get home." She looked tired and a bit harassed—thin lines I hadn't noticed before showing around her eyes and at the corners of her mouth. "You'll have to spend the night."

I was on guard instantly. "Where?"

"There's a very nice Y.M.C.A. They even have a pool. You could take a swim and there might be a movie in the auditorium. How does that sound?"

I thought about it for a moment. "All right," I said finally. I'd been wearing the same clothes for three days and the idea of the pool appealed to me. "As long as they don't lock me in."

"I'll give them a call. Harry Brian can come for you. You'll like him. And they won't lock you in if you promise to stay put."

"Okay."

She went behind the counter and picked up the nearest phone. After a few moments of conversation she listened, three fingers against the side of her head, her lower lip between her teeth, and then hung up.

"What's the matter?" I asked.

"They're full up. They don't have any room." She stared across the room at the blank wall. "I tried everything I could think of."

Very alert, moving unconsciously to the edge of my seat, I felt apprehension growing in me, a slow subtle buildup, like a color change, like the start of a long slide through the calm blues and greens toward the eventual terror of red. "Where do I go, then?"

"The Juvenile Home. It isn't as nice, of course, but you'll be perfectly comfortable."

Kangaroo court, my mind screamed in a blast of red. KANGAROO COURT KANGAROO COURT! "What kind of place is that?"

"Now don't worry. It's perfectly all right."

"Do they lock you up?"

"It isn't a prison."

"Do they lock you up?"

"They lock the doors, but they have to do that. I'll explain everything to them. It'll be all right. I promise you."

"Isn't there any place else?"

She turned back to the phone. "No," she said softly. "I'm sorry."

I was up and away so fast I doubt she had time to realize what was happening. Up, running, and through the door before she could turn her head.

A reckless, all-out dash through the station, astonished faces falling behind one by one, frozen by my speed. It was like running through a crowd of cardboard cutouts. I swerved, jumped, and dodged between them to the doors, slipping past the outstretched arms of a guard into the open roar of the street, into the twilight and the high, vaulting sky. Running headlong through the streets I felt my limbs go wild with freedom. My brain raced to keep up, ignoring the present, knowing only what was just ahead—a corner, a vacant lot, an overpass, a man with a dog. Dazed by the sweetness of surrender, I left everything behind me without a thought, all of it forever behind me, falling away, more and more distant with every stride, falling away, falling away, falling away.

Leaning against a high fence, both palms and the side of my head against the wood, I opened my eyes and saw half a boxcar. The rest of the world moved. Only the boxcar and myself were fixed in space. I watched until stillness settled and then moved along the fence. The boxcar stood by itself on a siding, a tall, wooden car without markings. Approaching, I could see weeds growing in the darkness underneath. I went around to the other side. A dilapidated loading shed nearby seemed deserted. The big sliding door of the boxcar was not completely closed and I slipped my hands into the crevice, pulling hard as I fell back along the length of the car. The door rolled open with a thunderous roar. I jumped away from the car and stared into the dark interior, ready to run should anyone emerge.

After a minute or two I moved cautiously to the open doorway and looked inside. The floor was strewn with large, empty paper sacks. I stood listening for a sound from the impenetrably black corners of the car but there was only silence. Holding on with one hand, I bent my knees and leaped like a high jumper rolling over the bar, tumbling in and getting to my feet in a matter of seconds. There was no sound except my own breathing. A vague sweet-sour smell hung in the air, the smell of some chemical. A light haze of white powder covered the floor and walls. Bent over, skittish, ready to bolt at the first sound or the first movement, I went over the entire car and satisfied myself there was no one in it. I picked up one of the bags, white powder trailing from its torn mouth, and read that it had contained chemical fertilizer. I shook it out and prepared a place to sleep in the darkest corner of the car.

"Surrender" to what?

Sitting in the open doorway, my legs dangling in the air, I watched the approach of night. Over the roof of the loading shed stars began to appear, faint at first, growing brighter as the sky turned from lavender to purple to black. Every now and then I would lean forward and look to the left and the right to make sure no one was coming. When it got so dark I couldn't see more than a car length in each direction I got up and went to the corner. Slipping into the bag I'd cleaned, I pulled three or four more over me for camouflage and went to sleep.

It started to rain just after dawn, a heavy downpour that crashed against the roof of the car and woke me up. I raised my head, saw the slanting white lines through the doorway, and then went back to sleep.

Hours later, when I crawled out of the bag and got to my feet, the rain was still falling. I stood by the door and slapped at my clothes to get the powder out. Clouds of it drifted from my head as I ruffled my hair. I waited for a lull in the rain and jumped to the ground.

It took me some time to find my way back. I was amazed how far I'd run—at least a mile. Wet to the skin, I walked through the station doors, crossed the huge waiting room, and opened the door to Travelers Aid. She was there, standing behind the counter, her head coming up as I closed the door. I avoided her eye.

"I hope you spent a pleasant night," she said.

"I slept in a boxcar."

She went to the end of the counter and raised the leaf. "Well, it's traditional I suppose. Very foolish, though. You could have been locked in." Holding up the leaf with one arm she said, "Come on. You're soaking wet."

"It's all right."

"Please don't argue. You can dry off in the bathroom."

I moved down the counter and slipped under her arm.

"My God, you smell awful. What was in the car?"

"Fertilizer."

"You'd better wash too. There's only a sink but you can't go home like that."

"Did you get him?"

"Yes. Before he left for work."

"What did he say?"

"I explained the situation and he agreed to wire your fare."

"Nothing else?"

She hesitated. "He asked if you were all right and I said you were." I knew she was lying but I remained silent. She opened the door to the bathroom. "Take your things off and hand them to me through the door. I'll see what I can do. I brought my iron." She walked me to the bus station, both of us moving under her umbrella. After a few steps I took the shaft. "Let me hold that," I said, shifting it to give her better protection. We covered the short distance in silence.

At the terminal I stood by the bus while she went inside to get my ticket. I felt a flash of annoyance at Jean. He was too cheap to send the extra couple of dollars for the train, which I would have enjoyed, so I had to take the bus, which I hated.

"Here's your ticket," she said at my shoulder. "And a dollar. Twenty cents is for carfare and eighty for a sandwich and milk at the rest stop."

"Thank you." People elbowed past us. "I guess I'd better go on in."

"Yes, if you go now you might get a window seat."

"I'm sorry I had to run away last night."

"That's all right. Think about what's ahead now." She took a step back.

I climbed into the bus. There was a window seat in the rear, on the far side, and I moved quickly and sat down. Staring through the rain-streaked glass I watched the white puddles on the black asphalt of the empty parking area. After a while the driver climbed in, pulled the door shut, and started the engine. Turning back to the window I saw her standing outside, under her umbrella, watching me. She'd come around the back of the bus and stood about twenty feet away. Neither of us moved. Then, very slowly, the bus rolled forward and she was gone.

Where do you run *when faith has evaporated*
and the imagination is dead?

Where do you stop? Why?

7
SECTIO

The Last Poem

When
the game has ended
and the roar of the crowd
has faded into the past
and only the cleaning brooms
click-clack echoes
on the empty rows of seats
drumming through
the dim lit concrete corridors
of the stadium what
then?

Does the next poem, "Ex-Basketball Player" (p.144), answer this question?

—Tom Meschery

Ex-Basketball Player

Pearl Avenue runs past the high-school lot,
Bends with the trolley tracks, and stops, cut off
Before it has a chance to go two blocks,
At Colonel McComsky Plaza. Berth's Garage
Is on the corner facing west, and there,
Most days, you'll find Flick Webb, who helps Berth out.

Flick stands tall among the idiot pumps—
Five on a side, the old bubble-head style,
Their rubber elbows hanging loose and low.
One's nostrils are two S's, and his eyes
An E and O. And one is squat, without
A head at all—more of a football type.

Once Flick played for the high-school team, the Wizards.
He was good: in fact, the best. In '46
He bucketed three hundred ninety points,
A county record still. The ball loved Flick.
I saw him rack up thirty-eight or forty
In one home game. His hands were like wild birds.

He never learned a trade, he just sells gas,
Checks oil, and changes flats. Once in a while,
As a gag, he dribbles an inner tube,
But most of us remember anyway.
His hands are fine and nervous on the lug wrench.
It makes no difference to the lug wrench, though.

Off work, he hangs around Mae's Luncheonette.
Grease-grey and kind of coiled, he plays pinball,
Sips lemon cokes, and smokes those thin cigars;
Flick seldom speaks to Mae, just sits and nods
Beyond her face towards bright applauding tiers
Of Necco Wafers, Nibs, and Juju Beads.

In the original version (1957), the term used here was "lemon phosphates." Would students know what that term means? Are they able to recognize the candies in line 30? Is this poem doomed? Should Updike continually update it?

—John Updike

She imagines a grainy photograph, a newspaper photograph of herself. It has been taken of her against the front of the high school, showing the steps and the big front doors; one of the windows, newly broken, is patched up with cardboard.

How We Fall in Love

Joyce Carol Oates

She dreams of this mysterious photograph of herself, a young teacher, her eyes squinting seriously into the camera, the skin about her mouth slightly puckered with the intensity of the moment.

She is being photographed for a reason. But what is the reason?

But when violence comes the newspaper photographs are old ones, always. They are prettily posed, innocent pictures of faces taken at leisure, in a time of innocence and ignorance, months or even years ago. So it is, this miracle, that the past self blends violently into the present self. . . . She imagines a picture of herself, a young woman two years out of college, a young dedicated teacher with an armful of books, looking like one of her own students; the photograph glimpsed on an inside page of the evening newspaper will be blurred, blurry, a little out of focus as if with the intensity of this young woman's stare. Her hair is pulled back from her face, to show its angular, delicate lines, the lines of cheekbones high beneath her eyes, and to show the enormous stare of her eyes, which have always been too large. Alarm enlarges them. Excitement enlarges them. Behind her are the dingy steps of the school, the front steps. They are empty. At the top are the front doors, all six of them, and one of them is patched up hurriedly with a piece of cardboard.

She dreams of this. . . .

Waking, she cuts off the dream; she moves into life with the rapidity of a child dressing in the morning, eager to be dressed and on her way. No time for breakfast. Eating at seven in the morning is repulsive, she thinks herself too pure for it, harsh and virginal in her tawdry bathroom mirror. She takes a shower. Her heart pounds beneath the airy weight of warm water; she is a girl on her way to an adventure. Her heart has been pounding like this during the night, off and on, when her secret mysterious dreams take over . . . but she cannot quite retrieve them, except for the newspaper photograph. Suddenly she is thinking of her family, a hundred miles away, reading the newspaper, and of friends from college and high school, coming upon her photograph and crying out, "Look, it's Corinne

Holland!" She rubs soap onto her face, thoughtfully. Her heart still pounds. The morning has begun, the day has begun, the second hand of her watch will move relentlessly forward and nothing, absolutely nothing, can prevent her from driving to school, parking in the faculty lot, entering the school, entering her homeroom, entering the confused, jostling world of her students, whom she loves. . . .

She washes her face for several minutes, silently. In the mirror she looks very young. She is twenty-three now but she looks much younger. Always she has been impatient with her frailty, the delicate bones of her face and pelvis, boyish bones, and the silent alarmed look of her eyes. Her hair is red-blond. Puffed out about her face it would make her too pretty, unimportant, but pulled back bluntly behind her ears it makes her stern, serious, a woman on her way to an adventure.

. . . It was time for her to be married and yet she could not fall in love. Younger, easier, she had known a number of people, she had moved without fear among them, but in the end those people had drawn back, as if confused by her. There was a distance around her, about her—as if she were an island in the center of a confused element, a confused air, everything troubled and threatening as invisible shapes, ghosts walking at will. She sometimes shivered convulsively, as if one of these shapes had brushed against her. . . .

She imagines the newspaper photograph again. What she cannot imagine is the caption.

She parks her car in the faculty lot and, hurrying to the school, falls in step with another teacher. He is a man in his fifties, heavy and perspiring, his coat open upon a soiled white shirt. He teaches shop. Corinne, the youngest teacher in the school, teaches English. She feels sharp and virginal, like a bride, walking alongside this tired dumpy man, talking brightly to him about the school assembly last Friday . . . about the staff meeting coming up. . . . "Too much politicking. I can't take it," he says with a snort of disgusted laughter.

In the women's lounge she sits to gather her thoughts, pressing her palms flat against her knees. She is struck at these times by a silence inside herself, an almost sacred carefulness, as if she must listen to something, some voice, out of her own memory, to guide her through the day. But she never hears anything. Other women are talking. Their voices lift with laughter, with surprises. They like to talk, they like to laugh; teachers' lounges are always filled with laughter. It is important, this gathering together to talk and laugh; it stirs the blood, shoots energy into the veins, inspires them with a slightly hysterical courage. Today they are talking about a meeting of the Detroit Federation of Teachers, but Corinne hasn't caught the drift of the conversation, thinking it more crucial to listen to herself, the silence inside herself. Her palms are damp and cold. She is a young teacher, fiercely dedicated, in love with her job, and yet her hands are cold though she has been teaching for two years.

"Do you ever get used to it? To teaching?" she asked one of the women, once.

"Never," the woman said bluntly.

And it was true.

In her homeroom there are forty-three students, all but eight of them Negroes. The room shakes with their footsteps and their voices, she feels the persistent, exasperating tug of their eyes, the slight surge of rebellion when she enters the room, always—all this is familiar. Yet she is not quite accustomed to it. The final bell rings; she takes attendance. Alert, impersonal, she glances up and down the rows of seats. *Bailey, Irene.* Absent. *Rutherford, Samuel.* Absent all week. She slips cards out of a file, stacks them together. She reads to her students four announcements on mimeographed sheets. One of the boys, a white boy named Ronnie Brock, stares at her with his mouth slightly open, showing the tip of his tongue. He sits right in front of her. A big Negro girl named Sarah, who is sometimes very jolly and friendly to Corinne and sometimes sullen, inexplicably, snatches up her purse from the floor and takes out an emery board and begins filing her nails. Her face is black with anger.

A boy already marked absent enters the room at the back door. Snickers. Someone calls out his name. Corinne marks him *tardy.* She reads them the announcement about the school nurse, the clinic . . . out of the corner of her eye she sees someone's desk being lifted, on his big knees, lifted slowly and let back down, slowly. . . . Yawns. Everyone is sleepy. They are strangely handsome when sleepy, like animals too innocent to wake up. She stares fully at them, wondering. The Negro boys have strong, clear faces. She thinks the marvel of their white, white eyes and their dark skins something that must be praised, but they have no thought for one another, they do not "see" one another at all. The girls see everything, perky and curious. Their skins range from very dark to very light, their hair ranges from wild and bushy to slick, processed, bleached hair, hair light as egg shell, fluffed out in iridescent haloes. One of the girls, Faith Smith, has a beautiful pale face and a slender, columnar neck; she smiles all the time, especially at Corinne. The arch of her eyebrows is exotic, as if she had copied that face from a photograph, careful to erase the smutty smudgy lines of Detroit and to replace them with the graceful lines of some West Indian island. It was rumored that Faith had been beaten up, that she'd had a miscarriage, but nothing shows on her lovely small face except a perpetual smile. Behind her a boy named Jock, black and heavy, ducks his head behind the top of his desk to take a bite of something—it is a Tootsie Roll and he tears off half of it in his teeth, twisting his head.

The bell rings. Desk tops are dropped shut, there is a jostling at the door, sudden noise. Corinne waits. Ronnie brushes against another white boy and is shoved back viciously, but pretends not to notice; he walks stooped over, as if plotting to himself. He comes to school occasionally to sit staring and dreaming and gaping, then he disappears again, probably working on junked cars out in the streets of Detroit, abandoned cars found everywhere in the hillbilly neighborhoods. Corinne thinks briefly of him, her heart pounding, for she believes she can see in his slow, gaping stare something that is a threat . . . something that will come to be a threat, when he understands what it is. Then she forgets about him.

She teaches two classes in a row, grammar. Her book is smudged from two years of teaching, thumbprints and fingerprints, the sweat of anxiety. There is a steady din in the room, a sense as of waves rocking gently, relentlessly. She raises her voice to be heard. Up and down the aisles she asks questions, sensitive to the abrupt tug and fall of interest in the room, the tension that shoots up when someone does not answer and she repeats her question. . . . Everyone thinks: *Is something going to happen?* Sometimes a student will shrug his shoulders angrily, and she goes on past him, showing no anger herself. She never shows anger though she feels it. Sometimes a student will falter, licking his lips, as if unable to think at all . . . and someone will snicker, inevitably . . . but the moment passes. Sometimes, at the conclusion of a two or three minute bout of will, she feels her heart leap as if it were ready to surrender. *Is something going to happen?*

But only yawns. The picking of noses, crossing of legs. An overheated room makes them all drowsy. They see her facing them and they interpret correctly the tense cords of her neck, which means she will not back down. When she smiles they interpret correctly her strange love for them, which is not for any individuals among them but for the whole room, the rows of legs and restless arms. . . . Does she imagine it, or does the room surge magically with a single thought, sometimes: *We got to be good to this teacher!* At other times it sighs, the entire room: *What the hell. . . .*

Noon hour. Snatched minutes having coffee with her colleagues—everyone in a hurry, oddly excited, always excited beneath their weariness. At any age they are excited; their hearts pound. A woman says in a bright anecdotal voice: "One of my girls fainted today! I thought all the girls would faint, the room was so hot and it caught on and I felt faint myself!" Everyone laughs breathlessly. Once Corinne had been teaching on an ordinary overcast morning, her ten o'clock class, and a rock had crashed through the window. It struck the blackboard and fell to the floor. The kids had jumped up, amazed, shouting. Corinne shouted back at them. *Sit down! Sit still!* She walked on broken glass, feeling it splinter beneath her feet, advancing on them though she feared another rock flying through the window, or some gunfire. "Sit down! It's all over!" she had cried.

They sat down. It was all over.

She went on teaching and tried to avoid stepping on the broken glass. When the bell rang she went to report the incident to the principal's office.

The other teachers had questioned her about it, attracted by her trouble, eager to sympathize with her and to sniff out more danger. They were always eager for signs of danger, always sniffing it out. "But what did you do? Weren't you afraid?" they asked. "Yes," Corinne said, "but I kept on teaching." "You mean you just kept on teaching?" they asked. "I kept on teaching because what else could I do?" she explained. She was shy in front of them. "I kept on because I couldn't stop, it was as if I was paralyzed or hypnotized, everything was mixed up . . . I couldn't remember where I was. . . ."

And they had stared at her, understanding. They were a little repelled by her.

Windows are always broken—in the stairways, in the basement, in classrooms. It takes days, sometimes weeks, to have them replaced. There is no money. *Detroit is running out of money!* everyone cries, breathless with danger and delight. *And then what will happen. . . ?* Gangs of kids run loose, throwing rocks, shooting off guns . . . suddenly black schools are demanded, all-black schools . . . and in class the boys are polite to Corinne, as if embarrassed, and the hefty motherly girls smile at her, straining their faces. . . . She thinks often of the glass underfoot, mixing it up with her persistent, mysterious dream of the photograph, and the crunch of glass surprises her. No rock ever came through a window again in her classes. No rock. But she thinks of it, ducks in her sleep, hears it crash against the blackboard and fall to the floor. . . .

In the faculty dining room a man has dropped a cup of coffee. The cup has broken. "Jesus, it slipped right through my hands, must have been wet," the man grumbles. The cup has broken into thick white chunks. No crunching underfoot, no danger from tiny, delicate, invisible splinters.

Another noon hour.

She hurries to her next class, her "good" class. She is eager for the intoxication of a fifty-minute ride, floating and soaring across the field of her students' vision, until perspiration begins to form on her face and body, a secret to them. She asks them questions. Her voice is thin and high-pitched. Several hands are raised; she smiles in praise of them. At the end of the hour she is almost giddy with pleasure, as if she has been inhaling something magical along with the heat and sweat of the room. She thinks joyfully, as she has thought so many times in the past: *This is my job, teaching is my job. . . .* After this class someone always stops to talk to her. The excitement is still in the air. A Negro boy in a flannel shirt many sizes too small asks her something about a television program, she hasn't seen it, she is sorry, genuinely sorry. . . . the boy's shyness is like his breath close upon her, intimate. A girl comes up to her. She seems to be flirting with Corinne, all the time, but then she flirts with everyone, always, unable to keep her eyes and mouth still. Her cheeks are richly dimpled. Her hair is processed and very greasy, her skirt is short and uneven, showing part of a pink slip. Jingly with bracelets, her bosom plump beneath her sheer blouse, she has a wonderful catch in her throat as if, while laughing, she must suck back part of her laughter because it is too daring.

"Oh man, oh Jesus Christ!" she exclaims, flirting with Corinne.

Her chatter is rapid, lilting, hilarious; her laughter is hiccuppy. Corinne smiles and wonders if she is being teased. The girl says, "Oh man, that Casper—let me tell you, Miss Holland, honey—that son of a bitch ain't good like you think! He don't do the lesson! Let me tell you, hon, he puts it over on the teachers—" And she giggles, as if drunk with joy, sucking half the giggle back into her throat. "I known him for a long time, I ain't putting him down or anything—but—anyway—he likes you real well, Miss Holland. That's the truth. He likes you, but he says he got no use for the rest of them."

And that is the point of the strange little conversation: a gift of love.

The girl leaves and the odor of the room closes in upon Corinne again, an odor of heat, loneliness, staleness, silence. . . . In the stillness of the air there is the memory of voices, of whispers and nudges, the shapes of invisible people; Corinne glances up, as if expecting to see someone. The giddiness drops from her suddenly. It occurs to her that she must live out the rest of the day —another class and a study hall and then a staff meeting—and she feels oddly numb, sober, a little surprised.

After the staff meeting her head aches. The corridors are lonely, smelly. Dirt and papers on the floor. Lockers are bent, some of them twisted open, their locks broken. Lipstick scrawls on the wall. Corinne's eyesight is blurry at this time of day, five-thirty, she is exhausted and thinks she sees things out of the corner of her eye, a rat scurrying across the hall, a kid jerking back around a corner. . . .

Some of her colleagues are still arguing. There is an odor of perspiration about them, stains of sweat. The women's faces are greasy. Oil has clogged up the pores of their faces, worked its way through their makeup. The men's faces are dark, greasy, exhausted. They are lined with worry and exasperation. Corinne moves among them, silent, her head aching, her heart no longer pounding but heavy with weariness, in a kind of adult shame. She tries to recall the excitement of her one o'clock class, but it seems to be drifting from her. She would like to talk about it with one of the other teachers, but no teacher is interested in another teacher's good classes; only bad classes. No teacher is interested in another teacher's good students; only the bad students are prized for conversation . . . *What do you think of him! Isn't he something?* . . . The teachers here are wary of their students, girls and boys, and they walk with their arms held against their bodies as if to protect themselves. The lines on their faces are protective too. Even the Negro teachers walk like this—they understand what a temptation their bodies are, they understand that the soft spaces between their ribs is a temptation to any knife blade.

Corinne drives home alone. She is very tired, dizzy with the memory of excitement, a little baffled as if she cannot quite understand what has happened to her excitement. The day might have been a dream, turned inside-out with the night. She has had to keep pace with a dream, and who can keep pace with a dream's leaps and turns? She recalls the one o'clock class . . . she recalls the boy that morning with his insolent idiot stare . . . she recalls the principal and his sarcasm, bullying them this afternoon . . . the odor of cigarettes in the room . . . the glimpse of a rat out of the corner of her eye, or had she imagined that?

Broken glass underfoot—she had stepped on some broken glass that day, in one of the halls, mysterious broken glass.

Her apartment building never catches the eye, there are several buildings like it in a single block, grimy with Detroit's perpetual smog, solid enough, like fortresses. Old, dependable, ugly, unsurprising. Corinne has never made a break with her family but sees them rarely now, since they disapprove so strongly of her career and her independence, and yet, in choosing a place to live, she has been drawn inevitably to a building that resembles the one in which they live—it is a perfect setting, in its ugliness, for her life of dedication. In the foyer she glances at the row of mailboxes. They have not been broken into. But her own is empty, no mail; she is relieved. Then, pausing, she forces herself to check again and she sees that yes, yes, she does have a letter after all. She unlocks the mailbox . . . the letter is from her mother.

Ascending these stairs she thinks of herself ascending the stairs of her school, every Monday morning of her life—her thin, strong legs carrying her up, to the women's lounge, to her homeroom. She is ready for anything. Sometimes her eyes dart anxiously in her face, as if ready for something that had not yet been imagined; by the end of the first class period her lipstick is partly worn off and hardened into a curious little line of crust, on her lower lip.

She unlocks her apartment door and enters. Silence. There is always a look about this neat apartment of silence, stealthiness, as if someone had just ducked back out of sight. She takes off her coat and stretches. Her body feels strangely young and disappointed. Upstairs people are arguing . . . a family with several children arguing, or laughing. The television set is on as always. Corinne glances up at the ceiling and sees only the pattern of familiar thin cracks, a gray, blank-gray ceiling. She sits in a chair and presses her hands against her knees, in the attitude of thinking, although she is not thinking. After a while she opens her mother's letter.

She draws one of the sheets of paper out and catches a glimpse of her mother's slanted, tiny handwriting: *. . . told us about Father Stract and his sister. . . .* She turns the letter over quickly and reads: *. . . in fact we are all very worried about you. . . .* That is enough of the letter for now; she puts it down, her hands slightly trembling. She sits for a while thinking of the letter she must write to her mother, explaining her life. It is her own life now, not theirs. She is not theirs any longer. Each of the girls in the family had a certain quality, a fictional quality that had hardened about her until she, herself, had not existed—so the family had no need to look at them, to "see" them any longer. One of the girls was "beautiful," one was "brilliant," one was "dependable," one was . . . Now, living away from home, alone, Corinne has no need to "see" them either, to think of them. She is free. She feels a peculiar radiance about her, a glowing of her face and skin.

Why should she explain to her mother that she is in love with the air of Thomas Wylie High School, with its long gray cluttered corridors, its rows and rows of battered lockers, its silence after school, its mobs of students during the day. . . . why should she explain that?

She is restless and so she goes out to the drugstore and buys the evening paper. The drugstore's front windows are protected by wire screens that had once been taken up during the day, but are now left on all the time. On the street automobiles pass quickly. The air is noisy with cars, horns, shouts; it is that time of day. She passes a group of kids, girls and boys, sitting out in the chilly March air, smoking. She catches a scent of something sweet about them—marijuana?—and shivers with the nearness of their legs, their dangling, dangerous arms, their lively eyes. A few of the younger teachers at school smoke marijuana themselves. It is private life. Corinne does not think about private life. These kids do not acknowledge her and she does not acknowledge them, though for all she knows some of them are her own students. She does not look at them. She is aware of them, fiercely, her sense of them mounting almost to pain in her body.

. . . In the corridors of Thomas Wylie their good natures explode daily into fist-fights and skirmishes. White people fear them, but they attack one another, mostly—the girls scream and claw, the boys punch and kick, there is a terrible violence in them that must free itself. Yet Corinne thinks of them as children, in whom something drastic and innocent slumbers, slumbering on in spite of the violence. The pregnant girls especially are children: their faces sleepy, dazed, with the mystery of being children who are having children, their own private children, babies growing inside them.

She makes supper for herself, opening cans. Now the family upstairs is in their kitchen overhead, arguing. A man walks heavily across the floor across Corinne's ceiling. She glances up automatically but sees nothing. She eats and reads the paper, the *Detroit News,* reading the paper through page after page, picking up the continuation of stories when she comes to them. She can juggle ten or twelve stories in her mind at once. A story about Negro boys pouring gasoline on a dance floor and setting fire to it makes her think of the fire that had been started in some trash at school, once, and the fire alarms ringing like mad. . . . She tries to think of her one o'clock class but the memory fades, teasingly; she is reading a story about burglary. She finds herself thinking of lunch at school one day last week when a man jabbered about a fight in the basement none of them had even heard about —a white boy named Baxter, whom Corinne had had the year before, had been slashed in the face with a razor. A long thin wound, right across his face. The police had been called but hadn't come for an hour. Blood, bleeding. . . . "Right across his ugly little face," the man said.

After supper she goes through her lessons for the next day. She is fond of her books, her annotations, even her own handwriting. But when she finishes it is only a little after eight . . . she decides to go out, to a movie in the neighborhood. She goes to the theater often, it is only a few blocks away.

She buys a candy bar at the refreshment counter and sits in the back row, not wanting safety but wanting anonymity. Students of hers come to this theater often. The movie is a suspense story about a kidnapping; she has come in fifteen minutes late. The audience is sparse tonight. She feels herself not quite anonymous. On the screen the pretty young victim is taking a shower . . . she stares up into the water, her face running smooth and very young with water . . . now she is staring into a gilt-edged mirror . . . she is arranging the face that will be frozen into a look of terror, photographed for the posters that advertise this movie . . . she is preparing the body that will be beaten. Like a bride she is light on her feet and tense and distracted; it looks as if a melody must be shaping itself in her brain. There is a strange, light, almost erotic expectation about her. . . . Now she is hurrying down a fashionable street, and an automobile awaits her at the corner, everything awaits her. . . .

Corinne bites off the end of her candy bar. It is stale, musty chocolate like wax, she is sorry she has bought it. The movie passes quickly before her eyes. It comes to an end. Corinne is disappointed that it is ended so soon. She gets up, in no hurry. She glances around to see who is here tonight. A few couples, middle-aged. Neighborhood people. A few kids, boys and girls. They are already joking and fooling around. Mysterious men, alone, their faces splotched and apologetic. When the movie ends they are all expelled: that minute of walking across the well-lighted foyer is an ugly minute.

Corinne goes home and picks up her mother's letter again. The final sentence: . . . *in fact we are all very worried about you. . . .*

She decides to go to bed early. She sleeps.

Note that the story begins and ends in "sleep," and that in between the beginning and the ending Corrine moves (or Miss Oates' prose *moves her*) as if caught in a fragmented state of suspension, a dream. What does this technique have to do with the dimension of love so delicately explored in the story?

Literary Sort: If that's "how we fall in love," I don't want it! Give me Romeo and Juliet's love any day.

Editor: Oh, were *they* different?

Literary Sort: But that girl, Corinne, is flirting with danger, with violent danger.

Editor: And Romeo and Juliet?

Cool Girl

STUDS TERKEL

This selection is one of the interviews with Chicago people in Mr. Terkel's book, *Division Street, America.*

Jan Powers, 24

She's on the staff of a magazine, popular with cool young men. Her job pays well and it's easy. She comes from a working-class family, and occasionally sees her mother and two younger brothers. She has an apartment of her own in a new high-rent high-rise on the Near North Side. She is engaged to Steven, a medical student.

I don't notice the world. I'm very bored. I really don't know how I feel. I'm nice and cordial but people sense something about me. I don't know, maybe I don't like them. Maybe I feel I'm above them. I can't think of anyone I love or respect. I can't be bothered with the news. I just can't get interested. I can't care less. I *should* care, it's terrible. (Laughs lightly.)

See ruled passage on page 171. Coincidence?

Vietnam? Isn't that a shame? (Laughs softly.) I saw a film on Vietnam, it showed the actual fighting. It looked ridiculous, just a bunch of kids. It was actually embarrassing to watch that, people were actually shooting and shouting. I saw Vietnam. I looked at a map once. I'm concerned with Vietnam if my brother has to go, otherwise, no.

My interest in life is me. It's a shame. I wish I could pick up a newspaper and read it. What I hear about things is heard from other people.

I hope I'll make it. I think it's marriage, to someone who is successful. Highland Park,° a couple of kids. I'm not too crazy about children, though. You're sitting in a room, and all of a sudden five kids'll come in and they'll go to another girl in the room. Same with dogs.

Is this "making it"? Is it part of The American Dream?

I'm worried about the next couple of years. Here I'm putting all this time and feeling into this relationship with Steven, and to have it not work out, it would be terrible. I don't know what I'd do. I'd probably find someone else and be just as happy.

Nothing touches me. I wonder why I don't care about these things. The Bomb doesn't bother me. I don't read the papers. There isn't much I can do about it, so I'm not worried. What is important now is my friend and me. The rest of the world can go.

If I were God, I'd make a world with a lot of me's in it. (Laughs.) No, no, I'd leave it the way it is. We have to have war, there's been wars through all the ages, apparently everyone gets enjoyment out of it. If we removed this part from man, it would be boring. Otherwise things would be sort of dull.

I love my building, I just love it. If I'm on a bus going to my mother's, I look at these people and get a nauseous feeling. On Michigan Avenue, I respect them more. Home gives me a sick feeling.

Is this attitude a natural follow-up to having "made it"?

It's a shame Negroes don't like me and children don't like me and dogs don't run up to me.

° HIGHLAND PARK: a suburb of Chicago

How did "Cool Girl" do in high school, do you suppose? How do you explain her?

INTERLOCK WITH CLUSTER 6:
A topical link: two views of and from two women

6

For a Lady I Know

She even thinks that up in heaven
Her class lies late and snores,
While poor black cherubs rise at seven
To do celestial chores.

—Countee Cullen

Cluster 6: pp. 156-179
An affective cluster
Focus: contrast, mostly humorous

INTERLOCK WITH CLUSTER 5:
A topical link: two views of
and from two women

What Counts Is Knowledge. And Feeling.

STUDS TERKEL

This selection is one of the interviews from Mr. Terkel's book, *Division Street, America*.

Lucy Jefferson, 52

When I first came from Mississippi, I was so young and ignorant. But I was freer, you know? I think I had a little bit more room to move around in than I have now. Because I think the white man wasn't so afraid then. There wasn't enough of us. There's too many of us now, I think that's what frightened him. Nobody noticed you then. You were there but nobody bothered about seeing you.

She lives in the low-rise Robert Brooks Housing Project on the Near West Side. Hers is described as a row house. It was neatly furnished; some pies were in the oven; there were books all over.

My supervisor once said to me, "Now, Lucy, you sit out here at this desk and answer the phone. And I think you should tell me what's going on because people here say things to you that they wouldn't dare say to me. And because, after all, you're just part of the furniture." Oh boy, did I give a chuckle. Yeah. I laughed to myself and I said, now here's a chance for all the hate in the world. But you know what really happened? I felt so sorry for the poor thing. Some Negro went out to the steel mill and he shot up a lot of people, and after that—Oh, I tell ya, I'm very wicked—after that I'd take her arm and say, "Miss Pruner, I want to talk to you about somethin'." And I slammed the door and she'd freeze. I wasn't going to do anything to her, but she . . . (Prolonged laughter.) I am just telling you how wicked I am. I'm an awful louse. (Soft chuckle.)

I walk down the street; I smoke a cigarette. Well, ladies aren't supposed to do that. But I'm no lady. (Laughs.) I just have the best old time. Sometimes, it amuses, you know. When I get blue and disgusted, I go get me some beer and get cockeyed drunk, stay at home. I don't go out. I don't believe in taverns. Then you say, why the hell do you drink beer? Because I like it. There's a lot of things that I don't like.

I just don't like doles. I wouldn't accept one dime from anybody. I'm not gonna raise my children on Aid. Why should I? There's enough money in America for me to raise my children. Now one is seventeen; one is twenty-one. And I absolutely refused to accept these handouts from anybody. How am I gonna teach these children of mine what a pleasure it is in accomplishment? Do you realize what it means if I'm gonna sit here and accept this check? We can't go to the zoo because there's carfare. Everything has to be pinpointed.

We took the little money that we made, brought it home, and we said, "Okay, Melvin would count it maybe one day, Corrine would count it the next payday." And they'd say, "Okay, what are you going to do this time, Mom? Does the rent have to be paid?" And I'd say, "No, not this time." "Well, then, we can go to the show?" and I'd say, "Yes, we can go to the show this time. Meet me downtown when I get off from work." I'd go to the ten-cent store when I got off from work and buy a pound of candy, mixed. I'd meet 'em at the show. We'd go in. Now this means, this is about five dollars and some cents out of this paycheck. We don't go but about every two—three months. Or maybe less. I always had a picnic basket and picnic jugs and all this junk. Because these things are essential wherein they could get around and see what is happening.

I worked at Wesley Hospital for about eleven years. As an aid in physical therapy. I worked part-time and went to school part-time, as a practical nurse. There was this woman that was very kind

Note the significance of the point made here. "You" is "white people"—the middle class, the *system.* An extension of her argument was made recently by a New York City Black Panther leader when he said that the white establishment uses welfare payments to bribe ghetto blacks. Thus the establishment is able to forestall the black revolution by maintaining the eternal ghetto-suburb relationship between blacks and whites by giving the blacks just enough money barely to survive where they live. What do students think? Some might like to re-read "Cool Girl" before or after they respond.

to me. She used to tell me, "Lucy, why don't you get on Public Aid until you can finish school. Don't let your pride stop you." Maybe I didn't realize exactly what she meant by pride. But I just—gave it up. With all the stuff attached to it, maybe that's why . . . the publicity, the degradation, see?

Everybody's screaming now: Oh, these women on ADC.° Why hasn't somebody told these people that they're on ADC because you gave all this money to keep from hirin' 'em? Years and years ago. This didn't just start, you know. You don't keep people in a certain category for hundreds of years and expect them to come out and do all these things. For generations and generations they've been just barely making it. Now what do you expect? Plums?

Hell, we're as poor as Joseph's goat, as far as that goes. We pinch pennies every day, but truly we don't think anything about it. When I get paid we know exactly what we're gonna eat for two weeks. I buy whatever sale is on, that's what we eat. I go to Hillman's or George's or something, whatever's on sale. Say, for instance, we're gonna make spareribs today. That's okay. We might have spareribs and sauerkraut. If the steak's cheap enough, we might even have steak once in a while. But for two long weeks we know exactly what kind of meat we're gonna have. So what we do, we wrap it around, we got potatoes in the house, we got rice in the house, we got frozen vegetables in the house, so we build a meal around this thing. So far as being poor is concerned, boy, I bet I got a monopoly on that. (Laughs.)

Foodstores in Chicago

It's a very fashionable hospital, Wesley. The clientele there are usually people that's got money. To me they were fascinating. All those beautiful clothes. You know, I could dream and see myself in this role. Then naturally I continued to read, self-educated almost. This man came in one day and he suffers from a backache. He usually gets a heat and massage to the low back. He knew me and of course all the clientele called me by my first name, which I resented. But it turned out to be an asset. So he came in and said, "Lucy, what are you reading?" And I said, *The Status Seekers.* And he said, "Don't read that junk." And I said, "By the way, you're in the advertising business." I had loads of fun, loads of fun.

Because she is (a) black and (b) seen in a servant role.

An expose of advertising practices and ethics, by Vance Packard.

They call you by the first name, the students, everybody. You see, this was the policy to keep the Negro in his place. But I happened to be the kind of Negro that became controversial, because I read such things as *The American Dilemma,* and I walk around with the book in my hand, see? I defied them in so many ways. I almost terrified 'em.

By Gurnar Myrdal, a book about race relations (conflict) in the U. S.

You know, it got so every time I got on an elevator—"What are you reading? What are you reading? What are you reading?"

°ADC: Aid to Dependent Children

(Laughs.) And I'd begin to enjoy this thing, you know. I was having the best old time. I was absolutely terrifying 'em. Everybody was yelling: "Lucy, Lucy!" Maybe that's why I say, the first name, it came in very handy. Because if they hadda just said, "Jefferson," nobody probably'd ever knowed it was me. But by making this so commonplace, here's this Negro woman, every time you see her she's reading a different book. You know what I'd do? I'd go to the library and get these books, and I'd just dash back home and read these. And truly it became a game with me. I don't think I ever had more fun in my life than I had working right there.

I guess I was darn near fifty then. That's the reason why I say I was havin' a ball. I'm carrying the book by Faulkner, paperback, in my pocket, you know. But this particular time I didn't realize that the heading of the book was sticking out just a little above. The students, doctors, interns got on . . . "Faulkner!!" (Prolonged laughter.)

What is it they're afraid of?

"stereotype"

This is what—you are just breaking down this stereo thing that all Negroes are ignorant, they won't read, they won't do this, they won't help themselves. Once they see you're trying to do it . . . You see what? They're not really worrying so much about the Negro, they're worried about themselves. When I really want to fight them, you know what I do, I glare at 'em. They cringe. (Laughter.)

I have learned that a Negro woman can do anything she wants to do if she's got enough nerve. So can a white man. But a white woman and a Negro man are slaves until this day. I'll tell you why. The white man has set his woman up on a pedestal. He's trying to prove to her how superior he is. Truly he's not superior; he's just another little boy. She has to stay there if she wants to be anybody. But if she ever learns anything and she strays, she's an outcast. Me, you know what I can do? I can do any cotton-pickin' thing I feel like doin'.

The white woman is more a slave than you?

Oh, by all standards. The black woman has to have nerve, though. She has to have experience. And she needs a little education to go along with it. You know this is such a strange thing. I don't know why people like mystery. Love is so beautiful. It can be beautiful, with any group of people . . . Florence Scala and I can sit here . . .

A white woman who opposed destruction of an old, established neighborhood on the West Side in Chicago. The area was to be used as a site for the Chicago campus of the University of Illinois.

We talk about all facets of our lives, things we wouldn't dare say to anybody else in public. And somebody else, even a Negro, walks in my back door, we shut up. Because it's taboo. They might say it was Uncle Tomming, or they could make it look ugly. These things are hard to understand. Two human beings could have so much in common that they can really sit down and talk about their own lives, their own failures, their own misgivings, and truly speaking tell you about some of my absolute traits that I don't like. Two women, we're just two women. So here is this cloak of mystery. Everybody, even the neighbors, gawking. When she comes in, you know. The curtains are moving, or they come boldly to the door and watch, as though, well, here is the enemy.

Florence, with Florence what I tried to teach in this particular neighborhood, here's a woman everybody says, oh well, she's Italian, she doesn't have the interest. Damn that, this is a woman that you *need* to talk to. She doesn't live on Lake Shore Drive. I tried to show them the little, simple, down-to-earth qualities about this particular woman. But, my God, this Petrillo,° whoever the hell he is, what are you going to tell him? The man has no interest in white or black. If you're poor, see? He's living in another world altogether.

This is the Berlin Wall right over here. You see, we don't even have a ten-cent store. Woolworth doesn't find it profitable. We don't have a bank. After all, everybody here is on Welfare. So if you want to get your check cashed, I go downtown to the bank. I usually go to Sears' or Ward's or somewhere where I've got a charge account. This is where you get a check cashed, unless you want to go to the currency exchange and pay somebody to get your check cashed. Well, I don't make that kind of money to give somebody money to cash my check. We don't have any facilities here that poor folks need. On Michigan Avenue, where people can get along without it, you got your ten-cent stores. I did all my shopping in a ten-cent store when I worked at Wesley.

Here again, it's the white man's standards. You know, I laugh sometimes. Just like these books we have in our schools. Dick and Jane, here's this pretty rosy-cheeked white woman and she's got on a pretty dress and a lovely little apron and she's standing out on this lawn and here's this big huge driveway, goes to two, three acres. All this stuff, and she's waving goodbye to her son. He's off on his way to school, you know. And this is what they teach the children in projects. (Laughter.) Boy, this is really something.

I was trying to live by white man's standards myself. I didn't realize it. One day the school sent for me. I'm kind of a stickler for not laying off the job, so I sent my mother. The principal told her Melvin was a problem child. He must have been about seven then. When I got off from work at five o'clock, I chased myself home to fix supper. I couldn't see the forest from the trees. I was so busy trying to get home, trying to get dinner, trying to help with homework, trying to get him to bed, so he'd get enough sleep. Do you realize what a

° DONALD PARILLO: Florence Scala's victorious machine-backed opponent in a 1964 Chicago election

An insight about her particular situation. Daniel P. Moynihan has generalized this individual perception in his famous theory about the destruction of the Negro family. See *Talks*, p. 61.

vicious cycle this is? I didn't realize what I was doing to my children. Because I was rushing them to death. I was rushing myself to death.

I asked for help. I realized that all the voices Melvin heard were female voices. My voice, his sister's voice, his grandmother's voice, his teacher's voice. I began to get frightened. I went down to the I.S.U. something; I talked with them. They decided I was the one needed the psychoanalyzing. They had me in a conference and there were about twelve psychiatrists, all around. Somebody was taking notes and what have you. Nobody said one word about tomorrow. I explained to the people that my child, he's wandering away and I'm afraid he needs male companionship. I'm not asking you to give him anything, just a few minutes of your time. Till this day I didn't get it.

This is what would happen at work. Instead of sending a card: Mrs. Jefferson, come to school to see about your son . . . they'd call up. When the phone would ring, honest to God, you know what? My blood pressure would rise, because now I was so afraid. "Lucy!" Whenever a call came in, I knew something was wrong. And when this truant officer would phone, one of the girls would answer.

Boy, oh boy, here I go. I didn't like this, see? I was furious, because I thought this was invading my private life. The way I raise my children was my own private business. Let's say I was ashamed. This would be a better word. I wouldn't have admitted it then, but I can admit it now. Because, you see, the stigma of all Negro children are lazy, they don't do this, they don't do that, you know. See, I didn't want anybody to think my children wasn't up to par, or wasn't up to the white man's standards. Well, I blowed that long ago. (Laughs.)

I couldn't afford to go to the PTA meetings. They don't do a damn thing but drink coffee anyway. I like coffee and I like to drink it in the morning, but I have to go to work, and they had PTA meetings at one o'clock in the day. I couldn't lay off my job to go down there to chitchat with them. I think they had PTA meetings twice in the last ten years at night. They're no damn good anyway.

Melvin was doing very poorly and I was getting letters. You know, they send you all these little items. Come to see me, come to school, because your child is not working up to his capacity. I don't know why they just don't tell you the truth about it, instead of using all these vague, false phrases. I thought he was just being lazy, but the child couldn't read. He couldn't spell. He was at Crane High, out there in the ghetto. I laid off from work the next day. I got up, cocked my hat up Miss Johnny Aside . . . I wanted to let him know I was plenty mad then. Oh yeah, I visited Crane. Melvin was having three study periods in a row. Gee, this is kind of crazy, studying what? I went to see this study hall. And this is the auditorium. It has a false ceiling, and there's very few lights, and there's children everywhere, male and female, and about the only thing they can do there is make love. Most of the kids can't read anyway, but if they could, they wouldn't be able to see. So I went to the counselor and he said, "It costs $10,000 to put up this business of putting lights in and the school system doesn't have the money" and blah, blah, blah. I said, "But in the meantime, what are you going to do about all these children in there, these boys and girls, these young men and women?" I said, "Maybe they can't read but they can do other things in there, such as getting babies." He said, "Well, well . . . we don't have anywhere else to put 'em."

One who gives counsel or advice.

?!? See above definition.

You're talking about teachers. I bet he never had the same teacher twice in two weeks in two years. It's a disgrace to keep on calling these places schools. I think the best thing we can say about them, these are meeting places where people get up every morning, give their children a dollar, seventy-five cents, or whatever the heck they give 'em, and these kids go off. Schools you learn in. They could take a store front on Roosevelt Road or anywhere and clean it up, put some seats in there, and put some books in. But see, you can't learn anything where there is no books. Melvin went a whole half year at Crane, didn't have a book. If I woke up in a house that didn't have a book in, I'd just burn it down, it wouldn't be any good. To me, they're my life blood. Types of caps, gowns, all that crap, it don't mean nothing.

Oh, what am I *really* looking for? For my daughter to have her baby. This is her first. Her marriage turned out bad. I would like for her to finish her college education. She's gonna need it to help her child, to rear her child. The only thrill left for me is to see my grandchild come and see what I can do about him. Won't that be fun? You know, I'll be able to afford things that would give him incentive to paint, music, literature, all these things that would free his little soul. Other than that, no bother. Melvin? Am I going to give him a chance to be a man or not? I took that chance when I let him go to Selma. I was scared to death. And I was very proud. I was afraid he was too young, because he was only sixteen, to know what was really happening. But I couldn't afford to tell him. I wouldn't have given him a chance to be a man. This was his chance. And I didn't want to steal it.

In Alabama, site of Martin Luther King, Jr.'s Freedom Marches in 1965.

Let's face it. What counts is knowledge. And feeling. You see, there's such a thing as a feeling tone. One is friendly and one is hostile. And if you don't have this, baby, you've had it. You're dead.

Literary Sort: What a horrible woman!

Editor: I thought she was beautiful.

Literary Sort: But she was too real for my taste.

Editor: But she *was* real . . . with feeling, wasn't she?

Snapshot of a Dog

James Thurber

I ran across a dim photograph of him the other day, going through some old things. He's been dead twenty-five years. His name was Rex (my two brothers and I named him when we were in our early teens) and he was a bull terrier. "An American bull terrier," we used to say, proudly; none of your English bulls. He had one brindle eye that sometimes made him look like a clown and sometimes reminded you of a politician with derby hat and cigar. The rest of him was white except for a brindle saddle that always seemed to be slipping off and a brindle stocking on a hind leg. Nevertheless, there was a nobility about him. He was big and muscular and beautifully made. He never lost his dignity even when trying to accomplish the extravagant tasks my brothers and myself used to set for him. One of these was the bringing of a ten-foot wooden rail into the yard through the back gate. We would throw it out into the alley and tell him to go get it. Rex was as powerful as a wrestler, and there were not many things that he couldn't manage somehow to get hold of with his great jaws and lift or drag to wherever he wanted to put them, or wherever we wanted them put. He would catch the rail at the balance and lift it clear of the ground and trot with great confidence toward the gate. Of course, since the gate was only four feet wide or so, he couldn't bring the rail in broadside. He found that out when he got a few terrific jolts, but he wouldn't give up. He finally figured out how to do it, by dragging the rail, holding onto one end, growling. He got a great, wagging satisfaction out of his work. We used to bet kids who had never seen Rex in action that he could catch a baseball thrown as high as they could throw it. He almost never let us down.

Rex could hold a baseball with ease in his mouth, in one cheek, as if it were a chew of tobacco.

He was a tremendous fighter, but he never started fights. I don't believe he liked to get into them, despite the fact that he came from a line of fighters. He never went for another dog's throat but for one of its ears (that teaches a dog a lesson), and he would get his grip, close his eyes, and hold on. He could hold on for hours. His longest fight lasted from dusk until almost pitch-dark, one Sunday. It was fought in East Main Street in Columbus with a large, snarly nondescript that belonged to a big colored man. When Rex finally got his ear grip, the brief whirlwind of snarling turned to screeching. It was frightening to listen to and watch. The Negro boldly picked the dogs up somehow and began swinging them around his head, and finally let them fly like a hammer in a hammer throw, but although they landed ten feet away with a great plump, Rex still held on.

The two dogs eventually worked their way to the middle of the car tracks, and after a while two or three streetcars were held up by the fight. A motorman tried to pry Rex's jaws open with a switch rod; somebody lighted a fire and made a torch of a stick and held that to Rex's tail, but he paid no attention. In the end, all the residents and storekeepers in the neighborhood were on hand, shouting this, suggesting that. Rex's joy of battle, when battle was joined, was almost tranquil. He had a kind of pleasant expression during fights, not a vicious one, his eyes closed in what would have seemed to be sleep had it not been for the turmoil of the struggle. The Oak Street Fire Department finally had to be sent for—I don't know why nobody thought of it sooner. Five or six pieces of apparatus arrived, followed by a battalion chief. A hose was attached and a powerful stream of water was turned on the dogs. Rex held on for several moments more while the torrent buffeted him about like a log in a freshet. He was a hundred yards away from where the fight started when he finally let go.

The story of that Homeric fight got all around town, and some of our relatives looked upon the incident as a blot on the family name. They insisted that we get rid of Rex, but we were very happy with him, and nobody could have made us give him up. We would have left town with him first, along any road there was to go. It would have been different, perhaps, if he had ever started fights, or looked for trouble. But he had a gentle disposition. He never bit a person in the ten strenuous years that he lived, nor ever growled at anyone except prowlers. He killed cats, that is true, but quickly and neatly and without especial malice, the way men kill certain animals. It was the only thing he did that we could never cure him of doing. He never killed, or even chased, a squirrel. I don't know why. He had his own philosophy about such things. He never ran barking after wagons or automobiles. He didn't seem to see the idea in pursuing something you couldn't catch, or something you couldn't do anything with, even if you did catch it. A wagon was one of the things he couldn't tug along with his mighty jaws, and he knew it. Wagons, therefore, were not a part of his world.

Swimming was his favorite recreation. The first time he ever saw a body of water (Alum Creek), he trotted nervously along the steep bank for a while, fell to barking wildly, and finally plunged in from a height of eight feet or more. I shall always remember that shining, virgin dive. Then he swam upstream and back just for the pleasure of it, like a man. It was fun to see him battle upstream against a stiff current, struggling and growling every foot of the way. He had as much fun in the water as any person I have known. You didn't have to throw a stick in the water to get him to go in. Of course, he would bring back a stick to you if you did throw one in. He would even have brought back a piano if you had thrown one in.

That reminds me of the night, way after midnight, when he went a-roving in the light of the moon and brought back a small chest of drawers that he found somewhere—how far from the house nobody ever knew; since it was Rex, it could easily have been half a mile.

There were no drawers in the chest when he got it home, and it wasn't a good one—he hadn't taken it out of anybody's house; it was just an old cheap piece that somebody had abandoned on a trash heap. Still, it was something he wanted, probably because it presented a nice problem in transportation. It tested his mettle. We first knew about his achievement when, deep in the night, we heard him trying to get the chest up onto the porch. It sounded as if two or three people were trying to tear the house down. We came downstairs and turned on the porch light. Rex was on the top step trying to pull the thing up, but it had caught somehow and he was just holding his own. I suppose he would have held his own till dawn if we hadn't helped him. The next day we carted the chest miles away and threw it out. If we had thrown it out in a nearby alley, he would have brought it home again, as a small token of his integrity in such matters. After all, he had been taught to carry heavy wooden objects about, and he was proud of his prowess.

I am glad Rex never saw a trained police dog jump. He was just an amateur jumper himself, but the most daring and tenacious I have ever seen. He would take on any fence we pointed out to him. Six feet was easy for him, and he could do eight by making a tremendous leap and hauling himself over finally by his paws, grunting and straining; but he lived and died without knowing that twelve- and sixteen-foot walls were too much for him. Frequently, after letting him try to go over one for a while, we would have to carry him home. He would never have given up trying.

There was in his world no such thing as the impossible. Even death couldn't beat him down. He died, it is true, but only, as one of his admirers said, after "straight-arming the death angel" for more than an hour. Late one afternoon he wandered home, too slowly and too uncertainly to be the Rex that had trotted briskly homeward up our avenue for ten years. I think we all knew when he came through the gate that he was dying. He had apparently taken a terrible beating, probably from the owner of some dog that he had got into a fight with. His head and body were scarred. His heavy collar with the teeth marks of many a battle on it was awry; some of the big brass studs in it were sprung loose from the leather. He licked at our hands and, staggering, fell, but got up again. We could see that he was looking for someone. One of his three masters was not home. He did not get home for an hour. During that hour the bull terrier fought against death as he had fought against the cold, strong current of Alum Creek, as he had fought to climb twelve-foot walls. When the person he was waiting for did come through the gate, whistling, ceasing to whistle, Rex walked a few wabbly paces toward him, touched his hand with his muzzle, and fell down again. This time he didn't get up.

Oh, Did I Have Dreams! STUDS TERKEL

This selection is one of the interviews from Mr. Terkel's book, *Division Street, America*.

Jesus Lopez, 42

He is a first helper at the open hearth, U. S. Steel Company. His work is highly skilled. He earns about $10,000 a year and is due for a thirteen-week vacation. On past excursions, he had visited relatives in Mexico, as well as his town of birth. "As I remember it, it was a big town; but when I went back a couple of years ago, it was just a tiny, little thing. It's nothing there, little shacks. It made me sick. Squalor, unbelievable, really unbelievable that people could live like that. You see rows of kids standing like that with their hands out."

His American boyhood was in Joliet and South Chicago, among "Polacks, Hunkies," and other Mexicans. "It was called the bush then. Oh, we had some grand old fights." He was a brilliant student at school, without too much effort, but he bypassed a chance at college to make some money fast.

He was once an outgoing person, with many friends and many curiosities: theater, literature, politics. Today, he lives with his Anglo wife in a modest-income suburb, to the city's southwest. Their only child, a girl, died during one of their trips to Mexico. He is convinced it was malpractice.

He has had a few drinks.

I smash cars up left and right. I have a Corvair out there, you see it? It's all smashed up, not fixed. I got a Hudson sitting in a garage, one of these Green Hornets. It's green, too. And it's a Hornet. (Laughs.) And something's wrong with the transmission or something. I don't know what, and it has to be fixed. I got a '64 Le Mans in the garage that's gettin' fixed. That's one I'm gonna pick up Saturday.

It's mixed around here. Polacks next door. Over here's a German, I think. And next to that there, that's another Polack. And there's a Filipino.

I noticed a bar over here where other people were paying thirty cents a bottle and I was paying thirty-five cents a bottle for beer. I stopped goin'. I wouldn't bother to ask. I know. A lot of things that I would fight at the drop a hat years ago, I just let go and think about it maybe. Like that business about the five cents. You may get sore inside, but you no longer make an issue of it, even though I feel sick inside most of the time. No, I've become a moral coward.

What do I mean by that? Let's say these principles and all that, I let them slide under to keep things at an even keel and all that. In other words, I've fallen into that pattern that everybody's cryin' about. That security. I'm forty-two years of age now. If I get fired from my job, what am I gonna do? How many first helpers do they want there in the back yard?

Like I happen to ride in Oklahoma City last summer and there was a motel, very fancy motel. They got those big neon signs and flashy lighted things around. And it was late, about 12:30 A.M. Drove in. I was with my mother. I was taking her down to Nogales. My sister's graduating from school down there. And there was nobody in there but one man. I asked for a room and I got it. I went and took my mother and got her settled and all that.

And there was some guy that looked like a salesman. Oh, when I walked in, I knew what he was talking about. About those people and all that business. When I walked in, he said, the Negroes, you know. And the man who was behind the desk, he said, "We have to take them." I almost started to make an issue right then and there. Because I saw this guy looking at me and you sort of sense these things. I mean you get a feeling when you've lived with it. And I asked him, "How about let's say a Mexican citizen or something like that?"

He didn't know that the papers in my pocket says that I'm a citizen of the United States by Act of Congress. I put that in when I was sold this house. The real-estate agent . . . I paid a substantial down payment and all that business. Went to the loan outfit for the balance. The minute we get back in the real-estate agent's office, after the thing was to be all settled, phone call. Real-estate agent answered the phone, he talks, then he asks me, "Are you a citizen?" (Laughs.) I told him "By Act of Congress. Who wants to know? Tell him by Act of Congress." And how many people can say that? By Act of Congress. In other words, I was made a citizen of the United States of America through service in World War Two. And I gotta put that in. When somebody asks me: Are you a citizen? I tell 'im by Act of Congress.

The guy next door, he mentioned to me that somebody came to visit him one time, and I was out mowing the lawn and he asked since when were niggers living around here? So he said, "He's not a nigger." (Laughs.) Sometimes in the summertime . . .

A couple time my car's been on blocks. One winter I had my car blocked, all four wheels, you know. I was standing on the corner, 95th and Central, waiting for a bus, and cars, kids: "Hi, Nigger," and all that. All I can do is forget it. A moral coward. Oh, well, I could carry a gun. Shoot somebody. I could carry a six-inch blade and kill somebody. Oh yeah, I used to fight at the drop of a hat. I used to be called the cock o' the walk. Yeah, I quit that long ago.

It is important to make sure that students understand his point. ("Useless" because he is "foreign," in spite of the "Act of Congress." What do students have to say about that?)

At the YMCA, I learned how to box. I became a very good boxer. I was small, light, I could move fast, I could hit fast. Featherweight. I was cock o' the walk for a while, and I found that a good feeling. You know, to be a big so-and-so in the Junior Golden Gloves and things like that. Yeah, it felt good.

Oh, did I have dreams! High school, sciences, mathematics, all A's. Did I have ideas! I wanted to be a violinist. I played violin and I was good. And then—I gave it up. Useless. (He takes a long swig at the can of beer.)

I'm a perfectionist, you know. That's a problem I found with my coworkers at the time. Let's say I don't lose my temper fast or easy. But when I want a job done, I want it done right and all things like that. Once in a while I see a guy lackadaisical or something, I'll go up to him and say, "Didn't your daddy ever tell you that if a job is worth doing, it's worth doing well?" My dad taught me that. I don't believe that, do I? (Laughs.)

Is he parodying middle-class norms and slogans?

But the work you do, you do. And that's another problem of this modern age. The majority that are coming up right now, they're gonna do the least they can and get away with. And I don't like that. I mean, I'm not built that way. This job of first helper, I try to do the best of my ability.

True? Or is this his own stereotype?

You can't go higher on the open hearth. From there you go to management. Being first helper is quite good for the ego, you know. You're the boss. 'Cause even bosses, I can tell 'em off. Quite a bit of independence. That's one reason why I like the work. Besides, we are men of steel, that could be. Actually, we're all soft, anyway, anyhow.

I run the furnace. Ostensibly I'm the boss of my second helper and the third helper. I say ostensibly because a lot of third helpers try to tell us how to run furnaces and things like that.

It's skilled, if skill is something you learn through practice. Half the moves we make are just an educated guess. We have seven doors and you have to be able to see in your mind what's happening in there and to interpret. We also take the temperature and test the carbon content. We're supposed to know exactly what moves to make. Intuition plays a great part. There's the son of a smelter foreman that's working there, he tells me it's an art. Well, it used to be an art before we had all these oxygen analyzers that will regulate your fuel. But they go on the blink a lot of times.

Actually the first helper is the man who's responsible. Two guys directly under me, and when I tap out the furnace, there's about seven or eight. If anything goes wrong, it's us . . . it's *we* (Laughs.)

. . . Oh, everybody's scared. Especially about this automation. You ought to hear it on the job. With these oxygen furnaces you know, they're gonna knock out all the open hearths. Well, it might. But I understand there will have to be some open hearths, because I don't believe oxygen furnaces can make all that steel, like some of the alloys we make, and things like that. But then I'm not a metallurgist. I'm just what is called an overpaid laborer. (Laughs.) That's exactly what they call us, overpaid laborers and like that. Actually we don't notice this fear among the furnace workers. It's the machine operators like the charging-car operators, the crane operators, and things like that there. They seem more worried about it, I don't know why.

So . . . at work and all that, what do we talk about and have a few beers? Work. Problems we've had there and what somebody should have done and didn't do. Oh, once in a while you hear them about—what? What Johnson's doing in Santo Domingo? Well, nobody knows what the hell he's doing there. What's he doing in Vietnam? Nobody wants to know, either. That's a fact, they don't. Actually I've come to the conclusion that people are more indrawn toward themselves and all that business.

See ruled passage on page 154.

So I stick to myself and I'm sort of a loner. Once in a while I'll get with a couple of guys and we might have identical thoughts and ideas and something like that. But the majority of the time, I keep to myself. Everybody's concerned more about themselves and why that is I don't know. They're letting things like Mayor Daley and all that, let them take care of outside things. We'll take care of themselves, just "me."

Boy, these kids today are different. They're a hell of a lot smarter than when I was their age. Also a lot more belligerent.

I remember how shocked I was when I came back from the war. It was 1946. I was only twenty-three years old. I had a run-in with a guy at the bar. This character came back with a couple of friends and he was gonna take care of me. Couple of friends came that I knew. They were younger than I was. So we got in a corner and had a nice little fist fight. The guy that started it all, I wasn't involved with him. Another guy hit him and he couldn't knock him down. So I told him, "You stand out of the way. I'll show you how to knock him down." I did. I hit him and knocked him down. And then the two characters I was with, they started kicking him. And I said, "Hey!"

I remember when we had a street fight and we knocked a man down; we stood up there and let the man get up again, if he wanted to, and continue to fight. If he didn't want any more, he gave up and you were the winner. All of a sudden, it wasn't done any more. All of a sudden, why, the minute you get him down, stomp him, kick him, what the hell. Now mind you, I came back from a war where I was shot at and wounded and doing a little kicking myself. But still I had, what? You would call them . . . ideals? Of a fair fight and things like that. Now what did I find? You knock him down, he was fair prey for kicking, kick him in the head, kick him in the ribs, kick him wherever, any place.

When you hollered "Hey!" did they stop?

They didn't answer me. They didn't give me an answer. Anyway, I quit getting involved in tavern brawls. I walk away. I remember the owner of a tavern told me about it once. The guys were saying I was chicken. "What the hell," I told him, "who's gonna profit? For what purpose? Look, I'm a grown man now, I'm not gonna get in a fight with anybody, and if I do, it's gonna be for keeps."

Have you found any hope, some other kind of people?

Hardly, hardly. When it comes to Negroes, I'm a little more than halfway neutral. (Laughs.) I can put myself in their shoes, because of things that happened to me. I did tell one, though: "You're not gonna get anywhere by wearing a chip on your shoulder." Any word that anybody says, you might say in a kidding way, they take it serious. I found too many people like that. But I don't care, that's the city of Chicago.

Is it true you don't care?

No, it's not really true. It's a world I have to live in, how can I not care? But the thing is *what can I do about it?* There we go. The Bomb. Nobody ever talks about it, nobody ever says boo about it. There's no such thing.

I was an idealist. I, oh boy! Now I feel we should all be happy as monkeys. No problems, just eat, sleep and—what's after that? It hurts me to think. For the last three years I just about given up thinking. I'm just going along day to day and day to day, like that.

What do you do in your leisure time?

I drink. (Laughs.) And read—*Playboy.* Look at the nude girls. I stopped being disturbed when I got over age for the draft. (Laughs.) Yeah.

You think the world's going to hell?

(Astonished.) Why, don't you think so?

I have a sense of humor. In this day and age, how could you survive without a sense of humor? Ask my wife if I have a sense of humor. She complains I sit here like a bump on a log, hours and hours. I'm doing nothing but thinking. What am I thinking? I better not be thinking. I hate myself. I'm weak. I'm too weak. (Takes a long swig out of the beer can.)

The Dog That Bit People

James Thurber

Probably no one man should have as many dogs in his life as I have had, but there was more pleasure than distress in them for me except in the case of an Airedale named Muggs. He gave me more trouble than all the other fifty-four or -five put together, although my moment of keenest embarrassment was the time a Scotch terrier named Jeannie, who had just had six puppies in the clothes closet of a fourth floor apartment in New York, had the unexpected seventh and last at the corner of Eleventh Street and Fifth Avenue during a walk she had insisted on taking. Then, too, there was the prize-winning French poodle, a great big black poodle—none of your little, untroublesome white miniatures—who got sick riding in the rumble seat of a car with me on her way to the Greenwich Dog Show. She had a red rubber bib tucked around her throat and, since a rain storm came up when we were half way through the Bronx, I had to hold over her a small green umbrella, really more of a parasol. The rain beat down fearfully and suddenly the driver of the car drove into a big garage, filled with mechanics. It happened so quickly that I forgot to put the umbrella down and I will always remember, with sickening distress, the look of incredulity mixed with hatred that came over the face of the particular hardened garage man that came over to see what we wanted, when he took a look at me and the poodle. All garage men, and people of that intolerant stripe, hate poodles with their curious haircut, especially the pom-poms that you got to leave on their hips if you expect the dogs to win a prize.

But the Airedale, as I have said, was the worst of all my dogs. He really wasn't my dog, as a matter of fact: I came home from a vacation one summer to find that my brother Roy had bought him while I was away. A big, burly, choleric dog, he always acted as if he thought I wasn't one of the family. There was a slight advantage in being one of the family, for he didn't bite the family as often as he bit strangers. Still, in the years that we had him he bit everybody but mother, and he made a pass at her once but missed. That was during the month when we suddenly had mice, and Muggs refused to do anything about them. Nobody ever had mice exactly like the mice we had that month. They acted like pet mice, almost like mice somebody had trained. They were so friendly that one night when mother entertained at dinner the Friraliras, a club she and my father had belonged to for twenty years, she put down a lot of little dishes with food in them on the pantry floor so that the mice would be satisfied with that and wouldn't come into the dining room. Muggs stayed out in the pantry with the mice, lying on the floor, growling to himself—not at the mice, but about all the people in the next room that he would have liked to get at. Mother slipped out into the pantry once to see how everything was going. Everything was going fine. It made her so mad to see Muggs lying there, oblivious of the mice—they came running up to her—that she slapped him and he slashed at her, but didn't make it. He was sorry immediately, mother said. He was always sorry, she said, after he bit someone, but we could not understand how she figured this out. He didn't act sorry.

Mother used to send a box of candy every Christmas to the people the Airedale bit. The list finally contained forty or more names. Nobody could understand why we didn't get rid of the dog. I didn't understand it very well myself, but we didn't get rid of him. I think that one or two people tried to poison Muggs—he acted poisoned once in a while—and old Major Moberly fired at him once with his service revolver near the Seneca Hotel in East Broad Street—but Muggs lived to be almost eleven years old and even when he could hardly get around he bit a Congressman who had called to see my father on business. My mother had never liked the Congressman—she said the signs of his horoscope showed he couldn't be trusted (he was Saturn with the moon in Virgo)—but she sent him a box of candy that Christmas. He sent it right back, probably because he suspected it was trick candy. Mother persuaded herself it was all for the best that the dog had bitten him, even though father lost an important business association because of it. "I wouldn't be associated with such a man," mother said. "Muggs could read him like a book."

We used to take turns feeding Muggs to be on his good side, but that didn't always work. He was never in a very good humor, even after a meal. Nobody knew exactly what was the matter with him, but whatever it was it made him irascible, especially in the mornings. Roy never felt very well in the morning, either, especially before breakfast, and once when he came downstairs and found that Muggs had moodily chewed up the morning paper he hit him in the face with a grapefruit and then jumped up on the dining room table, scattering dishes and silverware and spilling the coffee. Muggs' first free leap carried him all the way across the table and into a brass fire screen in front of the gas grate but he was back on his feet in a moment and in the end he got Roy and gave him a pretty vicious bite in the leg. Then he was all over it; he never bit anyone more than once at a time. Mother always mentioned that as an argument in his favor; she said he had a quick temper but that he didn't hold a grudge. She was forever defending him. I think she liked him because he wasn't well. "He's not strong," she would say, pityingly, but that was inaccurate; he may not have been well but he was terribly strong.

One time my mother went to the Chittenden Hotel to call on a woman mental healer who was lecturing in Columbus on the subject of "Harmonious Vibrations." She wanted to find out if it was possible to get harmonious vibrations into a dog. "He's a large tan-colored Airedale," mother explained. The woman said that she had never treated a dog but she advised my mother to hold the thought that he did not bite and would not bite. Mother was holding the thought the very next morning when Muggs got the iceman but she blamed that slip-up on the iceman. "If you didn't think he would bite you, he wouldn't," mother told him. He stomped out of the house in a terrible jangle of vibrations.

One morning when Muggs bit me slightly, more or less in passing, I reached down and grabbed his short stumpy tail and hoisted him into the air. It was a foolhardy thing to do and the last time I saw my mother, about six months ago, she said she didn't know what possessed me. I don't either, except that I was pretty mad. As long as I held the dog off the floor by his tail he couldn't get at me, but he twisted and jerked so, snarling all the time, that I realized I couldn't hold him that way very long. I carried him to the kitchen and flung him onto the floor and shut the door on him just as he crashed against it. But I forgot about the backstairs. Muggs went up the backstairs and down the frontstairs and had me cornered in the living room. I managed to get up onto the mantelpiece above the fireplace, but it gave way and came down with a tremendous crash throwing a large marble clock, several vases, and myself heavily to the floor. Muggs was so alarmed by the racket that when I picked myself up he had disappeared. We couldn't find him anywhere, although we whistled and shouted, until old Mrs. Detweiler called after dinner that night. Muggs had bitten her once, in the leg, and she came into the living room only after we assured her that Muggs had run away. She had just seated herself when, with a great growling and scratching of claws, Muggs emerged from under a davenport where he had been quietly hiding all the time, and bit her again. Mother examined the bite and put arnica on it and told Mrs. Detweiler that it was only a bruise. "He just bumped you," she said. But Mrs. Detweiler left the house in a nasty state of mind.

Lots of people reported our Airedale to the police but my father held a municipal office at the time and was on friendly terms with the police. Even so, the cops had been out a couple times—once when Muggs bit Mrs. Rufus Sturtevant and again when he bit Lieutenant-Governor Malloy—but mother told them that it hadn't been Muggs' fault but the fault of the people who were bitten. "When he starts for them, they scream," she explained, "and that excites him." The cops suggested that it might be a good idea to tie the dog up, but mother said that it mortified him to be tied up and that he wouldn't eat when he was tied up.

Muggs at his meals was an unusual sight. Because of the fact that if you reached toward the floor he would bite you, we usually put his food plate on top of an old kitchen table with a bench alongside the table. Muggs would stand on the bench and eat. I remember that my mother's Uncle Horatio, who boasted that he was the third man up Missionary Ridge, was splutteringly indignant when he found out that we fed the dog

Civil War battle, near Chattanooga

on a table because we were afraid to put his plate on the floor. He said he wasn't afraid of any dog that ever lived and that he would put the dog's plate on the floor if we would give it to him. Roy said that if Uncle Horatio had fed Muggs on the ground just before the battle he would have been the first man up Missionary Ridge. Uncle Horatio was furious. "Bring him in! Bring him in now!" he shouted. "I'll feed the ——— on the floor!" Roy was all for giving him a chance, but my father wouldn't hear of it. He said that Muggs had already been fed. "I'll feed him again!" bawled Uncle Horatio. We had quite a time quieting him.

In his last year Muggs used to spend practically all of his time outdoors. He didn't like to stay in the house for some reason or other—perhaps it held too many unpleasant memories for him. Anyway, it was hard to get him to come in and as a result the garbage man, the iceman, and the laundryman wouldn't come near the house. We had to haul the garbage down to the corner, take the laundry out and bring it back, and meet the iceman a block from home. After this had gone on for some time we hit on an ingenious arrangement for getting the dog in the house so that we could lock him up while the gas meter was read, and so on. Muggs was afraid of only one thing, an electrical storm. Thunder and lightning frightened him out of his senses (I think he thought a storm had broken the day the mantelpiece fell). He would rush into the house and hide under a bed or in a clothes closet. So we fixed up a thunder machine out of a long narrow piece of sheet iron with a wooden handle on one end. Mother would shake this vigorously when she wanted to get Muggs into the house. It made an excellent imitation of thunder, but I suppose it was the most roundabout system for running a household that was ever devised. It took a lot out of mother.

A few months before Muggs died, he got to "seeing things." He would rise slowly from the floor, growling low, and stalk stiff-legged and menacing toward nothing at all. Sometimes the Thing would be just a little to the right or left of a visitor. Once a Fuller Brush salesman got hysterics. Muggs came wandering into the room like Hamlet following his father's ghost. His eyes were fixed on a spot just to the left of the Fuller Brush man, who stood it until Muggs was about three slow, creeping paces from him. Then he shouted. Muggs wavered on past him into the hallway grumbling to himself but the Fuller man went on shouting. I think mother had to throw a pan of cold water on him before he stopped. That was the way she used to stop us boys when we got into fights.

Muggs died quite suddenly one night. Mother wanted to bury him in the family lot under a marble stone with some such inscription as "Flights of angels sing thee to thy rest" but we persuaded her it was against the law. In the end we just put up a smooth board above his grave along a lonely road. On the board I wrote with an indelible pencil "Cave Canem." Mother was quite pleased with the simple classic dignity of the old Latin epitaph.

Miss Gee: A Ballad

W. H. Auden

Let me tell you a little story
  About Miss Edith Gee;
She lived in Clevedon Terrace
  At Number 83.

She'd a slight squint in her left eye,
  Her lips they were thin and small,
She had narrow sloping shoulders
  And she had no bust at all.

She'd a velvet hat with trimmings,
  And a dark grey serge costume;
She lived in Clevedon Terrace
  In a small bed-sitting room.

She'd a purple mac for wet days, Mackintosh: raincoat
  A green umbrella too to take,
She'd a bicycle with shopping basket
  And a harsh back-pedal brake.

The Church of Saint Aloysius
  Was not so very far;
She did a lot of knitting,
  Knitting for that Church Bazaar.

Miss Gee looked up at the starlight
  And said: "Does anyone care
That I live in Clevedon Terrace
  On one hundred pounds a year?" About $240

She dreamed a dream one evening
  That she was the Queen of France
And the Vicar of Saint Aloysius
  Asked Her Majesty to dance.

But a storm blew down the palace,
  She was biking through a field of corn,
And a bull with the face of the Vicar
  Was charging with lowered horn.

She could feel his hot breath behind her,
  He was going to overtake;
And the bicycle went slower and slower
  Because of that back-pedal brake.

Summer made the trees a picture,
  Winter made them a wreck;
She bicycled to the evening service
  With her clothes buttoned up to her neck.

She passed by the loving couples,
  She turned her head away;
She passed by the loving couples
  And they didn't ask her to stay.

Miss Gee sat down in the side-aisle,
  She heard the organ play;
And the choir it sang so sweetly
  At the ending of the day,

Miss Gee knelt down in the side-aisle,
  She knelt down on her knees:
"Lead me not into temptation
  But make me a good girl, please."

The days and nights went by her
  Like waves round a Cornish wreck; — Off the coast of Cornwall
She bicycled down to the doctor
  With her clothes buttoned up to her neck.

She bicycled down to the doctor,
  And rang the surgery bell:
"O, doctor, I've a pain inside me,
  And I don't feel very well."

Doctor Thomas looked her over,
  And then he looked some more;
Walked over to his wash-basin,
  Said, "Why didn't you come before?"

Doctor Thomas sat over his dinner,
  Though his wife was waiting to ring;
Rolling his bread into pellets,
  Said, "Cancer's a funny thing."

His wife she rang for the servant,
  Said, "Don't be so morbid, dear."
He said: "I saw Miss Gee this evening
  And she's a goner, I fear."

They took Miss Gee to the hospital,
  She lay there a total wreck,
Lay in the ward for women
  With the bedclothes right up to her neck.

They laid her on the table,
  The students began to laugh;
And Mr Rose the surgeon
  He cut Miss Gee in half.

Mr Rose he turned to his students,
  Said, "Gentlemen, if you please,
We seldom see a sarcoma
  As far advanced as this."

They took her off the table,
  They wheeled away Miss Gee
Down to another department
  Where they study Anatomy.

They hung her from the ceiling,
  Yes, they hung up Miss Gee;
And a couple of Oxford Groupers
  Carefully dissected her knee.

See *Talks,* p. 44.

Editor: Another *type,* would you say?

Literary Sort: Clearly Mr. Auden thought her so. But I confess I do not like the attitude he seems to take toward poor Miss Gee.

Editor: But she *did* get what she *really* wanted.

Literary Sort: Oh?

INTERLOCK WITH CLUSTER 7:
An authorial link: W. H. Auden
A generic link: ballads

7

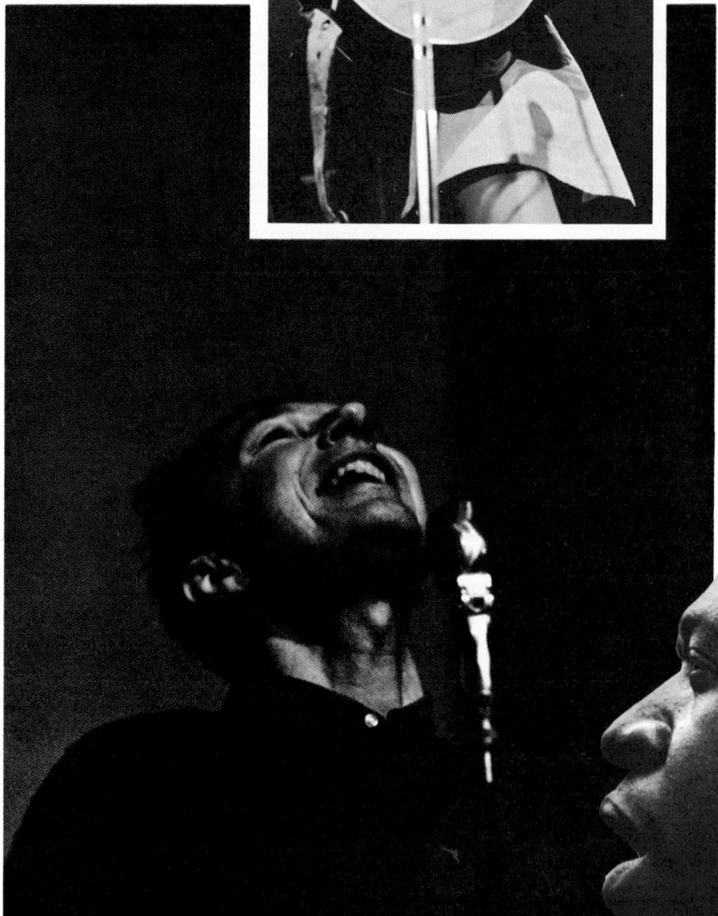

Cluster 7: pp. 180-201
A generic cluster
Focus: the ballad

INTERLOCK WITH CLUSTER 6:
An authorial link: W. H. Auden
A generic link: ballads

ON BALLADS

People who study ballads often treat them somewhat ambiguously. They acknowledge the impact of the stories the ballads tell, but they seem to be somewhat put off by the verse and the language. Some scholars have even suggested that the ballad ought to be treated as the ''literary debris'' of the Middle Ages.

The fact is that ballads—both ancient and modern—are popular songs, songs belonging to the people, especially to the common people. We can tell from historical references in classical ballads that many go back to the twelfth or thirteenth centuries. They have come down to us by oral transmission, from folk singer to folk singer in public performances, and also, no doubt, from parents to children as a part of family tradition. Ballads, then, can be seen as part of the oral culture, along with jump-rope rhymes, counting-out formulas, riddles, work songs, and the like.

The oral culture, however, seems little regarded in the schools, and cultivated folk tend to depreciate it. Perhaps the response of many adults to the Beatles when they first came on the scene is a contemporary example of this cultural snobbishness, a snobbishness which often views new forms in art with suspicion, even to the point of labeling them ''barbaric.''

All this seems rather amusing when you consider that today's over-thirty group, including some scholars, have difficulty identifying with the acid-rock of Jimi Hendrix or with singers like Blood, Sweat & Tears, but are at leisure with the lyricism of Joan Baez, Pete Seeger, Bob Dylan, and other contemporary balladeers. As you read the ballads that follow, you'll no doubt find some that turn you on and some that turn you off. Why do *you* relate to some and not to others? It makes you wonder whether art—ballads, in this case—is for all ages or for the culturally elite. And just who are the culturally elite?

The Quarry

W. H. Auden

The woman is speaking. Note the irony in her use of this romantic and pleasing word, especially when her husband (lover?) seems to be the quarry.

O what is that sound which so thrills the ear
Down in the valley drumming, drumming?
Only the scarlet soldiers, dear,
The soldiers coming.

O what is that light I see flashing so clear
Over the distance brightly, brightly?
Only the sun on their weapons, dear,
As they step lightly.

O what are they doing with all that gear,
What are they doing this morning, this morning?
Only their usual maneuvers, dear,
Or perhaps a warning.

O why have they left the road down there,
Why are they suddenly wheeling, wheeling?
Perhaps a change in their orders, dear.
Why are you kneeling?

Presumably she has realized the situation; see line 16. Is she hoping that her understanding is wrong?

O haven't they stopped for the doctor's care,
Haven't they reined their horses, their horses?
Why, they are none of them wounded, dear,
None of these forces.

O is it the parson they want, with white hair,
Is it the parson, is it, is it?
No, they are passing his gateway, dear,
Without a visit.

O it must be the farmer who lives so near.
It must be the farmer so cunning, so cunning?
They have passed the farmyard already, dear,
And now they are running.

O where are you going? Stay with me here!
Were the vows you swore deceiving, deceiving?
No, I promised to love you, dear,
But I must be leaving.

A curiously flat speech. What is the effect?

O it's broken the lock and splintered the door,
O it's the gate where they're turning, turning;
Their boots are heavy on the floor
And their eyes are burning.

The Noble Peere While He Lived Here: A Song of the Duke of Buckingham

Note we have retained "Peere" for "Pier" in the title, but we have changed "liued" and "heere" to "lived" and "here." And in line 103 we changed the double "s" in "prisson" to the same spelling as in line 99. Our changes, although minor, might afford some idea of how much and often ballads change from generation to generation, from editor to editor, and from singer to singer! And often it is not merely the spelling here and there but the actual content that undergoes major surgery.

Anonymous

The noble Peere, while he liued heere,
the worthie Duke of *Buckingham,*
Whoe florisht in king *Edwardes* raigne,
the fourth king of that name;

Which did in seruice keepe a man,
of meane and low degree,
Which of° a child he had brought vp
from base to dignitie, —

From "base" (illegitimate) birth.

He gaue him landes and liuinge good,
of which he was noe heire,
And married him to a galant Dame,
as rich as she was faire.

"Living." ("U"is consistently used for "v," and "v" for "u.")

It came to passe in tract of time
his wealth did soe excell,
His riches did surpasse them all
that in that shire did dwell.

Who was soe braue as *Banister?*
or who durst with him contend?
Which wold not be desirous still
to be his daylye friend?

°OF: as

But out, alas! it came to passe,
  and soe the strife beganne,
The maister he constrainèd was
  to seeke succour at the man.

If scansion is regular, this *e* should be pro
nounced; approximately the sound symb
by the *a* in "sofa." The other final *e's* all
to be silent.

King *Richard* the third he got the sword,
  forswore himselfe t' bee king;
Murdered two princes in their beddes,
  the which much strife did bringe.

This noble Duke when he saw that,
  that vile and wicked deed,
Against this Tyrant rais'd an hoast
  of armèd men with speede.

But when the king that he heard tell,
  a mightie hoast he sent
Against the Duke of *Buckingham,*
  his purpose to prevent.

When the Duke his souldiers they heard tell,
  feare pearst their hartes eich one; "pierced" "each"
That all his souldiers fled by night
  and left this worthie Duke alone.

Then in extreame neede he tooke his steede,
  and poasted night and day;
Vnto his owne man *Banister,*
  these wordes to him did say:

"O *Banister,* sweete *Banister,*
  pittie thou my cause," quoth hee;
"And hyde me from my cruell foes,
  which thus pursueth mee."

"O you are welcome, my maister deere,
  you are hartelie welcome heere; "heartily"
And like a friend I will you keepe,
  although it cost me deere."

His velvet sute then he put off, "suit"
  his chaine of gould likewise;
And ould letherne coate he put vpon,
  and all to blinde the people's eise.

Sayinge, "*Banister,* O *Banister,*
O *Banister,* be true!"
"*Christ* his curse then light on me and myne,
if ever I be false to you."

In another rendition of this same ballad, a stan
was added here to give emphasis to the Duke's
misfortune and disguise:

An old felt hat vpon his head,
with 20 holes therin;
And soe in labor he spent the time,
as tho some drudge he had beene.

(See title note on page 183.)

An ould felt hat he put on his head,
ould letherne slopes° also;
A hedginge bill vpon his necke,
and soe to the woodes did goe.

This worthie Duke went to the woodes,
as did not him beseeme,
And soe in sorrow spent his dais,
as he some drudge had beene.

A nobleman ought not to have had to take to the woods.

And there he liued long vnknowen,
and still vnknowne might bee,
Til *Banister* for hope of gaine
betray'd him Judaslye.

Note that we did not change here.

A proclamation there was made,
whosoeuer then could bringe
Newes of the Duke of *Buckingham*
vnto *Richard* the kinge,

A thousand pound should be his fee,
of gould and money bright,
And he preferrèd by his grace
and made a worthie knight.

When *Banister* that he heard tell,
he to the Court did hye;
And he betraid his maister deere
for luker of that fee.

"gain," "reward in that amount"

King *Richard* then he sent in hast
a mightie hoast with arrowes good,
And for to take this worthie Duke,
as he was wanderinge in the wood.

°SLOPES: trousers

And when the Duke that he saw that,
  he wronge his handes with wooe.
"O false *Banister,*" quoth he,
  "why hast thou serued thy maister soe?

"O *Banister,* false *Banister,*
  woe worth thy fainèd hart! "false"
Thou hast betraid thy maister deere,
  and play'd a treator's part!"

The noble Duke to *London* was brought,
  in his great feare and dread,
And straight in prison he was cast
  and judg'd to loase his head.

Then *Banister* went to the court,
  hopeinge these gifts to haue;
And straight in prison he was cast,
  and hard his life to saue.

Noe frend he found in his distresse,
  nor yet noe frend at neede,
But euerie man revilèd him
  for his most hatefull wicked deed.

His eldest sonne starke mad did runne;
  his daughter drounèd was
Within a shallow runninge streame,
  which did all danger passe.

Accordinge to his owne desyre,
  godes curse did on him fale;
That all his wealth consumèd quyte,
  and soe was wasted all.

Younge *Banister* liu'd longe in shame,
  but at the length did dye;
And soe our lord he shew'd his wrath
  for his father's villanye.

Good lord, preserue our noble kinge, James I
  and send him longe proceede;
And god send euerie distressèd man
  a better frend at need!

Finis

JOHNNY OF COCKLEY'S WELL

Anonymous

Johnny he's risen up in the morn,
  Called for water to wash his han's;
But little knew he that his bloody hounds
  Were bound in iron banns,
  Were bound in iron banns.

Johnny's mother she's gotten word of that,
  And care-bed she has ta'en:
"O, Johnny, for my benison, "blessing"
  I beg you'll bide at hame;
For the wine so red, and the well-baken bread,
  My Johnny he shall want nane.

"There are seven forsters at Pickram Side, "foresters," "game keepers"
  At Pickram where they dwell,
And for a drop of thy hearte's blood,
  They would ride the fords of Hell."

The *e* is sounded, hence the apostrophe (which represents the lost vowel of Old English) is unnecessary. A good example of uncertainty in a time of rapid linguistic change.

Johnny he's gotten word of that,
  And he's turned wondrous keen;
He's put him off the red scarlett,
  And he's put on the Lincoln green.

That is, disguising himself in the sort of cloth foresters wore

With a sheaf of arrows by his side,
  And a bent bow in his hand,
He's mounted on a prancing steed,
  And ridden fast o'er the land.

He's up in Braidhouplee, and down in Braidslee,
  And under a buss° of broom,
And there he found a good dun deer, "brown"
  Feeding in little room.°

Johnny shot, and the dun deer leapt,
  And she leapt wondrous wide,
Until they came to the wan water, Presumably Scottish for "dark"
  And he stemmed her of her pride.

°BUSS: bush

°ROOM: space

He's taken out the little pen-knife,
'Twas full three quarters long,
And he's taken out of that dun deer
The liver but and the tongue. Read "and also."

They ate of the flesh, and they drank of the blood,
And the blood it was so sweet,
Which causèd Johnny and his bloody hounds
To fall in a deep sleep.

By then came an old palmer, A pilgrim who has been to the Holy Land and, hence, wears crossed palms.
And an ill death may he die!
For he's away to Pickram Side,
As fast as he can drie.°

"What news, what news?" says one of the forsters,
"What news have ye brought to me?"
"I have no news," the palmer said,
"But what I saw with my ee."

"High up in Braidhouplee, low down in Braidslee,
And under a buss of scroggs,°
O there I spied a well-wight° man
Sleeping among his dogs."

"His coat it was of the light Lincoln,
And his breeches of the same,
His shoes were of the Cordovan leather,
And gold buckles tying them."

Up bespoke the seven forsters,
Up bespoke they one and all:
"O, that is Johnny of Cockley's Well,
And on him we shall fall."

O, the first stroke that they gave him,
They struck him by the knee;
Then up bespoke his sister's son;
"O, the next'll gar° him dee!" "die"

°DRIE: manage

°SCROGGS: stunted bushes

°WELL-WIGHT: sturdy

°GAR: make

"O, some they count° ye well-wight men,
But I do count ye nane; "none"
For you might well have wakened me,
And asked gin I would be ta'en.°

"The wildest wolf in all this wood
Would not have done so by me;
She'd have wet her foot in the wan water,
And sprinkled it o'er my brae, "brow"
And if that would not have wakened me,
She'd have gone and let me be.

"O, bow of yew, if ye be true,
In London, where ye were bought,
Fingers five, get up belive,°
Manhood shall fail me nought!"

Johnny he's killed the seven forsters,
He's killed them all but ane, "one"
And that won scarce to Pickram Side,
To carry the bode-words hame.

"Is there never a boy in all this wood
That will tell what I can say;
That will go for me to Cockley's Well,
Tell my mother to fetch me away?

"O, I often took to my mother's house
The dun roe and the hare;
But today I'll send to my mother's house
Much sorrow but and much care." "and also"

There was a boy into that wood,
That told what Johnny would say,
And many an ane was the well-wight man "a one"
At the fetching of Johnny away.

°COUNT: value

°GIN . . . TA'EN: whether I would surrender

°BELIVE: soon

Graeme and Bewick

Anonymous

Good Lord Graeme is to Carlisle gane,
"gone"
Sir Robert Bewick there met he,
And arm in arm to the wine they did go,
And they drank till they were both merrie.

Good Lord Graeme, he has ta'en the cup:
"Sir Robert Bewick, and here's to thee!
And here's to our twa sons at hame
And billies° together aye may they be!"

A "scholar"—"able to read and write"
"O, were your son a clerk like mine,
And learned some books that he could read,
They might have been two brethren bold,
And they might have bragged° the Border side.

"Aye, were your son a clerk like mine,
Well learned in the grammarie!
Perhaps the term shares some of the meaning of its cognate *glamor.* In any event, it means more than "grammar," rather "learning in general."
But your son's a lad, and he is but bad,
"thoroughly"
And billy to my son he cannot be."

Good Lord Graeme has a reckoning called,
A reckoning full then called he;
And he paid a crown, and it went roun',
It was all for the good wine and free.

And he has to the stable gane,
Where there stood thirty steeds and three;
He's taken his ain horse among them all,
"own"
And hame he rade sae hastily.

"Welcome, my father!" said Christie Graeme,
"But where sae long from hame were ye?"
"It's I have been at Carlisle town,
And a baffled° man by thee I be.

°BILLIES: companions-in-arms

°BRAGGED: defied

°BAFFLED: disgraced

"For I have been at Carlisle town,
  Where Sir Robert Bewick he met me;
He says ye're a lad, and ye are but bad,
  And billy to his son ye cannot be.

"I sent ye to school, and ye would not learn;
  I bought ye books, and ye would not read;
Therefore my blessing ye shall never earn,
  Till I see with Bewick thou save my head.°"

"Now, God forbid, my dear father,
  That ever such thing should be!
Billy Bewick was my master, and I was his scholar,
  And aye sae well as he learnèd me."

"And I learned very well what he taught me." (Note the similarity to "My teacher learned me English good,"—a phrasing that *does* upset a few teachers.)

"O, hold thy tongue, thou limmer loon,
  And of thy talking let me be!
If thou doest not end me this quarrel soon,
  There is my glove, I'll fight wi' thee."

"worthless lout"

Then Christie Graeme he stoopèd low
  Unto the ground, you shall understand.
"O father, put on your glove again
  The wind has blown it from your hand."

"What's that thou sayest, thou limmer loon?
  How darest thou stand to speak to me?
If thou dost not end this quarrel soon,
  There's my right hand, thou shalt fight with me."

Then Christie Graeme's to his chamber gane,
  To consider well what then should be;
Whether he should fight with his old father,
  Or with his billy Bewick, he.

"If I should kill my billy dear,
  God's blessing I shall never win;
But if I strike at my old father,
  I think 'twould be a mortal sin.

"And if I kill my billy dear,
  That is God's will, so let it be;
But I make a vow, ere I gang from hame,
  That I shall be the next man dee.°"

°HEAD: name

°DEE: to die

Then he's put on his back a good old jack,°
And on his head a cap of steel,
And sword and buckler by his side;
O, gin he did not become them weel!

We'll leave off talking of Christie Graeme,
And talk of him again belive; "by and by"
And we will talk of bonny Bewick,
Where he was teaching his scholars five.

When he had taught them well to fence,
And handle swords without any doubt,
He took his ain sword under his arm,
And he walked his father's close° about.

He looked between him and the sun,
And all to espy what there might be,
Till he saw a man in armour bright,
Was riding that way most hastily.

"O, who is yon, that comes this way.
So hastily that hither came?
I think it be my brother dear,
I think it be young Christie Graeme.

"Ye're welcome here, my billy dear,
And thrice ye're welcome unto me!"
"But I'm woe to say, I've seen the day
When I am come to fight with thee.

"My father's gane to Carlisle town,
With your father Bewick there met he:
He says I'm a lad, and I am but bad,
And a baffled man I trow I be. "believe"

"He sent me to school, and I would not learn;
He bought me books, and I would not read;
So my father's blessing I'll never earn,
Till he see how my arm can save his head!"

°JACK: coat of mail

°CLOSE: garden

"O, God forbid, my billy dear,
  That ever such a thing should be!
We'll take three men on either side,
  And see if we can our fathers agree."

"O, hold thy tongue now, billy Bewick,
  And of thy talking let me be!
But if thou'rt a man, as I'm sure thou art,
  Come o'er the dyke, and fight with me."

"But I have no harness, billy, on my back,
  As well I see is now on thine."
"But as little harness as is on thy back,
  As little, billy, shall be on mine."

Then he's thrown off his coat of mail,
  His cap of steel away flung he;
He stuck his spear into the ground,
  And he tied his horse unto a tree.

Then Bewick has thrown off his cloak,
  And his psalter-book from his hand flung he;
He laid his hand upon the dyke,
  And over he leapt most manfully.

O, they have fought for twa lang hours;
  When twa lang hours were come and gane,
The sweat drapped fast from off them both,
  But a drop of blood could not be seen.

Till Graeme gave Bewick an awkward stroke,
  An awkward stroke strucken sickerly;°
He has hit him under the left breast,
  And dead-wounded to the ground fell he.

"Rise up, rise up now, billy dear,
  Arise and speak three words to me!
Whether thou hast gotten thy deadly wound,
  Or if God and good leeching may succour thee?"

"On horse, on horse now, billy Graeme,
  And get thee far from hence with speed;
And get thee out of this countrie,
  That none may know who has done the deed."

°SICKERLY: surely

"O, I have slain thee, billy Bewick,
  If this be true thou tellest to me;
But I made a vow, ere I came from hame,
  That aye the next man I would be."

He has pitched his sword in a moodie-hill,°
  And he has leapt twenty lang feet and three,
And on his own sword's point he leapt,
  And dead upon the ground fell he.

'Twas then came up Sir Robert Bewick,
  And his brave alive saw he;
"Rise up, rise up, my son," he said.
  "For I think ye have gotten the victory."

"O, hold your tongue, my father dear,
  Of your prideful talking let me be!
Ye might have drunken your wine in peace,
  And let your son and his billy be.

"Go, dig a grave, both wide and deep,
  And a grave to hold both him and me;
But lay Christie Graeme on the sunny side,
  For I'm sure he won the victory."

"Alack! O, woe!" old Bewick cried,
  "Alack! was I not much to blame?
I'm sure I have lost the liveliest lad
  That e'er was born unto my name."

"Alack! O, woe!" quoth good Lord Graeme,
  "I'm sure I have lost the deeper lack!
I durst have ridden the Border through,
  Had Christie Graeme been at my back.

"Had I been led through Liddesdale,
  And thirty horsemen guarding me,
And Christie Graeme been at my back,
  So soon would he have set me free!

"I've lost my hopes, I've lost my joy,
  I've lost the key but and the lock; "and also"
I durst have ridden the world around,
  Had Christie Graeme been at my back."

°MOODIE-HILL: mole hill

Come On, Good Fellowe, Make an End . . .

Anonymous

DEATH

Come on, good fellowe, make an end,
for you and I must talke;
You may noe longer soiburne here, "i" for "j"
but hence you must goe walke.

YOUTH

What wofull wordes, alas,
be theise that I do heare?
Alas, and shall I now forthewith
forsake my lyfe so deare?

DEATH

Come on, come on, and lynger not,
ye tryfle but the tyme;
Ye make too muche of that, Iwis,°
which is but dirt and slyme.

YOUTH

O cursèd death, what dost thou mean,
so cruell for to be,
To him that neuer thought thee harm
nor once offended thee?

O death, behold; I am but younge
and of a pleasaunt age:
Take thou some old and crokèd wight,
and spare me in thy rage.

Behold, my lymmes be lyvely now, "limbs"
my mynd and courage strong, Probably "heart"
And by the verdit of all men "verdict"
lyke to continew long;

°Iwis: indeed

My bewty like the rose so red,
  my heare like glistring gold; —
"hair"
And canst thou now of pity then
  transforme me into molde?

O gentle death, be not extreme;
  thy mercy heare I craue;
It is not for thyne honor nowe
  to fetche me to my grave:

But rather let me lyve a while,
  till youth consumèd be, —
When crookèd age doth me opres,
  then welcome death to me.

DEATH

O foolishe man, what dost thou meane
  to strive against the streame?
Nothing there is that can thee nowe
  out of my handes redeame.

Thy time is past, thy daies are gone,
  thy race is fully runne;
Thou must of force nowe make an end,
  as thou hadst onse begunne.

O foole, why dost thou beag and boast
  of theise thy youthfull dayes? —
Which passeth fast and fadeth swifte,
  as flowers freshe decayes.

Both youth and age to me be one —
  I care not whome I stryke:
The child, the man, the father old,
  doe I reward alyke.

The proudest of them all, Iwis,
  can not escape my darte:
The lady fayre, the lazer fowlle,
  shall both posses a parte.

Thou art not nowe the first, I say,
  that I have earèd° vppe;
Ne yet shalt be the last, pardy,
  that drincketh of my cuppe;

For he that doth vs now behold, —
  perusing this our talke, —
He knoweth not yet how sone, god wot,
  with thee and me to walke!

Dispatche, therfore, and make an end,
  for needes you must obey;
And as thou camest into this world,
  so shalt thou nowe away.

YOUTH

And must I passe out of this world
  in-dede, and shall I soe?
May noe man me restrayn a while,
  but needes nowe must I goe?

Why, then, farewell my lyfe and landes,
  adiew my pleasures all!
Loe dredfull deth doth vs departe,°
  and me away doth call.

My chearfull dayes be worne a-way,
  my pleasaunt tyme is past,
My youthfull yeares are spent and gone,
  my lyfe it may not last;

And I (for lacke of lyfe and breath)
  whose like hath not bene sene,
Shall straight consumèd be to dust,
  as I had never bene.

But thoughe I yeld as now to thee,
    when nothing me can save,
Yet I am sure that I shall lyve
  when thou thy death shalt haue.

Finis

°EARÈD: ploughed up

°DEPARTE: separate

Ode to Billy Joe

BOBBIE GENTRY

It was the third of June, another sleepy, dusty, delta day,
I was out choppin' cotton and my brother was bailin' hay;
And at dinner time we stopped and walked back to the house to eat,
And Mama hollered at the back door, "Y'all remember to wipe your feet."
Then she said, "I got some news this mornin' from Choctaw Ridge,
Today Billy Joe McAllister jumped off the Tallahatchee Bridge."

Papa said to Mama, as he passed around the black-eyed peas,
"Well, Billy Joe never had a lick o' sense, pass the biscuits please,
There's five more acres in the lower forty I've got to plow,"
And Mama said it was a shame about Billy Joe anyhow.
Seems like nothin' ever comes to no good up on Choctaw Ridge,
And now Billy Joe McAllister's jumped off the Tallahatchee Bridge.

Brother said he recollected when he and Tom and Billy Joe,
Put a frog down my back at the Carroll County picture show,
And wasn't I talkin' to him after Church last Sunday night,
I'll have another piece of apple pie, you know, it don't seem right.
I saw him at the sawmill yesterday on Choctaw Ridge,
And now you tell me Billy Joe's jumped off the Tallahatchee Bridge.

Mama said to me, "Child, what's happened to your appetite?
I been cookin' all mornin' and you haven't touched a single bite,
That nice young preacher Brother Taylor dropped by today,
Said he'd be pleased to have dinner on Sunday. Oh, by the way,
He said he saw a girl that looked a lot like you up on Choctaw Ridge
And she an' Billy Joe was throwin' somethin' off the Tallahatchee Bridge."

A year has come and gone since we heard the news 'bout Billy Joe,
Brother married Becky Thompson, they bought a store in Tupelo,
There was a virus goin' 'round, Papa caught it and he died last spring,
And now Mama doesn't seem to want to do much of anything.
And me I spend a lot of time pickin' flowers up on Choctaw Ridge,
And drop them into the muddy water off the Tallahatchee Bridge.

AN CAISIDEACH BÂN
(Fair Cassidy)

Donagh MacDonagh

I left my prayers and the kneeling pilgrims
And went wild running down the holy Reek
And all who saw me said: "That is Cassidy
Who abandoned God for a girl's cheek."

The first time I saw her I was a student
Reading my prayer-book, I raised my eyes
But they betrayed me, raced to embrace her,
And I had not slept at the next sunrise.

When I was at college they taught me English
And praised my accent, but with that first sight
The only language that I knew was love-talk
And all my thoughts were turned to birds in flight.

I have no land, no stock nor money
To win that girl to me, I cannot pray,
But I'd mount the Reek on my bleeding knees
If I could have her on her wedding-day.

She could cheat my heart to believe in marvels,
That no grass would grow, that no moon would shine,
That the stars are lightless, that she could love me;
And oh! Christ in Heaven that she were mine.

The sun will cool and the moon will darken
And fishes swim in an empty sea,
The floods will rise above the mountains
And Cassidy still be in slavery.

She passes by and I curse the mother
Who bore that daughter to torture me—
Ah sweet, if we could elope together
I'd risk my neck on the gallows tree.

There is no hill and there's no valley,
No road, no bog that she passes by
But is filled with music, heart-breaking music,
And may Christ have mercy on Cassidy.

All in green went my love riding

e. e. cummings

All in green went my love riding
on a great horse of gold
into the silver dawn.

four lean hounds crouched low and smiling
the merry deer ran before.

Fleeter be they than dappled dreams
the swift sweet deer
the red rare deer.

Four red roebuck at a white water
the cruel bugle sang before.

Horn at hip went my love riding
riding into the echo down
into the silver dawn.

four lean hounds crouched low and smiling
the level meadows ran before.

Softer be they than slippered sleep
the lean lithe deer
the fleet flown deer.

Four fleet does at a gold valley
the famished arrow sang before.

Bow at belt went my love riding
riding the mountain down
into the silver dawn.

four lean hounds crouched low and smiling
the sheer peaks ran before.

Paler be they than daunting death
the sleek slim deer
the tall tense deer.

Four tall stags at a green mountain
the lucky hunter sang before.

All in green went my love riding
on a great horse of gold
into the silver dawn.

four lean hounds crouched low and smiling
my heart fell dead before.

INTERLOCK WITH CLUSTER 8:
A topical link: thoughts of love

"Sumer is icumen in,
Lhude sing cuccu!
Groweth sed, and bloweth med,
And springeth the wude nu—
Sing cuccu!"

"Cuccu, cuccu, well singes thu, cuccu:
Ne swike thu naver nu;
Sing cuccu, nu, sing cuccu,
Sing cuccu, sing cuccu, nu!"

"What the hell do you suppose that was all about?"

8

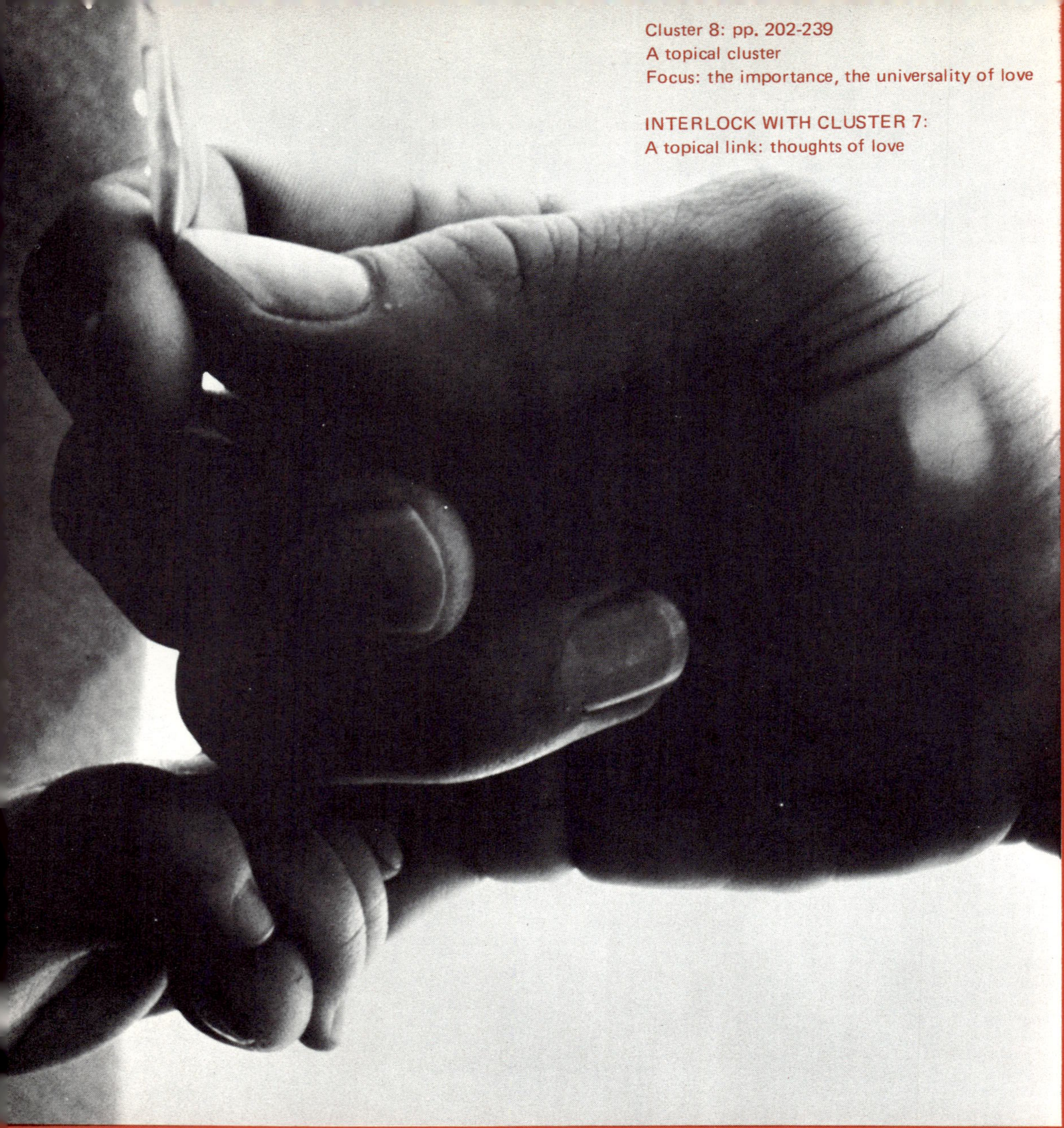

Cluster 8: pp. 202-239
A topical cluster
Focus: the importance, the universality of love

INTERLOCK WITH CLUSTER 7:
A topical link: thoughts of love

love is a
love is a bit
love is a bitter
love is a bitter mist
love is a bitter mystery
love is a bitter mystery
love is a bitter mist
love is a bitter
love is a bit
love is a

In the Midnight Hour

Adrian Henri

When we meet
in the midnight hour
country girl
I will bring you nightflowers
colored like your eyes
in the moonlight
in the midnight
hour

I remember

Your cold hand
held for a moment among strangers
held for a moment among dripping trees
in the midnight hour

I remember

Your eyes colored like the autumn landscape
walking down muddy lanes
watching sheep eating yellow roses
walking in city squares in winter rain.

kissing in darkened hallways
walking in empty suburban streets
saying goodnight in deserted alleyways

in the midnight hour

Andy Williams singing "We'll Keep a Welcome
in the Hillsides" for us
When I meet you at the station
The Beatles singing "We Can Work It Out" with
James Ensor at the harmonium
Rita Hayworth in a nightclub singing "Amade Mia"

I will send you armadas
of love vast argosies of flowers
in the midnight hour
country girl

when we meet

in the
moonlight
midnight
hour
country girl

I will bring you

yellow
white
eyes
bright
moon
light
mid
night
flowers

in the midnight hour.

The Sick Rose

O Rose, thou art sick!
The invisible worm,
That flies in the night,
In the howling storm,

Has found out thy bed
Of crimson joy;
And his dark secret love
Does thy life destroy.

—William Blake

My Last Duchess

Robert Browning

Ferrara

That's my last Duchess painted on the wall,
Looking as if she were alive. I call
That piece a wonder, now: Fra Pandolf's hands
Worked busily a day, and there she stands.
Will't please you sit and look at her? I said
"Fra Pandolf" by design, for never read   Past tense
Strangers like you that pictured countenance,
The depth and passion of its earnest glance,
But to myself they turned (since none puts by
The curtain I have drawn for you, but I)
And seemed as they would ask me, if they durst,
How such a glance came there; so, not the first
Are you to turn and ask thus. Sir, 'twas not
Her husband's presence only, called that spot
Of joy into the Duchess' cheek: perhaps
Fra Pandolf chanced to say, "Her mantle laps
Over my lady's wrist too much," or "Paint
Must never hope to reproduce the faint

Half-flush that dies along her throat"; such stuff
Was courtesy, she thought, and cause enough
For calling up that spot of joy. She had
A heart—how shall I say?—too soon made glad,
Too easily impressed; she liked whate'er
She looked on, and her looks went everywhere.
Sir, 'twas all one! My favor at her breast,
The dropping of the daylight in the west,
The bough of cherries some officious fool
Broke in the orchard for her, the white mule
She rode with round the terrace—all and each
Would draw from her alike the approving speech,
Or blush, at least. She thanked men—good! but thanked
Somehow—I know not how—as if she ranked
My gift of a nine-hundred-years-old name
With anybody's gift. Who'd stoop to blame
This sort of trifling? Even had you skill
In speech—(which I have not)—to make your will
Quite clear to such an one, and say, "Just this
Or that in you disgusts me; here you miss,
Or there exceed the mark"—and if she let
Herself be lessoned so, nor plainly set
Her wits to yours, forsooth, and made excuse,
—E'en then would be some stooping; and I choose
Never to stoop. Oh sir, she smiled, no doubt,
Whene'er I passed her; but who passed without
Much the same smile? This grew; I gave commands;
Then all smiles stopped together. There she stands
As if alive. Will't please you rise? We'll meet
The company below, then. I repeat,
The Count your master's known munificence
Is ample warrant that no just pretence
Of mine for dowry will be disallowed;
Though his fair daughter's self, as I avowed
At starting, is my object. Nay, we'll go
Together down, sir. Notice Neptune, though,
Taming a sea horse, thought a rarity,
Which Claus of Innsbruck cast in bronze for me!

Editor: That Ferrara is a possessive tyrant!

Literary Sort: But it was the Duchess' heart that was "too soon made glad"!

Editor: Yes, but who said that?

Here is a modern man, jealous of another heart
too soon made glad. . . .
There is a reconciliation. But afterwards?

The White Stocking

D. H. Lawrence

I

"I'm getting up, Teddilinks," said Mrs. Whiston, and she sprang out of bed briskly.

"What the Hanover's got you?" asked Whiston.

"Nothing. Can't I get up?" she replied animatedly.

It was about seven o'clock, scarcely light yet in the cold bedroom. Whiston lay still and looked at his wife. She was a pretty little thing, with her fleecy, short black hair all tousled. He watched her as she dressed quickly, flicking her small, delightful limbs, throwing her clothes about her. Her slovenliness and untidiness did not trouble him. When she picked up the edge of her petticoat, ripped off a torn string of white lace, and flung it on the dressing-table, her careless abandon made his spirit glow. She stood before the mirror and roughly scrambled together her profuse little mane of hair. He watched the quickness and softness of her young shoulders, calmly, like a husband, and appreciatively.

"Rise up," she cried, turning to him with a quick wave of her arm—"and shine forth."

They had been married two years. But still, when she had gone out of the room, he felt as if all his light and warmth were taken away, he became aware of the raw, cold morning. So he rose himself, wondering casually what had roused her so early. Usually she lay in bed as late as she could.

Note!

Whiston fastened a belt round his loins and went downstairs in shirt and trousers. He heard her singing in her snatchy fashion. The stairs creaked under his weight. He passed down the narrow little passage, which she called a hall, of the seven and sixpenny house which was his first home.

Rent per week

He was a shapely young fellow of about twenty-eight, sleepy now and easy with well-being. He heard the water drumming into the kettle, and she began to whistle. He loved the quick way she dodged the supper cups under the tap to wash them for breakfast. She looked an untidy

She is somewhat pretentious. In British usage, a hall is a large room.

An independent, flirtatious young woman

minx, but she was quick and handy enough.

"Teddilinks," she cried.

"What?"

"Light a fire, quick."

She wore an old, sack-like dressing-jacket of black silk pinned across her breast. But one of the sleeves, coming unfastened, showed some delightful pink upper-arm.

"Why don't you sew your sleeve up?" he said, suffering from the sight of the exposed soft flesh.

and stimulated by

"Where?" she cried, peering round. "Nuisance," she said, seeing the gap, then with light fingers went on drying the cups.

The kitchen was of fair size, but gloomy. Whiston poked out the dead ashes.

Suddenly a thud was heard at the door down the passage.

"I'll go," cried Mrs. Whiston, and she was gone down the hall.

The postman was a ruddy-faced man who had been a soldier. He smiled broadly, handing her some packages.

"They've not forgot you," he said impudently.

"No—lucky for them," she said, with a toss of the head. But she was interested only in her envelopes this morning. The postman waited inquisitively, smiling in an ingratiating fashion. She slowly, abstractedly, as if she did not know anyone was there, closed the door in his face, continuing to look at the addresses on her letters.

She tore open the thin envelope. There was a long, hideous, cartoon valentine. She smiled briefly and dropped it on the floor. Struggling with the string of a packet, she opened a white cardboard box, and there lay a white silk handkerchief packed neatly under the paper lace of the box, and her initial, worked in heliotrope, fully displayed. She smiled pleasantly, and gently put the box aside. The third envelope contained another white packet—apparently a cotton handkerchief neatly folded. She shook it out. It was a long white stocking, but there was a little weight in the toe. Quickly, she thrust down her arm, wriggling her fingers into the toe of the stocking, and brought out a small box. She peeped inside the box, then hastily opened a door on her left hand, and went into the little cold sitting-room. She had her lower lip caught earnestly between her teeth.

With a little flash of triumph, she lifted a pair of pearl earrings from the small box, and she went to the mirror. There, earnestly, she began to hook them through her ears, looking at herself sideways in the glass. Curiously concentrated and intent she seemed as she fingered the lobes of her ears, her head bent on one side.

Then the pearl earrings dangled under her rosy, small ears. She shook her head sharply, to see the swing of the drops. They went chill against her neck, in little, sharp touches. Then she stood still to look at herself, bridling her head in the dignified fashion. Then she simpered at herself. Catching her own eye, she could not help winking at herself and laughing.

Drawing her head up and chin in. To do so, "in the dignified fashion," must mean "as a person of social rank would." A reference to her pretentiousness again.

She turned to look at the box. There was a scrap of paper with this posy:

"Pearls may be fair, but
thou art fairer.
Wear these for me, and
I'll love the wearer."

She made a grimace and a grin. But she was drawn to the mirror again, to look at her earrings.

Whiston had made the fire burn, so he came to look for her. When she heard him, she started round quickly, guiltily. She was watching him with intent blue eyes when he appeared.

He did not see much, in his morning-drowsy warmth. He gave her, as ever, a feeling of warmth and slowness. His eyes were very blue, very kind, his manner simple.

"What ha' you got?" he asked.

"Valentines," she said briskly, ostentatiously turning to show him the silk handkerchief. She thrust it under his nose. "Smell how good," she said.

"Who's that from?" he replied, without smelling.

"It's a valentine," she cried. "How do I know who it's from?"

"I'll bet you know," he said.

"Ted!—I don't!" she cried, beginning to shake her head, then stopping because of the earrings.

He stood still a moment, displeased.

"They've no right to send you valentines now," he said.

"Ted!—Why not? You're not jealous, are you? I haven't the least idea who it's from. Look—there's my initial"—she pointed with an emphatic finger at the heliotrope embroidery—

"E for Elsie,
Nice little gelsie,"

"girlie"

she sang.

"Get out," he said. "You know who it's from."

"Truth, I don't," she cried.

He looked round, and saw the white stocking lying on a chair.

"Is this another?" he said.

"No, that's a sample," she said. "There's only a comic." And she fetched in the long cartoon.

He stretched it out and looked at it solemnly.

"Fools!" he said, and went out of the room.

She flew upstairs and took off the earrings. When she returned, he was crouched before the fire blowing the coals. The skin of his face was flushed, and slightly pitted, as if he had had smallpox. But his neck was white and smooth and goodly. She hung her arms round his neck as he crouched there, and clung to him. He balanced on his toes.

"This fire's a slow-coach," he said.

"And who else is a slow-coach?" she said.

"One of us two, I know," he said, and he rose carefully. She remained clinging round his neck, so that she was lifted off her feet.

"Ha!—swing me," she cried.

He lowered his head, and she hung in the air, swinging from his neck, laughing. Then she slipped off.

"The kettle is singing," she sang, flying for the teapot. He bent down again to blow the fire. The veins in his neck stood out, his shirt collar seemed too tight.

"Doctor Wyer,
Blow the fire,
Puff! puff! puff!"

she sang, laughing.

He smiled at her.

She was so glad because of her pearl earrings.

Over the breakfast she grew serious. He did not notice. She became portentous in her gravity. Almost it penetrated through his steady good humor to irritate him.

"Teddy!" she said at last.

"What?" he asked.

"I told you a lie," she said, humbly tragic.

His soul stirred uneasily.

"Oh, aye?" he said casually.

She was not satisfied. He ought to be more moved.

"Yes," she said.

He cut a piece of bread.

"Was it a good one?" he asked.

She was piqued. Then she considered—*was* it a good one? Then she laughed.

"No," she said, "it wasn't up to much."

"Ah!" he said easily, but with a steady strength of fondness for her in his tone. "Get it out then."

It became a little more difficult.

"You know that white stocking," she said earnestly. "I told you a lie. It wasn't a sample. It was a valentine."

A little frown came on his brow.

"Then what did you invent it as a sample for?" he said. But he knew this weakness of hers. The touch of anger in his voice frightened her.

"I was afraid you'd be cross," she said pathetically.

"I'll bet you were vastly afraid," he said.

"I *was,* Teddy."

There was a pause. He was resolving one or two things in his mind.

"And who sent it?" he asked.

"I can guess," she said, "though there wasn't a word with it—except—"

She ran to the sitting-room and returned with a slip of paper.

"Pearls may be fair, but
thou art fairer.
Wear these for me, and
I'll love the wearer."

He read it twice, then a dull red flush came on his face.

"And *who* do you guess it is?" he asked, with a ringing of anger in his voice.

"I suspect it's Sam Adams," she said, with a little virtuous indignation.

Whiston was silent for a moment.

"Fool!" he said. "An' what's it got to do with pearls?—and how can he say 'wear these for me' when there's only one? He hasn't got the brain to invent a proper verse."

The humor here adds an interesting dimension to Teddy's character. Is it surface humor? Is there something more intense and less controlled behind it? (See *Talks,* p. 53.)

He screwed the slip of paper into a ball and flung it into the fire.

"I suppose he thinks it'll make a pair with the one last year," she said.

"Why, did he send one then?"

"Yes. I thought you'd be wild if you knew."

His jaw set rather sullenly.

Presently he rose, and went to wash himself, rolling back his sleeves and pulling open his shirt at the breast. It was as if his fine, clear-cut temples and steady eyes were degraded by the lower, rather brutal part of his face. But she loved it.

As she whisked about, clearing the table, she loved the way in which he stood washing himself. He was such a man. She liked to see his neck glistening with water as he swilled it. It amused her and pleased her and thrilled her. He was so sure, so permanent, he had her so utterly in his power. It gave her a delightful, mischievous sense of liberty. Within his grasp, she could dart about excitingly.

British: "to clean by flooding with water"

He turned round to her, his face red from the cold water, his eyes fresh and very blue.

"You haven't been seeing anything of him, have you?" he asked roughly.

"Yes," she answered, after a moment, as if caught guilty. "He got into the tram with me, and he asked me to drink a coffee and a Benedictine in the Royal."

"You've got it off fine and glib," he said sullenly. "And did you?"

"Yes," she replied, with the air of a traitor before the rack.

The blood came up into his neck and face, he stood motionless, dangerous.

"It was cold, and it was such fun to go into the Royal," she said.

"You'd go off with a nigger for a packet of chocolate," he said, in anger and contempt, and some bitterness. Queer how he drew away from her, cut her off from him.

Compare with note on p. 211.

"Ted—how beastly!" she cried. "You know quite well—" She caught her lip, flushed, and the tears came to her eyes.

He turned away, to put on his necktie. She went about her work, making a queer pathetic little mouth, down which occasionally dripped a tear.

He was ready to go. With his hat jammed down on his head, and his overcoat buttoned up to his chin, he came to kiss her. He would be miserable all the day if he went without. She allowed herself to be kissed. Her cheek was wet under his lip, and his heart burned. She hurt him so deeply. And she felt aggrieved, and did not quite forgive him.

In a moment she went upstairs to her earrings. Sweet they looked nestling in the little drawer—sweet! She examined them with voluptuous pleasure, she threaded them in her ears, she looked at herself, she posed and postured and smiled and looked sad and tragic and winning and appealing, all in turn before the mirror. And she was happy, and very pretty.

She wore her earrings all morning, in the house. She was self-conscious, and quite brilliantly winsome, when the baker came, wondering if he'd notice. All the tradesmen left her door with a glow in them, feeling elated, and unconsciously favoring the delightful little creature, though there had been nothing to notice in her behavior.

She was stimulated all the day. She did not think about her husband. He was the permanent basis from which she took these giddy little flights into nowhere. At night, like chickens and curses, she would come home to him, to roost.

Meanwhile Whiston, a traveler and confidential support of a small firm, hastened about his work, his heart all the while anxious for her, yearning for surety, and kept tense by not getting it.

"salesm

II

She had been a warehouse girl in Adams's lace factory before she was married. Sam Adams was her employer. He was a bachelor of forty, growing stout, a man well dressed and florid, with a large brown moustache and thin hair. From the rest of his well-groomed, showy appearance, it was evident his baldness was a chagrin to him. He had a good presence, and some Irish blood in his veins.

Note transition in time.

His fondness for the girls, or the fondness of the girls for him, was notorious. And Elsie, quick, pretty, almost witty little thing—she *seemed* witty, although, when her sayings were repeated, they were entirely trivial—she had a great attraction for him. He would come into the warehouse dressed in a rather sporting reefer coat, of fawn color, and trousers of fine black-and-white check, a cap with a big peak and scarlet carnation in his button-hole, to impress her. She was only half impressed. He was too loud for her good taste. Instinctively perceiving this, he sobered down to navy blue. Then a well-built man, florid, with large brown whiskers, smart navy blue suit, fashionable boots, and manly hat, he was the irreproachable. Elsie was impressed.

But meanwhile Whiston was courting her, and she made splendid little gestures, before her bedroom mirror, of the constant-and-true sort.

"True, true till death—"

That was her song. Whiston was made that way, so there was no need to take thought for him.

Perhaps, as far as Lawrence was concerned, it was "good taste."

Every Christmas Sam Adams gave a party at his house, to which he invited his superior work-people—not factory hands and laborers, but those above. He was a generous man in his way, with a real warm feeling for giving pleasure.

Two years ago Elsie had attended this Christmas party for the last time. Whiston had accompanied her. At that time he worked for Sam Adams.

She had been very proud of herself, in her close-fitting, full-skirted dress of blue silk. Whiston called for her. Then she tripped beside him, holding her large cashmere shawl across her breast. He strode with long strides, his trousers handsomely strapped under his boots, and her silk shoes bulging the pocket of his full-skirted overcoat.

They passed through the park gates, and her spirits rose. Above them the Castle Rock loomed grandly in the night, the naked trees stood still and dark in the frost, along the boulevard.

in Nottingham

They were rather late. Agitated with anticipation, in the cloak-room she gave up her shawl, donned her silk shoes, and looked at herself in the mirror. The loose bunches of curls on either side her face danced prettily, her mouth smiled.

She hung a moment in the door of the brilliantly lighted room. Many people were moving within the blaze of lamps, under the crystal chandeliers, the full skirts of the women balancing and floating, the side-whiskers and white cravats of the men bowing above. Then she entered the light.

In an instant Sam Adams was coming forward, lifting both his arms in boisterous welcome. There was a constant red laugh on his face.

"Come late, would you," he shouted, "like royalty."

He seized her hands and led her forward. He opened his mouth wide when he spoke, and the effect of the warm, dark opening behind the brown whiskers was disturbing. But she was floating into the throng on his arm. He was very gallant.

He can fill her whole card, have every dance, if he wants.

"Now then," he said, taking her card to write down the dances, "I've got *carte blanche,* haven't I?"

"Mr. Whiston doesn't dance," she said.

"I am a lucky man!" he said, scribbling his initials. "I was born with an *amourette* in my mouth."

Ambiguous here, but probably means "little love object" or "mistress." In any event, Lawrence is using the word to excite, especially in context with their sensual word play about "mouth." Two flittering flirts here, and Lawrence subtly conveys that sensuality without destroying its effect.

He wrote on, quietly. She blushed and laughed, not knowing what it meant.

"Why, what is that?" she said.

"It's you, even littler than you are, dressed in little wings," he said.

"I should have to be pretty small to get in your mouth," she said.

"You think you're too big, do you!" he said easily.

He handed her her card, with a bow.

"Now I'm set up, my darling, for this evening," he said.

Then, quick, always at his ease, he looked over the room. She waited in front of him. He was ready. Catching the eye of the band, he nodded. In a moment, the music began. He seemed to relax, giving himself up.

"Now then, Elsie," he said, with a curious caress in his voice that seemed to lap the outside of her body in a warm glow, delicious. She gave herself to it. She liked it.

He was an excellent dancer. He seemed to draw her close in to him by some male warmth of attraction, so that she became all soft and pliant to him, flowing to his form, whilst he united her with him and they lapsed along in one movement. She was just carried in a kind of strong, warm flood, her feet moved of themselves, and only the music threw her away from him, threw her back to him, to his clasp, in his strong form moving against her, rhythmically, deliciously.

When it was over, he was pleased and his eyes had a curious gleam which thrilled her and yet had nothing to do with her. Yet it held her. He did not speak to her. He only looked straight into her eyes with a curious, gleaming look that disturbed her fearfully and deliciously. But also there was in his look some of the automatic irony of the *roué*.° It left her partly cold. She was not carried away.

She went, driven by an opposite, heavier impulse, to Whiston. He stood looking gloomy, trying to admit that she had a perfect right to enjoy herself apart from him. He received her with rather grudging kindliness.

"Aren't you going to play whist?" she asked.

"Aye," he said. "Directly."

"I do wish you could dance."

"Well, I can't," he said. So you enjoy yourself."

"But I should enjoy it better if I could dance with you."

"Nay, you're all right," he said. "I'm not made that way."

°ROUÉ: a rake, a man devoted to sensual pleasure

"Then you ought to be!" she cried.

"Well, it's my fault, not yours. You enjoy yourself," he bade her. Which she proceeded to do, a little bit irked.

She went with anticipation to the arms of Sam Adams, when the time came to dance with him. It *was* so gratifying, irrespective of the man. And she felt a little grudge against Whiston, soon forgotten when her host was holding her near to him, in a delicious embrace. And she watched his eyes, to meet the gleam in them, which gratified her.

She was getting warmed right through, the glow was penetrating into her, driving away everything else. Only in her heart was a little tightness, like conscience.

When she got a chance, she escaped from the dancing-room to the cardroom. There, in a cloud of smoke, she found Whiston playing cribbage. Radiant, roused, animated, she came up to him and greeted him. She was too strong, too vibrant a note in the quiet room. He lifted his head, and a frown knitted his gloomy forehead.

"Are you playing cribbage? Is it exciting? How are you getting on," she chattered.

He looked at her. None of these questions needed answering, and he did not feel in touch with her. She turned to the cribbage-board.

"Are you white or red?" she asked.

"He's red," replied the partner.

"Then you're losing," she said, still to Whiston. And she lifted the red peg from the board. "One—two—three—four—five—six—seven—eight— Right up there you ought to jump—"

"Now put it back in its right place," said Whiston.

"Where was it?" she asked gaily, knowing her transgression. He took the little red peg away from her and stuck it in its hole.

The cards were shuffled.

"What a shame you're losing," said Elsie.

"You'd better cut for him," said the partner.

She did so hastily. The cards were dealt. She put her hand on his shoulder, looking at his cards.

"It's good," she cried, "isn't it?"

He did not answer, but threw down two cards. It moved him more strongly than was comfortable, to have her hand on his shoulder, her curls dangling and touching his ears, whilst she was roused to another man. It made the blood flame over him.

At that moment Sam Adams appeared, florid and boisterous, intoxicated more with himself, with the dancing, than with wine. In his eye the curious, impersonal light gleamed.

"I thought I should find you here, Elsie," he cried boisterously, a disturbing, high note in his voice.

"What made you think so?" she replied, the mischief rousing in her.

The florid, well-built man narrowed his eyes to a smile.

"I should never look for you among the ladies," he said, with a kind of intimate, animal call to her.

He laughed, bowed, and offered her his arm.

"Madam, the music waits."

She went almost helplessly, carried along with him, unwilling, yet delighted.

That dance was an intoxication to her. After the first few steps, she felt herself slipping away from herself. She almost knew she was going, she did not even want to go. Yet she must have chosen to go. She lay in the arm of the steady, close man with whom she was dancing, and she seemed to swim away out of contact with the room, into him. She had passed into another, denser element of him, an essential privacy. The room was all vague around her, like an atmosphere, like under sea, with a flow of ghostly, dumb movements. But she herself was held real against her partner, and it seemed she was connected with him, as if the movements of his body and limbs were her own movements, yet not her own movements—and oh, delicious! He also was given up, oblivious, concentrated, into the dance. His eye was unseeing. Only his large, voluptuous body gave off a subtle activity. His fingers seemed to search into her flesh. Every moment, and every moment, she felt she would give way utterly, and sink molten: the fusion point was coming when she would fuse down into perfect unconsciousness at his feet and knees. But he bore her round the room in the dance, and he seemed to sustain all her body with his limbs, his body, and his warmth seemed to come closer into her, nearer, till it would fuse right through her, and she would be as liquid to him as an intoxication only.

It was exquisite. When it was over, she was dazed, and was scarcely breathing. She stood with him in the middle of the room as if she were alone in a remote place. He bent over her. She expected his lips on her bare shoulder, and waited. Yet they were not alone, they were not alone. It was cruel.

"'Twas good, wasn't it, my darling?" he said to her, low and delighted. There was a strange impersonality about his low, exultant call that appealed to her irresistibly. Yet why was she aware of some part shut off in her? She pressed his arm, and he led her towards the door.

She was not aware of what she was doing, only a little grain of resistant trouble was in her. The man, possessed, yet with a superficial presence of mind, made way to the dining room, as if to give her refreshment, cunningly working to his own escape with her. He was molten hot, filmed over with presence of mind, and bottomed with cold disbelief. In the dining room was Whiston, carrying coffee to the plain, neglected ladies. Elsie saw him, but felt as if he could not see her. She was beyond his reach and ken. A sort of fusion existed between her and the large man at her side. She ate her custard, but an incomplete fusion all the while sustained and contained within the being of her employer.

But she was growing cooler. Whiston came up. She looked at him, and saw him with different eyes. She saw his slim, young man's figure real and enduring before her. That was he. But she was in the spell with the other man, fused with him, and she could not be taken away.

"Have you finished your cribbage?" she asked, with hasty evasion of him.

"Yes," he replied. "Aren't you getting tired of dancing?"

"Not a bit," she said.

"Not she," said Adams heartily. "No girl with any spirit gets tired of dancing. Have something else, Elsie. Come—sherry. Have a glass of sherry with us, Whiston."

Whilst they sipped the wine, Adams watched Whiston almost cunningly, to find his advantage.

"We'd better be getting back—there's the music," he said. "See the women get something to eat, Whiston, will you, there's a good chap."

And he began to draw away. Elsie was drifting helplessly with him. But Whiston put himself beside them, and went along with them. In silence they passed through to the dancing-room. There Adams hesitated, and looked round the room. It was as if he could not see.

A man came hurrying forward, claiming Elsie, and Adams went to his other partner. Whiston stood watching during the dance. She was conscious of him standing there observant of her, like a ghost, or a judgment, or a guardian angel. She was also conscious, much more intimately and impersonally, of the body of the other man moving somewhere in the room. She still belonged to him, but a feeling of distraction possessed her, and helplessness. Adams danced on, adhering to Elsie, waiting his time, with the persistence of cynicism.

The dance was over. Adams was detained. Elsie found herself beside Whiston. There was something shapely about him as he sat, about his knees and his distinct figure, that she clung to. It was as if he had enduring form. She put her hand on his knee.

"Are you enjoying yourself?" he asked.

"*Ever* so," she replied, with a fervent, yet detached tone.

"It's going on for one o'clock," he said.

"Is it?" she answered. It meant nothing to her.

"Should we be going?" he said.

She was silent. For the first time for an hour or more an inkling of her normal consciousness returned. She resented it.

"What for?" she said.

"I thought you might have had enough," he said.

A slight soberness came over her, an irritation at being frustrated of her illusion.

"Why?" she said.

"We've been here since nine," he said.

That was no answer, no reason. It conveyed nothing to her. She sat detached from him. Across the room Sam Adams glanced at her. She sat there exposed for him.

"You don't want to be too free with Sam Adams," said Whiston cautiously, suffering. "You know what he is."

"How, free?" she asked.

"Why—you don't want to have too much to do with him."

She sat silent. He was forcing her into consciousness of her position. But he could not get hold of her feelings, to change them. She had a curious, perverse desire that he should not.

"I like him," she said.

"What do you find to like in him?" he said, with a hot heart.

"I don't know—but I like him," she said.

She was immutable. He sat feeling heavy and dulled with rage. He was not clear as to what he felt. He sat there unliving whilst she danced. And she, distracted, lost to herself between the opposing forces of the two men, drifted. Between the dances, Whiston kept near to her. She was scarcely conscious. She glanced repeatedly at her card, to see when she would dance again with Adams, half in desire, half in dread. Sometimes she met his steady, glaucous eye as she passed him in the dance. Sometimes she saw the steadiness of his flank as he danced. And it was always as if she rested on his arm, were borne along, upborne by him, away from herself. And always there was present the other's antagonism. She was divided.

The time came for her to dance with Adams. Oh, the delicious closing of contact with him, of his limbs touching her limbs, his arm supporting her. She seemed to resolve. Whiston had not made himself real to her. He was only a heavy place in her consciousness.

But she breathed heavily, beginning to suffer from the closeness of strain. She was nervous. Adams also was constrained. A tightness, a tension was coming over them all. And he was exasperated, feeling something counteracting physical magnetism, feeling a will stronger with her than his own, intervening in what was becoming a vital necessity to him.

Elsie was almost lost to her own control. As she went forward with him to take her place at the dance, she stooped for her pocket handkerchief. The music sounded for quadrilles. Everybody was ready. Adams stood with his body near her, exerting his attraction over her. He was tense and fighting. She stooped for her pocket handkerchief, and shook it as she rose. It shook out and fell from her hand. With agony, she saw she had taken a white stocking instead of a handkerchief. For a second it lay on the floor, a twist of white stocking. Then, in an instant, Adams picked it up, with a little, surprised laugh of triumph.

"That'll do for me," he whispered—seeming to take possession of her. And he stuffed the stocking in his trousers pocket, and quickly offered her his handkerchief.

The dance began. She felt weak and faint, as if her will were turned to water. A heavy sense of loss came over her. She could not help herself any more. But it was peace.

When the dance was over, Adams yielded her up. Whiston came to her.

"What was it as you dropped?" Whiston asked.

"I thought it was my handkerchief—I'd taken a stocking by mistake," she said, detached and muted.

"And he's got it?"

"Yes."

"What does he mean by that?"

She lifted her shoulders.

"Are you going to let him keep it?" he asked.

"I don't let him."

There was a long pause.

"Am I to go and have it out with him?" he asked, his face flushed, his blue eyes going hard with opposition.

"No," she said, pale.

"Why?"

"No—I don't want you to say anything about it."

He sat exasperated and nonplussed.

"You'll let him keep it, then?" he asked.

She sat silent and made no form of answer.

"What do you mean by it?" he said, dark with fury. And he started up.

"No!" she cried. "Ted!" And she caught hold of him, sharply detaining him.

It made him black with rage.

"Why?" he said.

The something about her mouth was pitiful to him. He did not understand, but he felt she must have her reasons.

"Then I'm not stopping here," he said. "Are you coming with me?"

She rose mutely, and they went out of the room. Adams had not noticed.

In a few moments they were in the street.

"What the hell do you mean?" he said, in a black fury.

She went at his side, in silence, neutral.

"That great hog, an' all," he added.

Then they went a long time in silence through the frozen, deserted darkness of the town. She felt she could not go indoors. They were drawing near her house.

"I don't want to go home," she suddenly cried in distress and anguish. "I don't want to go home."

He looked at her.

"Why don't you?" he said.

"I don't want to go home," was all she could sob.

He heard somebody coming.

"Well, we can walk a bit farther," he said.

She was silent again. They passed out of the town into the fields. He held her by the arm—they could not speak.

"What's a-matter?" he asked at length, puzzled.

She began to cry again.

At last he took her in his arms, to soothe her. She sobbed by herself, almost unaware of him.

"Tell me what's a-matter, Elsie," he said. "Tell me what's a-matter—my dear—tell me, then—"

He kissed her wet face, and caressed her. She made no response. He was puzzled and tender and miserable.

At length she became quiet. Then he kissed her, and she put her arms round him, and clung to him very tight, as if for fear and anguish. He held her in his arms, wondering.

"Ted!" she whispered, frantic. "Ted!"

"What, my love?" he answered, becoming also afraid.

"Be good to me," she cried. "Don't be cruel to me."

"No, my pet," he said, amazed and grieved. "Why?"

"Oh, be good to me," she sobbed.

And he held her very safe, and his heart was white-hot with love for her. His mind was amazed. He could only hold her against his chest that was white-hot with love and belief in her. So she was restored at last.

III

She refused to go to her work at Adams's any more. Her father had to submit and she sent in her notice—she was not well. Sam Adams was ironical. But he had a curious patience. He did not fight.

In a few weeks, she and Whiston were married. She loved him with passion and worship, a fierce little abandon of love that moved him to the depths of his being, and gave him a permanent surety and sense of realness in himself. He did not trouble about himself any more: he felt he was fulfilled and now he had only the many things in the world to busy himself about. Whatever troubled him, at the bottom was surety. He had found himself in this love.

They spoke once or twice of the white stocking.

"Ah!" Whiston exclaimed. "What does it matter?"

He was impatient and angry, and could not bear to consider the matter. So it was left unresolved.

She was quite happy at first, carried away by her adoration of her husband. Then gradually she got used to him. He always was the ground of her happiness, but she got used to him, as to the air she breathed. He never got used to her in the same way.

Inside of marriage she found her liberty. She was rid of the responsibility of herself. Her husband must look after that. She was free to get what she could out of her time.

So that, when, after some months, she met Sam Adams, she was not quite as unkind to him as she might have been. With a young wife's new and exciting knowledge of men, she perceived he was in love with her, she knew he had always kept an unsatisfied desire for her. And, sportive, she could not help playing a little with this, though she cared not one jot for the man himself.

When Valentine's day came, which was near the first anniversary of her wedding day, there arrived a white stocking with a little amethyst brooch. Luckily Whiston did not see it, so she said nothing of it to him. She had not the faintest intention of having anything to do with Sam Adams, but once a little brooch was in her possession, it was hers, and she did not trouble her head for a moment how she had come by it. She kept it.

Now she had the pearl earrings. They were a more valuable and a more conspicuous present. She would have to ask her mother to give them to her, to explain their presence. She made a little plan in her head. And she was extraordinarily pleased. As for Sam Adams, even if he saw her wearing them, he would not give her away. What fun, if he saw her wearing his earrings!

Note time.

Note shift in time again; picks up where time on page 212 stopped.

There is a suggestion that Elsie's mother's family is from a somewhat higher level in society than her father's. So Lawrence and his mother felt about her family.

She would pretend she had inherited them from her grandmother, her mother's mother. She laughed to herself as she went downtown in the afternoon, the pretty drops dangling in front of her curls. But she saw no one of importance.

Whiston came home tired and depressed. All day the male in him had been uneasy, and this had fatigued him. She was curiously against him, inclined, as she sometimes was nowadays, to make mock of him and jeer at him and cut him off. He did not understand this, and it angered him deeply. She was uneasy before him.

She knew he was in a state of suppressed irritation. The veins stood out on the backs of his hands, his brow was drawn stiffly. Yet she could not help goading him.

"What did you do wi' that white stocking?" he asked, out of a gloomy silence, his voice strong and brutal.

"I put it in a drawer—why?" she replied flippantly.

"Why didn't you put it on the fire-back?" he said harshly. "What are you hoarding it up for?"

"I'm not hoarding it up," she said. "I've got a pair."

He relapsed into gloomy silence. She, unable to move him, ran away upstairs, leaving him smoking by the fire. Again she tried on the earrings. Then another little inspiration came to her. She drew on the white stockings, both of them.

Presently she came down in them. Her husband still sat immovable and glowering by the fire.

"Look!" she said. "They'll do beautifully."

And she picked up her skirts to her knees, and twisted round, looking at her pretty legs in the neat stockings.

He filled with unreasonable rage, and took the pipe from his mouth.

"Don't they look nice?" she said. "One from last year and one from this, they just do. Save you buying a pair."

And she looked over her shoulders at her pretty calves, and at the dangling frills of her knickers.

"Put your skirts down and don't make a fool of yourself," he said.

"Why a fool of myself?" she asked.

And she began to dance slowly round the room, kicking up her feet half reckless, half jeering, in ballet dancer's fashion. Almost fearful, yet in defiance, she kicked up her legs at him, singing as she did so. She resented him.

"You little fool, ha' done with it," he said. "And you'll backfire them stockings, I'm telling you." He was angry. His face flushed dark, he kept his head bent. She ceased to dance.

"I shan't," she said. "They'll come in very useful."

He lifted his head and watched her, with lighted, dangerous eyes.

"You'll put 'em on the fire-back, I tell you," he said.

It was a war now. She bent forward, in a ballet dancer's fashion, and put her tongue between her teeth.

"I shan't back-fire them stockings," she sang, repeating his words, "I shan't, I shan't, I shan't."

And she danced round the room doing a high kick to the tune of her words. There was a real biting indifference in her behavior.

"We'll see whether you will or not," he said, "trollop! You'd like Sam Adams to know you was wearing 'em, wouldn't you? That's what would please you."

"Yes, I'd like him to see how nicely they fit me, he might give me some more then."

And she looked down at her pretty legs.

He knew somehow that she *would* like Sam Adams to see how pretty her legs looked in the white stockings. It made his anger go deep, almost to hatred.

"Yer nasty trolley," he cried. "Put yer petticoats down, and stop being so foul-minded."

222

"I'm not foul-minded," she said. "My legs are my own. And why shouldn't Sam Adams think they're nice?"

There was a pause. He watched her with eyes glittering to a point.

"Have you been havin' owt to do with him?" he asked.

Note that in anger his speech becomes dialect. Is Lawrence suggesting anything here?

"I've just spoken to him when I've seen him," she said. "He's not as bad as you would make out."

"Isn't he?" he cried, a certain wakefulness in his voice. "Them who has anything to do wi' him is too bad for me, I tell you."

"Why, what are you frightened of him for?" she mocked.

She was rousing all his uncontrollable anger. He sat glowering. Every one of her sentences stirred him up like a red-hot iron. Soon it would be too much. And she was afraid herself; but she was neither conquered nor convinced.

A curious little grin of hate came on his face. He had a long score against her.

"What am I frightened of him for?" he repeated automatically. "What am I frightened of him for? Why, for you, you stray-running little bitch."

She flushed. The insult went deep into her, right home.

"Well, if you're so dull—" she said, lowering her eyelids, and speaking coldly, haughtily.

"If I'm so dull I'll break your neck the first word you speak to him," he said, tense.

"Pf!" she sneered. "Do you think I'm frightened of you?" She spoke coldly, detached.

She was frightened, for all that, white round the mouth.

His heart was getting hotter.

"You *will* be frightened of me, the next time you have anything to do with him," he said.

"Do you think *you'd* ever be told—ha!"

Her jeering scorn made him go white-hot, molten. He knew he was incoherent, scarcely responsible for what he might do. Slowly, unseeing, he rose and went out of doors, stifled, moved to kill her.

He stood leaning against the garden fence, unable either to see or hear. Below him, far off, fumed the lights of the town. He stood still, unconscious with a black storm of rage, his face lifted to the night.

Presently, still unconscious of what he was doing, he went indoors again. She stood, a small, stubborn figure with tight-pressed lips and big, sullen, childish eyes, watching him, white with fear. He went heavily across the floor and dropped into his chair.

There was a silence.

"*You're* not going to tell me everything I shall do, and everything I shan't," she broke out at last.

He lifted his head.

"I tell you *this,*" he said, low and intense. "Have anything to do with Sam Adams, and I'll break your neck."

She laughed, shrill and false.

"How I hate your word 'break your neck'," she said, with a grimace of the mouth. "It sounds so common and beastly. Can't you say something else—"

There was a dead silence.

"And besides," she said, with a queer chirrup of mocking laughter, "what do you know about anything? He sent me an amethyst brooch and a pair of pearl earrings."

"He what?" said Whiston, in a suddenly normal voice. His eyes were fixed on her.

"Sent me a pair of pearl earrings, and an amethyst brooch," she repeated, mechanically, pale to the lips.

And her big, black, childish eyes watched him, fascinated, held in her spell.

He seemed to thrust his face and his eyes forward at her, as he rose slowly and came to her. She watched transfixed in terror. Her throat made a small sound, as she tried to scream.

Then, quick as lightning, the back of his hand struck her with a crash across the mouth, and she was flung black-blinded against the wall. The shock shook a queer sound out of her. And then she saw him still coming on, his eyes holding her, his fist drawn back, advancing slowly. At any instant the blow might crash into her.

Mad with terror, she raised her hands with a queer clawing movement to cover her eyes and her temples, opening her mouth in a dumb shriek. There was no sound. But the sight of her slowly arrested him. He hung before her, looking at her fixedly, as she stood crouched against the wall with open, bleeding mouth, and wide-staring eyes, and two hands clawing over her temples. And his lust to see her bleed, to break her and destroy her, rose from an old source against her. It carried him. He wanted satisfaction.

But he had seen her standing there, a piteous, horrified thing, and he turned his face aside in shame and nausea. He went and sat heavily in his chair, and a curious ease, almost like sleep, came over his brain.

She walked away from the wall towards the fire, dizzy, white to the lips, mechanically wiping her small, bleeding mouth. He sat motionless. Then, gradually, her breath began to hiss, she shook, and was sobbing silently, in grief for herself. Without looking, he saw. It made his mad desire to destroy her come back.

At length he lifted his head. His eyes were glowing again, fixed on her.

"And what did he give them you for?" he asked, in a steady, unyielding voice.

Her crying dried up in a second. She also was tense.

"They came as valentines," she replied, still not subjugated, even if beaten.

"When, today?"

"The pearl earrings today—the amethyst brooch last year."

"You've had it a year?"

"Yes."

She felt that now nothing would prevent him if he rose to kill her. She could not prevent him any more. She was yielded up to him. They both trembled in the balance, unconscious.

"What have you had to do with him?" he asked, in a barren voice.

"I've not had anything to do with him," she quavered.

"You just kept 'em because they were jewelry?" he said.

A weariness came over him. What was the worth of speaking any more of it? He did not care any more. He was dreary and sick.

She began to cry again, but he took no notice. She kept wiping her mouth on her handkerchief. He could see it, the blood-mark. It made him only more sick and tired of the responsibility of it, the violence, the shame.

When she began to move about again, he raised his head once more from his dead, motionless position.

"Where are the things?" he said.

"They are upstairs," she quavered. She knew the passion had gone down in him.

"Bring them down," he said.

"I won't," she wept, with rage. "You're not going to bully me and hit me like that on the mouth."

And she sobbed again. He looked at her in contempt and compassion and in rising anger.

"Where are they?" he said.

"They're in the little drawer under the looking-glass," she sobbed.

He went slowly upstairs, struck a match, and found the trinkets. He brought them downstairs in his hand.

"These?" he said, looking at them as they lay in his palm.

She looked at them without answering. She was not interested in them any more.

He looked at the little jewels. They were pretty.

"It's none of their fault," he said to himself.

The kind of line (and knowledge of human beings) that makes a great author.

And he searched round slowly, persistently, for a box. He tied the things up and addressed them to Sam Adams. Then he went out in his slippers to post the little package.

When he came back she was still sitting crying.

"You'd better go to bed," he said.

She paid no attention. He sat by the fire. She still cried.

"I'm sleeping down here," he said. "Go you to bed."

In a few moments she lifted her tear-stained, swollen face and looked at him with eyes all forlorn and pathetic. A great flash of anguish went over his body. He went over, slowly, and very gently took her in his hands. She let herself be taken. Then as she lay against his shoulder, she sobbed aloud:

"I never meant—"

"My love—my little love—" he cried, in anguish of spirit, holding her in his arms.

The River-Merchant's Wife: A Letter

Li T'ai Po

While my hair was still cut straight across my forehead
I played about the front gate, pulling flowers.
You came by on bamboo stilts, playing horse,
You walked about my seat, playing with blue plums.
And we went on living in the village of Chokan:
Two small people, without dislike or suspicion.

At fourteen I married My Lord, you.
I never laughed, being bashful.
Lowering my head, I looked at the wall.
Called to, a thousand times, I never looked back.

At fifteen I stopped scowling,
I desired my dust to be mingled with yours
Forever and forever and forever.
Why should I climb the lookout?

At sixteen you departed,
You went into far Ku-to-yen, by the river of swirling eddies,
And you have been gone five months.
The monkeys make sorrowful noise overhead.

You dragged your feet when you went out.
By the gate now, the moss is grown, the different mosses,
Too deep to clear them away!
The leaves fall early this autumn, in wind.
The paired butterflies are already yellow with August
Over the grass in the West garden;
They hurt me. I grow older.
If you are coming down through the narrows of the river Kiang,
Please let me know beforehand,
And I will come out to meet you
As far as Cho-fu-Sa.

—Translated by Ezra Pound

Leda and the Swan

A sudden blow: the great wings beating still
Above the staggering girl, her thighs caressed
By the dark webs, her nape caught in his bill,
He holds her helpless breast upon his breast.

How can those terrified vague fingers push
The feathered glory from her loosening thighs?
And how can body, laid in that white rush,
But feel the strange heart beating where it lies?

A shudder in the loins engenders there
The broken wall, the burning roof and tower
And Agamemnon dead.
                    Being so caught up,
So mastered by the brute blood of the air,
Did she put on his knowledge with his power
Before the indifferent beak could let her drop?

—William Butler Yeats

Literary Sort: I have always *loved* that poem.

Editor: That's nice, but does the poem make much sense if you don't know who Helen was?

Literary Sort: What does *she* have to do with it? The poem doesn't mention her.

Editor: No, but it refers to "Agamemnon dead," and he certainly wouldn't have been killed by his wife Clytemnestra (who, by the way, was Helen's half-sister) if he hadn't gone off to the Trojan Wars to rescue the captured Helen.

Literary Sort: But Yeats doesn't mention Helen in *this* poem?

Editor: Oh, she's in there all right. You see, the swan who rapes Leda is really the god Zeus. And according to the myth, the offspring was Helen.

Literary Sort: Oh, I see now. This poem is just packed with facts.

Editor: No . . . not really. But "Agamemnon dead" does bring to mind the whole myth.

This poem shows that the cultivated Greeks, even in the sixth century B.C., found some fun at least in the *story* of Helen's birth.

People Do Gossip

Sappho

People do gossip

And they say about
Leda, that she

Once found an egg
hidden under

wild hyacinths

—*Translated by Mary Barnard*

I Knew a Woman

I knew a woman, lovely in her bones,
When small birds sighed, she would sigh back at them;
Ah, when she moved, she moved more ways than one:
The shapes a bright container can contain!
Of her choice virtues only gods should speak,
Or English poets who grew up on Greek
(I'd have them sing in chorus, cheek to cheek).

How well her wishes went! She stroked my chin,
She taught me Turn, and Counter-turn, and Stand;
She taught me Touch, that undulant white skin;
I nibbled meekly from her proffered hand;
She was the sickle; I, poor I, the rake,
Coming behind her for her pretty sake
(But what prodigious mowing we did make).

Love likes a gander, and adores a goose:
Her full lips pursed, the errant note to seize;
She played it quick, she played it light and loose;
My eyes, they dazzled at her flowing knees;
Her several parts could keep a pure repose,
Or one hip quiver with a mobile nose
(She moved in circles, and those circles moved).

Let seed be grass, and grass turn into hay:
I'm martyr to a motion not my own;
What's freedom for? To know eternity.
I swear she cast a shadow white as stone.
But who would count eternity in days?
These old bones live to learn her wanton ways:
(I measure time by how a body sways).

—Theodore Roethke

Upon Julia's Clothes

When as in silks my *Julia* goes,
Then, then (me thinks) how sweetly flowes
That liquefaction of her clothes.

Next, when I cast mine eyes and see
That brave Vibration each way free;
O how that glittering taketh me!

—*Robert Herrick*

love is more thicker than forget

e. e. cummings

love is more thicker than forget
more thinner than recall
more seldom than a wave is wet
more frequent than to fail

it is most mad and moonly
and less it shall unbe
than all the sea which only — The antecedent is "it," not "sea."
is deeper than the sea

love is less always than to win
less never than alive
less bigger than the least begin
less littler than forgive

it is most sane and sunly
and more it cannot die
than all the sky which only — The antecedent is "it," not "sky."
is higher than the sky

MY OEDIPUS COMPLEX

Frank O'Connor

Father was in the army all through the war—the first war, I mean—so, up to the age of five, I never saw much of him, and what I saw did not worry me. Sometimes I woke and there was a big figure in khaki peering down at me in the candlelight. Sometimes in the early morning I heard the slamming of the front door and the clatter of nailed boots down the cobbles of the lane. These were Father's entrances and exits. Like Santa Claus he came and went mysteriously.

In fact, I rather liked his visits, though it was an uncomfortable squeeze between Mother and him when I got into the big bed in the early morning. He smoked, which gave him a pleasant musty smell, and shaved, an operation of astounding interest. Each time he left a trail of souvenirs—model tanks and Gurkha knives with handles made of bullet cases, and German helmets and cap badges and button-sticks, and all sorts of military equipment—carefully stowed away in a long box on top of the wardrobe, in case they ever came in handy. There was a bit of the magpie about Father; he expected everything to come in handy. When his back was turned, Mother let me get a chair and rummage through his treasures. She didn't seem to think so highly of them as he did.

The war was the most peaceful period of my life. The window of my attic faced southeast. My mother had curtained it, but that had small effect. I always woke with the first light and, with all the responsibilities of the previous day melted, feeling myself rather like the sun, ready to illumine and rejoice. Life never seemed so simple and clear and full of possibilities as then. I put my feet out from under the clothes—I called them Mrs. Left and Mrs. Right—and invented dramatic situations for them in which they discussed the problems of the day. At least Mrs. Right did; she was very demonstrative, but I hadn't the same control of Mrs. Left, so she mostly contented herself with nodding agreement.

They discussed what Mother and I should do during the day, what Santa Claus should give a fellow for Christmas, and what steps should be taken to brighten the home. There was that little matter of the baby, for instance. Mother and I could never agree about that. Ours was the only house in the terrace without a new baby, and Mother said we couldn't afford one till Father came back from the war because they cost seventeen and six. That showed how simple she was. The Geneys up the road had a baby, and everyone knew they couldn't afford seventeen and six. It was probably a cheap baby, and Mother wanted something really good, but I felt she was too exclusive. The Geneys' baby would have done us fine.

Seventeen pounds and six shillings; about $41.52

Having settled my plans for the day, I got up, put a chair under the attic window, and lifted the frame high enough to stick out my head. The window overlooked the front gardens of the terrace behind ours, and beyond these it looked over a deep valley to the tall, redbrick houses terraced up the opposite hillside, which were all still in shadow, while those at our side of the valley were all lit up, though with long strange shadows that made them seem unfamiliar—rigid and painted.

After that I went into Mother's room and climbed into the big bed. She woke and I began to tell her of my schemes. By this time, though I never seem to have noticed it, I was petrified in my nightshirt, and I thawed as I talked until, the last frost melted, I fell asleep beside her and woke again only when I heard her below in the kitchen, making the breakfast.

After breakfast we went into town; heard Mass at St. Augustine's and said a prayer for Father, and did the shopping. If the afternoon was fine we either went for a walk in the country or a visit to Mother's great friend in the convent, Mother St. Dominic. Mother had them all praying for Father, and every night, going to bed, I asked God to send him back safe from the war to us. Little, indeed, did I know what I was praying for!

One morning, I got into the big bed, and there, sure enough, was Father in his usual Santa Claus manner, but later, instead of uniform, he put on his best blue suit, "streetcars"

and Mother was as pleased as anything. I saw nothing to be pleased about, because, out of uniform, Father was altogether less interesting, but she only beamed, and explained that our prayers had been answered, and off we went to Mass to thank God for having brought Father safely home.

The irony of it! That very day when he came in to dinner he took off his boots and put on his slippers, donned the dirty old cap he wore about the house to save him from colds, crossed his legs, and began to talk gravely to Mother, who looked anxious. Naturally, I disliked her looking anxious, because it destroyed her good looks, so I interrupted him.

"Just a moment, Larry!" she said gently.

This was only what she said when we had boring visitors, so I attached no importance to it and went on talking.

"Do be quiet, Larry!" she said impatiently. "Don't you hear me talking to Daddy?"

This was the first time I had heard those ominous words, "talking to Daddy," and I couldn't help feeling that if this was how God answered prayers, he couldn't listen to them very attentively.

"Why are you talking to Daddy?" I asked with as great a show of indifference as I could muster.

"Because Daddy and I have business to discuss. Now, don't interrupt again!"

In the afternoon, at Mother's request, Father took me for a walk. This time we went into town instead of out the country, and I thought at first, in my usual optimistic way, that it might be an improvement. It was nothing of the sort. Father and I had quite different notions of a walk in town. He had no proper interest in trams, ships, and horses, and the only thing that seemed to divert him was talking to fellows as old as himself. When I wanted to stop he simply went on, dragging me behind him by the hand; when he wanted to stop I had no alternative but to do the same. I noticed that it seemed to be a sign that he wanted to stop for a long time whenever he leaned against a wall. The second time I saw him do it I got wild. He seemed to be settling himself forever. I pulled him by the coat and trousers, but, unlike Mother, who, if you were too persistent, got into a wax and said: "Larry, if you don't behave yourself, I'll give you a good slap," Father had an extraordinary capacity for amiable inattention. I sized him up and wondered would I cry, but he seemed to be too remote to be annoyed even by that. Really, it was like going for a walk with a mountain! He either ignored the wrenching and pummeling entirely, or else glanced down with a grin of amusement from his peak. I had never met anyone so absorbed in himself as he seemed.

At teatime, "talking to Daddy" began again, complicated this time by the fact that he had an evening paper, and every few minutes he put it down and told Mother some-

"got angry"

thing new out of it. I felt this was foul play. Man for man, I was prepared to compete with him any time for Mother's attention, but when he had it all made up for him by other people it left me no chance. Several times I tried to change the subject without success.

"You must be quiet while Daddy is reading, Larry," Mother said impatiently.

It was clear that she either genuinely liked talking to Father better than talking to me, or else that he had some terrible hold on her which made her afraid to admit the truth.

"Mummy," I said that night when she was tucking me up, "do you think if I prayed hard God would send Daddy back to the war?"

She seemed to think about that for a moment.

"No, dear," she said with a smile. "I don't think he would."

"Why wouldn't he, Mummy?"

"Because there isn't a war any longer, dear."

"But, Mummy, couldn't God make another war, if He liked?"

"He wouldn't like to, dear. It's not God who makes wars, but bad people."

"Oh!" I said.

I was disappointed about that. I began to think that God wasn't quite what he was cracked up to be.

Next morning I woke at my usual hour, feeling like a bottle of champagne. I put out my feet and invented a long conversation in which Mrs. Right talked of the trouble she had with her own father till she put him in the Home. I didn't quite know what the Home was but it sounded like the right place for Father. Then I got my chair and stuck my head out of the attic window. Dawn was just breaking, with a guilty air that made me feel I had caught it in the act. My head bursting with stories and schemes, I stumbled in next door, and in the half-darkness scrambled into the big bed. There was no room at Mother's side so I had to get between her and Father. For the time being I had forgotten about him, and for several minutes I sat bolt upright, racking my brains to know what I could do with him. He was taking up more than his fair share of the bed, and I couldn't get comfortable, so I gave him several kicks that made him grunt and stretch. He made room all right, though. Mother waked and felt for me. I settled back comfortably in the warmth of the bed with my thumb in my mouth.

"Mummy!" I hummed, loudly and contentedly.

"Sssh! dear," she whispered. "Don't wake Daddy!"

This was a new development, which threatened to be even more serious than "talking to Daddy." Life without my early-morning conferences was unthinkable.

"Why?" I asked severely.

"Because poor Daddy is tired."

This seemed to me a quite inadequate reason, and I was sickened by the sentimentality of her "poor Daddy." I never liked that sort of gush; it always struck me as insincere.

"Oh!" I said lightly. Then in my most winning tone: "Do you know where I want to go with you today, Mummy?"

"No, dear," she sighed.

"I want to go down the Glen and fish for thornybacks with my new net, and then I want to go out to the Fox and Hounds, and—"

"Don't-wake-Daddy!" she hissed angrily, clapping her hand across my mouth.

But it was too late. He was awake, or nearly so. He grunted and reached for the matches. Then he stared incredulously at his watch.

"Like a cup of tea, dear?" asked Mother in a meek, hushed voice I had never heard her use before. It sounded almost as though she were afraid.

"Tea?" he exclaimed indignantly. "Do you know what the time is?"

"And after that I want to go up the Rathcooney Road," I said loudly, afraid I'd forget something in all those interruptions.

"Go to sleep at once, Larry!" she said sharply.

I began to snivel. I couldn't concentrate, the way that pair went on, and smothering my early-morning schemes was like burying a family from the cradle.

Father said nothing, but lit his pipe and sucked it, looking out into the shadows without minding Mother or me. I knew he was mad. Every time I made a remark Mother hushed me irritably. I was mortified. I felt it wasn't fair; there was even something sinister in it. Every time I had pointed out to her the waste of making two beds when we could both sleep in one, she had told me it was healthier like that, and now here was this man, this stranger sleeping with her without the least regard for her health!

He got up early and made tea but though he brought Mother a cup he brought none for me.

"Mummy," I shouted, "I want a cup of tea, too."

"Yes, dear," she said patiently. "You can drink from Mummy's saucer."

That settled it. Either Father or I would have to leave the house. I didn't want to drink from Mother's saucer; I wanted to be treated as an equal in my own home, so, just to spite her, I drank it all and left none for her. She took that quietly, too.

But that night when she was putting me to bed she said gently:

"Larry, I want you to promise me something."

"What is it?" I asked.

"Not to come in and disturb poor Daddy in the morning. Promise?"

"Poor Daddy" again! I was becoming suspicious of everything involving that quite impossible man.

"Why?" I asked.

"Because poor Daddy is worried and tired and he doesn't sleep well."

"Why doesn't he, Mummy?"

"Well, you know, don't you, that while he was at the war

Mummy got the pennies from the Post Office?"

"From Miss MacCarthy?"

"That's right. But now, you see, Miss MacCarthy hasn't any more pennies, so Daddy must go out and find us some. You know what would happen if he couldn't?"

"No," I said, "tell us."

"Well, I think we might have to go out and beg for them like the poor old woman on Fridays. We wouldn't like that, would we?"

"No," I agreed. "We wouldn't."

"So you'll promise not to come in and wake him?"

"Promise."

Mind you, I meant that. I knew pennies were a serious matter, and I was all against having to go out and beg like the old woman on Fridays. Mother laid out all my toys in a complete ring round the bed so that, whatever way I got out, I was bound to fall over one of them.

When I woke I remembered my promise all right. I got up and sat on the floor and played—for hours, it seemed to me. Then I got my chair and looked out the attic window for more hours. I wished it was time for Father to wake; I wished someone would make me a cup of tea. I didn't feel in the least like the sun; instead, I was bored and so very, very cold! I simply longed for the warmth and depth of the big featherbed.

At last I could stand it no longer. I went into the next room. As there was still no room at Mother's side I climbed over her and she woke with a start.

"Larry," she whispered, gripping my arm very tightly, "what did you promise?"

"But I did, Mummy," I wailed, caught in the very act. "I was quiet for ever so long."

"Oh, dear, and you're perished!" she said sadly, feeling me all over. "Now, if I let you stay will you promise not to talk?"

"But I want to talk, Mummy," I wailed.

"That has nothing to do with it," she said with a firmness that was new to me. "Daddy wants to sleep. Now, do you understand that?"

I understood it only too well. I wanted to talk, he wanted to sleep—whose house was it, anyway?

"Mummy," I said with equal firmness, "I think it would be healthier for Daddy to sleep in his own bed."

That seemed to stagger her, because she said nothing for a while.

"Now, once for all," she went on, "you're to be perfectly quiet or go back to your own bed. Which is it to be?"

The injustice of it got me down. I had convicted her out of her own mouth of inconsistency and unreasonableness, and she hadn't even attempted to reply. Full of spite, I gave Father a kick, which she didn't notice but which made him grunt and open his eyes in alarm.

"What time is it?" he asked in a panic-stricken voice, not looking at Mother but at the door, as if he saw someone there.

"It's early yet," she replied soothingly. "It's only the child. Go to sleep again. . . . Now, Larry," she added, getting out of bed, "you've wakened Daddy and you must go back."

This time, for all her quiet air, I knew she meant it, and knew that my principal rights and privileges were as good as lost unless I asserted them at once. As she lifted me, I gave a screech, enough to wake the dead, not to mind Father. He groaned.

"That damn child! Doesn't he ever sleep?"

"It's only a habit, dear," she said quietly, though I could see she was vexed.

"Well, it's time he got out of it," shouted Father, beginning to heave in the bed. He suddenly gathered all the bedclothes about him, turned to the wall, and then looked back over his shoulder with nothing showing only two small, spiteful, dark eyes. The man looked very wicked.

To open the bedroom door, Mother had to let me down, and I broke free and dashed for the farthest corner, screeching. Father sat bolt upright in bed.

"Shut up, you little puppy!" he said in a choking voice.

I was so astonished that I stopped screeching. Never, never had anyone spoken to me in that tone before. I looked at him incredulously and saw his face convulsed with rage. It was only then that I fully realized how God had codded me, listening to my prayers for the safe return of this monster.

"Shut up, you!" I bawled, beside myself.

"What's that you said?" shouted Father, making a wild leap out of the bed.

"Mick, Mick!" cried Mother. "Don't you see the child isn't used to you?"

"I see he's better fed than taught," snarled Father, waving his arms wildly. "He wants his bottom smacked."

All his previous shouting was as nothing to these obscene words referring to my person. They really made my blood boil.

"Smack your own!" I screamed hysterically. "Smack your own! Shut up! Shut up!"

At this he lost his patience and let fly at me. He did it with the lack of conviction you'd expect of a man under Mother's horrified eyes, and it ended up as a mere tap, but the sheer indignity of being struck at all by a stranger, a total stranger who had cajoled his way back from the war into our big bed as a result of my innocent intercession, made me completely dotty. I shrieked and shrieked, and danced in my bare feet, and Father, looking awkward and hairy in nothing but a short grey army shirt, glared down at me like a mountain out for murder. I think it must have been then that I realized he was jealous too. And there stood Mother in her nightdress, looking as if her heart was broken between us. I hoped she felt as she looked. It seemed to me that she deserved it all.

From that morning out my life was a hell. Father and I were enemies, open and avowed. We conducted a series of skirmishes against one another, he trying to steal my time with Mother and I his. When she was sitting on my bed, telling me a story, he took to looking for some pair of old boots which he alleged he had left behind him at the beginning of the war. While he talked to Mother I played loudly with my toys to show my total lack of concern. He created a terrible scene one evening when he came in from work and found me at his box, playing with his regimental badges, Gurkha knives, and button-sticks. Mother got up and took the box from me.

"You mustn't play with Daddy's toys unless he lets you, Larry," she said severely. "Daddy doesn't play with yours."

For some reason Father looked at her as if she had struck him and then turned away with a scowl.

"Those are not toys," he growled, taking down the box again to see had I lifted anything. "Some of those curios are very rare and valuable."

But as time went on I saw more and more how he managed to alienate Mother and me. What made it worse was that I couldn't grasp his method or see what attraction he had for Mother. In every possible way he was less winning than I. He had a common accent and made noises at his tea. I thought for a while that it might be the newspapers she was interested in, so I made up bits of news of my own to read to her. Then I thought it might be the smoking, which I personally thought attractive, and took his pipes and went round the house dribbling into them till he caught me. I even made noises at my tea, but Mother only told me I was disgusting. It all seemed to hinge round that unhealthy habit of sleeping together, so I made a point of dropping into their bedroom and nosing round, talking to myself, so that they wouldn't know I was watching them, but they were never up to anything that I could see. In the end it beat me. It seemed to depend on being grown up and giving people rings, and I realized I'd have to wait.

But at the same time I wanted him to see that I was only waiting, not giving up the fight. One evening when he was being particularly obnoxious, chattering away well above my head, I let him have it.

"Mummy," I said, "do you know what I'm going to do when I grow up?"

"No, dear," she replied. "What?"

"I'm going to marry you," I said quietly.

Father gave a great guffaw out of him, but he didn't take me in. I knew it must only be pretense. And Mother, in spite of everything, was pleased. I felt she was probably relieved to know that one day Father's hold on her would be broken.

"Won't that be nice?" she said with a smile.

"It'll be very nice," I said confidently. "Because we're going to have lots and lots of babies."

"That's right, dear," she said placidly. "I think we'll have one soon, and then you'll have plenty of company."

I was no end pleased about that because it showed that in spite of the way she gave in to Father she still considered my wishes. Besides, it would put the Geneys in their place.

It didn't turn out like that, though. To begin with, she was very preoccupied—I suppose about where she would get the seventeen and six—and though Father took to staying out late in the evenings it did me no particular good. She stopped taking me for walks, became as touchy as blazes, and smacked me for nothing at all. Sometimes I wished I'd never mentioned the confounded baby—I seemed to have a genius for bringing calamity on myself.

And calamity it was! Sonny arrived in the most appalling hullabaloo—even that much he couldn't do without a fuss—and from the first moment I disliked him. He was a difficult child—so far as I was concerned he was always difficult—and demanded far too much attention. Mother was simply silly about him, and couldn't see when he was only showing off. As company he was worse than useless. He slept all day, and I had to go round the house on tiptoe to avoid waking him. It wasn't any longer a question of not waking Father. The slogan now was "Don't-wake-Sonny!" I couldn't understand why the child wouldn't sleep at the proper time, so whenever Mother's back was turned I woke him. Sometimes to keep him awake I pinched him as well. Mother caught me at it one day and gave me a most unmerciful flaking.

One evening, when Father was coming in from work, I was playing trains in the front garden. I let on not to notice him; instead, I pretended to be talking to myself, and said in a loud voice: "If another bloody baby comes into this house, I'm going out."

Father stopped dead and looked at me over his shoulder.

"What's that you said?" he asked sternly.

"I was only talking to myself," I replied, trying to conceal my panic. "It's private."

He turned and went in without a word. Mind you, I intended it as a solemn warning, but its effect was quite different. Father started being quite nice to me. I could understand that, of course. Mother was quite sickening about Sonny. Even at mealtimes she'd get up and gawk at him in the cradle with an idiotic smile, and tell Father to do the same. He was always polite about it, but he looked so puzzled you could see he didn't know what she was talking about. He complained of the way Sonny cried at night, but she only got cross and said that Sonny never cried except when there was something up with him—which was a flaming lie, because Sonny never had anything up with him, and only cried for attention. It was really painful to see how simple-minded she was. Father wasn't attractive, but he had a fine intelligence. He saw through Sonny, and now he knew that I saw through him as well.

One night I woke with a start. There was someone beside me in the bed. For one wild moment I felt sure it must be Mother, having come to her senses and left Father for good, but then I heard Sonny in convulsions in the next room, and Mother saying: "There! There! There!" and I knew it wasn't she. It was Father. He was lying beside me, wide awake, breathing hard and apparently as mad as hell.

After a while it came to me what he was mad about. It was his turn now. After turning me out of the big bed, he had been turned out himself. Mother had no consideration now for anyone but that poisonous pup, Sonny. I couldn't help feeling sorry for Father. I had been through it all myself, and even at that age I was magnanimous. I began to stroke him down and say: "There! There!" He wasn't exactly responsive.

"Aren't you asleep either?" he snarled.

"Ah, come on and put your arm around us, can't you?" I said, and he did, in a sort of way. Gingerly, I suppose, is how you'd describe it. He was very bony but better than nothing.

At Christmas he went out of his way to buy me a really nice model railway.

INTERLOCK WITH CLUSTER 9:
A topical link: relationships between parents and children

9

Cluster 9: pp. 240-279
A topical cluster
Focus: parent-child relationships

INTERLOCK WITH CLUSTER 8:
A topical link: relationships between parents and children

FROST AT MIDNIGHT

Samuel Taylor Coleridge

This poem is a soliloquy, a meditation, in which we follow Coleridge's thought about a present moment, his own past, the future he wants for his child. (Or perhaps it is the past that he wishes he had had.)

The Frost performs its secret ministry,
Unhelp'd by any wind. The owlet's cry
Came loud—and hark, again! loud as before.
The inmates of my cottage, all at rest,

> cottage: At Nether Stowey, near the residence of Thomas Poole, one of Coleridge's friends and patrons

Have left me to that solitude, which suits
Abstruser musings: save that at my side
My cradled infant slumbers peacefully.
'Tis calm indeed! so calm, that it disturbs
And vexes meditation with its strange
And extreme silentness. Sea, hill, and wood,
This populous village! Sea, and hill, and wood,
With all the numberless goings on of life,
Inaudible as dreams! the thin blue flame
Lies on my low burnt fire, and quivers not;
Only that film, which flutter'd on the grate,
Still flutters there, the sole unquiet thing.
Methinks, its motion in this hush of nature
Gives it dim sympathies with me who live,
Making it a companionable form,
To which the living spirit in our frame,
That loves not to behold a lifeless thing,
Transfuses its own pleasures, its own will.

How oft, at school, with most believing mind,
Presageful, have I gaz'd upon the bars,

> bars: Of the grate in his room or dormitory at Christ's Hospital School

To watch that fluttering *stranger!* and as oft
With unclosed lids, already had I dreamt
Of my sweet birth-place, and the old church-tower,
Whose bells, the poor man's only music, rang
From morn to evening, all the hot fair day,
So sweetly, that they stirred and haunted me
With a sweet pleasure, falling on mine ear
Most like articulate sounds of things to come!
So gaz'd I, till the soothing things, I dreamt,
Lull'd me to sleep, and sleep prolong'd my dreams!
And so I brooded all the following morn,

Aw'd by the stern preceptor's face, mine eye
Fix'd with mock study on my swimming book:
Save if the door half open'd, and I snatch'd
A hasty glance, and still my heart leapt up,
For still I hop'd to see the *stranger's* face,
Townsman, or aunt, or sister more beloved,
My play-mate when we both were cloth'd alike!

David Hartley Coleridge, born in September, 1796

Dear Babe, that sleepest cradled by my side,
Whose gentle breathings, heard in this dead calm,
Fill'd up the interspersed vacancies
And momentary pauses of the thought!
My Babe so beautiful! it fills my heart
With tender gladness, thus to look at thee,
And think that thou shalt learn far other lore
And in far other scenes! For I was rear'd
In the great city, pent 'mid cloisters dim,
And saw nought lovely but the sky and stars.
But *thou,* my babe! shalt wander like a breeze
By lakes and sandy shores, beneath the crags
Of ancient mountain, and beneath the clouds
Which image in their bulk both lakes and shores
And mountain crags: so shalt thou see and hear
The lovely shapes and sounds intelligible
Of that eternal language, which thy God
Utters, who from eternity doth teach
Himself in all, and all things in himself.
Great universal Teacher! he shall mould
Thy spirit, and by giving make it ask.

These lines are probably a very early reflection of plans to move to the Lake Country, as soon as Wordsworth could establish residence there.

Therefore all seasons shall be sweet to thee,
Whether the summer clothe the general earth
With greenness, or the redbreast sit and sing
Betwixt the tufts of snow on the bare branch
Of mossy apple-tree, while the nigh thatch
Smokes in the sun-thaw; whether the eve-drops fall,
Heard only in the traces of the blast,
Or if the secret ministry of frost
Shall hang them up in silent icicles,
Quietly shining to the quiet Moon.

Literary Sort: What a thoughtful, humane man.

Editor: But isn't he only a romantic dreamer?

MY PAPA'S WALTZ

The whiskey on your breath
Could make a small boy dizzy;
But I hung on like death:
Such waltzing was not easy.

We romped until the pans
Slid from the kitchen shelf;
My mother's countenance
Could not unfrown itself.

The hand that held my wrist
Was battered on one knuckle;
At every step you missed
My right ear scraped a buckle.

You beat time on my head
With a palm caked hard by dirt,
Then waltzed me off to bed
Still clinging to your shirt.

—Theodore Roethke

But they don't believe that God is going to touch these white people's hearts and change them tomorrow. Things change through action. By no other way.

The Sky Is Gray

Ernest J. Gaines

Go'n be coming in a few minutes. Coming 'round that bend down there full speed. And I'm go'n get out my hankercher and I'm go'n wave it down, and us go'n get on it and go.

A noteworthy piece of writing that sets both the time of the year and the cold; it's like describing a valley through the surrounding hills and deep shadows, without ever mentioning the valley.

I keep on looking for it, but Mama don't look that way no more. She looking down the road where us jest come from. It's a long old road, and far's you can see you don't see nothing but gravel. You got dry weeds on both sides, and you got trees on both sides, and fences on both sides, too. And you got cows in the pastures and they standing close together. And when us was coming out yer to catch the bus I seen the smoke coming out o' the cow's nose.

I look at my mama and I know what she thinking. I been with Mama so much, jest me and her, I know what she thinking all the time. Right now it's home—Auntie and them. She thinking if they got 'nough wood—if she left 'nough there to keep 'em warm till us get back. She thinking if it go'n rain and if any of 'em go'n have to go out in the rain. She thinking 'bout the hog—if he go'n get out, and if Ty and Val be able to get him back in. She always worry like that when she leave the house. She don't worry too much if she leave me there with the smaller ones 'cause she know I'm go'n look after 'em and look after Auntie and everything else. I'm the oldest and she say I'm the man.

See questions on page 264.

I look at my mama and I love my mama. She wearing that black coat and that black hat and she looking sad. I love my mama and I want put my arm 'round her and tell her. But I'm not s'pose to do that. She say that's weakness and that's cry-baby stuff, and she don't want no cry-baby 'round her. She don't want you to be scared neither. 'Cause Ty scared of ghosts and she always whipping him. I'm scared of the dark, too. But I make 'tend I ain't. I make 'tend I ain't 'cause I'm the oldest, and I got to set a good sample for the rest. I can't ever be scared and I can't ever cry. And that's the reason I didn't never say nothing 'bout my teef. It been hurting me and hurting me close to a month now.

But I didn't say it. I didn't say it 'cause I didn't want act like no cry-baby, and 'cause I know us didn't have 'nough money to have it pulled. But, Lord, it been hurting me. And look like it won't start till at night when you trying to get little sleep. Then soon's you shet your eyes—umm-umm, Lord, look like it go right down to your heart string.

"Hurting, hanh?" Ty'd say.

I'd shake my head, but I wouldn't open my mouth for nothing. You open your mouth and let that wind in, and it almost kill you.

I'd jest lay there and listen to 'em snore. Ty, there, right 'side me, and Auntie and Val over by the fireplace. Val younger 'an me and Ty, and he sleep with Auntie. Mama sleep 'round the other side with Louis and Walker.

I'd jest lay there and listen to 'em, and listen to that wind out there, and listen to that fire in the fireplace. Sometime it'd stop long enough to let me get little rest. Sometime it jest hurt, hurt, hurt. Lord, have mercy.

II

Auntie knowed it was hurting me. I didn't tell nobody but Ty, 'cause us buddies and he ain't go'n tell nobody. But some kind o' way Auntie found out. When she asked me, I told her no, nothing was wrong. But she knowed it all the time. She told me to mash up a piece o' aspirin and wrap it in some cotton and jugg it down in that hole. I did it, but it didn't do no good. It stopped for a little while, and started right back again. She wanted to tell Mama, but I told her Uh-uh. 'Cause I knowed it didn't have no money, and it jest was go'n make her mad again. So she told Monsieur Bayonne, and Monsieur Bayonne came to the house and told me to kneel down 'side him on the fireplace. He put his finger in his mouth and made the Sign of the Cross on my jaw. The tip of Monsieur Bayonne finger is some hard, 'cause he always playing on that guitar. If us sit outside at night us can always hear Monsieur Bayonne playing on his guitar. Sometime us leave him out there playing on the guitar.

He made the Sign of the Cross over and over on my jaw, but that didn't do no good. Even when he prayed and told me to pray some, too, that teef still hurt.

"How you feeling?" he say.

"Same," I say.

He kept on praying and making the Sign of the Cross and I kept on praying, too.

"Still hurting?" he say.

"Yes, sir."

Monsieur Bayonne mashed harder and harder on my jaw. He mashed so hard he almost pushed me on Ty. But then he stopped.

"What kind o' prayers you praying, boy?" he say.

"Baptist," I say.

"Well, I'll be—no wonder that teef still killing him. I'm going one way and he going the other. Boy, don't you know any Catholic prayers?"

"Hail Mary," I say.

"Then you better start saying it."

"Yes, sir."

He started mashing again, and I could hear him praying at the same time. And, sure 'nough, afterwhile it stopped.

Me and Ty went outside where Monsieur Bayonne two hounds was, and us started playing with 'em. "Let's go hunting," Ty say. "All right," I say; and us went on back in the pasture. Soon the hounds got on a trail, and me and Ty followed 'em all cross the pasture and then back in the woods, too. And then they cornered this little old rabbit and killed him, and me and Ty made 'em get back, and us picked up the rabbit and started on back home. But it had started hurting me again. It was hurting me plenty now, but I wouldn't tell Monsieur Bayonne. That night I didn't sleep a bit, and first thing in the morning Auntie told me go back and let Monsieur Bayonne pray over me some more. Monsieur Bayonne was in his kitchen making coffee when I got there. Soon's he seen me, he knowed what was wrong.

"All right, kneel down there 'side that stove," he say. "And this time pray Catholic. I don't know nothing 'bout Baptist, and don't want know nothing 'bout him."

III

Last night Mama say: "Tomorrow us going to town."

"It ain't hurting me no more," I say. "I can eat anything on it."

"Tomorrow us going to town," she say.

And after she finished eating, she got up and went to bed. She always go to bed early now. 'Fore Daddy went in the Army, she used to stay up late. All o' us sitting out on the gallery or 'round the fire. But now, look like soon's she finish eating she go to bed.

This morning when I woke up, her and Auntie was standing 'fore the fireplace. She say: " 'Nough to get there and back. Dollar and a half to have it pulled. Twenty-five for me to go, twenty-five for him. Twenty-five for me to come back, twenty-five for him. Fifty cents left. Guess I get a little piece o' salt meat with that."

"Sure can use a piece," Auntie say. "White beans and no salt meat ain't white beans."

"I do the best I can," Mama say.

They was quiet after that, and I made 'tend I was still sleep.

"James, hit the floor," Auntie say.

I still made 'tend I was sleep. I didn't want 'em to know I was listening.

"All right," Auntie say, shaking me by the shoulder. "Come on. Today's the day."

I pushed the cover down to get out, and Ty grabbed it and pulled it back.

"You, too, Ty," Auntie say.

"I ain't getting no teef pulled," Ty say.

"Don't mean it ain't time to get up," Auntie say. "Hit it, Ty."

Ty got up grumbling.

"James, you hurry up and get in your clothes and eat your food," Auntie say. "What time y'all coming back?" she say to Mama.

In parts of the U. S., especially the southern and border states, "evening" is a generally used term to designate the period between noon and dusk. The Mother can't afford to lose a full day's work.

"That 'leven o'clock bus," Mama say. "Got to get back in that field this evening."

"Get a move on you, James," Auntie say.

I went in the kitchen and washed my face, then I ate my breakfast. I was having bread and syrup. The bread was warm and hard and tasted good. And I tried to make it last a long time.

Ty came back there, grumbling and mad at me.

"Got to get up," he say. "I ain't having no teef pulled. What I got to be getting up for."

Ty poured some syrup in his pan and got a piece of bread. He didn't wash his hands, neither his face, and I could see that white stuff in his eyes.

"You the one getting a teef pulled," he say. "What I got to get up for. I bet you if I was getting a teef pulled, you wouldn't be getting up. Shucks, syrup again. I'm getting tired of this old syrup. Syrup, syrup, syrup. I want me some bacon sometime."

"Go out in the field and work and you can have bacon," Auntie say. She stood in the middle door looking at Ty. "You better be glad you got syrup. Some people ain't got that—hard's time is."

"Shucks," Ty say. "How can I be strong."

"I don't know too much 'bout your strength," Auntie say; "but I know where you go'n be hot, you keep that grumbling up. James, get a move on you; your mama waiting."

I ate my last piece of bread and went in the front room. Mama was standing 'fore the fireplace warming her hands. I put on my coat and my cap, and us left the house.

IV

I look down there again, but it still ain't coming. I almost say, "It ain't coming, yet," but I keep my mouth shet. 'Cause that's something else she don't like. She don't like for you to say something just for nothing. She can see it ain't coming, I can see it ain't coming, so why say it ain't coming. I don't say it, and I turn and look at the river that's back o' us. It so cold the smoke jest raising up from the water. I see a bunch of pull-doos not too far out —jest on the other side the lilies. I'm wondering if you can eat pull-doos. I ain't too sure, 'cause I ain't never ate none. But I done ate owls and black birds, and I done ate red birds, too. I didn't want kill the red birds, but she made me kill 'em. They had two of 'em back there. One in my trap, one in Ty trap. Me and Ty was go'n play with 'em and let 'em go. But she made me kill 'em 'cause us needed the food.

"I can't," I say. "I can't."

"Here," she say. "Take it."

"I can't," I say. "I can't. I can't kill him, Mama. Please."

"Here," she say. "Take this fork, James."

"Please, Mama, I can't kill him," I say.

I could tell she was go'n hit me. And I jecked back, but I didn't jeck back soon enough.

"Take it," she say.

I took it and reached in for him, but he kept hopping to the back.

"I can't, Mama," I say. The water just kept running down my face. "I can't."

"Get him out o' there," she say.

I reached in for him and he kept hopping to the back. Then I reached in farther, and he pecked me on the hand.

"I can't, Mama," I say.

She slapped me again.

I reached in again, but he kept hopping out my way. Then he hopped to one side, and I reached there. The fork got him on the leg and I heard his leg pop. I pulled my hand out 'cause I had hurt him.

"Give it here," she say, and jecked the fork out my hand.

She reached and got the little bird right in the neck. I heard the fork go in his neck, and I heard it go in the ground. She brought him out and helt him right in front o' me.

"That's one," she say. She shook him off and gived me the fork. "Get the other one."

"I can't, Mama. I do anything. But I can't do that."

She went to the corner o' the fence and broke the biggest switch over there. I knelt 'side the trap crying.

"Get him out o' there," she say.

"I can't, Mama."

She started hitting me cross the back. I went down on the ground crying.

"Get him," she say.

"Octavia," Auntie say.

'Cause she had come out o' the house and she was standing by the tree looking at us.

"Get him out o' there," Mama say.

"Octavia," Auntie say; "explain to him. Explain to him. Jest don't beat him. Explain to him."

But she hit me and hit me and hit me.

I'm still young. I ain't no more'an eight. But I know now. I know why I had to. (They was so little, though. They was so little. I 'member how I picked the feathers off 'em and cleaned 'em and helt 'em over the fire. Then us all ate 'em. Ain't had but little bitty piece, but us all had little bitty piece, and ever'body jest looked at me, 'cause they was so proud.) S'pose she had to go away? That's why I had to do it. S'pose she had to go away like Daddy went away? Then who was go'n look after us? They had to be somebody left to carry on. I didn't know it then, but I know it now. Auntie and Monsieur Bayonne talked to me and made me see. *See what?*

V

"the bus"

Time I see it, I get out my hankercher and start waving. It still way down there, but I keep waving anyhow. Then it come closer and stop and me and Mama get on. Mama tell me go sit in the back while she pay. I do like she say, and the people look at me. When I pass the little sign that say White and Colored, I start looking for a seat. I jest see one of 'em back there, but I don't take it, 'cause I want my mama to sit down herself. She come in the back and sit down, and I lean on the seat. They got seats in the front, but I know I can't sit there, 'cause I have to sit back o' the sign. Anyhow, I don't want sit there if my mama go'n sit back here.

They got a lady sitting 'side my mama and she look at me and grin little bit. I grin back, but I don't open my mouth, 'cause the wind'll get in and make that teef hurt. The lady take out a pack o' gum and reach me a slice, but I shake my head. She reach Mama a slice, and Mama shake her head. The lady jest can't understand why a little boy'll turn down gum, and she reached me a slice again. This time I point to my jaw. The lady understand and grin little bit, and I grin little bit, but I don't open my mouth, though.

They got a girl sitting 'cross from me. She got on a red overcoat, and her hair plaited in one big plait. First, I make 'tend I don't even see her. But then I start looking at her little bit. She make 'tend she don't see me neither, but I catch her looking that way. She got a cold, and ever' now and then she hist that that little hankercher to her nose. She ought to blow it, but she don't. Must think she too much a lady or something.

Ever' time she hist that little hankercher, the lady 'side her say something in her yer. She shake her head and lay her hands in her lap again. Then I catch her kind o' looking where I'm at. I grin at her. But think she'll grin back? No. She turn up her little old nose like I got some snot on my face or something. Well, I show her both o' us can turn us head. I turn mine, too, and look out at the river.

The river is gray. The sky is gray. They have pull-doos on the water. The water is wavy, and the pull-doos go up and down. The bus go 'round a turn, and you got plenty trees hiding the river. Then the bus go 'round another turn, and I can see the river again.

I look to the front where all the white people sitting. Then I look at that little old gal again. I don't look right at her, 'cause I don't want all them people to know I love her. I jest look at her little bit, like I'm looking out that window over there. But she know I'm looking that way, and she kind o' look at me, too. The lady sitting 'side her catch her this time, and she lean over and say something in her yer.

"I don't love him nothing," that little old gal say out loud.

Ever'body back there yer her mouth, and all of 'em look at us and laugh.

"I don't love you, neither," I say. "So you don't have to turn up your nose, Miss."

"You the one looking," she say.

"I wasn't looking at you," I say. "I was looking out that window, there."

"Out that window, my foot," she say. "I seen you. Ever' time I turn 'round you look at me."

"You must o' been looking yourself if you seen me all them times," I say.

"Shucks," she say. "I got me all kinds o' boyfriends."

"I got girlfriends, too," I say.

The "Stars and Bars"; the flag of the Confederacy

"Well, I just don't want you to get your hopes up," she say.

I don't say no more to that little old gal, 'cause I don't want have to bust her in the mouth. I lean on the seat where Mama sitting, and I don't even look that way no more. When us get to Bayonne, she jugg her little old tongue out at me. I make 'tend I'm go'n hit her, and she duck down side her mama. And all the people laugh at us again.

VI

Me and Mama get off and start walking in town. Bayonne is a little bitty town. Baton Rouge is a hundred times bigger 'an Bayonne. I went to Baton Rouge once—me, Ty, Mama, and Daddy. But that was 'way back yonder—'fore he went in the Army. I wonder when us go'n see him again. I wonder when. Look like he ain't ever coming home. . . . Even the pavement all cracked in Bayonne. Got grass shooting right out the sidewalk. Got weeds in the ditch, too; jest like they got home.

It some cold in Bayonne. Look like it colder 'an it is home. The wind blow in my face, and I feel that stuff running down my nose. I sniff. Mama say use that hankercher. I blow my nose and put it back.

Us pass a school and I see them white children playing in the yard. Big old red school, and them children jest running and playing. Then us pass a café, and I see a bunch of 'em in there eating. I wish I was in there 'cause I'm cold. Mama tell me keep my eyes in front where they blonks.

Us pass stores that got dummies, and us pass another café, and then us pass a shoe shop, and that baldhead man in there fixing on a shoe. I look at him and I butt into that white lady, and Mama jeck me in front and tell me stay there.

Us come to the courthouse, and I see the flag waving there. This one yer ain't like the one us got at school. This one yer ain't got but a handful of stars. One at school got a big pile of stars—one for ever' state. Us pass it and us turn and there it is—the dentist office. Me and Mama go in, and they got people sitting ever'where you look. They even got a little boy in there younger 'an me.

Me and Mama sit on that bench, and a white lady come in there and ask me what my name. Mama tell her, and the white lady go back. Then I yer somebody hollering in there. And soon's that little boy hear him hollering, he start hollering, too. His mama pat him and pat him, trying to make him hush up, but he ain't thinking 'bout her.

The man that was hollering in there come out holding his jaw.

"Got it, hanh?" another man say.

The man shake his head.

"Man, I thought they was killing you in there," the other man say. "Hollering like a pig under a gate."

The man don't say nothing. He jest head for the door, and the other man follow him.

"John Lee," the white lady say. "John Lee Williams."

The little boy jugg his head down in his mama lap and holler more now. His mama tell him go with the nurse, but he ain't thinking 'bout her. His mama tell him again, but he don't even yer. His mama pick him up and take him in there, and even when the white lady shet the door I can still hear him hollering.

"I often wonder why the Lord let a child like that suffer," a lady say to my mama. The lady's sitting right in front o' us on another bench. She got on a white dress and a black sweater. She must be a nurse or something herself, I reckoned.

"Not us to question," a man say.

"Sometimes I don't know if we shouldn't," the lady say.

"I know definitely we shouldn't," the man say. The man look like a preacher. He big and fat and he got on a black suit. He got a gold chain, too.

"Why?" the lady say.

"Why anything?" the preacher say.

"Yes," the lady say. "Why anything?"

"Not us to question," the preacher say.

The lady look at the preacher a little while and look at Mama again.

"And look like it's the poor who do most the suffering," she say. "I don't understand it."

"Best not to even try," the preacher say. "He works in mysterious ways. Wonders to perform."

Right then Little John Lee bust out hollering, and ever'body turn they head.

"He's not a good dentist," the lady say. "Dr. Robillard is much better. But more expensive. That's why most of the colored people come here. The white people go to Dr. Robillard. Y'all from Bayonne?"

"Down the river," my mama say. And that's all she go'n say, 'cause she don't talk much. But the lady keep on looking at her, and so she say: "Near Morgan."

"I see," the lady say.

VII

"That's the trouble with the black people in this country today," somebody else say. This one yer sitting on the same side me and Mama sitting, and he kind o' sitting in front of that preacher. He look like a teacher or somebody that go to college. He got on a suit, and he got a book that he been reading. "We don't question is exactly the trouble," he say. "We should question and question and question. Question everything."

The preacher jest look at him a long time. He done put a toothpick or something in his mouth, and he jest keep turning it and turning it. You can see he don't like that boy with that book.

"Maybe you can explain what you mean," he say.

"I said what I meant," the boy say. "Question everything. Every stripe, every star, every word spoken. Everything."

"It 'pears to me this young lady and I was talking 'bout God, young man," the preacher say.

"Question Him, too," the boy say.

"Wait," the preacher say. "Wait now."

"You heard me right," the boy say. "His existence as well as everything else. Everything."

The preacher jest look cross the room at the boy. You can see he getting madder and madder. But mad or no mad, the boy ain't thinking 'bout him. He look at the preacher jest's hard's the preacher look at him.

"Is this what they coming to?" the preacher say. "Is this what we educating them for?"

"You're not educating me," the boy say. "I wash dishes at night to go to school in the day. So even the words you spoke need questioning."

The preacher jest look at him and shake his head.

"When I come in this room and seen you there with your book, I said to myself, 'There's an intelligent man.' How wrong a person can be."

"Show me one reason to believe in the existence of a God," the boy say.

"My heart tell me," the preacher say.

"My heart tells me," the boy say. "My heart tells me. Sure, my heart tells me. And as long as you listen to what your heart tells you, you will have only what the white man gives you and nothing more. Me, I don't listen to my heart. The purpose of the heart is to pump blood throughout the body, and nothing else."

"Who's your paw, boy?" the preacher say.

"Why?"

"Who is he?"

"He's dead."

"And your mom?"

"She's in Charity Hospital with pneumonia. Half killed herself working for nothing."

"And 'cause he's dead and she sick, you mad at the world?"

"I'm not mad at the world. I'm questioning the world. I'm questioning it with cold logic, sir. What do words like *Freedom, Liberty, God, White, Colored* mean? I want to know. That's why *you* are sending us to school, to read and to ask questions. And because we ask these questions, you call us mad. No, sir, it is not us who are mad."

"You keep saying 'us'?"

" 'Us' . . . why not? I'm not alone."

The preacher jest shake his head. Then he look at ever'body in the room—ever'body. Some of the people look down at the floor, keep from looking at him. I kind o' look 'way myself, but soon's I know he done turn his head, I look that way again.

"I'm sorry for you," he say.

"Why?" the boy say. "Why not be sorry for yourself? Why are you so much better off than I am? Why aren't you sorry for these other people in here? Why not be sorry for the lady who had to drag her child into the dentist office? Why not be sorry for the lady sitting on that bench over there? Be sorry for them. Not for me. Some way or other I'm going to make it."

"No, I'm sorry for you," the preacher say.

"Of course. Of course," the boy say, shaking his head. "You're sorry for me because I rock that pillar you're leaning on."

"You can't ever rock the pillar I'm leaning on, young man. It's stronger than anything man can ever do."

"You believe in God because a man told you to believe in God. A white man told you to believe in God. And why? To keep you ignorant, so he can keep you under his feet."

"So now, we the ignorant?"

"Yes," the boy say. "Yes." And he open his book again.

The preacher jest look at him there. The boy done forgot all about him. Ever'body else make 'tend they done forgot 'bout the squabble, too.

Then I see that preacher getting up real slow. Preacher a great big old man, and he got to brace hisself to get up. He come 'cross the room where the boy is. He jest stand there looking at him, but the boy don't raise his head.

"Stand up, boy," preacher say.

The boy look up at him, then he shet his book real slow and stand up. Preacher jest draw back and hit him in the face. The boy fall 'gainst the wall, but he straighten hisself up and look right back at that preacher.

"You forgot the other cheek," he say.

The preacher hit him again on the other side. But this time the boy don't fall.

"That hasn't changed a thing," he say.

The preacher jest look at the boy. The preacher breathing real hard like he jest run up a hill. The boy sit down and open his book again.

"I feel sorry for you," the preacher say. "I never felt so sorry for a man before."

The boy make 'tend he don't even hear that preacher. He keep on reading his book. The preacher go back and get his hat off the chair.

"Excuse me," he say to us. "I'll come back some other time. Y'all, please excuse me."

And he look at the boy and go out the room. The boy hist his hand up to his mouth one time, to wipe 'way some blood. All the rest o' the time he keep on reading.

VIII

The lady and her little boy come out the dentist, and the nurse call somebody else in. Then little bit later they come out, and the nurse call another name. But fast's she call somebody in there, somebody else come in the place where we at, and the room stay full.

The people coming in now, all of 'em wearing big coats. One of 'em say something 'bout sleeting, and another one say he hope not. Another one say he think it ain't nothing but rain. 'Cause, he say, rain can get awful cold this time o' year.

All 'cross the room they talking. Some of 'em talking to people right by 'em, some of 'em talking to people clare 'cross the room, some of 'em talking to anybody'll listen. It's a little bitty room, no bigger 'an us kitchen, and I can see ever'body in there. The little old room 's full of smoke, 'cause you got two old

Is there something beyond the "pink wind" and "green [or] black grass" being discussed here?

men smoking pipes. I think I feel my teef thumping me some, and I hold my breath and wait. I wait and wait, but it don't thump me no more. Thank God for that.

I feel like going to sleep, and I lean back 'gainst the wall. But I'm scared to go to sleep: Scared 'cause the nurse might call my name and I won't hear her. And Mama might go to sleep, too, and she be mad if neither us heard the nurse.

I look up at Mama. I love my mama. I love my mama. And when cotton come I'm go'n get her a newer coat. And I ain't go'n get a black one neither. I think I'm go'n get her a red one.

"They got some books over there," I say. "Want read one of 'em?"

Mama look at the books, but she don't answer me.

"You got yourself a little man there," the lady say.

Mama don't say nothing to the lady, but she must 'a' grin a little bit, 'cause I seen the lady grinning back. The lady look at me a little while, like she feeling sorry for me.

"You sure got that preacher out here in a hurry," she say to that other boy.

The boy look up at her and look in his book again. When I grow up I want be jest like him. I want clothes like that and I want keep a book with me, too.

See questions on page 264.

"You really don't believe in God?" the lady say.

"No," he say.

"But why?" the lady say.

"Because the wind is pink," he say.

"What?" the lady say.

The boy don't answer her no more. He jest read in his book.

"Talking 'bout the wind is pink," that old lady say. She sitting on the same bench with the boy, and she trying to look in his face. The boy make 'tend the old lady ain't even there. He jest keep reading. "Wind is pink," she say again. "Eh, Lord, what children go'n be saying next?"

The lady 'cross from us bust out laughing.

"That's a good one," she say. "The wind is pink. Yes, sir, that's a good one."

"Don't you believe the wind is pink?" the boy say. He keep his head down in the book.

"Course I believe it, Honey," the lady say. "Course I do." She look at us and wink her eye. "And what color is grass, Honey?"

"Grass? Grass is black."

She bust out laughing again. The boy look at her.

"Don't you believe grass is black?" he say.

The lady quit laughing and look at him. Ever'body else look at him now. The place quiet, quiet.

"Grass is green, Honey," the lady say. "It was green yesterday, it's green today, and it's go'n be green tomorrow."

"How do you know it's green?"

"I know because I know."

"You don't know it's green. You believe it's green because someone told you it was green. If someone had told you it was black you'd believe it was black."

"It's green," the lady say. "I know green when I see green."

"Prove it's green."

"Surely, now," the lady say. "Don't tell me it's coming to that?"

"It's coming to just that," the boy say. "Words mean nothing. One means no more than the other."

"That's what it all coming to?" that old lady say. That old lady got on a turban and she got on two sweaters. She got a green sweater under a black sweater. I can see the green sweater 'cause some of the buttons on the other sweater missing.

"Yes, ma'am," the boy say. "Words mean nothing. Action is the only thing. Doing. That's the only thing."

"Other words, you want the Lord to come down here and show Hisself to you?" she say.

"Exactly, ma'am."

"You don't mean that, I'm sure?"

"I do, ma'am."

"Done, Jesus," the old lady say, shaking her head.

"I didn't go 'long with that preacher at first," the other lady say; "but now—I don't know. When a person say the grass is black, he's either a lunatic or something wrong."

"Prove to me that it's green."

"It's green because the people say it's green."

"Those same people say we're citizens of the United States."

"I think I'm a citizen."

"Citizens have certain rights. Name me one right that you have. One right, granted by the Constitution, that you can exercise in Bayonne."

The lady don't answer him. She jest look at him like she don't know what he talking 'bout. I know I don't.

"Things changing," she say.

"Things are changing because some black men have begun to follow their brains instead of their hearts."

"You trying to say these people don't believe in God?"

"I'm sure some of them do. Maybe most of them do. But they don't believe that God is going to touch these white people's hearts and change them tomorrow. Things change through action. By no other way."

Ever'body sit quiet and look at the boy. Nobody say a thing. Then the lady 'cross from me and Mama jest shake her head.

"Let's hope that not all your generation feel the same way you do," she say.

"Think what you please, it doesn't matter," the boy say. "But it will be men who listen to their heads and not their hearts who will see that your children have a better chance than you had."

"Let's hope they ain't all like you, though," the old lady say. "Done forgot the heart absolutely."

"Yes, ma'am, I hope they aren't all like me," the boy say. "Unfortunately I was born too late to believe in your God. Let's hope that the ones who come after will have your faith—if not in your God, then in something else, something definitely that they can lean on. I haven't anything. For me, the wind is pink; the grass is black."

IX

The nurse come in the room where us all sitting and waiting and say the doctor won't take no more patients till one o'clock this evening. My mama jump up off the bench and go up to the white lady.

"Nurse, I have to go back in the field this evening," she say.

"The doctor is treating his last patient now," the nurse say. "One o'clock this evening."

"Can I at least speak to the doctor?" my mama say.

"I'm his nurse," the lady say.

"My little boy sick," my mama say. "Right now his teef almost killing him."

The nurse look at me. She trying to make up her mind if to let me come in. I look at her real pitiful. The teef ain't hurting me a tall, but Mama say it is, so I make 'tend for her sake.

"This evening," the nurse say, and go back in the office.

"Don't feel 'jected, Honey," the lady say to Mama. "I been 'round 'em a long time--they take you when they want to. If you was white, that's something else; but you the wrong shade."

Mama don't say nothing to the lady, and me and her go outside and stand 'gainst the wall. It's cold out there. I can feel that wind going through my coat. Some of the other people come out of the room and go up the street. Me and Mama stand there a little while and start to walking. I don't know where us going. When us come to the other street us jest stand there.

"You don't have to make water, do you?" Mama say.

"No, ma'am," I say.

Us go up the street. Walking real slow. I can tell Mama don't know where she going. When us come to a store us stand there and look at the dummies. I look at a little boy with a brown overcoat. He got on brown shoes, too. I look at my old shoes and look at his'n again. You wait till summer, I say.

Me and Mama walk away. Us come up to another store and us stop and look at them dummies, too. Then us go again. Us pass a café where the white people in there eating. Mama tell me keep my eyes in front where they blonks, but I can't help from seeing them people eat. My stomach start to growling 'cause I'm hungry. When I see people eating, I get hungry; when I see a coat, I get cold.

A man whistle at my mama when us go by a filling station. She make 'tend she don't even see him. I look back and I feel like hitting him in the mouth. If I was bigger, I say. If I was bigger, you see.

Us keep on going. I'm getting colder and colder, but I don't say nothing. I feel that stuff running down my nose and I sniff.

"That rag," she say.

I git it out and wipe my nose. I'm getting cold all over now—my face, my hands, my feet, ever'thing. Us pass another little café, but this'n for white people, too, and us can't go in there neither. So us jest walk. I'm so cold now, I'm 'bout ready to say it. If I knowed where us was going, I wouldn't be so cold, but I don't know where us going. Us go, us go, us go. Us walk clean out o' Bayonne. Then us cross the street and us come back. Same thing I seen when I got off the bus. Same old trees, same old walk, same old weeds, same old cracked pave—same old ever'thing.

I sniff again.

"That rag," she say.

I wipe my nose real fast and jugg that hankercher back in my pocket 'fore my hand get too cold. I raise my head and I can see David hardware store. When us come up to it, us go in. I don't know why, but I'm glad.

It's warm in there. It so warm in there you don't want ever leave. I look for the heater, and I see it over by them ba'ls. Three white men standing 'round the heater talking in Creole. One of 'em come to see what Mama want.

"Got any ax handle?" she say.

Me, Mama, and the white man start to the back, but Mama stop me when us come to the heater. Her and the white man go on. I hold my hand over the heater and look at 'em. They go all the way in the back, and I see the white man point to the ax handle 'gainst the wall. Mama take one of 'em and shake it like she trying to figure out how much it weigh. Then she rub her hand over it from one end to the other end. She turn it over and look at the other side, then she shake it again, and shake her head and put it back. She get another one and she do it jest like she did the first one, then she shake her head. Then she get a brown one and do it that, too. But she don't like this one neither. Then she get another one, but 'fore she shake it or anything, she look at me. Look like she trying to say something to me, but I don't know what it is. All I know is I done got warm now and I'm feeling right smart better. Mama shake this ax handle jest like she done the others, and shake her head and say something to the white man. The white man jest look at his pile of ax handle, and when Mama pass by him to come to the front, the white man jest scratch his head and follow her. She tell me come on, and us go on out and start walking again.

Us walk and walk, and no time at all I'm cold again. Look like I'm colder now 'cause I can still remember how good it was back there. My stomach growl and I suck it in to keep Mama from yering it. She walking right 'side me, and it growl so loud you can yer it a mile. But Mama don't say a word.

X

When us come up to the courthouse, I look at the clock. It got quarter to twelve. Means us got another hour and a quarter to be out yer in the cold. Us go and stand side a building. Something hit my cap and I look up at the sky. Sleet falling.

I look at Mama standing there. I want stand close 'side her, but she don't like that. She say that's crybaby stuff. She say you got to stand for yourself, by yourself.

"Let's go back to that office," she say.

Creole: French dialect of many Louisiana residents

Us cross the street. When us get to the dentist I try to open the door, but I can't. Mama push me on the side and she twist the knob. But she can't open it neither. She twist it some more, harder, but she can't open it. She turn 'way from the door. I look at her, but I don't move and I don't say nothing. I done seen her like this before and I'm scared.

"You hungry?" she say. She say it like she mad at me, like I'm the one cause of ever'thing.

"No, ma'am," I say.

"You want eat and walk back, or you rather don't eat and ride?"

"I ain't hungry," I say.

I ain't jest hungry, but I'm cold, too. I'm so hungry and I'm so cold I want to cry. And look like I'm getting colder and colder. My feet done got numb. I try to work my toes, but I can't. Look like I'm go'n die. Look like I'm go'n stand right here and freeze to death. I think about home. I think about Val and Auntie and Ty and Louis and Walker. It 'bout twelve o'clock and I know they eating dinner. I can hear Ty making jokes. That's Ty. Always trying to make some kind o' joke. I wish I was right there listening to him. Give anything in the world if I was home 'round the fire.

"Come on," Mama say.

Us start walking again. My feet so numb I can't hardly feel 'em. Us turn the corner and go back up the street. The clock start hitting for twelve.

The sleet's coming down plenty now. They hit the pave and bounce like rice. Oh, Lord; oh, Lord, I pray. Don't let me die. Don't let me die. Don't let me die, Lord.

XI

Now I know where us going. Us going back o' town where the colored people eat. I don't care if I don't eat. I been hungry before. I can stand it. But I can't stand the cold.

I can see us go'n have a long walk. It 'bout a mile down there. But I don't mind. I know when I get there I'm go'n warm myself. I think I can hold out. My hands numb in my pockets and my feet numb, too, but if I keep moving I can hold out. Jest don't stop no more, that's all.

The sky's gray. The sleet keep falling. Falling like rain now—plenty, plenty. You can hear it hitting the pave. You can see it bouncing. Sometime it bounce two times 'fore it settle.

Us keep going. Us don't say nothing. Us jest keep going, keep going.

I wonder what Mama thinking. I hope she ain't mad with me. When summer come I'm go'n pick plenty cotton and get her a coat. I'm go'n get her a red one.

I hope they make it summer all the time. I be glad if it was summer all the time—but it ain't. Us got to have winter, too. Lord, I hate the winter. I guess ever'body hate the winter.

I don't sniff this time. I get out my hankercher and wipe my nose. My hand so cold I can hardly hold the hankercher.

I think us getting close, but us ain't there yet. I wonder where ever'body is. Can't see nobody but us. Look like us the only two people moving 'round today. Must be too cold for the rest of the people to move 'round.

I can hear my teefes. I hope they don't knock together too hard and make that bad one hurt. Lord, that's all I need, for that bad one to start off.

I hear a church bell somewhere. But today ain't Sunday. They must be ringing for a funeral or something.

I wonder what they doing at home. They must be eating. Monsieur Bayonne might be there with his guitar. One day Ty played with Monsieur Bayonne guitar and broke one o' the string. Monsieur Bayonne got some mad with Ty. He say Ty ain't go'n never 'mount to nothing. Ty can go jest like him when he ain't there. Ty can make ever'body laugh mocking Monsieur Bayonne.

I used to like to be with Mama and Daddy. Us used to be happy. But they took him in the Army. Now, nobody happy no more. . . . I be glad when he come back.

Monsieur Bayonne say it wasn't fair for 'em to take Daddy and give Mama nothing and give us nothing. Auntie say, Shhh, Etienne. Don't let 'em yer you talk like that. Monsieur Bayonne say, It's God truth. What they giving his children? They have to walk three and a half mile to school hot or cold. That's anything to give for a paw? She got to work in the field rain or shine jest to make ends meet. That's anything to give for a husband? Auntie say, Shhh, Etienne, shhh. Yes, you right, Monsieur Bayonne say. Best don't say it in front of 'em now. But one day they go'n find out. One day. Yes, s'pose so, Auntie say. Then what, Rose Mary? Monsieur Bayonne say. I don't know, Etienne, Auntie say. All us can do is us job, and leave ever'thing else in His hand. . . .

Compare with arguments on pp. 253-5.

Us getting closer, now. Us getting closer. I can see the railroad tracks.

Us cross the tracks, and now I see the café. Jest to get in there, I say. Jest to get in there. Already I'm starting to feel little better.

XII

Us go in. Ahh, it good. I look for the heater; there 'gainst the wall. One of them little brown ones. I jest stand there and hold my hand over it. I can't open my hands too wide 'cause they almost froze.

Mama standing right 'side me. She done unbuttoned her coat. Smoke rise out the coat, and the coat smell like a wet dog.

I move to the side so Mama can have more room. She open out her hands and rub 'em together. I rub mine together, too, 'cause this keep 'em from hurting. If you let 'em warm too fast, they hurt you sure. But if you let 'em warm jest little bit at a time, and you keep rubbing 'em, they be all right ever' time.

They got jest two more people in the café. A lady back o' the counter, and a man on this side the counter. They been watching us ever since us come in.

Mama get out the hankercher and count the money. Both o' us know how much money she got there. Three dollars. No, she ain't got three dollars. 'Cause she had to pay us way up here. She ain't got but two dollars and a half left. Dollar and a half to get my teef pulled, and fifty cents for us to go back on, and fifty cents worse o' salt meat.

She stir the money 'round with her finger. Most o' the money is change 'cause I can hear it rubbing together. She stir it and stir it. Then she look at the door. It still sleeting. I can yer it hitting 'gainst the wall like rice.

"I ain't hungry, Mama," I say.

"Got to pay 'em something for they heat," she say.

She take a quarter out the hankercher and tie the hankercher up again. She look over her shoulder at the people, but she still don't move. I hope she don't spend the money. I don't want her spend it on me. I'm hungry, I'm almost starving I'm so hungry, but I don't want her spending the money on me.

She flip the quarter over like she thinking. She must be thinking 'bout us walking back home. Lord, I sure don't want walk home. If I thought it done any good to say something, I say it. But my mama make up her own mind.

She turn way from the heater right fast, like she better hurry up and do it 'fore she change her mind. I turn to look at her go to the counter. The man and the lady look at her, too. She tell the lady something and the lady walk away. The man keep on looking at her. Her back turn to the man, and Mama don't even know he standing there.

The lady put some cakes and a glass o' milk on the counter. Then she pour a cup o' coffee and set it side the other stuff. Mama pay her for the things and come back where I'm at. She tell me sit down at that table 'gainst the wall.

The milk and the cakes for me. The coffee for my mama. I eat slow, and I look at her. She looking outside at the sleet. She looking real sad. I say to myself, I'm go'n make all this up one day. You see, one day, I'm go'n make all this up. I want to say it now. I want to tell how I feel right now. But Mama don't like for us to talk like that.

"I can't eat all this," I say.

They got just three little cakes there. And I'm so hungry right now, the Lord know I can eat a hundred times three. But I want her to have one.

She don't even look my way. She know I'm hungry. She know I want it. I let it stay there a while, then I get it and eat it. I eat jest on my front teefes, 'cause if it tech that back teef I know what'll happen. Thank God it ain't hurt me a tall today.

After I finish eating I see the man go to the juke box. He drop a nickel in it, then he jest stand there looking at the record. Mama tell me keep my eyes in front where they blonks. I turn my head like she say, but then I yer the man coming towards us.

"Dance, Pretty?" he say.

Mama get up to dance with him. But 'fore you know it, she done grabbed the little man and done throwed him 'side the wall. He hit the wall so hard he stop the juke box from playing.

"Some pimp," the lady back o' the counter say. "Some pimp."

The little man jump up off the floor and start towards my mama. 'Fore you know it, Mama done sprung open her knife and she waiting for him.

"Come on," she say. "Come on. I'll cut you from your neighbo to your throat. Come on."

I go up to the little man to hit him, but Mama make me come and stand 'side her. The little man look at me and Mama and go back to the counter.

"Some pimp," the lady back o' the counter say. "Some pimp." She start laughing and pointing at the little man. "Yes, sir, you a pimp, all right. Yes, sir."

XIII

"Fasten that coat. Let's go," Mama say.

"You don't have to leave," the lady say.

Mama don't answer the lady, and us right out in the cold again. I'm warm right now—my hands, my yers, my feet—but I know this ain't go'n last too long. It done sleet so much now you got ice ever'where.

Us cross the railroad tracks, and soon's us do, I get cold. That wind go through this little old coat like it ain't nothing. I got a shirt and a sweater under it, but that wind don't pay 'em no mind. I look up and I can see us got a long way to go. I wonder if us go'n make it 'fore I get too cold.

Us cross over to walk on the sidewalk. They got jest one sidewalk back here. It's over there.

After us go jest a little piece, I smell bread cooking. I look, then I see a baker shop. When us get closer, I can smell it more better. I shet my eyes and make 'tend I'm eating. But I keep 'em shet too long and I butt up 'gainst a telephone post. Mama grab me and see if I'm hurt. I ain't bleeding or nothing and she turn me loose.

I can feel I'm getting colder and colder, and I look up to see how far us still got to go. Uptown is 'way up yonder. A half mile, I reckoned. I try to think of something. They say think and you won't get cold. I think of that poem, *Annabel Lee.* I ain't been to school in so long—this bad weather—I reckoned they done passed *Annabel Lee.* But passed it or not, I'm sure Miss Walker go'n make me recite it when I get there. That woman don't never forget nothing. I ain't never seen nobody like that.

I'm still getting cold. *Annabel Lee* or no *Annabel Lee,* I'm still getting cold. But I can see us getting closer. Us getting there gradually.

Soon's us turn the corner, I see a little old white lady up in front o' us. She the only lady on the street. She all in black and she got a long black rag over her head.

"Stop," she say.

Pronounce "et." The pronunciation is standard in England, old-fashioned or dialect in the U.S. Here it is *not* an indication of low social status or lack of education.

A deft political touch. The woman may be poor, but she is white. So she can simply phone and make arrangements. (Perhaps she is also a "lady"? The whole episode is full of an old and literary sense of *noblesse oblige*. Notice that "yall" is her only dialect word.)

Me and Mama stop and look at her. She must be crazy to be out in all this sleet. Ain't got but a few other people out there, and all of 'em men.

"Yall done ate?" she say.

"Jest finished," Mama say.

"Yall must be cold then?" she say.

"Us headed for the dentist," Mama say. "Us'll warm up when us get there."

"What dentist?" the old lady say. "Mr. Bassett?"

"Yes, ma'am," Mama say.

"Come on in," the old lady say. "I'll telephone him and tell him yall coming."

Me and Mama follow the old lady in the store. It's a little bitty store, and it don't have much in there. The old lady take off her head piece and fold it up.

"Helena?" somebody call from the back.

"Yes, Alnest?" the old lady say.

"Did you see them?"

"They're here. Standing beside me."

"Good. Now you can stay inside."

The old lady look at Mama. Mama waiting to hear what she brought us in here for. I'm waiting for that, too.

"I saw yall each time you went by," she say. "I came out to catch you, but you were gone."

"Us went back o' town," Mama say.

"Did you eat?"

"Yes, ma'am."

The old lady look at Mama a long time, like she thinking Mama might be jest saying that. Mama look right back at her. The old lady look at me to see what I got to say. I don't say nothing. I sure ain't going 'gainst my mama.

"There's food in the kitchen," she say to Mama. "I've been keeping it warm."

Mama turn right around and start for the door.

"Just a minute," the old lady say. Mama stop. "The boy'll have to work for it. It isn't free."

"Us don't take no handout," Mama say.

"I'm not handing out anything," the old lady say. "I need my garbage moved to the front. Ernest has a bad cold and can't go out there."

"James'll move it for you," Mama say.

"Not unless you eat," the old lady say. "I'm old, but I have my pride, too, you know."

Mama can see she ain't go'n beat this old lady down, so she jest shake her head.

"All right," the old lady say. "Come into the kitchen."

She lead the way with that rag in her hand. The kitchen is a little bitty little thing, too. The table and the stove jest about fill it up. They got a little room to the side. Somebody in there laying cross the bed. Must be the person she was talking with: Alnest or Ernest—I forget what she call him.

"Sit down," the old lady say to Mama. "Not you," she say to me. "You have to move the cans."

"Helena?" somebody say in the other room.

"Yes, Alnest?" the old lady say.

"Are you going out there again?"

"I must show the boy where the garbage is," the old lady say.

"Keep that shawl over your head," the old man say.

"You don't have to remind me. Come, boy," the old lady say.

Us go out in the yard. Little old back yard ain't no bigger 'an the store or the kitchen. But it can sleet here jest like it can sleet in any big back yard. And 'fore you know it I'm trembling.

"There," the old lady say, pointing to the cans. I pick up one of the cans. The can so light I put it back down to look inside o' it.

"Here," the old lady say. "Leave that cap alone."

I look at her in the door. She got that black rag wrapped 'round her shoulders, and she pointing one of her fingers at me.

"Pick it up and carry it to the front," she say. I go by her with the can. I'm sure the thing 's empty. She could 'a' carried the thing by herself, I'm sure. "Set it on the sidewalk by the door and come back for the other one," she say.

I go and come back, Mama look at me when I pass her. I get the other can and take it to the front. It don't feel no heavier 'an the other one. I tell myself to look inside and see just what I been hauling. First, I look up and down the street. Nobody coming. Then I look over my shoulder. Little old lady done slipped there jest 's quiet 's mouse, watching me. Look like she knowed I was go'n try that.

"Ehh, Lord," she say. "Children, children. Come in here, boy, and go wash your hands."

I follow her into the kitchen, and she point, and I go to the bathroom. When I come out, the old lady done dished up the food. Rice, gravy, meat, and she even got some lettuce and tomato in a saucer. She even got a glass o' milk and a piece o' cake there, too. It look so good. I almost start eating 'fore I say my blessing.

"Helena?" the old man say.

"Yes, Alnest?" she say.

"Are they eating?"

"Yes," she say.

"Good," he say. "Now you'll stay inside."

The old lady go in there where he is and I can hear 'em talking. I look at Mama. She eating slow like she thinking. I wonder what's matter now. I reckoned she think 'bout home.

The old lady come back in the kitchen.

"I talked to Dr. Bassett's nurse," she say. "Dr. Bassett will take you as soon as you get there."

"Thank you, ma'am," Mama say.

"Perfectly all right," the old lady say. "Which one is it?"

Mama nod towards me. The old lady look at me real sad. I look sad, too.

"You're not afraid, are you?" she say.

"No'm," I say.

"That's a good boy," the old lady say. "Nothing to be afraid of."

When me and Mama get through eating, us thank the old lady again.

"Helena, are they leaving?" the old man say.

"Yes, Alnest."

"Tell them I say good-by."

"They can hear you, Alnest."

"Good-by both mother and son," the old man say. "And may God be with you."

Me and Mama tell the old man good-by, and us follow the old lady in the front. Mama open the door to go out, but she stop and come back in the store.

"You sell salt meat?" she say.

"Yes."

"Give me two bits worse."

"That isn't very much salt meat," the old lady say.

"That's all I have," Mama say.

The old lady go back o' the counter and cut a big piece off the chunk. Then she wrap it and put it in a paper bag.

"Two bits," she say.

"That look like awful lot of meat for a quarter," Mama say.

"Two bits," the old lady say. "I've been selling salt meat behind this counter twenty-five years. I think I know what I'm doing."

"You got a scale there," Mama say.

"What?" the old lady say.

"Weigh it," Mama say.

"What?" the old lady say. "Are you telling me how to run my business?"

"Thanks very much for the food," Mama say.

"Just a minute," the old lady say.

"James," Mama say to me. I move towards the door.

"Just one minute, I said," the old lady say.

Me and Mama stop again and look at her. The old lady take the meat out the bag and unwrap it and cut 'bout half o' it off. Then she wrap it up again and jugg it back in the bag and give it to Mama. Mama lay the quarter on the counter.

"Your kindness will never be forgotten," she say. "James," she say to me.

Us go out, and the old lady come to the door to look at us. After us go a little piece I look back, and she still there watching us.

The sleet's coming down heavy, heavy now, and I turn up my collar to keep my neck warm. My mama tell me turn it right back down.

"You not a bum," she say. "You a man."

What do you think Mama means when she says to James, "You not a bum . . . You a man"?

The problem, of course, is what she means by *man*.

Leaving

Willie Morris

This selection comes from Willie Morris's autobiography *North Toward Home.* Willie Morris had to leave home to find home, and then he could only go north *toward* home.

One day that spring, two months before I was to graduate from high school, my father gave me some unexpected advice. He was reading the *Commercial Appeal* in our front room, and he turned to me and told me, quite simply, to get the hell out of Mississippi. I do not quite know why. Perhaps he knew something about doom, though his argument, he said, was based on a lack of *opportunity.*

At first I ignored this advice. I was obsessed with Belle Prairie and the blond belle who graced its gullies, swamps, and tenant shacks. I had my heart set, at the age of seventeen, on entering Mississippi's educated landed gentry—by taking a degree at Ole Miss, as all my friends planned to do, and by returning to that plantation with my majorette, to preside there on the banks of the Yazoo over boll weevils big enough to wear dog tags, pre-Earl Warren darkies, and the young squirearchy from the plantations abutting on Carter, Eden, Holly Bluff, Sidon, and Tchula.

Chief Justice of the Supreme Court 1953-69; a symbol to those who oppose the 1954 decision holding segregated schools to be unconstitutional.

I saw no reason to leave. I was athlete, sports announcer, valedictorian, and, my greatest pride, editor of the *Flashlight.* I knew Mississippi and I loved what I saw. I had just been voted most likely to succeed. In Yazoo I knew every house and every tree in the white section of town. Each street and hill was like a map on my consciousness; I loved the contours of its land, and the slow changing of its seasons. I was full of the regional graces and was known as a perfect young gentleman. I was pleasant, enthusiastic, and happy. On any question pertaining to God or man I would have cast my morals on the results of a common plebiscite of the white voters of Yazoo County. "One shudders at the thought of the meaninglessness of life," I read years later in *Winesburg, Ohio,* in a moment when I was trying to remember these years, "while at the same instant, and if the people of the town are his people, one loves life so intensely that tears come into the eyes."

By Sherwood Anderson, a collection of short stories about small-town life.

Faulkner's hometown

Yet more than being desperately in love, I was sorrowfully ignorant—ignorant of myself, ignorant of the world of moving objects I was about to enter. One hundred miles to the north of Yazoo, Faulkner was writing his great tales of violence and the destruction of honor. In the spring of my senior year, when I was at Oxford for a convention, I watched as they filmed the jail scenes for the movie *Intruder in the Dust,* yet this did not inspire me much one way or the other. Had I known that great books were for one's own private soul rather than mere instrumentalities for achieving those useless trinkets on which all American high schools, including small ones in Mississippi, base their existence, perhaps I would have found in Faulkner some dark chord, some suggestion of how this land had shaped me, how its isolation and its guilt-ridden past had already settled so deeply into my bones. Unfortunately this was to come later. Then I joined easily and thoughtlessly in the Mississippi middle-class consensus that Faulkner, the chronicler and moralist, was out for the Yankee dollar.

Grades, diplomas, etc.

My first seventeen years had been lived rich in experience—in sensual textures, in unusual confrontations. I had moved easily among many kinds of people, I had seen something of cruelty and madness, and I had survived fundamentalist religion. My father had taught me the woods; from everyone I had had love. The town in which I had grown up had yet to be touched by the great television culture, or by the hardening emotions and the defensive hostilities unloosed by the Supreme Court in 1954. Something was left, if but an oblique recollection: a Southern driftlessness, a closeness to the earth, a sense of time standing still, a lingering isolation from America's relentless currents of change and homogeneity. Something else also remained, some innocent and exposed quality that made possible, in the heart of a young and vulnerable boy, an allegiance and a love for a small, inconsequential place. Only retrospect would tell me I was to take something of these things with me forever, through my maturing into my manhood. But then I could not connect them, because I had yet to go beyond the most fundamental awareness of myself.

What was it, then, that led me to leave, to go to a place where I did not know a soul, and eventually to make such a sharp break with my own past that I still suffer from the pain of that alienation? Was there some small grain of sand there, something abrasive and unrecognized in my perception of things, some hidden ambition and independence that finally led me away from everything I knew and honored? Was there something in me that needed some stark removal from my deepest loyalties?

In trying to recapture a turning point in one's life at such an age, it is almost impossible to ascribe tangible motives to some great change in one's direction, to isolate a thought, or a decision. But there are a handful of things that stand out so clearly that they become, after many years, almost symbol. They embody in retrospect the very substance of one's existence at a given moment. They may be fleeting recollections, chance encounters, the thread of an old thought, but they are revealing in themselves, and they become more than memory.

My father took out one day for Austin, Texas, to see the campus of what we had sometimes heard was the best and certainly the biggest state university in the South. Four or five days later, my friend Bubba Barrier and I, quite by chance, ran into him in the lobby of the Edwards House in Jackson. He had just returned. "That's one hell of a place they got out there," he said. They had a main building 30 stories high, a baseball field dug right out of stone, artificial moonlight for street lamps, the biggest state capitol in the Republic, and the goddamndest student newspaper you ever saw. "I think you ought to go to school out there," he said. "Can't nuthin' in *this* state match it."

I would wander off by myself to that place of my childhood, the town cemetery. Here I would walk among all those graves I knew that had given me such a sense of the town when I was a boy—of the reprobates and early settlers, the departed gospelists and bootleggers, and all the boys we had buried with the American Legionnaires. I cannot remember what my thoughts were on these excursions, except that I had the most dramatic conception of imminent departure. Something different was stirring around in my future, and I would brood over the place where I was and some place where I would end up, and for days I carried a map of the University of Texas in my shirt pocket. I was bathing in self-drama; perhaps it was my *imagination,* which had never failed me even as a child, that sought some unknown awakening.

Is there something special about small-town life that magnetizes the local cemeteries? Note Edgar Lee Masters' ***Spoon River Anthology.*** Perhaps some of those epitaphs could be used to illustrate Morris' point.

I had been commissioned to write the prophecy of the Class of 1952 of Yazoo High School, and I delivered it on class day that spring in the school auditorium. Afterward one of the senior class teachers cornered me and said it was the most disgusting thing she had ever heard, that only the day before she had recommended me to two FBI agents as promising material for that agency, but that she was going to write a letter telling them I was unfit for their service. These were unusual words for me, the favorite of every teacher in school and the winner of the American Legion Citizenship Award, but on rereading this curious statement I saw what had aroused her. I had consigned each member of the fifty-two-member graduating class to destruction. Honest Ed Upton, the salutatorian, was to die an agonizing death in quicksand in a Mississippi swamp. Billy Bonner would be shot down by Italians in the streets of Brooklyn. All the others were to go the way

This may be another cue to ***Spoon River*** or, even better, to the stories in ***Winesburg, Ohio*** or Joyce's ***Dubliners.*** Note also Morris' reference to "doom" in the first paragraph of the selection and the meditation on Faulkner.

of violence, treachery, corruption, and oblivion, except myself, their chronicler, who did not figure in the predictions. "You just as well get out of here to Texas," that teacher said, "because it's pretty clear you don't appreciate the people around you." On graduation night in the school gymnasium, on a wet spring night in June, my comrades who were doomed to destruction and I stood finally on the podium and sang the last lines of our alma mater: *"Yazoo, Yazoo, in closing let us say . . . that forever and a day . . . we'll be thinking of you, Yazoo . . . Yazoo."*

And one cold, dark morning in the early fall, sick with leaving for the first time the place where I grew up, and the blond majorette whom I had said good-bye to for the first and as it proved the last time in my old DeSoto car near the railroad tracks the night before, I caught a Southern Trailways bus in Vicksburg for Austin. My mother, as the story always goes, cried, and my father looked thin as death as the bus pulled out to cross the great bridge into Louisiana. I turned on the red portable radio the local radio station had given me as a farewell present, and I remember the song that came on over in Louisiana, a popular song of that time:

Fly the ocean in a silver plane,
See the jungle when it's wet with rain,
Just remember 'til you're home again
You belong to me.

my father moved through dooms of love

e. e. cummings

my father moved through dooms of love
through sames of am through haves of give,
singing each morning out of each night
my father moved through depths of height

"Morning" is the object of "singing," which is a kind of synonym for "creating."

this motionless forgetful where
turned at his glance to shining here;
that if (so timid air is firm)
under his eyes would stir and squirm

The subject is "if," with "that" the demonstrative.

newly as from unburied which
floats the first who, his april touch
drove sleeping selves to swarm their fates
woke dreamers to their ghostly roots

and should some why completely weep
my father's fingers brought her sleep:
vainly no smallest voice might cry
for he could feel the mountains grow.

The child as questioner

Lifting the valleys of the sea
my father moved through griefs of joy;
praising a forehead called the moon
singing desire into begin

joy was his song and joy so pure
a heart of star by him could steer
and pure so now and now so yes
the wrists of twilight would rejoice

Even a heart of star-like quality, reading "star" as "guide"

keen as midsummer's keen beyond
conceiving mind of sun will stand,
so strictly (over utmost him
so hugely) stood my father's dream

Compare with "it is most sane and sunly" in "Love is more thicker than forget" (p. 229).

The intensive "so"

A particularly fine stanza and sentiment. But why does Cummings use "dooms" with "feel"? (Also, note title.) Compare sentiment with that in line 66.

his flesh was flesh his blood was blood;
no hungry man but wished him food;
no cripple wouldn't creep one mile
uphill to only see him smile.

Scorning the pomp of must and shall
my father moved through dooms of feel;
his anger was as right as rain
his pity was as green as grain

septembering arms of year extend
less humbly wealth to foe and friend
than he to foolish and to wise
offered immeasurable is

The object of "extend"

A sense of "being/living"; more important than "wealth"

proudly and (by octobering flame
beckoned) as earth will downward climb,
so naked for immortal work
his shoulders marched against the dark

Probably="thus"

his sorrow was as true as bread:
no liar looked him in the head;
if every friend became his foe
he'd laugh and build a world with snow.

My father moved through theys of we,
singing each new leaf out of each tree
(and every child was sure that spring
danced when she heard my father sing)

then let men kill which cannot share,
let blood and flesh be mud and mire,
scheming imagine, passion willed,
freedom a drug that's bought and sold

Read "that which."

giving to steal and cruel kind,
a heart to fear, to doubt a mind,
to differ a disease of same,
conform the pinnacle of am

though dull were all we taste as bright,
bitter all utterly things sweet,
maggoty minus and dumb death
all we inherit, all bequeath

and nothing quite so least as truth
—i say though hate were why men breathe—
because my father lived his soul
love is the whole and more than all

Do Not Go Gentle Into That Good Night

Do not go gentle into that good night,
Old age should burn and rave at close of day;
Rage, rage against the dying of the light.

Though wise men at their end know dark is right,
Because their words had forked no lightning they
Do not go gentle into that good night.

Good men, the last wave by, crying how bright
Their frail deeds might have danced in a green bay,
Rage, rage against the dying of the light.

Wild men who caught and sang the sun in flight,
And learn, too late, they grieved it on its way,
Do not go gentle into that good night.

Grave men, near death, who see with blinding sight
Blind eyes could blaze like meteors and be gay,
Rage, rage against the dying of the light.

And you, my father, there on the sad height,
Curse, bless, me now with your fierce tears, I pray.
Do not go gentle into that good night.
Rage, rage against the dying of the light.

—Dylan Thomas

I Stand Here Ironing

Tillie Olsen

I stand here ironing, and what you asked me moves tormented back and forth with the iron. Who is that "you

272

"I wish you would manage the time to come in and talk with me about your daughter. I'm sure you can help me understand her. She's a youngster who needs help and whom I'm deeply interested in helping."

"Who needs help." Even if I came, what good would it do? You think because I am her mother I have a key, or that in some way you could use me as a key? She has lived for nineteen years. There is all that life that has happened outside of me, beyond me.

And when is there time to remember, to sift, to weigh, to estimate, to total? I will start and there will be an interruption and I will have to gather it all together again. Or I will become engulfed with all I did or did not do, with what should have been and what cannot be helped.

She was a beautiful baby. The first and only one of our five that was beautiful at birth. You do not guess how new and uneasy her tenancy in her now-loveliness. You did not know her all those years she was thought homely, or see her poring over her baby pictures, making me tell her over and over how beautiful she had been—and would be, I would tell her—and was now, to the seeing eye. But the seeing eyes were few or nonexistent. Including mine.

I nursed her. They feel that's important nowadays. I nursed all the children, but with her, with all the fierce rigidity of first motherhood, I did like the books then said. Though her cries battered me to trembling and my breasts ached with swollenness, I waited till the clock decreed.

Why do I put that first? I do not even know if it matters, or if it explains anything.

She was a beautiful baby. She blew shining bubbles of sound. She loved motion, loved light, loved color and music and textures. She would lie on the floor in her blue overalls patting the surface so hard in ecstasy her hands and feet would blur. She was a miracle to me, but when she was eight months old I had to leave her daytimes with the woman downstairs to whom she was no miracle at all, for I worked or looked for work and for Emily's father, who "could no longer endure" (he wrote in his good-by note) "sharing want with us."

I was nineteen. It was the pre-relief, pre-WPA world of the depression. I would start running as soon as I got off the streetcar, running up the stairs, the place smelling sour, and awake or asleep to startle awake, when she saw me she would break into a clogged weeping that could not be comforted, a weeping I can yet hear.

After a while I found a job hashing at night so I could be with her days, and it was better. But it came to where I had to bring her to his family and leave her.

A waitress in a roadside diner

It took a long time to raise the money for her fare back. Then she got chicken pox and I had to wait longer. When she finally came, I hardly knew her, walking quick and nervous like her father, looking like her father, thin, and dressed in a shoddy red that yellowed her skin and glared at the pock marks. All the baby loveliness gone.

She was two. Old enough for nursery school they said, and I did not know then what I know now—the fatigue of the long day, and the lacerations of group life in nurseries that are only parking places for children.

Except that it would have made no difference if I had known. It was the only place there was. It was the only way we could be together, the only way I could hold a job.

And even without knowing, I knew. I knew the teacher that was evil because all these years it has curdled into my memory, the little boy hunched in the corner, her rasp, "Why aren't you outside, because Alvin hits you? that's no reason, go out, scaredy." I knew Emily hated it even if she did not clutch and implore "Don't go, Mommy" like the other children, mornings.

She always had a reason why we should stay home. Momma, you look sick, Momma. I feel sick. Momma, the teachers aren't there today, they're sick. Momma, there was a fire there last night. Momma, it's a holiday today, no school, they told me.

But never a direct protest, never rebellion. I think of our others in their three-, four-year-oldness—the explosions, the tempers, the denunciations, the demands—and I feel suddenly ill. I put the iron down. What in me demanded that goodness in her? And what was the cost, the cost to her of such goodness?

The old man living in the back once said in his gentle way: "You should smile at Emily more when you look at her." What *was* in my face when I looked at her? I loved her. There were all the acts of love.

It was only with the others I remembered what he said, and it was the face of joy, and not of care or tightness or worry I turned to them—too late for Emily. She does not smile easily, let alone almost always as her brothers and sisters do. Her face is closed and somber, but when she wants, how fluid. You must have seen it in her pantomimes; you spoke of her rare gift for comedy on the stage that rouses a laughter out of the audience so dear they applaud and applaud and do not want to let her go.

Where does it come from, that comedy? There was none of it in her when she came back to me that second time, after I had had to send her away again. She had a new daddy now to learn to love, and I think perhaps it was a better time. Except when we left her alone nights, telling ourselves she was old enough.

"Can't you go some other time, Mommy, like tomorrow?" she would ask. "Will it be just a little while you'll be gone? Do you promise?"

The time we came back, the front door open, the clock on the floor in the hall. She rigid awake. "It wasn't just a little while. I didn't cry. Three times I called you, just three times, and then I ran downstairs to open the door so you could come faster. The clock talked loud. I threw it away, it scared me what it talked."

She said the clock talked loud again that night I went to the hospital to have Susan. She was delirious with the fever that comes before red measles, but she was fully conscious all the week I was gone and the week after we were home when she could not come near the new baby or me.

She did not get well. She stayed skeleton thin, not wanting to eat, and night after night she had nightmares. She would call for me, and I would rouse from exhaustion to sleepily call back, "You're all right, darling—go to sleep—it's just a dream," and if she still called, in a sterner voice, "now go to sleep Emily, there's nothing to hurt you." Twice, only twice, when I had to get up for Susan anyhow, I went in to sit with her.

Now when it is too late (as if she would let me hold and comfort her like I do the others) I get up and go to her at once at her moan or restless stirring. "Are you awake, Emily? Can I get you something, dear?" And the answer is always the same: "No, I'm all right, go back to sleep, Mother."

They persuaded me at the clinic to send her away to a convalescent home in the country where "she can have the kind of food and care you can't manage for her, and you'll be free to concentrate on the new baby." They still send children to that place. I see pictures on the society page of sleek young women planning affairs to raise money for it, or dancing at the affairs, or decorating Easter eggs or filling Christmas stockings for the children.

They never have a picture of the children, so I do not know if the girls still wear those gigantic red bows and the ravaged looks on the every other Sunday when parents can come to visit "unless otherwise notified"—as we were notified the first six weeks.

Oh it is a handsome place, green lawns and tall trees and fluted flower beds. High up on the balconies of each cottage the children stand, the girls in their red bows and white dresses, the boys in white suits and giant red ties. The parents stand below shrieking up to be heard and the children shriek down to be heard, and between them the invisible wall "Not To Be Contaminated by Parental Germs or Physical Affection."

There was a tiny girl who always stood hand in hand with Emily. Her parents never came. One visit she was gone. "They moved her to Rose Cottage," Emily shouted in explanation. "They don't like you to love anybody here."

She wrote once a week, the labored writing of a seven-year-old. "I am fine. How is the baby. If I write my leter nicly I will have a star. Love." There never was a star. We wrote every other day, letters she could never hold or keep but only hear read—once. "We simply do not have room for children to keep any personal possessions," they patiently explained when we pieced one Sunday's shrieking together to plead how much it would mean to Emily, who loved so to keep things, to be allowed to keep her letters and cards.

Each visit she looked frailer. "She isn't eating," they told us. (They had runny eggs for breakfast or mush with lumps, Emily said later, I'd hold it in my mouth and not swallow. Nothing ever tasted good, just when they had chicken.)

It took us eight months to get her released home, and only the fact that she gained back so little of her seven lost pounds convinced the social worker.

What is a "social worker"? Note irony here.

I used to try to hold and love her after she came back, but her body would stay stiff, and after a while she'd push away. She ate little. Food sickened her, and I think much of life too. Oh she had physical lightness and brightness, twinkling by on skates, bouncing like a ball up and down, up and down, over the jump rope, skimming over the hill; but these were momentary.

She fretted about her appearance, thin and dark and foreign-looking at a time when every little girl was supposed to look or thought she should look a chubby blonde replica of Shirley Temple. The doorbell sometimes rang for her, but no one seemed to come and play in the house or be a best friend. Maybe because we moved so much.

There was a boy she loved painfully through two school semesters. Months later she told me how she had taken pennies from my purse to buy him candy. "Licorice was his favorite and I brought him some every day, but he still liked Jennifer better'n me. Why, Mommy?" A question I could never answer.

School was a worry to her. She was not glib or quick in a world where glibness and quickness were easily confused with ability to learn. To her overworked and exasperated teachers she was an over-conscientious "slow learner" who kept trying to catch up and was absent entirely too often.

I let her be absent, though sometimes the illness was imaginary. How different from my now-strictness about attendance with the others. I wasn't working. We had a new baby, I was home anyhow. Sometimes, after Susan grew old enough, I would keep her home from school, too, to have them all together.

Mostly Emily had asthma, and her breathing, harsh and labored, would fill the house with a curiously tranquil sound. I would bring the two old dresser mirrors and her boxes of collections to her bed. She would select beads and single earrings, bottle tops and shells, dried flowers and pebbles, old postcards and scraps, all sorts of oddments; then she and Susan would play Kingdom, setting up landscapes and furniture, peopling them with action.

Those were the only times of peaceful companionship between her and Susan. I have edged away from it, that poisonous feeling between them, that terrible balancing of hurts and needs I had to do between the two, and did so badly, those earlier years.

Oh there are conflicts between the others too, each one human, needing, demanding, hurting, taking—but only between Emily and Susan, no, Emily toward Susan, that corroding resentment. It seems so obvious on the surface, yet it is not obvious. Susan, the second child, Susan, golden- and curly-haired and chubby, quick and articulate and assured, everything in appearance and manner Emily was not. Susan, not able to resist Emily's precious things, losing or sometimes clumsily breaking them; Susan telling jokes and riddles to company for applause, while Emily sat silent (to say to me later: that was *my* riddle, Mother, I told it to Susan); Susan, who for all the five years' difference in age was just a year behind Emily in developing physically.

I am glad for that slow physical development that widened the difference between her and her contemporaries, though she suffered over it. She was too vulnerable for that terrible world of youthful competition, of preening and parading, of constant measuring of yourself against every other, of envy, "If I had that copper hair," "If I had that skin. . . ." She tormented herself enough about not looking like the others, there was enough of the unsureness, the having to be conscious of words before you speak, the constant caring—what are they thinking of me?—without having it all magnified by the merciless physical drives.

Ronnie is calling. He is wet and I change him. It is rare there is such a cry now. That time of motherhood is almost behind me when the ear is not one's own but must always be racked and listening for the child cry, the child call. We sit for a while and I hold him, looking out over the city spread in charcoal with its soft aisles of light. *"Shoogily,"* he breathes and curls closer. I carry him back to bed, asleep. *Shoogily.* A funny word, a family word, inherited from Emily, invented by her to say: *comfort.*

In this and other ways she leaves her seal, I say aloud. And startle at my saying it. What do I mean? What did I start to gather together, to try and make coherent? I was at the terrible, growing years. War years. I do not remember them well. I was working, there were four smaller ones now, there was not time for her. She had to help be a mother, and housekeeper, and shopper. She had to set her seal. Mornings of crisis and near hysteria trying to get lunches packed, hair combed, coats and shoes found, everyone to school or Child Care on time, the baby ready for transportation. And always the paper scribbled on by a smaller one, the book looked at by Susan then mislaid, the homework not done. Running out to that huge school where she was one, she was lost, she was a drop; suffering over the unpreparedness, stammering and unsure in her classes.

There was so little time left at night after the kids were bedded down. She would struggle over books, always eating (it was in those years she developed her enormous appetite that is legendary in our family) and I would be ironing, or preparing food for the next day, or writing V-mail to Bill, or tending the baby. Sometimes, to make me laugh, or out of her despair, she would imitate happenings or types at school.

I think I said once: "Why don't you do something like this in the school amateur show?" One morning she phoned me at work, hardly understandable through the weeping: "Mother, I did it. I won, I won; they gave me first prize; they clapped and clapped and wouldn't let me go."

Now suddenly she was Somebody, and as imprisoned in her difference as she had been in anonymity.

She began to be asked to perform at other high schools, even in colleges, then at city and state-wide affairs. The first one we went to, I only recognized her that first moment when thin, shy, she almost drowned herself into the curtains. Then: Was this Emily? the control, the command, the convulsing and deadly clowning, the spell, then the roaring, stamping audience, unwilling to let this rare and precious laughter out of their lives.

Afterwards: You ought to do something about her with a gift like that—but without money or knowing how, what does one do? We have left it all to her, and the gift has as often eddied inside, clogged and clotted, as been used and growing.

She is coming. She runs up the stairs two at a time with her light graceful step, and I know she is happy tonight. Whatever it was that occasioned your call did not happen today.

"Aren't you ever going to finish the ironing, Mother? Whistler painted his mother in a rocker. I'd have to paint mine standing over an ironing board." This is one of her communicative nights and she tells me everything and nothing as she fixes herself a plate of food out of the icebox.

She is so lovely. Why did you want me to come in at all? Why were you concerned? She will find her way.

She starts up the stairs to bed. "Don't get me up with the rest in the morning." "But I thought you were having midterms." "Oh, those," she comes back in, kisses me, and says quite lightly, "in a couple of years when we'll all be atom-dead they won't matter a bit."

She has said it before. She *believes* it. But because I have been dredging the past, and all that compounds a human being is so heavy and meaningful in me, I cannot endure it tonight.

I will never total it all. I will never come in to say: She was a child seldom smiled at. Her father left me before she was a year old. I worked her first six years when there was work, or I sent her home and to his relatives. There were years she had care she hated. She was dark and thin and foreign-looking in a world where the prestige went to blondness and curly hair and dimples; she was slow where glibness was prized. She was a child of anxious, not proud, love. We were poor and could not afford for her the soil of easy growth. I was a young mother, I was a distracted mother. There were the other children pushing up, demanding. Her younger sister was all that she was not. There were years she did not want me to touch her. She kept too much in herself, her life was such she had to keep too much in herself. My wisdom came too late. She has much to her and probably nothing will come of it. She is a child of her age, of depression, of war, of fear.

Let her be. So all that is in her will not bloom—but in how many does it? There is still enough left to live by. Only help her to know—help make it so there is cause for her to know that she is more than this dress on the ironing-board, helpless before the iron.

Literary Sort: I am rather surprised that you are calling attention to this story. I should have thought you would find it sentimental.

Editor: Perhaps it is. But there are times—aren't there?—when we need to release ourselves to obvious and no doubt direct and also simple responses, to what I call, though with apologies, "the troubles of living," or even "life's sadness."

Literary Sort: Oh, I've tried to . . . but I just can't identify with that woman. . . . Eight pages of ironing. I mean *really*. . . . Pass the cream, please.

INTERLOCK WITH CLUSTER 10:
A generic link: short stories
An affective link: pathos

10

If nothing will survive of life besides what artists report of it, we have no right to report what we know to be lies.

—*From* Real People *by Alison Lurie*

Cluster 10: pp. 280-315
An affective cluster
Focus: the eliciting of sorrow, frustration, or resignation

INTERLOCK WITH CLUSTER 9:
A generic link: short stories
An affective link: pathos

A GOOD MAN IS HARD TO FIND

Flannery O'Connor

The grandmother didn't want to go to Florida. She wanted to visit some of her connections in east Tennessee and she was seizing at every chance to change Bailey's mind. Bailey was the son she lived with, her only boy. He was sitting on the edge of his chair at the table, bent over the orange sports section of the *Journal.* "Now look here, Bailey," she said, "see here, read this," and she stood with one hand on her thin hip and the other rattling the newspaper at his bald head. "Here this fellow that calls himself The Misfit is aloose from the Federal Pen and headed toward Florida and you read here what it says he did to these people. Just you read it. I wouldn't take my children in any direction with a criminal like that aloose in it. I couldn't answer to my conscience if I did."

Bailey didn't look up from his reading so she wheeled around then and faced the children's mother, a young woman in slacks, whose face was as broad and innocent as a cabbage and was tied around with a green headkerchief that had two points on the top like rabbit's ears. She was sitting on the sofa, feeding the baby his apricots out of a jar. "The children have been to Florida before," the old lady said. "You all ought to take them somewhere else for a change so they would see different parts of the world and be broad. They never have been to east Tennessee."

The children's mother didn't seem to hear her but the eight-year-old boy, John Wesley, a stocky child with glasses, said, "If you don't want to go to Florida, why dontcha stay at home?" He and the little girl, June Star, were reading the funny papers on the floor.

"She wouldn't stay at home to be queen for a day," June Star said without raising her yellow head.

"Yes and what would you do if this fellow, The Misfit, caught you?" the grandmother asked.

"I'd smack his face," John Wesley said.

"She wouldn't stay at home for a million bucks," June Star said. "Afraid she'd miss something. She has to go everywhere we go."

"All right, Miss," the grandmother said. "Just remember that the next time you want me to curl your hair."

June Star said her hair was naturally curly.

The next morning the grandmother was the first one in the car, ready to go. She had her big black valise that looked like the head of a hippopotamus in one corner, and underneath it she was hiding a basket with Pitty Sing, the cat, in it. She didn't intend for the cat to be left alone in the house for three days because he would miss her too much and she was afraid he might brush against one of the gas burners and accidentally asphyxiate himself. Her son, Bailey, didn't like to arrive at a motel with a cat.

She sat in the middle of the back seat with John Wesley and June Star on either side of her. Bailey and the children's mother and the baby sat in the front and they left Atlanta at eight forty-five with the mileage on the car at 55890. The grandmother wrote this down because she thought it would be interesting to say how many miles they had been when they got back. It took them twenty minutes to reach the outskirts of the city.

The old lady settled herself comfortably, removing her white cotton gloves and putting them up with her purse on the shelf in front of the back window. The children's mother still had on slacks and still had her head tied up in a green kerchief, but the grandmother had on a navy blue straw sailor hat with a bunch of white violets on the brim and a navy blue dress with a small white dot in the print. Her collar and cuffs were white organdy trimmed with lace and at her neckline she had pinned a purple spray of cloth violets containing a sachet. In case of an accident, anyone seeing her dead on the highway would know at once that she was a lady.

She said she thought it was going to be a good day for driving, neither too hot nor too cold, and she cautioned Bailey that the speed limit was fifty-five miles an hour and that the patrolmen hid themselves behind billboards and small clumps of trees and sped out after you before you had a chance to slow down. She pointed out interesting details of the scenery: Stone Mountain; the blue granite that in some places came up to both sides of the highway; the brilliant red clay banks slightly streaked with purple; and the various crops that made rows of green lace-work on the ground. The trees were full of silver-white sunlight and the meanest of them sparkled. The children were reading comic magazines and their mother had gone back to sleep.

"Let's go through Georgia fast so we won't have to look at it much," John Wesley said.

"If I were a little boy," said the grandmother, "I wouldn't talk about my native state that way. Tennessee has the mountains and Georgia has the hills."

"Tennessee is just a hillbilly dumping ground," John Wesley said, "and Georgia is a lousy state too."

"You said it," June Star said.

"In my time," said the grandmother, folding her thin veined fingers, "children were more respectful of their native states and their parents and everything else. People did right then. Oh look at the cute little pickaninny!" she said and pointed to a Negro child standing in the door of a

See overprinted note at top of p. 284.

This passage is a good example of O'Connor's distance from her material. She never intrudes to comment on the idiosyncrasies of her characters; instead they reveal themselves through their own acts and words. Solid, subtle writing.

shack. "Wouldn't that make a picture, now?" she asked and they all turned and looked at the little Negro out of the back window. He waved.

"He didn't have any britches on," June Star said.

"He probably didn't have any," the grandmother explained. "Little niggers in the country don't have things like we do. If I could paint, I'd paint that picture," she said.

Why would she paint *that* picture?

The children exchanged comic books.

The grandmother offered to hold the baby and the children's mother passed him over the front seat to her. She set him on her knee and bounced him and told him about the things they were passing. She rolled her eyes and screwed up her mouth and stuck her leathery thin face into his smooth bland one. Occasionally he gave her a faraway smile. They passed a large cotton field with five or six graves fenced in the middle of it, like a small island. "Look at the graveyard!" the grandmother said, pointing it out. "That was the old family burying ground. That belonged to the plantation."

Allusion to the novel and film, both of which focused on the Civil War and the loss of the aristocratic-plantation-way-of-life. Note that the grandmother laughs.

"Where's the plantation?" John Wesley asked.

"Gone with the Wind," said the grandmother. "Ha. Ha."

When the children finished all the comic books they had brought, they opened the lunch and ate it. The grandmother ate a peanut butter sandwich and an olive and would not let the children throw the box and the paper napkins out the window. When there was nothing else to do they played a game by choosing a cloud and making the other two guess what shape it suggested. John Wesley took one the shape of a cow and June Star guessed a cow and John Wesley said, no, an automobile, and June Star said he didn't play fair, and they began to slap each other over the grandmother.

The grandmother said she would tell them a story if they would keep quiet. When she told a story, she rolled her eyes and waved her head and was very dramatic. She said once when she was a maiden lady she had been courted by a Mr. Edgar Atkins Teagarden from Jasper, Georgia. She said he was a very good-looking man and a gentleman and that he brought her a watermelon every Saturday afternoon with his initials cut in it, E.A.T. Well, one Saturday, she said, Mr. Teagarden brought the watermelon and there was nobody at home and he left it on the front porch and returned in his buggy to Jasper, but she never got the watermelon, she said, because a nigger boy ate it when he saw the initials, E.A.T.! This story tickled John Wesley's funny bone and he giggled and giggled but June Star didn't think it was any good. She said she wouldn't marry a man that just brought her a watermelon on Saturday. The grandmother said she would have done well to marry Mr. Teagarden because he was a gentleman and had bought Coca-Cola stock when it first came out and that he had died only a few years ago, a very wealthy man.

See first over-printed note above.

They stopped at The Tower for barbecued sandwiches. The Tower was a part stucco and part wood filling station and dance hall set in a clearing outside of Timothy. A fat man named Red Sammy Butts ran it and there were signs stuck here and there on the building and for miles up and down the highway saying, TRY RED SAMMY'S FAMOUS BARBECUE. NONE LIKE FAMOUS RED SAMMY'S! RED SAM! THE FAT BOY WITH THE HAPPY LAUGH. A VETERAN! RED SAMMY'S YOUR MAN!

Red Sammy was lying on the bare ground outside The Tower with his head under a truck while a gray monkey about a foot high, chained to a small chinaberry tree, chattered nearby. The monkey sprang back into the tree and got on the highest limb as soon as he saw the children jump out of the car and run toward him.

Inside, The Tower was a long dark room with a counter at one end and tables at the other and dancing space in the middle. They all sat down at a broad table next to the nickelodeon and Red Sam's wife, a tall burnt-brown woman with hair and eyes lighter than her skin, came and took their order. The children's mother put a dime in the machine and played "The Tennessee Waltz," and the grandmother said that tune always made her want to dance. She asked Bailey if he would like to dance but he only glared at her. He didn't have a naturally sunny disposition like she did and trips made him nervous. The grandmother's brown eyes were very bright. She swayed her head from side to side and pretended she was dancing in her chair. June Star said play something she could tap to so the children's mother put in another dime and played a fast number and June Star stepped out onto the dance floor and did her tap routine.

"Ain't she cute?" Red Sam's wife said, leaning over the counter. "Would you like to come be my little girl?"

"No, I certainly wouldn't," June Star said. "I wouldn't live in a broken-down place like this for a million bucks!" and she ran back to the table.

"Ain't she cute?" the woman repeated, stretching her mouth politely.

"Aren't you ashamed?" hissed the grandmother.

Red Sam came in and told his wife to quit lounging on the counter and hurry up with these people's order. His khaki trousers reached just to his hip bones and his stomach hung over them like a sack of meal swaying under his shirt. He came over and sat down at a table nearby and let out a combination sigh and yodel. "You can't win," he said. "You can't win," and he wiped his sweating red face off with a gray handkerchief. "These days you don't know who to trust," he said. "Ain't that the truth?"

"People are certainly not nice like they used to be," said the grandmother.

This is the second time she has said this.
What does "used to be" mean to the grandmother?

"Two fellers come in here last week," Red Sammy said, "driving a Chrysler. It was a old beat-up car but it was a good one and these boys looked all right to me. Said they worked at the mill and you know I let them fellers charge the gas they bought? Now why did I do that?"

"Because you're a good man!" the grandmother said at once.

"Yes'm, I suppose so," Red Sam said as if he were struck with this answer.

His wife brought the orders, carrying the five plates all at once without a tray, two in each hand and one balanced on her arm. "It isn't a soul in this green world of God's that you can trust," she said. "And I don't count nobody out of that, not nobody," she repeated, looking at Red Sammy.

"Did you read about that criminal, The Misfit, that's escaped?" asked the grandmother.

"I wouldn't be a bit surprised if he didn't attact this place right here," said the woman. "If he hears about it being here, I wouldn't be none surprised to see him. If he hears it's two cent in the cash register, I wouldn't be a tall surprised if he . . ."

"That'll do," Red Sam said. "Go bring these people their Co'Colas," and the woman went off to get the rest of the order.

"A good man is hard to find," Red Sammy said. "Everything is getting terrible. I remember the day you could go off and leave your screen door unlatched. Not no more."

He and the grandmother discussed better times. The old lady said that in her opinion Europe was entirely to blame for the way things were now. She said the way Europe acted you would think we were made of money and Red Sam said it was no use talking about it, she was exactly right. The children ran outside into the white sunlight and looked at the monkey in the lacy chinaberry tree. He was busy catching fleas on himself and biting each one carefully between his teeth as if it were a delicacy.

They drove off again into the hot afternoon. The grandmother took cat naps and woke up every few minutes with her own snoring. Outside of Toombsboro she woke up and recalled an old plantation that she had visited in this neighborhood once when she was a young lady. She said the house had six white columns across the front and that there was an avenue of oaks leading up to it and two little wooden trellis arbors on either side in front where you sat down with your suitor after a stroll in the garden. She recalled exactly which road to turn off to get to it. She knew that Bailey would not be willing to lose any time looking at an old house, but the more she talked about it, the more she wanted to see it once again and find out if the little twin arbors were still standing. "There was a secret panel in this house," she said craftily, not telling the truth but wishing that she were, "and the story went that all the family silver was hidden in it when Sherman came through but it was never found . . ."

"Hey!" John Wesley said. "Let's go see it! We'll find it! We'll poke all the woodwork and find it! Who lives there? Where do you turn off at? Hey, Pop, can't we turn off there?"

"We never have seen a house with a secret panel!" June Star shrieked. "Let's go to the house with the secret panel! Hey, Pop, can't we go see the house with the secret panel!"

"It's not far from here, I know," the grandmother said. "It wouldn't take over twenty minutes."

Bailey was looking straight ahead. His jaw was as rigid as a horseshoe. "No," he said.

The children began to yell and scream that they wanted to see the house with the secret panel. John Wesley kicked the back of the front seat and June Star hung over her mother's shoulder and whined desperately into her ear that they never had any fun even on their vacation, that they could never do what THEY wanted to do. The baby began to scream and John Wesley kicked the back of the seat so hard that his father could feel the blows in his kidney.

"All right!" he shouted and drew the car to a stop at the side of the road. "Will you all shut up? Will you all just shut up for one second? If you don't shut up, we won't go anywhere."

"It would be very educational for them," the grandmother murmured.

"All right," Bailey said, "but get this. This is the only time we're going to stop for anything like this. This is the one and only time."

"The dirt road that you have to turn down is about a mile back," the grandmother directed. "I marked it when we passed."

"A dirt road," Bailey groaned.

After they had turned around and were headed toward the dirt road, the grandmother recalled other points about the house, the beautiful glass over the front doorway and the candle-lamp in the hall. John Wesley said that the secret panel was probably in the fireplace.

"You can't go inside this house," Bailey said. "You don't know who lives there."

"While you all talk to the people in front, I'll run around behind and get in a window," John Wesley suggested.

"We'll all stay in the car," his mother said.

They turned onto the dirt road and the car raced roughly along in a swirl of pink dust. The grandmother recalled the times when there were no paved roads and thirty miles was a day's journey. The dirt road was hilly and there were sudden washes in it and sharp curves on dangerous embankments. All at once they would be on a hill, looking down over the blue tops of trees for miles around, then the next minute, they would be in a red depression with the dust-coated trees looking down on them.

"This place had better turn up in a minute," Bailey said, "or I'm going to turn around."

The road looked as if no one had traveled on it in months.

"It's not much farther," the grandmother said and just as she said it, a horrible thought came to her. The thought was so embarrassing that she turned red in the face and her eyes dilated and her feet jumped up, upsetting her valise in the corner. The instant the valise moved, the newspaper top she had over the basket under it rose with a snarl and Pitty Sing, the cat, sprang onto Bailey's shoulder.

The children were thrown to the floor and their mother, clutching the baby, was thrown out the door onto the ground; the old lady was thrown into the front seat. The car turned over once and landed right-side-up in a gulch on the side of the road. Bailey remained in the driver's seat with the cat—gray-striped with a broad white face and an orange nose—clinging to his neck like a caterpillar.

As soon as the children saw they could move their arms and legs, they scrambled out of the car, shouting, "We've had an ACCIDENT!" The grandmother was curled up under the dashboard, hoping she was injured so that Bailey's wrath would not come down on her all at once. The horrible thought she had had before the accident was that the house she had remembered so vividly was not in Georgia but in Tennessee.

Bailey removed the cat from his neck with both hands and flung it out the window against the side of a pine tree. Then he got out of the car and started looking for the children's mother. She was sitting against the side of the red gutted ditch, holding the screaming baby, but she only had a cut down her face and a broken shoulder. "We've had an ACCIDENT!" the children screamed in a frenzy of delight.

"But nobody's killed," June Star said with disappointment as the grandmother limped out of the car, her hat still pinned to her head but the broken front brim standing up at jaunty angle and the violet spray hanging off the side. They all sat down in the ditch, except the children, to recover from the shock. They were all shaking.

"Maybe a car will come along," said the children's mother hoarsely.

"I believe I have injured an organ," said the grandmother, pressing her side, but no one answered her. Bailey's teeth were clattering. He had on a yellow sport shirt with bright blue parrots designed in it and his face was as yellow as the shirt. The grandmother decided that she would not mention that the house was in Tennessee.

The road was about ten feet above and they could see only the tops of the trees on the other side of it. Behind the ditch they were sitting in there were more woods, tall and dark and deep. In a few minutes they saw a car some distance away on top of a hill, coming slowly as if the occupants were watching them. The grandmother stood up and waved both arms dramatically to attract their attention. The car continued to come on slowly, disappeared around a bend and appeared again, moving even slower, on top of the hill they had gone over. It was a big black battered hearse-like automobile. There were three men in it.

It came to stop just over them and for some minutes, the driver looked down with a steady expressionless gaze to where they were sitting, and didn't speak. Then he turned his head and muttered something to the other two and they got out. One was a fat boy in black trousers and a red sweat shirt with a silver stallion embossed on the front of it. He moved around on the right side of them and stood staring, his mouth partly open in a kind of loose grin. The other had on khaki pants and a blue striped coat and a gray hat pulled down very low, hiding most of his face. He came around slowly on the left side. Neither spoke.

The driver got out of the car and stood by the side of it, looking down at them. He was an older man than the other two. His hair was just beginning to gray and he wore silver-rimmed spectacles that gave him a scholarly look. He had a long creased face and didn't have on any shirt or undershirt. He had on blue jeans that were too tight for him and was holding a black hat and a gun. The two boys also had guns.

"We've had an ACCIDENT!" the children screamed.

The grandmother had the peculiar feeling that the bespectacled man was someone she knew. His face was as familiar to her as if she had known him all her life but she could not recall who he was. He moved away from the car and began to come down the embankment, placing his feet carefully so that he wouldn't slip. He had on tan and white shoes and no socks, and his ankles were red and thin. "Good afternoon," he said. "I see you all had you a little spill."

"We turned over twice!" said the grandmother.

"Oncet," he corrected. "We seen it happen. Try their car and see will it run, Hiram," he said quietly to the boy with the gray hat.

"What you got that gun for?" John Wesley asked. "Whatcha gonna do with that gun?"

"Lady," the man said to the children's mother, "would you mind calling them children to sit down by you? Children make me nervous. I want all you all to sit down right together there where you're at."

"What are you telling US what to do for?" June Star asked.

Behind them the line of woods gaped like a dark open mouth. "Come here," said their mother.

"Look here now," Bailey began suddenly, "we're in a predicament! We're in . . ."

The grandmother shrieked. She scrambled to her feet and stood staring.

"You're The Misfit!" she said. "I recognized you at once!"

"Yes'm," the man said, smiling slightly as if he were pleased in spite of himself to be known, "but it would have been better for all of you, lady, if you hadn't of reckernized me."

Bailey turned his head sharply and said something to his mother that shocked even the children. The old lady began to cry and The Misfit reddened.

"Lady," he said, "don't you get upset. Sometimes a man says things he don't mean. I don't reckon he meant to talk to you thataway."

"You wouldn't shoot a lady, would you?" the grandmother said and removed a clean handkerchief from her cuff and began to slap at her eyes with it.

The Misfit pointed the toe of his shoe into the ground and made a little hole and then covered it up again. "I would hate to have to," he said.

"Listen," the grandmother almost screamed, "I know you're a good man. You don't look a bit like you have common blood. I know you must come from nice people!"

"Yes mam," he said, "finest people in the world." When he smiled he showed a row of strong white teeth. "God never made a finer woman than my mother and my daddy's heart was pure gold," he said. The boy with the red sweat shirt had come around behind them and was standing with his gun at his hip. The Misfit squatted down on the ground. "Watch them children, Bobby Lee," he said. "You know they make me nervous." He looked at the six of them huddled together in front of him and he seemed to be embarrassed as if he couldn't think of anything to say. "Ain't a cloud in the sky," he remarked, looking up at it. "Don't see no sun but don't see no cloud neither."

"Yes, it's a beautiful day," said the grandmother. "Listen," she said, "you shouldn't call yourself The Misfit because I know you're a good man at heart. I can just look at you and tell."

"Hush!" Bailey yelled. "Hush! Everybody shut up and let me handle this!" He was squatting in the position of a runner about to sprint forward but he didn't move.

"I pre-chate that, lady," The Misfit said and drew a little circle in the ground with the butt of his gun.

"It'll take a half a hour to fix this here car," Hiram called, looking over the raised hood of it.

"Well, first you and Bobby Lee get him and that little boy to step over yonder with you," The Misfit said, pointing to Bailey and John Wesley. "The boys want to ast you something," he said to Bailey. "Would you mind stepping back in them woods there with them?"

"Listen," Bailey began, "we're in a terrible predicament! Nobody realizes what this is," and his voice cracked. His eyes were as blue and intense as the parrots in his shirt and he remained perfectly still.

The grandmother reached up to adjust her hat brim as if she were going to the woods with him but it came off in her hand. She stood staring at it and after a second she let it fall on the ground. Hiram pulled Bailey up by the arm as if he were assisting an old man. John Wesley caught hold of his father's hand and Bobby Lee followed. They went off toward the woods and just as they reached the dark edge, Bailey turned and supporting himself against a gray naked pine trunk, he shouted, "I'll be back in a minute, Mamma, wait on me!"

"Come back this instant!" his mother shrilled but they all disappeared into the woods.

"Bailey Boy!" the grandmother called in a tragic voice but she found she was looking at The Misfit squatting on the ground in front of her. "I just know you're a good man," she said desperately. "You're not a bit common!"

"Nome, I ain't a good man," The Misfit said after a second as if he had considered her statement carefully, "but I ain't the worst in the world neither. My daddy said I was a different breed of dog from my brothers and sisters. 'You know,' Daddy said, 'it's some that can live their whole life out without asking about it and it's others has to know why it is, and this boy is one of the latters. He's going to be into everything!' " He put on his black hat and looked up suddenly and then away deep into the woods as if he were embarrassed again. "I'm sorry I don't have on a shirt before you ladies," he said, hunching his shoulders slightly. "We buried our clothes that we had on when we escaped and we're just making do until we can get better. We borrowed these from some folks we met," he explained.

"That's perfectly all right," the grandmother said. "Maybe Bailey has an extra shirt in his suitcase."

"I'll look and see terrectly," The Misfit said.

"Where are they taking him?" the children's mother screamed.

"Daddy was a card himself," The Misfit said. "You couldn't put anything over on him. He never got in trouble with the Authorities though. Just had the knack of handling them."

"You could be honest too if you'd only try," said the grandmother. "Think how wonderful it would be to settle down and live a comfortable life and not have to think about somebody chasing you all the time."

The Misfit kept scratching in the ground with the butt of his gun as if he were thinking about it. "Yes'm, somebody is always after you," he murmured.

The grandmother noticed how thin his shoulder blades were just behind his hat because she was standing up looking down on him. "Do you ever pray?" she asked.

He shook his head. All she saw was the black hat wiggle between his shoulder blades. "Nome," he said.

There was a pistol shot from the woods, followed closely by another. Then silence. The old lady's head jerked around. She could hear the wind move through the tree tops like a long satisfied insuck of breath. "Bailey Boy!" she called.

"I was a gospel singer for a while," The Misfit said. "I been most everything. Been in the arm service, both land and sea, at home and abroad, been twict married, been an undertaker, been with the railroads, plowed Mother Earth, been in a tornado, seen a man burnt alive oncet," and he looked up at the children's mother and the little girl who were sitting close together, their faces white and their eyes glassy; "I even seen a woman flogged," he said.

"Pray, pray," the grandmother began, "pray, pray . . ."

"I never was a bad boy that I remember of," The Misfit said in an almost dreamy voice, "but somewheres along the line I done something wrong and got sent to the penitentiary. I was buried alive," and he looked up and held her attention to him by a steady stare.

"That's when you should have started to pray," she said. "What did you do to get sent to the penitentiary that first time?"

"Turn to the right, it was a wall," The Misfit said, looking up again at the cloudless sky. "Turn to the left, it was a wall. Look up it was a ceiling, look down it was a floor. I forget what I done, lady. I set there and set there, trying to remember what it was I done and I ain't recalled it to this day. Oncet in a while, I would think it was coming to me, but it never come."

"Maybe they put you in by mistake," the old lady said vaguely.

"Nome," he said. "It wasn't no mistake. They had the papers on me."

"You must have stolen something," she said.

The Misfit sneered slightly. "Nobody had nothing I wanted," he said. "It was a head-doctor at the penitentiary said what I had done was kill my daddy but I known that for a lie. My daddy died in nineteen ought nineteen of the epidemic flu and I never had a thing to do with it. He was buried in the Mount Hopewell Baptist churchyard and you can go there and see for yourself."

"If you would pray," the old lady said, "Jesus would help you."

"That's right," The Misfit said.

"Well then, why don't you pray?" she asked trembling with delight suddenly.

"I don't want no hep," he said. "I'm doing all right by myself."

Bobby Lee and Hiram came ambling back from the woods. Bobby Lee was dragging a yellow shirt with bright blue parrots in it.

"Throw me that shirt, Bobby Lee," The Misfit said. The shirt came flying at him and landed on his shoulder and he put it on. The grandmother couldn't name what the shirt reminded her of. "No, lady," The Misfit said while he was buttoning it up, "I found out the crime don't matter. You can do one thing or you can do another, kill a man or take a tire off his car, because sooner or later you're going to forget what it was you done and just be punished for it."

The children's mother had begun to make heaving noises as if she couldn't get her breath. "Lady," he asked, "would you and that little girl like to step off yonder with Bobby Lee and Hiram and join your husband?"

"Yes, thank you," the mother said faintly. Her left arm dangled helplessly and she was holding the baby, who had gone to sleep, in the other. "Hep that lady up, Hiram," The Misfit said as she struggled to climb out of the ditch, "and Bobby Lee, you hold onto that little girl's hand."

"I don't want to hold hands with him," June Star said. "He reminds me of a pig."

The fat boy blushed and laughed and caught her by the arm and pulled her off into the woods after Hiram and her mother.

Alone with The Misfit, the grandmother found that she had lost her voice. There was not a cloud in the sky nor any sun. There was nothing around her but woods. She wanted to tell him that he must pray. She opened and closed her mouth several times before anything came out. Finally she found herself saying, "Jesus. Jesus," meaning, Jesus will help you, but the way she was saying it, it sounded as if she might be cursing.

"Yes'm," The Misfit said as if he agreed. "Jesus thown everything off balance. It was the same case with Him as with me except He hadn't committed any crime and they could prove I had committed one because they had the papers on me. Of course," he said, "they never shown me my papers. That's why I sign myself now. I said long ago, you get you a signature and sign everything you do and keep a copy of it. Then you'll know what you done and you can hold up the crime to the punishment and see do they match and in the end you'll have something to prove you ain't been treated right. I call myself The Misfit," he said, "because I can't make what all I done wrong fit what all I gone through in punishment."

There was a piercing scream from the woods, followed closely by a pistol report. "Does it seem right to you, lady, that one is punished a heap and another ain't punished at all?"

"Jesus!" the old lady cried. "You've got good blood! I know you wouldn't shoot a lady! I know you come from nice people! Pray! Jesus, you ought not to shoot a lady. I'll give you all the money I've got!"

"Lady," The Misfit said, looking beyond her far into the woods, "there never was a body that give the undertaker a tip."

There were two more pistol reports and the grandmother raised her head like a parched old turkey hen crying for water and called, "Bailey Boy, Bailey Boy!" as if her heart would break.

"Jesus was the only One that ever raised the dead," The Misfit continued, "and He shouldn't have done it. He thown everything off balance. If He did what He said, then it's nothing for you to do but thow away everything and follow Him, and if He didn't then it's nothing for you to do but enjoy the few minutes you got left the best way you can—by killing somebody or burning down his house or doing some other meanness to him. No pleasure but meanness," he said and his voice had become almost a snarl.

"Maybe He didn't raise the dead," the old lady mumbled, not knowing what she was saying and feeling so dizzy that she sank down in the ditch with her legs twisted under her.

"I wasn't there so I can't say He didn't," The Misfit said. "I wisht I had of been there," he said, hitting the ground with his fist. "It ain't right I wasn't there because if I had of been there I would of known. Listen lady," he said in a high voice, "if I had of been there I would of known and I wouldn't be like I am now." His voice seemed about to crack and the grandmother's head cleared for an instant. She saw the man's face twisted close to her own as if he were going to cry and she murmured, "Why, you're one of my babies. You're one of my own children!" She reached out and touched him on the shoulder. The Misfit sprang back as if a snake had bitten him and shot her three times through the chest. Then he put his gun down on the ground and took off his glasses and began to clean them.

Hiram and Bobby Lee returned from the woods and stood over the ditch, looking down at the grandmother who half sat and half lay in a puddle of blood with her legs crossed under her like a child's and her face smiling up at the cloudless sky.

Without his glasses, The Misfit's eyes were red-rimmed and pale and defenseless-looking. "Take her off and thow her where you thown the others," he said, picking up the cat that was rubbing itself against his leg.

"She was a talker, wasn't she?" Bobby Lee said, sliding down the ditch with a yodel.

"She would of been a good woman," The Misfit said, "if it had been somebody there to shoot her every minute of her life."

"Some fun!" Bobby Lee said.

"Shut up, Bobby Lee," The Misfit said. "It's no real pleasure in life."

Students interested in this type of Southern Gothic writing might like to read one or more of the following:

Flannery O'Connor, *Everything That Rises Must Converge*
Carson McCullers, *Ballad of the Sad Cafe and Other Stories*
Truman Capote, *Grass Harp: Tree of Night and Other Stories*

The dragon is by the side of the road, watching those who pass.
Beware lest he devour you.
We go to the father of souls, but it is necessary to pass by the dragon.

—Saint Cyril of Jerusalem

William and Emily

There is something about Death
Like love itself!
If with someone with whom you have known passion,
And the glow of youthful love,
You also, after years of life
Together, feel the sinking of the fire,
And thus fade away together,
Gradually, faintly, delicately,
As it were in each other's arms,
Passing from the familiar room—
That is the power of unison between souls
Like love itself!

Compare with the last two lines of "After Long Silence" (p. 296).

—Edgar Lee Masters

After Long Silence

Speech after long silence; it is right,
All other lovers being estranged or dead,
Unfriendly lamplight hid under its shade,
The curtains drawn upon unfriendly night,
That we descant and yet again descant
Upon the supreme theme of Art and Song:
Bodily decrepitude is wisdom; young
We loved each other and were ignorant.

—William Butler Yeats

A very formal, learned word for *converse*

Compare with last two lines of "William and Emily" (p. 295).

THE BLACK AND WHITE

Harold Pinter

i. e., the woman

The FIRST OLD WOMAN *is sitting at a milk bar table. Small. A* SECOND OLD WOMAN *approaches. Tall. She is carrying two bowls of soup, which are covered by two plates, on each of which is a slice of bread. She puts the bowls down on the table carefully.*

SECOND: You see that one come up and speak to me at the counter?

She takes the bread plates off the bowls, takes two spoons from her pocket, and places the bowls, plates and spoons.

FIRST: You got the bread, then?

SECOND: I didn't know how I was going to carry it. In the end I put the plates on top of the soup.

FIRST: I like a bit of bread with my soup.

They begin the soup. Pause.

SECOND: Did you see that one come up and speak to me at the counter?

FIRST: Who?

SECOND: Comes up to me, he says, hullo, he says, what's the time by your clock? Bloody liberty. I was just standing there getting your soup.

FIRST: It's tomato soup.

SECOND: What's the time by your clock? he says.

FIRST: I bet you answered him back.

SECOND: I told him all right. Go on, I said, why don't you get back into your scraghole, I said, clear off out of it before I call a copper.

Pause.

FIRST: I not long got here.

SECOND: Did you get the all-night bus?

FIRST: I got the all-night bus straight here.

SECOND: Where from?

FIRST: Marble Arch. At western edge of Central London

SECOND: Which one?

FIRST: The two-nine-four, that takes me all the way to Fleet Street. Considerably to the east of where they seem to be

SECOND: So does the two-nine-one. [*Pause.*] I see you talking to two strangers as I come in. You want to stop talking to strangers, old piece of boot like you, you mind who you talk to.

FIRST: I wasn't talking to any strangers.

Pause. The FIRST OLD WOMAN *follows the progress of a bus through the window.*

That's another all-night bus gone down. [*Pause.*] Going up the other way. Fulham way. [*Pause.*] That was a two-nine-seven. [*Pause.*] I've never been up that way. [*Pause.*] I've been down to Liverpool Street. Farther east again

SECOND: That's up the other way.

FIRST: I don't fancy going down there, down Fulham way, and all up there.

SECOND: Uh-uh.

FIRST: I've never fancied that direction much.

Pause.

SECOND: How's your bread?

Pause.

Note "pauses"—as in Yeats' poem (p. 296), there appears to be much "silence" here.

FIRST: Eh?

SECOND: Your bread.

FIRST: All right. How's yours?

Pause.

SECOND: They don't charge for the bread if you have soup.

FIRST: They do if you have tea.

SECOND: If you have tea they do. [*Pause.*] You talk to strangers they'll take you in. Mind my word. Coppers'll take you in.

FIRST: I don't talk to strangers.

SECOND: They took me away in the wagon once.

FIRST: They didn't keep you though.

SECOND: They didn't keep me, but that was only because they took a fancy to me. They took a fancy to me when they got me in the wagon.

FIRST: Do you think they'd take a fancy to me?

SECOND: I wouldn't back on it. "bet"

The FIRST OLD WOMAN *gazes out of the window.*

FIRST: You can see what goes on from this top table. [*Pause.*] It's better than going down to that place on the embankment, anyway.

SECOND: Yes, there's not too much noise. Along the Thames River

FIRST: There's always a bit of noise.

SECOND: Yes, there's always a bit of life.

Pause.

FIRST: They'll be closing down soon to give it a scrub-round.

SECOND: There's a wind out.

Pause.

FIRST: I wouldn't mind staying.

SECOND: They won't let you.

FIRST: I know. [*Pause.*] Still, they only close hour and half, don't they? [*Pause.*] It's not long. [*Pause.*] You can go along, then come back.

SECOND: I'm going. I'm not coming back.

FIRST: When it's light I come back. Have my tea.

SECOND: I'm going. I'm going up to the Garden. Probably Covent Garden

FIRST: I'm not going down there. [*Pause.*] I'm going up to Waterloo Bridge.

SECOND: You'll just about see the last two-nine-six come up over the river.

FIRST: I'll just catch a look of it. Time I get up there. About due south of them

Pause.

It don't look like an all-night bus in daylight, do it?

A Summer Tragedy

Arna Bontemps

Old Jeff Patton, the black share farmer, fumbled with his bow tie. His fingers trembled and the high, stiff collar pinched his throat. A fellow loses his hand for such vanities after thirty or forty years of simple life. Once a year, or maybe twice if there's a wedding among his kinfolks, he may spruce up; but generally fancy clothes do nothing but adorn the wall of the big room and feed the moths. That had been Jeff Patton's experience. He had not worn his stiff-bosomed shirt more than a dozen times in all his married life. His swallow-tailed coat lay on the bed beside him, freshly brushed and pressed, but it was as full of holes as the overalls in which he worked on weekdays. The moths had used it badly. Jeff twisted his mouth into a hideous toothless grimace as he contended with the obstinate bow. He stamped his good foot and decided to give up the struggle.

"Jennie," he called.

"What's that, Jeff?" His wife's shrunken voice came out of the adjoining room like an echo. It was hardly bigger than a whisper.

"I reckon you'll have to he'p me wid this heah bow tie, baby," he said meekly. "Dog if I can hitch it up."

Her answer was not strong enough to reach him, but presently the old woman came to the door, feeling her way with a stick. She had a wasted, dead-leaf appearance. Her body, as scrawny and gnarled as a string bean, seemed less than nothing in the ocean of frayed and faded petticoats that surrounded her. These hung an inch or two above the tops of her heavy unlaced shoes and showed little grotesque piles where the stockings had fallen down from her negligible legs.

"You oughta could do a heap mo' wid a thing like that'n me—beingst as you got yo' good sight."

"Looks like I oughta could," he admitted. "But my fingers is gone democrat on me. I get all mixed up in the looking glass an' can't tell wicha way to twist the devilish thing."

Jennie sat on the side of the bed, and old Jeff Patton got down on one knee while she tied the bow knot. It was a slow and painful ordeal for each of them in this position. Jeff's bones cracked, his knee ached, and it was only after a half dozen attempts that Jennie worked a semblance of a bow into the tie.

"I got to dress maself now," the old woman whispered. "These is ma old shoes an' stockings, and I ain't so much as unwrapped ma dress."

"Well, don't worry 'bout me no mo', baby," Jeff said. "That 'bout finishes me. All I gotta do now is slip on that old coat 'n ves' an' I'll be fixed to leave."

Jennie disappeared again through the dim passage into the shed room. Being blind was no handicap to her in that black hole. Jeff heard the cane placed against the wall beside the door and knew that his wife was on easy ground. He put on his coat, took a battered top hat from the bed post, and hobbled to the front door. He was ready to travel. As soon as Jennie could get on her Sunday shoes and her old black silk dress, they would start.

Outside the tiny log house, the day was warm and mellow with sunshine. A host of wasps were humming with busy excitement in the trunk of a dead sycamore. Gray squirrels were searching through the grass for hickory nuts, and blue jays were in the trees, hopping from branch to branch. Pine woods stretched away to the left like a black sea. Among them were scattered scores of log houses like Jeff's, houses of black share farmers. Cows and pigs wandered freely among the trees. There was no danger of loss. Each farmer knew his own stock and knew his neighbor's as well as he knew his neighbor's children.

Down the slope to the right were the cultivated acres on which the colored folks worked. They extended to the river, more than two miles away, and they were today green with the unmade cotton crop. A tiny thread of a road, which passed directly in front of Jeff's place, ran through these green fields like a pencil mark.

Jeff, standing outside the door, with his absurd hat in his left hand, surveyed the wide scene tenderly. He had been forty-five years on these acres. He loved them with the unexplained affection that others have for the countries to which they belong.

The sun was hot on his head, his collar still pinched his throat, and the Sunday clothes were intolerably hot. Jeff transferred the hat to his right hand and began fanning with it. Suddenly the whisper that was Jennie's voice came out of the shed room.

"You can bring the car round front whilst you's waitin'," it said feebly. There was a tired pause; then it added, "I'll soon be fixed to go."

"A'right, baby," Jeff answered. "I'll get it in a minute."

But he didn't move. A thought struck him that made his mouth fall open. The mention of the car brought to his mind, with new intensity, the trip he and Jennie were about to take. Fear came into his eyes; excitement took his breath. Lord, Jesus!

"Jeff. . . . O Jeff," the old woman's whisper called.

He awakened with a jolt. "Hunh, baby?"

"What you doin'?"

"Nuthin. Jes studyin'. I jes been turnin' things round 'n round in ma mind."

"You could be gettin' the car," she said.

"Oh yes, right away, baby."

He started round to the shed, limping heavily on his bad leg. There were three frizzly chickens in the yard. All his other chickens had been killed or stolen recently. But the frizzly chickens had been saved somehow. That was fortunate indeed, for these curious creatures had a way of devouring "poison" from the yard and in that way protecting against conjure and black luck and spells. But even the frizzly chickens seemed now to be in a stupor. Jeff thought they had some ailment; he expected all three of them to die shortly.

The shed in which the old T-model Ford stood was only a grass roof held up by four corner poles. It had been built by tremulous hands at a time when the little rattletrap car had been regarded as a peculiar treasure. And, miraculously, despite wind and downpour, it still stood.

Jeff adjusted the crank and put his weight upon it. The engine came to life with a sputter and bang that rattled the old car from radiator to tail light. Jeff hopped into the seat and put his foot on the accelerator. The sputtering and banging increased. The rattling became more violent. That was good. It was good banging, good sputtering and rattling, and it meant that the aged car was still in running condition. She could be depended on for this trip.

Again Jeff's thought halted as if paralyzed. The suggestion of the trip fell into the machinery of his mind like a wrench. He felt dazed and weak. He swung the car out into the yard, made a half turn, and drove around to the front door. When he took his hands off the wheel, he noticed that he was trembling violently. He cut off the motor and climbed to the ground to wait for Jennie.

A few minutes later she was at the window, her voice rattling against the pane like a broken shutter.

"I'm ready, Jeff."

He did not answer, but limped into the house and took her by the arm. He led her slowly through the big room, down the step, and across the yard.

"You reckon I'd oughta lock the do'?" he asked softly.

They stopped and Jennie weighed the question. Finally she shook her head.

"Ne' mind the do'," she said. "I don't see no cause to lock up things."

"You right," Jeff agreed. "No cause to lock up."

Jeff opened the door and helped his wife into the car. A quick shudder passed over him. Jesus! Again he trembled.

"How come you shaking so?" Jennie whispered.

"I don't know," he said.

"You mus' be scairt, Jeff."

"No, baby, I ain't scairt."

He slammed the door after her and went around to crank up again. The motor started easily. Jeff wished that it had not been so responsive. He would have liked a few more minutes in which to turn things around in his head. As it was, with Jennie chiding him about being afraid, he had to keep going. He swung the car into the little pencil-mark road and started off toward the river, driving very slowly, very cautiously.

Chugging across the green countryside, the small battered Ford seemed tiny indeed. Jeff felt a familiar excitement, a thrill, as they came down the first slope to the immense levels on which the cotton was growing. He could not help reflecting that the crops were good. He knew what that meant, too; he had made forty-five of them with his own hands. It was true that he had worn out nearly a dozen mules, but that was the fault of old man Stevenson, the owner of the land. Major Stevenson had the odd notion that one mule was all a share farmer needed to work a thirty-acre plot. It was an expensive notion, the way it killed mules from overwork, but the old man held to it. Jeff thought it killed a good many share farmers as well as mules, but he had no sympathy for them. He had always been strong, and he had been taught to have no patience with weakness in men. Women or children might be tolerated if they were puny, but a weak man was a curse. Of course, his own children—

Jeff's thought halted there. He and Jennie never mentioned their dead children any more. And naturally, he did not wish to dwell upon them in his mind. Before he knew it, some remark would slip out of his mouth and that would make Jennie feel blue. Perhaps she would cry. A woman like Jennie could not easily throw off the grief that comes from losing five grown children within two years. Even Jeff was still staggered by the blow. His memory had not been much good recently. He frequently talked to himself. And, although he had kept it a secret, he knew that his courage had left him. He was terrified by the least unfamiliar sound at night. He was reluctant to venture far from home in the daytime. And that habit of trembling when he felt fearful was now far beyond his control. Sometimes he became afraid and trembled without knowing what had frightened him. The feeling would just come over him like a chill.

The car rattled slowly over the dusty road. Jennie sat erect and silent with a little absurd hat pinned to her hair. Her useless eyes seemed very large, very white in their deep sockets. Suddenly Jeff heard her voice, and he inclined his head to catch the words.

"Is we passed Delia Moore's house yet?" she asked.

"Not yet," he said.

"You must be drivin' mighty slow, Jeff."

"We just as well take our time, baby."

There was a pause. A little puff of steam was coming out of the radiator of the car. Heat wavered above the hood. Delia Moore's house was nearly half a mile away. After a moment Jennie spoke again.

"You ain't really scairt, is you, Jeff?"

"Nah, baby, I ain't scairt."

"You know how we agreed—we gotta keep on goin'."

Jewels of perspiration appeared on Jeff's forehead. His eyes rounded, blinked, became fixed on the road.

"I don't know," he said with a shiver, "I reckon it's the only thing to do."

"Hm."

A flock of guinea fowls, pecking in the road, were scattered by the passing car. Some of them took to their wings; others hid under bushes. A blue jay, swaying on a leafy twig, was annoying a roadside squirrel. Jeff held an even speed till he came near Delia's place. Then he slowed down noticeably.

Delia's house was really no house at all, but an abandoned store building converted into a dwelling. It sat near a crossroads, beneath a single black cedar tree. There Delia, a cattish old creature of Jennie's age, lived alone. She had been there more years than anybody could remember, and long ago had won the disfavor of such women as Jennie. For in her young days Delia had been gayer, yellower, and saucier than seemed proper in those parts. Her ways with menfolks had been dark and suspicious. And the fact that she had had as many husbands as children did not help her reputation.

"Yonder's old Delia," Jeff said as they passed.

"What she doin'?"

"Jes sittin' in the do'," he said.

"She see us?"

"Hm," Jeff said. "Musta did."

That relieved Jennie. It strengthened her to know that her old enemy had seen her pass in her best clothes. That would give the old she-devil something to chew her gums and fret about, Jennie thought. Wouldn't she have a fit if she didn't find out? Old evil Delia! This would be just the thing for her. It would pay her back for being so evil. It would also pay her, Jennie thought, for the way she used to grin at Jeff—long ago, when her teeth were good.

The road became smooth and red, and Jeff could tell by the smell of the air that they were nearing the river. He could see the rise where the road turned and ran along parallel to the stream. The car chugged on monotonously. After a long silent spell, Jennie leaned against Jeff and spoke.

"How many bale o' cotton you think we got standin'?" she said.

Jeff wrinkled his forehead as he calculated.

" 'Bout twenty-five, I reckon."

"How many you make las' year?"

"Twenty-eight," he said. "How come you ask that?"

"I's jes thinkin'," Jennie said quietly.

"It don't make a speck o' difference though," Jeff reflected. "If we get much or if we get little, we still gonna be in debt to old man Stevenson when he gets through counting up agin us. It's took us a long time to learn that."

Jennie was not listening to these words. She had fallen into a trance-like meditation. Her lips twitched. She chewed her gums and rubbed her gnarled hands nervously. Suddenly, she leaned forward, buried her face in the nervous hands, and burst into tears. She cried aloud in a dry, cracked voice that suggested the rattle of fodder on dead stalks. She cried aloud like a child, for she had never learned to suppress a genuine sob. Her slight old frame shook heavily and seemed hardly able to sustain such violent grief.

"What's the matter, baby?" Jeff asked awkwardly. "Why you cryin' like all that?"

"I's jes thinkin'," she said.

"So you the one what's scairt now, hunh?"

"I ain't scairt, Jeff. I's jes thinkin' 'bout leavin' eve'thing like this —eve'thing we been used to. It's right sad-like."

Jeff did not answer, and presently Jennie buried her face again and cried.

The sun was almost overhead. It beat down furiously on the dusty wagon-path road, on the parched roadside grass and the tiny battered car. Jeff's hands, gripping the wheel, became wet with perspiration; his forehead sparkled. Jeff's lips parted. His mouth shaped a hideous grimace. His face suggested the face of a man being burned. But the torture passed and his expression softened again.

"You mustn't cry, baby," he said to his wife. "We gotta be strong. We can't break down."

Jennie waited a few seconds, then said, "You reckon we oughta do it, Jeff? You reckon we oughta go 'head an' do it, really?"

Jeff's voice choked; his eyes blurred. He was terrified to hear Jennie say the thing that had been in his mind all morning. She had egged him on when he had wanted more than anything in the world to wait, to reconsider, to think things over a little longer. Now she was getting cold feet. Actually, there was no need of thinking the question through again. It would only end in making the same painful decision once more. Jeff knew that. There was no need of fooling around longer.

"We jes as well to do like we planned," he said. "They ain't nothin' else for us now—it's the bes' thing."

Jeff thought of the handicaps, the near impossibility, of making another crop with his leg bothering him more and more each week. Then there was always the chance that he would have another stroke, like the one that had made him lame. Another one might kill him. The least it could do would be to leave him helpless. Jeff gasped—Lord, Jesus! He could not bear to think of being helpless, like a baby, on Jennie's hands. Frail, blind Jennie.

The little pounding motor of the car worked harder and harder. The puff of steam from the cracked radiator became larger. Jeff realized that they were climbing a little rise. A moment later the road turned abruptly, and he looked down upon the face of the river.

"Jeff."

"Hunh?"

"Is that the water I hear?"

"Hm. Tha's it."

"Well, which way you goin' now?"

"Down this-a way," he said. "The road runs 'long 'side o' the water a lil piece."

She waited a while calmly. Then she said, "Drive faster."

"A'right, baby," Jeff said.

The water roared in the bed of the river. It was fifty or sixty feet below the level of the road. Between the road and the water there was a long smooth slope, sharply inclined. The slope was dry, the clay hardened by prolonged summer heat. The water below, roaring in a narrow channel, was noisy and wild.

"Jeff."

"Hunh?"

"How far you goin'?"

"Jes a lil piece down the road."

"You ain't scairt, is you, Jeff?"

"Nah, baby," he said trembling. "I ain't scairt."

"Remember how we planned it, Jeff. We gotta do it like we said. Brave-like."

"Hm."

Jeff's brain darkened. Things suddenly seemed unreal, like figures in a dream. Thoughts swam in his mind foolishly, hysterically, like little blind fish in a pool within a dense cave. They rushed again. Jeff soon became dizzy. He shuddered violently and turned to his wife.

"Jennie, I can't do it. I can't." His voice broke pitifully.

She did not appear to be listening. All the grief had gone from her face. She sat erect, her unseeing eyes wide open, strained and frightful. Her glossy black skin had become dull. She seemed as thin, as sharp and bony, as a starved bird. Now, having suffered and endured the sadness of tearing herself away from beloved things, she showed no anguish. She was absorbed with her own thoughts, and she didn't even hear Jeff's voice shouting in her ear.

Jeff said nothing more. For an instant there was light in his cavernous brain. The great chamber was, for less than a second, peopled by characters he knew and loved. They were simple, healthy creatures, and they behaved in a manner that he could understand. They had quality. But since he had already taken leave of them long ago, the remembrance did not break his heart again. Young Jeff Patton was among them, the Jeff Patton of fifty years ago who went down to New Orleans with a crowd of country boys to the Mardi Gras doings. The gay young crowd, boys with candy-striped shirts and rouged brown girls in noisy silks, was like a picture in his head. Yet it did not make him sad. On that very trip Slim Burns had killed Joe Beasley—the crowd had been broken up. Since then Jeff Patton's world had been the Greenbriar Plantation. If there had been other Mardi Gras carnivals, he had not heard of them. Since then there had been no time; the years had fallen on him like waves. Now he was old, worn out. Another paralytic stroke (like the one he had already suffered) would put him on his back for keeps. In that condition, with a frail blind woman to look after him, he would be worse off than if he were dead.

Suddenly Jeff's hands became steady. He actually felt brave. He slowed down the motor of the car and carefully pulled off the road. Below, the water of the stream boomed, a soft thunder in the deep channel. Jeff ran the car onto the clay slope, pointed it directly toward the stream, and put his foot heavily on the accelerator. The little car leaped furiously down the steep incline toward the water. The movement was nearly as swift and direct as a fall. The two old black folks, sitting quietly side by side, showed no excitement. In another instant the car hit the water and dropped immediately out of sight.

A little later it lodged in the mud of a shallow place. One wheel of the crushed and upturned little Ford became visible above the rushing water.

"William and Emily"

"A Summer Tragedy"

"THE BLACK AND WHITE"

"After Long Silence"

When there's nothing left, what then?

nobody loses all the time

e. e. cummings

nobody loses all the time

i had an uncle named
Sol who was a born failure and
nearly everybody said he should have gone
into vaudeville perhaps because my Uncle Sol could
sing McCann He Was A Diver on Xmas Eve like Hell Itself which
may or may not account for the fact that my Uncle

Sol indulged in that possibly most inexcusable
of all to use a highfalootin phrase
luxuries that is or to
wit farming and be
it needlessly
added

my Uncle Sol's farm
failed because the chickens
ate the vegetables so
my Uncle Sol had a
chicken farm till the
skunks ate the chickens when

my Uncle Sol
had a skunk farm but
the skunks caught cold and
died and so
my Uncle Sol imitated the
skunks in a subtle manner

or by drowning himself in the watertank
but somebody who'd given my Uncle Sol a Victor
Victrola and records while he lived presented to
him upon the auspicious occasion of his decease a
scrumptious not to mention splendiferous funeral with
tall boys in black gloves and flowers and everything and

i remember we all cried like the Missouri
when my Uncle Sol's coffin lurched because
somebody pressed a button
(and down went
my Uncle
Sol

and started a worm farm)

Tragedy overcomes distance. Comedy creates distance.
—Friedrich Durrenmatt

ULYSSES

Alfred, Lord Tennyson

Ulysses the sagacious, the cunning, the brave, the wily . . . now safely home in Ithaca, speaks of further adventures, of a search for a newer world.

It little profits that an idle king,
By this still hearth, among these barren crags,
Match'd with an aged wife, I mete and dole
Unequal laws unto a savage race,
That hoard, and sleep, and feed, and know not me.
I cannot rest from travel; I will drink
Life to the lees. All times I have enjoyed
Greatly, have suffer'd greatly, both with those
That loved me, and alone; on shore, and when
Thro' scudding drifts the rainy Hyades
Vext the dim sea. I am become a name;
For always roaming with a hungry heart
Much have I seen and known,—cities of men
And manners, climates, councils, governments,
Myself not least, but honor'd of them all,—

Stars that indicated approach of rain when they rose and set with the sun (17 October and 12 April).

Seems to be based on detail in the Invocation to the *Odyssey*.

And drunk delight of battle with my peers,
Far on the ringing plains of windy Troy. See overprinted note at bottom of p. 310.
I am a part of all that I have met;
Yet all experience is an arch wherethro'
Gleams that untravell'd world, whose margin fades
For ever and for ever when I move.
How dull it is to pause, to make an end,
To rust unburnish'd, not to shine in use!
As tho' to breathe were life! Life piled on life "[merely] to breathe"
Were all too little, and of one to me
Little remains; but every hour is saved
From that eternal silence, something more,
A bringer of new things; and vile it were
For some three suns to store and hoard myself,
And this gray spirit yearning in desire
To follow knowledge like a shrinking star,
Beyond the utmost bound of human thought.

This is my son, mine own Telemachus,
To whom I leave the scepter and the isle—
Well-loved of me, discerning to fulfill
This labor, by slow prudence to make mild
A rugged people, and thro' soft degrees
Subdue them to the useful and the good.
Most blameless is he, centered in the sphere
Of common duties, decent not to fail
In offices of tenderness, and pay "and won't fail to pay proper"
Meet adoration to my household gods,
When I am gone. He works his work, I mine.

There lies the port; the vessel puffs her sail;
There gloom the dark, broad seas. My mariners,
Souls that have toil'd, and wrought, and thought with me,—
That ever with a frolic welcome took
The thunder and the sunshine, and opposed
Free hearts, free foreheads,—you and I are old;
Old age hath yet his honor and his toil;
Death closes all; but something ere the end,
Some work of noble note, may yet be done,
Not unbecoming men that strove with Gods.
The lights begin to twinkle from the rocks;
The long day wanes; the slow moon climbs; the deep
Moans round with many voices. Come, my friends.
'Tis not too late to seek a newer world.

Hardly a Homeric view of the sailors; and anyway the ones who left Troy with Odysseus didn't make it home, because of their sin of eating the oxen of Hyperion. (Or is that final detail, Ulysses' forgetting that his men are *dead,* meant to be ironic?)

Push off, and sitting well in order smite
The sounding furrows; for my purpose holds
To sail beyond the sunset, and the baths
Of all the western stars, until I die.
It may be that the gulfs will wash us down;
It may be we shall touch the Happy Isles,
And see the great Achilles, whom we knew.
Tho' much is taken, much abides; and tho'
We are not now that strength which in old days
Moved earth and heaven, that which we are, we are,—
One equal temper of heroic hearts,
Made weak by time and fate, but strong in will
To strive, to seek, to find, and not to yield.

Happy Isles: At the extremity of the world (but not in Greek mythology), an abode of the dead heroes

Literary Sort: I never have been able to read that poem the way Tennyson must have wanted it read. All I can think of is Ulysses going on and on about what he had done and will do. And poor Telemachus and Penelope hearing again and again about the Happy Isles and Achilles and all the rest of it.

Editor: So you think Tennyson's Ulysses is a fool and a bore?

Literary Sort: Well, that depends upon how you read the poem. But it does seem to me as if Ulysses' virtuous striving is incompatible with his responsibilities to his family.

Editor: But does a hero have to be a knight in shining armor? It seems to me that Ulysses would get along very well in today's world.

THE LITTLE MAN

See *Talks,* (p. 69), for note on title.

Nicanor Parra

Whoever wants to go to the little man's heaven
has to go the way of art for art's sake
and swallow great quantities of saliva:
The apprenticeship is almost endless.

Is the "list" that follows one of the reasons for Ulysses' panic (p. 311, lines 33-43)?

Here is a list of what he will have to know:

How to fashion his necktie with a flair
how to slip a man a calling card
how to pop a shine on a pair of shoes
how to consult a Venetian mirror
to study himself in profile and full-face
how to take a shot of cognac
how to distinguish viola and violin
how to receive visitors in pajamas
how to slow the falling of his hair
and how to swallow great quantities of saliva.

He will need to have everything in his files.
If his wife is excited for someone else
I recommend the following:
shave with a razor
admire the natural beauties
crumple up a piece of paper
talk on the phone
shoot a pop-gun
pare the nails with the teeth
and swallow great quantities of saliva.

If he wants to shine at social gatherings
The little man
has to know how to run on four feet
to sneeze and smile at the same time
to waltz on the edge of a cliff
to deify the instruments of sex
undress in front of a mirror
defoliate a rose with a pencil
and swallow great buckets of saliva.

After this you can ask yourself
Was Jesus Christ a little man?

You can see
if you want to get to the paradise
of the little man you have to be
a perfect acrobat.
If you want to get to paradise
you have to be a perfect acrobat.

No wonder the true artist
passes the time killing dragon flies!
To break out of the vicious circle
the gratuitous act is recommended:

to appear and disappear
to move in a cataleptic state
to waltz on a pile of debris
to rock an old man in your arms
never taking your eyes from the old man's eyes
to ask a dying man what time it is
to spit in the hollow of your hand
to follow fire trucks in a dinner jacket
to cut through funeral processions
to go further than the female sex
to lift up that tombstone
to see if trees are growing underneath
and then to cross from one side to the other
with neither reason nor a time
for the sake of changing
with the moustache of a movie hero
and the speed of thought.

—Translated by Miller Williams

The Unknown Citizen W. H. Auden

(To JS/07/M/378
This Marble Monument
Is Erected by the State)

He was found by the Bureau of Statistics to be
One against whom there was no official complaint,
And all the reports on his conduct agree
That, in the modern sense of an old-fashioned word, he was a saint,
For in everything he did he served the Greater Community.
Except for the War till the day he retired
He worked in a factory and never got fired,
But satisfied his employers, Fudge Motors Inc.
Yet he wasn't a scab or odd in his views,
For his Union reports that he paid his dues,
(Our report on his Union shows it was sound)
And our Social Psychology workers found
That he was popular with his mates and liked a drink.
The Press are convinced that he bought a paper every day
And that his reactions to advertisements were normal in every way.
Policies taken out in his name prove that he was fully insured,
And his Health-card shows he was once in a hospital but left it cured.
Both Producers Research and High-Grade Living declare
He was fully sensible to the advantages of the Instalment Plan
And had everything necessary to the Modern Man,
A phonograph, a radio, a car and a frigidaire.
Our researchers into Public Opinion are content
That he held the proper opinions for the time of year;
When there was peace, he was for peace; when there was war, he went.
He was married and added five children to the population,
Which our Eugenist says was the right number for a parent of his generation,
And our teachers report that he never interfered with their education.

Was he free? Was he happy? The question is absurd:
Had anything been wrong, we should certainly have heard.

Do you think the Unknown Citizen and The Little Man belonged to the same Wednesday night bowling team?

INTERLOCK WITH CLUSTER 11:
A generic link: poems
A topical link: the forgotten man

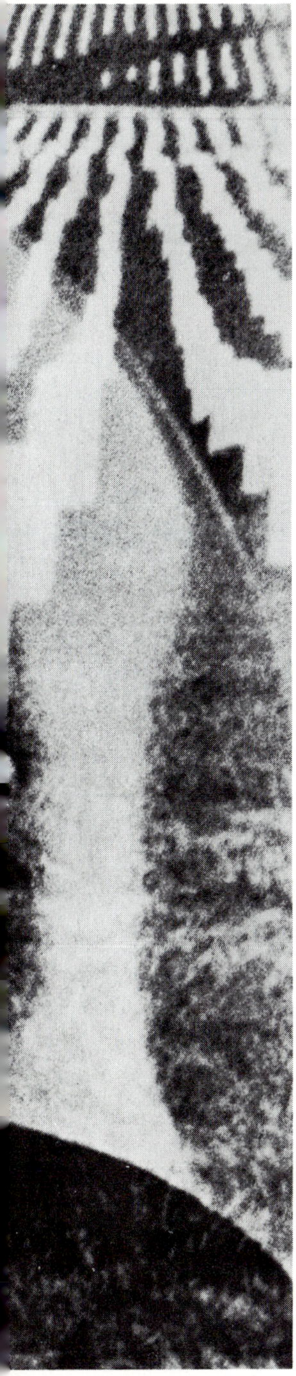

Cluster 11: pp. 316-341
A topical cluster
Focus: war and its effects

INTERLOCK WITH CLUSTER 10:
A generic link: poems
A topical link: the forgotten man

11

Western wind, when will thou blow?
The small rain down can rain.
Christ, that my love were in my arms,
And I in my bed again.

Read "So that . . ."

—Anonymous

War draws men closer together . . . it begets brotherly love —George Fitzhugh, Southern journalist, 1866

Thinking of My Brothers on A Moonlight Night

Tu Fu

Drums at the watch-towers beat,
And roads below clear of people;
I think of the frontier as I
Hear the wild geese's autumn cry;
Dew changes to frost, but I feel
Moonlight is not as bright as it was
Back in my old home; now my brothers
Are scattered, and there is no way
For me to know if they are alive
Or dead, for letters cannot come
And the war that keeps us apart
Seems unending.

—Translated by Rewi Alley

PITY FOR PRISONERS

Ly Dao Tai

They write letters with their blood, to send news home.
A lone wild goose flaps through the clouds.
How many families are weeping under this same moon?
The same thought wandering how far apart.

—Translated by Nguyen Ngoc Bich and Burton Raffel

mother, the wardrobe is full of infantrymen

Roger McGough talking:
I think poetry is about whatever one feels like in this particular poem. I think generally when people write about the Bomb and things it's too big, you know, too vast, to think about. I'm concerned about the person next door and the person next to me. I'm involved in a very claustrophobic environment—or envirusment!—rather than wide social things . . . . The Georgian poets were poets who tended their gardens while the factories were being built on the outskirts; in fact, what we're doing is that—while the mushroom cloud is growing outside on the horizon we're laying the birds in the back yard.

Roger McGough

Mother, the wardrobe is full of infantrymen
i did, i asked them
but they snarled saying it was a man's life

Mother, there is a centurion tank in the parlor
i did, i asked the officer
but he laughed saying queen's regulations,
piano was out of tune anyway

Mother, polish your identity bracelet
there is a mushroom cloud in the back garden
i did, i tried to bring in the cat
but it simply came to pieces in my hand
i did, i tried to whitewash the windows
but there weren't any
i did, i tried to hide under the stairs
but i couldn't get in for civil defense leaders
i did, i tried ringing Candid Camera
but they crossed their hearts

I went for a policeman but they were looting the town
i went out for a fire engine but they were all upside down
i went for a priest but they were all on their knees
mother don't just lie there say something please
mother don't just lie there say something please

From THE LIVERPOOL SCENE, 1968, edited by Edward Lucie-Smith. Reprinted by permission of Hope, Leresche & Steele, London.

Don Lee

HERO

(a poem for brig. general frederic davison, if he can dig it)

little willie
a hero in
the american tradition.
a blk/hero.
he
received the:
    bronze star: which read "meritorious action,"
      (his momma had to look the word up)
    good conduct medal,
    combat infantry badge,
    purple heart,
    national defense service medal,
    vietnam campaign ribbon,
    & some others i can't even spell.

little willie
a hero in
the american tradition.
a blk/hero.
he
received his medals

p
o
s
t
h
u
m
o
u
s
l
y
.
.
.

What is the difference between Gwendolyn Brooks' feelings about the pool players (p. 109) and Don Lee's about dead "little willie"?

"To die—even in the service of an impersonal cause—is always a personal and intimate affair."
—Arthur Koestler,
Dialogue With Death

An End of Empire

Bernard Fall

This selection is an excerpt from *Street Without Joy*.

. . . Sometimes, there occurs an almost irrelevant incident which, in the light of later developments, seems to have been a sign of the gods, a dreamlike warning which, if heeded, could have changed fate—or so it seems.

The French first attempted "pacification" of Southeast Asia; later, in the early 1960's the Americans began their version, "Vietnamization."

One such incident occurred to me in October, 1953, in Cambodia, at Siem-Réap, not far away from the fabulous temples of Angkor-Wat. I had been in the field with the 5th Cambodian Autonomous Infantry Company and was now in need of transportation back to Phnom-Penh, the capital of Cambodia. Siem-Réap, a quiet and pleasant little place with two hotels catering to the tourist trade and a few French archeologists working around the ruins of Angkor, might as well have been a small garrison town in southern France, such as Avignon or Nîmes.

A few French officers were still around, mainly as advisers to the newly-independent Cambodian Army. Their chores were light, there were no Communists in the area, and the handful of obsolescent "Renault" trucks and World War II-type weapons needed a minimum of maintenance and care. An assignment to Siem-Réap was as good a sinecure as could be found in Indochina in October, 1953, and the officers made the most of it.

When I went to the Transportation Office that afternoon at 1530, the Cambodian orderly told me apologetically that *"le Lieutenant est allé au mess jouer au tennis avec le Capitaine"* and that they might well stay there for the rest of the afternoon. Since a convoy which I expected to catch was supposed to leave at dawn, I decided to stroll over to the mess in order to get my travel documents signed there.

The Siem-Réap officers' mess was a pleasant and well-kept place; with its wide Cambodian-type verandahs, its parasol-shaded tables, and the well-manicured lawns and beautifully red-sanded tennis court, it was an exact replica of all the other colonial officers' messes from Port Said to Singapore, Saigon, or even Manila, wherever the white man had set his foot in the course of building his ephemeral empires.

I found the two officers at the tennis court, in gleaming white French square-bottomed shorts (no one in Europe would be caught dead in the ungainly Bermuda pants called "shorts" in the United States),

Named after René Lacoste, a French tennis player of the 1920's.

matching Lacoste tennis shirts and knee-long socks. Their skins had lost the unhealthy pallor of the jungle and taken on the handsome bronze of the vacationer engaging in outdoor sports; their wives, seated at a neighboring table, were beautifully groomed and wore deceptively simple (but, oh, so expensive!) cotton summer dresses clearly showing the hand of a Paris designer. Both officers played in the easy style of men who knew each other's game and were bent less on winning than on getting the fun and exercise of it. Three Cambodian servants, clad in impeccable white slacks and shirts, stood respectfully in the shadow of the verandah, awaiting the call of one of the officers or women for a new cool drink.

Since the men were in the midst of a set and I had little else to do, I sat down at a neighboring table after a courteous bow to the ladies and watched the game, gladly enjoying the atmosphere of genteel civility and forgetting for a moment the war. At the next table, the two women kept up the rapid-fire chatter which French women are prone to use when men are present. The two men also kept up a conversation of sorts, interrupted regularly by the "plop-plop" of the tennis ball.

Then emerged from the verandah a soldier in French uniform. His small stature, brown skin and Western-type features showed him to be a Cambodian. He wore the blue field cap with the golden anchor of the *Troupes Coloniales*—the French "Marines"—and the three golden chevrons of a master-sergeant. On his chest above the left breast pocket of his suntan regulation shirt were three rows of multi-colored ribbons: *croix de guerre* with four citations, campaign ribbons with the clasps of France's every colonial campaign since the Moroccan pacification of 1926, the Italian campaign of 1943, and the drive to the Rhine of 1945. In his left hand, he carried several papers crossed diagonally with a tri-colored ribbon—travel orders, like mine, which also awaited the signature of one of the officers.

He remained in the shadow of the verandah's awnings until the officers had interrupted their game and had joined the two women with their drinks, then strode over in a measured military step, came stiffly to attention in a military salute, and handed the orders for himself and his squad to the captain. The captain looked up in surprise, still with a half-smile on his face from the remark he had made previously. His eyes narrowed suddenly as he understood that he was being interrupted. Obviously, he was annoyed but not really furious.

"Sergeant, you can see that I'm busy. Please wait until I have time to deal with your travel orders. Don't worry. You will have them in time for the convoy."

The sergeant stood stiffly at attention, some of his almost white hair glistening in the sun where it peeked from under the cap, his wizened face betraying no emotion whatever.

"A vos ordres, mon Capitaine." A sharp salute, a snappy about-face. The incident was closed, the officers had had their drink and now resumed their game.

The sergeant resumed his watch near where the Cambodian messboys were following the game, but this time he had squatted down on his haunches, a favorite Cambodian position of repose which would leave most Europeans with partial paralysis for several hours afterwards. Almost without moving his head, he attentively followed the tennis game, his travel orders still tightly clutched in his left hand.

The sun began to settle behind the trees of the garden and a slight cooling breeze rose from the nearby Lake Tonlé-Sap, Cambodia's inland sea. It was 1700.

All of a sudden, there rose behind the trees, from the nearby French camp, the beautiful bell-clear sounds of a bugle playing "lower the flag"—the signal which, in the French Army, marks the end of the working day as the colors are struck.

Nothing changed at the tennis court; the two officers continued to play their set, the women continued their chatter, and the messboys their silent vigil.

Only the old sergeant had moved. He was now standing stiffly at attention, his right hand raised to the cap in the flat-palmed salute of the French Army, facing in the direction from which the bugle tones came; saluting, as per regulations, France's tricolor hidden behind the trees. The rays of the setting sun shone upon the immobile brown figure, catching the gold of the anchor and of the chevrons and of one of the tiny metal stars of his ribbons.

Something very warm welled up in me. I felt like running over to the little Cambodian who had fought all his life for my country, and apologizing to him for my countrymen here who didn't care about him, and for my countrymen in France who didn't even care about *their* countrymen fighting in Indochina . . .

And in one single blinding flash, I *knew* that we were going to lose the war.

"If we march together, endure together, share together, we shall succeed—we shall gloriously succeed together."

—General Dwight D. Eisenhower, 1951

To Lucasta,

on Going to the Wars

Tell me not, Sweet, I am unkind
  That from the nunnery
Of thy chaste breast and quiet mind
  To war and arms I fly.

True, a new mistress now I chase,
  The first foe in the field;
And with a stronger faith embrace
  A sword, a horse, a shield.

Yet this inconstancy is such
  As you too shall adore;
I could not love thee, Dear, so much,
  Loved I not Honor more.

—Richard Lovelace

Literary Sort: One of my favorites. Such a splendid sentiment!

Editor: But you do realize the sensuality implied in "I could not love thee, Dear, so much," don't you?

next to of course god . . .

e. e. cummings

"next to of course god america i
love you land of the pilgrims' and so forth oh
say can you see by the dawn's early my
country 'tis of centuries come and go
and are no more what of it we should worry
in every language even deafanddumb
thy sons acclaim your glorious name by gorry
by jingo by gee by gosh by gum
why talk of beauty what could be more beaut-
iful than these heroic happy dead
who rushed like lions to the roaring slaughter
they did not stop to think they died instead
then shall the voice of liberty be mute?"

He spoke. And drank rapidly a glass of water

"To make a people great it is necessary to send them into battle even if you have to kick them in the pants. This is what I shall do."

—Benito Mussolini, 1940

it's jolly/odd . . .

e. e. cummings

it's jolly
odd what pops into
your jolly tête when the
jolly shells begin dropping jolly fast you
hear the rrmp and
the nearerandnearerandNEARER
and before
you can

!

& we're

NOT
(oh—
—i say

that's jolly odd
old thing, jolly
odd, jolly
jolly odd isn't
it jolly odd.

"Just think, reader,
what will happen to you
if the truth of a mad beast
overpowers the sane truth of man."

—*Maxim Gorky,* Notes on the Russian Revolution, 1917–18

> "A man who has never lost himself in a cause bigger than himself has missed one of life's mountaintop experiences. Only in losing himself does he find himself. Only then does he discover all the latent strengths he never knew he had and which otherwise would have remained dormant."
>
> —*Richard M. Nixon,* Six Crises

look at this) . . .

e. e. cummings

look at this)
a 75 done
this nobody would
have believed
would they no
kidding this was my particular

pal
funny aint
it we was
buddies
i used to

know
him lift the
poor cuss
tenderly this side up handle

with care
fragile
and send him home

to his old mother in
a new nice pine box

(collect

"Do people think I am mad?
Do they think I fight for the fun of it?"

—*Napoleon Bonaparte*

first Jock he . . .

e. e. cummings

first Jock he
was kilt a handsome
man and James and
next let me
see yes Will that was
cleverest
he was kilt and my youngest
boy was kilt last with
the big eyes i loved like you can't
imagine Harry was o
god kilt he was kilt everybody was kilt

they called them the kilties

"War is the greatest element of modern civilization, and our destiny is conquest."

—Letter from South Carolinian novelist William G. Simms to South Carolinian Senator James H. Hammond, 1847

lis
-ten . . .

e. e. cummings

lis
-ten

you know what i mean when
the first guy drops you know
everybody feels sick or
when they throw in a few gas
and the oh baby shrapnel
or my feet getting dim freezing or
up to your you know what in water or
with the bugs crawling right all up
all everywhere over you all me everyone
that's been there knows what
i mean a god damned lot of
people don't and never
never
will know,
they don't want

to
no

Ten Days Leave

W. D. Snodgrass

He steps down from the dark train, blinking; stares
At trees like miracles. He will play games
With boys or sit up all night touching chairs.
Talking with friends, he can recall their names.

Noon burns against his eyelids, but he lies
Hunched in his blankets; he is half awake
But still lacks nerve to open up his eyes;
Supposing it were just his old mistake?

His old dream of waking up at home?

But no; it seems just like it seemed. His folks
Pursue their lives like toy trains on a track.
He can forsee each of his father's jokes
Like words in some old movie that's come back.

He is like days when you've gone some place new
To deal with certain strangers, though you never
Escape the sense in everything you do,
"We've done this all once. Have I been here, ever?"

But no; he thinks it must recall some old film, lit
By lives you want to touch; as if he'd slept
And must have dreamed this setting, peopled it,
And wakened out of it. But someone's kept

His dream asleep here like a small homestead
Preserved long past its time in memory
Of some great man who lived here and is dead.
They have restored his landscape faithfully:

The hills, the little houses, the costumes:
How real it seems! But he comes, wide awake,
A tourist whispering through the priceless rooms
Who must not touch things or his hand might break

Their sleep and black them out. He wonders when
He'll grow into his sleep so sound again.

An Irish Airman Foresees His Death

William Butler Yeats

I know that I shall meet my fate
Somewhere among the clouds above;
Those that I fight I do not hate,
Those that I guard I do not love;
My country is Kiltartan Cross,
My countrymen Kiltartan's poor,
No likely end could bring them loss
Or leave them happier than before.
Nor law, nor duty bade me fight,
Nor public men, nor cheering crowds,
A lonely impulse of delight
Drove to this tumult in the clouds;
I balanced all, brought all to mind,
The years to come seemed waste of breath,
A waste of breath the years behind
In balance with this life, this death.

"It is said that I might have refused to obey and indeed should have done so. This, however, is thought of only now. Under the circumstances at the time, such behavior was impossible. Nobody acted this way."

—Adolf Eichmann, upon his being sentenced to death for war crimes, 1961

Three Memorial Sonnets

George Barker

(For two young seamen lost overboard in a storm in Mid-Pacific, January 1940)

I

The seagull, spreadeagled, splayed on the wind,
Span backwards shrieking, belly facing upward,
Fled backward with a gimlet° in its heart
To see the two youths swimming hand in hand
Through green eternity. O swept overboard
Not could the thirty-foot jaws them part,
Or the flouncing skirts that swept them over
Separate what death pronounced was love.

I saw them, the hand flapping like a flag,
And another like a dolphin with a child
Supporting him. Was I the shape of Jesus
When to me hopeward their eyeballs swiveled,
Saw I was standing in the stance of vague
Horror; paralyzed with mere pity's peace?

II

From thorax of storms the voices of verbs
Shall call to me without sound, like the silence
Round which cyclones rage, to nurse my nerve
And hang my heart midway, where the balance
Meets. I taste sea swilling in my bowels
As I sit shivering in the swing of waves
Like a face in a bubble. As the hull heaves
I and my ghost tread water over hell.

°GIMLET: a piercing tool

The greedy bitch with sailors in her guts
Green as a dream and formidable as God,
Spitting at stars, gnawing at shores, mad randy,
Riots with us on her abdomen and puts
Eternity in our cabins, pitches our pod
To the mouth of the death for which no one is ready.

"The sea." These sonnets might well be compared to Stephen Crane's "To the Maiden."

III

At midday they looked up and saw their death
Standing up overhead as loud as thunder
As white as angels and as broad as God:
Then, then the shock, the last gasp of breath
As grazing the bulwark they swept over and under,
All the green arms around them that load
Their eyes their ears their stomachs with eternals,
Whirled away in a white pool to the stern.

But the most possible of all miracles
Is that the useless tear that did not fall
From the corner of their eyes, was the prize,
The flowers, the gifts, the crystal sepulchre,
The funeral contribution and memorial,
The perfect and nonexistent obsequies.°

°OBSEQUIES: funeral or burial rites

CORNFLOWER

Guillaume Apollinaire

Young man
of twenty
Who have seen such terrible things
What do you think of the grown men of your childhood
You
know
bravery and cunning
You
have
seen
death
face
to
face
more
than
a
hundred
times
you
do
not
know
what
life
is
Communicate your fearlessness
To those who will come
After you

Young man
You are full of joy your memory is full of blood
Your soul is also red
With joy
You have absorbed the life of those who died close to you
You have the quality of decision
It is 1700 hrs. and you would know how to
Die

If no better than your elders
At least more piously
For you know death better than life
O sweetness of other times
Immemorial slowness

—*Translated by Oliver Bernard*

CORNFLOWER from *Apollinaire: Selected Poems* (Penguin Books © 1965).
Translated by Oliver Bernard. Reprinted by permission.

Worried

Nguyen Binh Khiem

I hate war. I'm worried, of course,
yet content to be here, alone, bound in duty
to my old lord. How can I betray him to face the world?
An immortal must bide his time: I sing a little
to blend my soul with the landscape, I meditate
on Peace and Satisfaction. Modest perhaps, but then
not all of us can choose fame.

—Translated by Nguyen Ngoc Bich

From Memoirs of Chateaubriand

M. de Latour–Mauboug, one of Napoleon's officers, said to his weeping orderly after the Russian debacle, "What are you complaining about? You have only one boot to polish now."

The Complexities of modern Warfare require men of knowledge

Our weapons can be no better than the men who employ them. The complexities of modern weapons require soldiers of high skill.

The Complexities of modern Warfare require men of knowledge

h skill. Our weapons can be no better than the men who employ them. The com

The complexities of the modern world require men of broad outlook.
Our training programs have been expanded
to provide this greater wisdom."

—Lyndon B. Johnson, *My Hope for America*

Game

Donald Barthelme

Shotwell keeps the jacks and the rubber ball in his attaché case and will not allow me to play with them. He plays with them, alone, sitting on the floor near the console hour after hour, chanting "onesies, twosies, threesies, foursies" in a precise, well-modulated voice, not so loud as to be annoying, not so soft as to allow me to forget. I point out to Shotwell that two can derive more enjoyment from playing jacks than one, but he is not interested. I have asked repeatedly to be allowed to play by myself, but he simply shakes his head. "Why?" I ask. "They're mine," he says. And when he has finished, when he has sated himself, back they go into the attaché case.

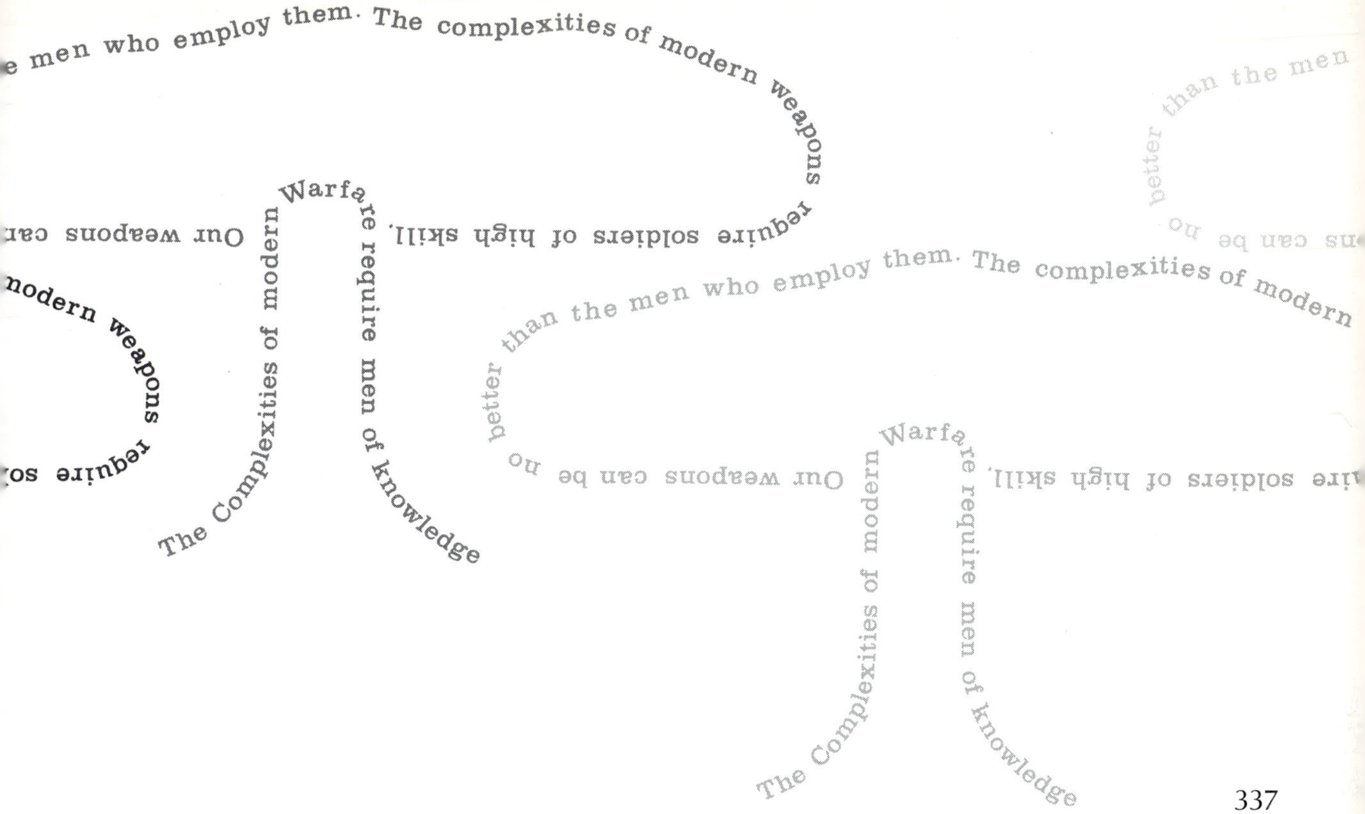

It is unfair but there is nothing I can do about it. I am aching to get my hands on them.

Shotwell and I watch the console. Shotwell and I live under the ground and watch the console. If certain events take place upon the console, we are to insert our keys in the appropriate locks and turn our keys. Shotwell has a key and I have a key. If we turn our keys simultaneously the bird flies, certain switches are activated and the bird flies. But the bird never flies. In one hundred thirty-three days the bird has not flown. Meanwhile Shotwell and I watch each other. We each wear a .45 and if Shotwell behaves strangely I am supposed to shoot him. If I behave strangely Shotwell is supposed to shoot me. We watch the console and think about shooting each other and think about the bird. Shotwell's behavior with the jacks is strange. Is it strange? I do not know. Perhaps he is merely a selfish bastard, perhaps his character is flawed, perhaps his childhood was twisted. I do not know.

Each of us wears a .45 and each of us is supposed to shoot the other if the other is behaving strangely. How strangely is strangely? I do not know. In addition to the .45 I have a .38 which Shotwell does not know about concealed in my attaché case, and Shotwell has a .25 calibre Beretta which I do not know about strapped to his right

A very interesting question, indeed.

calf. Sometimes instead of watching the console I pointedly watch Shotwell's .45, but this is simply a ruse, simply a maneuver, in reality I am watching his hand when it dangles in the vicinity of his right calf. If he decides I am behaving strangely he will shoot me not with the .45 but with the Beretta. Similarly Shotwell pretends to watch my .45 but he is really watching my hand resting idly atop my attaché case, my hand resting idly atop my attaché case, my hand. My hand resting idly atop my attaché case.

In the beginning I took care to behave normally. So did Shotwell. Our behavior was painfully normal. Norms of politeness, consideration, speech, and personal habits were scrupulously observed. But then it became apparent that an error had been made, that our relief was not going to arrive. Owing to an oversight. Owing to an oversight we have been here for one hundred thirty-three days. When it became clear that an error had been made, that we were not to be relieved, the norms were relaxed. Definitions of normality were redrawn in the agreement of January 1, called by us, The Agreement. Uniform regulations were relaxed, and mealtimes are no longer rigorously scheduled. We eat when we are hungry and sleep when we are tired. Considerations of rank and precedence were temporarily put aside, a handsome concession on the part of Shotwell, who is a captain, whereas I am only a first lieutenant. One of us watches the console at all times rather than two of us watching the console at all times, except when we are both on our feet. One of us watches the console at all times and if the bird flies then that one wakes the other and we turn our keys in the locks simultaneously and the bird flies. Our system involves a delay of perhaps twelve seconds but I do not care because I am not well, and Shotwell does not care because he is not himself. After the agreement was signed Shotwell produced the jacks and the rubber ball from his attaché case, and I began to write a series of descriptions of forms occurring in nature, such as a shell, a leaf, a stone, an animal. On the walls.

Shotwell plays jacks and I write descriptions of natural forms on the walls.

Shotwell is enrolled in a USAFI course which leads to a master's degree in business administration from the University of Wisconsin (although we are not in Wisconsin, we are in Utah, Montana, or Idaho). When we went down it was in either Utah, Montana, or Idaho, I don't remember. We have been here for one hundred thirty-three days owing to an oversight. The pale green reinforced concrete walls sweat and the air conditioning zips on and off erratically and Shotwell reads *Introduction to Marketing* by Lassiter and Munk, making notes with a blue ballpoint pen. Shotwell is not himself but I do not know it; he presents a calm aspect and reads *Introduction to Marketing* and makes his exemplary notes with a blue ballpoint pen, meanwhile controlling the .38 in my attaché case with one-third of his attention. I am not well.

We have been here one hundred thirty-three days owing to an oversight. Although now we are not sure what is oversight, what is plan. Perhaps the plan is for us to stay here permanently, or if not permanently at least for a year, for three hundred sixty-five days. Or if not for a year for some number of days known to them and not known to us, such as two hundred days. Or perhaps they are observing our behavior in some way, sensors of some kind, perhaps our behavior determines the number of days. It may be that they are pleased with us, with our behavior, not in every detail but in sum. Perhaps the whole thing is very successful, perhaps the whole thing is an experiment and the experiment is very successful. I do not know. But I suspect that the only way they can persuade sun-loving creatures into their pale green sweating reinforced concrete rooms under the ground is to say that the system is twelve hours on, twelve hours off. And then lock us below for some number of days known to them and not known to us. We eat well although the frozen enchiladas are damp when defrosted and the frozen devil's food cake is sour and untasty. We sleep uneasily and acrimoniously. I hear Shotwell shouting in his sleep, objecting, denouncing, cursing sometimes, weeping sometimes, in his sleep. When Shotwell sleeps I try to pick the lock on his attaché case, so as to get at the jacks. Thus far I have been unsuccessful. Nor has Shotwell been successful in picking the locks on my attaché case so as to get at the .38. I have seen the marks on the shiny surface. I laughed, in the latrine, pale green walls sweating and the air conditioning whispering in the latrine.

I write descriptions of natural forms on the walls, scratching them on the tile surface with a diamond. The diamond is a two and one-half carat solitaire I had in my attaché case when we went down. It was for Lucy. The south wall of the room containing the console is already covered. I have described a shell, a leaf, a stone, animals, a baseball bat. I am aware that the baseball bat is not a natural form. Yet I described it. "The baseball bat," I said, "is typically made of wood. It is typically one meter in length or a little longer, fat at one end, tapering to afford a comfortable grip at the other. The end with the handhold typically offers a slight rim, or lip, at the nether extremity, to prevent slippage." My description of the baseball bat ran to 4500 words, all scratched with a diamond on the south wall. Does Shotwell read what I have written? I do not know. I am aware that Shotwell regards my writing-behavior as a little strange. Yet it is no stranger than his jacks-behavior, or the day he appeared in black bathing trunks with the .25 calibre Beretta strapped to his right calf and stood over the console, trying to span with his two arms outstretched the distance between the locks. He could not do it, I had already tried, standing over the console with my two arms outstretched, the distance is too great. I was moved to comment but did not comment, comment would have provoked counter-comment, comment would have led God knows where. They had in their infinite patience, in their infinite foresight, in their infinite wisdom, already imagined a man standing over the console with his two arms outstretched, trying to span with his two arms outstretched the distance between the locks.

"Something given or received for something else." But more important is the tone implicit in the pampered, child-like reaction, "I insist on a quid pro quo." One must consider the larger situation here—whom these men work for and the nature of their work.

Shotwell is not himself. He has made certain overtures. The burden of his message is not clear. It has something to do with the keys, with the locks. Shotwell is a strange person. He appears to be less affected by our situation than I. He goes about his business stolidly, watching the console, studying *Introduction to Marketing*, bouncing his rubber ball on the floor in a steady, rhythmical, conscientious manner. He appears to be less affected by our situation than I am. He is stolid. He says nothing. But he has made certain overtures, certain overtures have been made. I am not sure that I understand them. They have something to do with the keys, with the locks. Shotwell has something in mind. Stolidly he shucks the shiny silver paper from the frozen enchiladas, stolidly he stuffs them into the electric oven. But he has something in mind. But there must be a quid pro quo. I insist on a quid pro quo. I have something in mind.

I am not well. I do not know our target. They do not tell us for which city the bird is targeted. I do not know. That is planning. That is not my responsibility. My responsibility is to watch the console and when certain events take place upon the console, turn my key in the lock. Shotwell bounces the rubber ball on the floor in a steady, stolid, rhythmical manner. I am aching to get my hands on the ball, on the jacks. We have been here one hundred thirty-three days owing to an oversight. I write on the walls. Shotwell chants "onesies, twosies, threesies, foursies" in a precise, well-modulated voice. Now he cups the jacks and the rubber ball in his hands and rattles them suggestively. I do not know for which city the bird is targeted. Shotwell is not himself.

Sometimes I cannot sleep. Sometimes Shotwell cannot sleep. Sometimes when Shotwell cradles me in his arms and rocks me to sleep, singing Brahms' "Guten abend, gut Nacht," or I cradle Shotwell in my arms and rock him to sleep, singing, I understand what it is Shotwell wishes me to do. At such moments we are very close. But only if he will give me the jacks. That is fair. There is something he wants me to do with my key, while he does something with his key. But only if he will give me my turn. That is fair. I am not well.

Seems to be the motif of the piece.

INTERLOCK WITH CLUSTER 12:
A topical link: "games"
A modal link: irony

We must build more weapons to keep the peace.
Who'll keep the weapons?

нает шагать в
и не останавл
ним едва поспе
Путники выход
синеющей вдал
заволокли сол
местечка. Тем
— Свят, свят;
Первые брызги

Cluster 12: pp. 342-381
An authorial cluster
Focus: Anton Chekhov

INTERLOCK WITH CLUSTER 11:
A topical link: "games"
A modal link: irony

12

That the world "swarms with male and female scum" is perfectly true. Human nature is imperfect, and it would, therefore, be strange to find only righteous people on this earth. But to think that the task of literature is to gather the pure grain from the muck heap, is to reject literature itself. Artistic literature is called so just because it depicts life as it really is. Its aim is truth,—unconditional and honest. . . .

To a chemist, nothing on earth is unclean. A writer must be as objective as a chemist; he must abandon the subjective line; he must know that dung-heaps play a very respectable part in a landscape, and that evil passions are as inherent in life as good ones.

—Anton Chekhov

In appearance, a woman may be all poetry and romance, goddess and angel, muslin and fluff. To look at her exterior is to be transported to heaven. But I have looked at her interior, Mrs. Popov, and what did I find there— in her very soul? A crocodile.

THE BRUTE

Anton Chekhov

Translated by Eric Bentley

CHARACTERS

MRS. POPOV, *widow and landowner, small, with dimpled cheeks.*
MR. GRIGORY S. SMIRNOV, *gentleman farmer, middle-aged.*
LUKA, *Mrs. Popov's footman, an old man.*
GARDENER, COACHMAN, HIRED MEN.

The drawing room of a country house. Mrs. Popov, in deep mourning, is staring hard at a photograph. Luka is with her.

LUKA: It's not right, ma'am, you're killing yourself. The cook has gone off with the maid to pick berries. The cat's having a high old time in the yard catching birds. Every living thing is happy. But you stay moping here in the house like it was a convent, taking no pleasure in nothing. I mean it, ma'am! It must be a full year since you set foot out of doors.

MRS. POPOV: I must never set foot out of doors again, Luka. Never! I have nothing to set foot out of doors *for*. My life is done. *He* is in his grave. I have buried myself alive in this house. We are *both* in our graves.

LUKA: You're off again, ma'am. I just won't listen to you no more. Mr. Popov is dead, but what can we do about that? It's God's doing. God's will be done. You've cried over him; you've done your share of mourning, haven't you? There's a limit to everything. You can't go on weeping and wailing forever. My old lady died, for that matter, and I wept and wailed over her a whole month long. Well, that was it. I couldn't weep and wail all my life; she just wasn't worth it. (*He sighs.*) As for the neighbors, you've forgotten all about them, ma'am. You don't visit them and you don't let them visit you. You and I are like a pair of spiders—excuse the expression, ma'am—here we are in this house like a pair of spiders, we never see the light of day. And it isn't like there was no nice people around either. The whole county's swarming with 'em. There's a regiment quartered at Riblov, and the officers are so good-looking! The girls can't take their eyes off them—There's a ball at the camp every Friday—The military band plays most every day of the week—What do you say, ma'am? You're young, you're pretty, you could enjoy yourself! Ten years from now you may want to strut and show your feathers to the officers, and it'll be too late.

MRS. POPOV (*firmly*): You must never bring this subject up again, Luka. Since Popov died, life has been an empty dream to me, you know that. *You* may think I am alive. Poor ignorant Luka! You are wrong. I am dead. I'm in my grave. Never more shall I see the light of day, never strip from my body this . . . raiment of death! Are you listening, Luka? Let his ghost learn how I love him! Yes, *I* know, and *you* know, he was often unfair to me, he was cruel to me, and he was unfaithful to me. What of it? *I* shall be faithful to *him,* that's all. I will show him how *I* can love. Hereafter, in a better world than this, he will welcome me back, the same loyal girl I always was—

LUKA: Instead of carrying on this way, ma'am, you should go out in the garden and take a bit of a walk, ma'am. Or why not harness Toby and take a drive? Call on a couple of the neighbors, ma'am?

MRS. POPOV (*breaking down*): Oh, Luka!

LUKA: Yes, ma'am? What have I said, ma'am? Oh dear!

MRS. POPOV: Toby! You said *Toby!* He adored that horse. When he drove me out to the Korchagins and the Vlasovs, it was always with Toby! He was a wonderful driver, do you remember, Luka? So graceful! So strong! I can see him now, pulling at those reins with all his might and main! Toby! Luka, tell them to give Toby an extra portion of oats today.

LUKA: Yes, ma'am.

A line to remember. See last line of play (p. 356).

[*A bell rings.*]

MRS. POPOV: Who is that? Tell them I'm not at home.

LUKA: Very good, ma'am. (*Exit.*)

MRS. POPOV (*gazing again at the photograph*): You shall see, my Popov, how a wife can love and forgive. Till death do us part. Longer than that. Till death reunite us forever! (*Suddenly a titter breaks through her tears.*) Aren't you ahsamed of yourself, Popov? Here's your little wife, being good, being faithful, so faithful she's locked up here waiting for her own funeral, while you—doesn't it make you ashamed, you naughty boy? You were terrible, you know. You made those awful scenes. You stormed out and left me alone for weeks—

[*Enter Luka.*]

LUKA (*upset*): There's someone asking for you, ma'am. Says he must—

MRS. POPOV: I suppose you told him that since my husband's death I see no one?

LUKA: Yes, ma'am. I did, ma'am. But he wouldn't listen, ma'am. He says it's urgent.

MRS. POPOV (*shrilly*): I see no one!!

LUKA: He won't take no for an answer, ma'am. He just curses and swears and comes in anyway. He's a perfect monster, ma'am. He's in the dining room right now.

MRS. POPOV: In the dining room, is he? I'll give him his comeuppance. Bring him in here this minute. (*Exit Luka. Suddenly sad again*) Why do they do this to me? Why? Insulting my grief, intruding on my solitude? (*She sighs.*) I'm afraid I'll have to enter a convent. I will, I *must* enter a convent!

[*Enter Mr. Smirnov and Luka.*]

SMIRNOV (*to Luka*): Dolt! Idiot! You talk too much! (*Seeing Mrs. Popov, with dignity*) May I have the honor of introducing myself, madam? Grigory S. Smirnov, landowner and lieutenant of artillery, retired. Forgive me, madam, if I disturb your peace and quiet, but my business is both urgent and weighty.

MRS. POPOV (*declining to offer him her hand*): What is it you wish, sir?

SMIRNOV: At the time of his death, your late husband—with whom I had the honor to be acquainted, ma'am—was in my debt to the tune of twelve hundred rubles. I have two notes to prove it. Tomorrow, ma'am, I must pay the interest on a bank loan. I have therefore no alternative, ma'am, but to ask you to pay me the money today.

MRS. POPOV: Twelve hundred rubles? But what did my husband owe it to you for?

SMIRNOV: He used to buy his oats from me, madam.

MRS. POPOV (*to Luka, with a sigh*): Remember what I said, Luka: tell them to give Toby an extra portion of oats today! (*Exit Luka.*) My dear Mr.—what was the name again?

SMIRNOV: Smirnov, ma'am.

MRS. POPOV: My dear Mr. Smirnov, if Mr. Popov owed you money, you shall be paid—to the last ruble, to the last kopeck. But today—you must excuse me, Mr.—what was it?

SMIRNOV: Smirnov, ma'am.

MRS. POPOV: Today, Mr. Smirnov, I have no ready cash in the house. (*Smirnov starts to speak.*) Tomorrow, Mr. Smirnov, no, the day after tomorrow, all will be well. My steward will be back from town. I shall see that he pays what is owing. Today, no. In any case, today is exactly seven months from Mr. Popov's death. On such a day you will understand that I am in no mood to think of money.

SMIRNOV: Madam, if you don't pay up now, you can carry me out feet foremost. They'll seize my estate.

MRS. POPOV: You can have your money. (*He starts to thank her.*) Tomorrow. (*He again starts to speak.*) That is: the day after tomorrow.

SMIRNOV: I don't need the money the day after tomorrow. I need it today.

MRS. POPOV: I'm sorry, Mr.—

SMIRNOV (*shouting*): Smirnov!

MRS. POPOV: (*sweetly*): Yes, of course. But you can't have it today.

SMIRNOV: But I can't wait for it any longer!

MRS. POPOV: Be sensible, Mr. Smirnov. How can I pay you if I don't have it?

SMIRNOV: You don't have it?

MRS. POPOV: I don't have it.

SMIRNOV: Sure?

MRS. POPOV: Positive.

SMIRNOV: Very well. I'll make a note to that effect. (*Shrugging*) And then they want me to keep cool. I meet the tax commissioner on the street, and he says, "Why are you always in such a bad humor, Smirnov?" Bad humor! How can I help it? I need money; I need it desperately. Take yesterday: I leave home at the crack of dawn; I call on all my debtors. Not a one of them pays up. Footsore and weary, I creep at midnight into some little dive, and try to snatch a few winks of sleep on the floor by the vodka barrel. Then today, I come here, fifty miles from home, saying to myself, "At last, at last, I can be sure of something," and you're not in the mood! You give me a mood! How can I help getting all worked up?

MRS. POPOV: I thought I'd made it clear, Mr. Smirnov, that you'll get your money the minute my steward is back from town?

SMIRNOV: What the hell do I care about your steward? Pardon the expression, ma'am. But it was you I came to see.

MRS. POPOV: What language! What a tone to take to a lady! I refuse to hear another word. (*Quickly, exit.*)

SMIRNOV: Not in the mood, huh? "Exactly seven months since Popov's death," huh? How about me? (*Shouting after her*) Is there this interest to pay, or isn't there? I'm asking you a question: is there this interest to pay, or isn't there? So your husband died, and you're not in the mood, and your steward's gone off some place, and so forth and so on, but what can *I* do about all that, huh? What do you think I should do? Take a running jump and shove my head through the wall? Take off in a balloon? You don't know my *other* debtors. I call on Gruzdeff. Not at home. I look for Yaroshevitch. He's hiding out. I find Kooritsin. He kicks up a row, and I have to throw him through the window. I work my way right down the list. Not a kopeck. Then I come to you, and you're not in the mood! (*Quietly, as he realizes he's talking to air*) I've spoiled them all, that's what; I've let them play me for a sucker. Well, I'll show them. I'll show this one. I'll stay right here till she pays up. Ugh! (*He shudders with rage.*) I'm in a rage! I'm in a positively towering rage! Every nerve in my body is trembling at forty to the dozen! I can't breathe, I feel ill, I think I'm going to faint. Hey, you there!

[*Enter Luka.*]

LUKA: Yes, sir. Is there anything you wish, sir?

SMIRNOV: Water! Water! No, make it vodka. (*Exit Luka.*) Consider the logic of it. A fellow creature is desperately in need of cash, so desperately in need that he has to seriously contemplate hanging himself, and this woman, this mere chit of a girl, won't pay up, and why not? Because, forsooth, she isn't in the mood! Oh, the logic of women! Come to that, I never have liked them, I could do without the whole sex. Talk to a woman? I'd rather sit on a barrel of dynamite, the very thought gives me gooseflesh. Women! Creatures of poetry and romance! Just to see one in the distance gets me mad. My legs start twitching with rage. I feel like yelling for help.

[*Enter Luka, handing Smirnov a glass of water.*]

LUKA: Mrs. Popov is indisposed, sir. She is seeing no one.

SMIRNOV: Get out. (*Exit Luka.*) Indisposed, is she? Seeing no one, huh? Well, she can see me or not, but I'll be here, I'll be right here till she pays up. If you're sick for a week, I'll be here for a week. If you're sick for a year, I'll be here for a year. You won't get around *me* with your widow's weeds and your schoolgirl dimples. I know all about dimples. (*Shouting through the window*) Semyon, let the horses out of those shafts, we're not leaving, we're staying, and tell them to give the horses some oats, yes, oats, you fool, what do you think? (*Walking away from the window*) What a mess, what an unholy mess! I didn't sleep last night, the heat is terrific today, not a damn one of 'em has paid up, and here's this—this skirt in mourning that's not in the mood! My head aches, where's that—(*He drinks from the glass.*) Water, ugh! You there!

[*Enter Luka.*]

LUKA: Yes, sir. You wish for something, sir?

SMIRNOV: Where's that confounded vodka I asked for? (*Exit Luka. Smirnov sits and looks himself over.*) Oof! A fine figure of a man *I* am! Unwashed, uncombed, unshaven, straw on my vest, dust all over me. The little woman must've taken me for a highwayman. (*Yawns.*) I suppose it wouldn't be considered polite to barge into a drawing room in this state, but who cares? I'm not a visitor; I'm a creditor—most unwelcome of guests, second only to Death.

[*Enter Luka.*]

LUKA (*handing him the vodka*): If I may say so, sir, you take too many liberties, sir.

SMIRNOV: What?!

LUKA: Oh, nothing, sir, nothing.

SMIRNOV: Who do you think you're talking to? Shut your mouth!

LUKA (*aside*): There's an evil spirit abroad. The Devil must have sent him. Oh! (*Exit Luka.*)

SMIRNOV: What a rage I'm in! I'll grind the whole world to powder. Oh, I feel ill again. You there!

[*Enter Mrs. Popov.*]

MRS. POPOV (*looking at the floor*): In the solitude of my rural retreat, Mr. Smirnov, I've long grown unaccustomed to the sound of the human voice. Above all, I cannot bear shouting. I must beg you not to break the silence.

SMIRNOV: Very well. Pay me my money and I'll go.

MRS. POPOV: I told you before, and I tell you again, Mr. Smirnov: I have no cash; you'll have to wait till the day after tomorrow. Can I express myself more plainly?

SMIRNOV: And *I* told *you* before, and *I* tell *you* again, that I need the money today, that the day after tomorrow is too late, and that if you don't pay, and pay now, I'll have to hang myself in the morning!

MRS. POPOV: But I have no cash. This is quite a puzzle.

SMIRNOV: You won't pay, huh?

MRS. POPOV: I *can't* pay, Mr. Smirnov.

SMIRNOV: In that case, I'm going to sit here and wait. (*Sits down.*) You'll pay up the day after tomorrow? Very good. Till the day after tomorrow, here I sit. (*Pause. He jumps up.*) Now look, do I have to pay that interest tomorrow, or don't I? Or do you think I'm joking?

MRS. POPOV: I must ask you not to raise your voice, Mr. Smirnov. This is not a stable.

SMIRNOV: Who said it was? Do I have to pay the interest tomorrow or not?

MRS. POPOV: Mr. Smirnov, do you know how to behave in the presence of a lady?

SMIRNOV: No, madam, I do not know how to behave in the presence of a lady.

MRS. POPOV: Just what I thought. I look at you and I say: ugh! I hear you talk, and I say to myself: "That man doesn't know how to talk to a lady."

Like Tolstoy and Dostoevsky, Chekhov enjoyed taking slaps at the Russian aristocracy's—and the upper middle class's—imitation of French manners, *comme il faut.*

SMIRNOV: You'd like me to come simpering to you in French, I suppose. "*Enchanté, madame! Merci beaucoup* for not paying zee money, *madame! Pardonnez-moi* if I 'ave disturbed you, *madame!* How *charmante* you look in mourning, *madame!*"

MRS. POPOV: Now you're being silly, Mr. Smirnov.

SMIRNOV (*mimicking*): "Now you're being silly, Mr. Smirnov." "You don't know how to talk to a lady, Mr. Smirnov." Look here, Mrs. Popov, I've known more women than you've known pussy cats. I've fought three duels on their account. I've jilted twelve, and been jilted by nine others. Oh, yes, Mrs. Popov, I've played the fool in my time, whispered sweet nothings, bowed and scraped and endeavored to please. Don't tell me I don't know what it is to love, to pine away with longing, to have the blues, to melt like butter, to be weak as water. I was full of tender emotion. I was carried away with passion. I squandered half my fortune on the sex. I chattered about women's emancipation. But there's an end to everything, dear madam. Burning eyes, dark eyelashes, ripe, red lips, dimpled cheeks, heaving bosoms, soft whisperings, the moon above, the lake below—I don't give a rap for that sort of nonsense any more, Mrs. Popov. I've found out about women. Present company excepted, they're liars. Their behavior is mere play acting; their conversation is sheer gossip. Yes, dear lady, women, young or old, are false, petty, vain, cruel, malicious, unreasonable. As for intelligence, any sparrow could give them points. Appearances, I admit, can be deceptive. In appearance, a woman may be all poetry and romance, goddess and angel, muslin and fluff. To look at her exterior is to be transported to heaven. But I have looked at her interior, Mrs. Popov, and what did I find there—in her very soul? A crocodile. (*He has gripped the back of the chair so firmly that it snaps.*) And, what is more revolting, a crocodile with an illusion, a crocodile that imagines tender sentiments are its own special province, a crocodile that thinks itself queen of the realm of love! Whereas, in sober fact, dear madam, if a woman can love anything except a lap dog you can hang me by the feet on that nail. For a man, love is suffering, love is sacrifice. A woman just swishes her train around and tightens her grip on your nose. Now, you're a woman, aren't you, Mrs. Popov? You must be an expert on some of this. Tell me, quite frankly, did you ever know a woman to be—faithful, for instance? Or even sincere? Only old hags, huh? Though some women are old hags from birth. But as for the others? You're right: a faithful woman is a freak of nature—like a cat with horns.

What would Kate Millet (Women's Liberation leader) have to say about this?

MRS. POPOV: Who *is* faithful, then? Who *have* you cast for the faithful lover? Not man?

SMIRNOV: Right first time, Mrs. Popov: man.

MRS. POPOV (*going off into a peal of bitter laughter*): Man! Man is faithful! That's a new one! (*Fiercely*) What right do you have to say this, Mr. Smirnov? Men faithful? Let me tell you something. Of all the men I have ever known my late husband Popov was the best. I loved him, and there are women who know how to love, Mr. Smirnov. I gave him my youth, my happiness, my life, my fortune. I worshiped the ground he trod on—and what happened? The best of men was unfaithful to me, Mr. Smirnov. Not once in a while. All the time. After he died, I found his desk drawer full of love letters. He squandered my money. He made love to other women before my very eyes. But, in spite of all, Mr. Smirnov, *I* was faithful. Unto death. And beyond. I am *still* faithful, Mr. Smirnov! Buried alive in this house, I shall wear mourning till the day I, too, am called to my eternal rest.

The real question here is *what* was she faithful to? And perhaps, we should also ask, "Why?"

SMIRNOV (*laughing scornfully*): Expect me to believe that? As if I couldn't see through all this hocus-pocus. Buried alive! Till you're called to your eternal rest! Till when? Till some little poet—or some little subaltern° with his first mustache—comes riding by and asks: "Can that be the house of the mysterious Tamara who for love of her late husband has buried herself alive, vowing to see no man?" Ha!

MRS. POPOV (*flaring up*): How dare you? How dare you insinuate—?

SMIRNOV: You may have buried yourself alive, Mrs. Popov, but you haven't forgotten to powder your nose.

MRS. POPOV (*incoherent*): How dare you? How—?

SMIRNOV: Who's raising his voice now? Just because I call a spade a spade. Because I shoot straight from the shoulder. Well, don't shout at me; I'm not your steward.

MRS. POPOV: I'm not shouting; you're shouting! Oh, leave me alone!

SMIRNOV: Pay me the money, and I will.

MRS. POPOV: You'll get no money out of me!

SMIRNOV: Oh, so that's it!

MRS. POPOV: Not a ruble, not a kopeck. Get out! Leave me alone!

SMIRNOV: Not being your husband, I must ask you not to make scenes with me. (*He sits.*) I don't like scenes.

MRS. POPOV (*choking with rage*): You're sitting down?

SMIRNOV: Correct, I'm sitting down.

MRS. POPOV: I asked you to leave!

SMIRNOV: Then give me the money. (*Aside*) Oh, what a rage I'm in, what a rage!

MRS. POPOV: The impudence of the man! I won't talk to you a moment longer. Get out. (*Pause*) Are you going?

SMIRNOV: No.

MRS. POPOV: No?!

SMIRNOV: No.

MRS. POPOV: On your head be it. Luka! (*Enter Luka.*) Show the gentleman out, Luka.

LUKA (*approaching*): I'm afraid, sir, I'll have to ask you, um, to leave, sir, now, um—

SMIRNOV (*jumping up*): Shut your mouth, you old idiot! Who do you think you're talking to? I'll make mincemeat of you.

°SUBALTERN: an officer below the rank of captain

LUKA (*clutching his heart*): Mercy on us! Holy saints above! (*He falls into an armchair.*) I'm taken sick! I can't breathe!!

MRS. POPOV: Then where's Dasha? Dasha! Dasha! Come here at once! (*She rings.*)

LUKA: They've gone picking berries, ma'am, I'm alone here—Water, water, I'm taken sick!

MRS. POPOV (*to Smirnov*): Get out, you!

SMIRNOV: Can't you even be polite with me, Mrs. Popov?

MRS. POPOV (*clenching her fists and stamping her feet*): With you? You're a wild animal, you were never housebroken!

SMIRNOV: What? What did you say?

MRS. POPOV: I said you were a wild animal, you were never housebroken.

SMIRNOV (*advancing upon her*): And what right do you have to talk to me like that?

MRS. POPOV: Like what?

SMIRNOV: You have insulted me, madam.

MRS. POPOV: What of it? Do you think I'm scared of you?

SMIRNOV: So you think you can get away with it because you're a woman. A creature of poetry and romance, huh? Well, it doesn't go down with me. I hereby challenge you to a duel.

LUKA: Mercy on us! Holy saints alive! Water!

SMIRNOV: I propose we shoot it out.

MRS. POPOV: Trying to scare me again? Just because you have big fists and a voice like a bull? You're a brute.

SMIRNOV: No one insults Grigory S. Smirnov with impunity! And I don't care if you *are* a female.

MRS. POPOV (*trying to outshout him*): Brute, brute, brute!

SMIRNOV: The sexes are equal, are they? Fine: then it's just prejudice to expect men alone to pay for insults. I hereby challenge—

See overprinted note on page 356.

MRS. POPOV (*screaming*): All right! You want to shoot it out? All right! Let's shoot it out!

SMIRNOV: And let it be here and now!

MRS. POPOV: Here and now! All right! I'll have Popov's pistols here in one minute! (*Walks away, then turns.*) Putting one of Popov's bullets through your silly head will be a pleasure! *Au revoir.* (*Exit.*)

How should this very funny line be delivered? (Note annotation on page 350.)

SMIRNOV: I'll bring her down like a duck, a sitting duck. I'm not one of your little poets; I'm no little subaltern with his first mustache. No sir, there's no weaker sex where I'm concerned!

LUKA: Sir! Master! (*He goes down on his knees.*) Take pity on a poor old man, and do me a favor: go away. It was bad enough before, you nearly scared me to death. But a duel—!

SMIRNOV (*ignoring him*): A duel! That's equality of the sexes for you! That's women's emancipation! Just as a matter of principle I'll bring her down like a duck. But what a woman! "Putting one of Popov's bullets through your silly head . . ." Her cheeks were flushed, her eyes gleaming! And she's accepted the challenge! I never knew a woman like this before!

LUKA: Sir! Master! Please go away! I'll always pray for you!

SMIRNOV (*again ignoring him*): What a woman! Phew!! *She's* no sour puss; *she's* no cry baby. She's fire and brimstone. She's a human cannon ball. What a shame I have to kill her!

LUKA (*weeping*): Please, kind sir, please, go away!

SMIRNOV (*as before*): I like her, isn't that funny? With those dimples and all? I like her. I'm even prepared to consider letting her off that debt. And where's my rage? It's gone. I never knew a woman like this before.

[*Enter Mrs. Popov with pistols.*]

MRS. POPOV (*boldly*): Pistols, Mr. Smirnov! (*Matter of fact*) But before we start, you'd better show me how it's done; I'm not too familiar with these things. In fact I never gave a pistol a second look.

LUKA: Lord, have mercy on us, I must go hunt up the gardener and the coachman. Why has this catastrophe fallen upon us, O Lord? (*Exit.*)

SMIRNOV (*examining the pistols*): Well, it's like this. There are several makes: one is the Mortimer, with capsules, especially constructed for dueling. What you have here are Smith and Wesson triple-action revolvers, with extractor, first-rate job, worth ninety rubles at the very least. You hold it this way. (*Aside*) My God, what eyes she has! They're setting me on fire.

MRS. POPOV: This way?

SMIRNOV: Yes, that's right. You cock the trigger, take aim like this, head up, arm out like this. Then you just press with this finger here, and it's all over. The main thing is, keep cool, take slow aim, and don't let your arm jump.

MRS. POPOV: I see. And if it's inconvenient to do the job here, we can go out in the garden.

SMIRNOV: Very good. Of course, I should warn you: I'll be firing in the air.

MRS. POPOV: What? This is the end. Why?

SMIRNOV: Oh, well—because—for private reasons.

MRS. POPOV: Scared, huh? (*She laughs heartily.*) Now don't you try to get out of it, Mr. Smirnov. My blood is up. I won't be happy till I've drilled a hole through that skull of yours. Follow me. What's the matter? Scared?

SMIRNOV: That's right. I'm scared.

MRS. POPOV: Oh, come on, what's the matter with you?

SMIRNOV: Well, um, Mrs. Popov, I, um, I like you.

MRS. POPOV (*laughing bitterly*): He likes me, does he? The gall of the man. (*Showing him the door*) You may leave, Mr. Smirnov.

SMIRNOV (*quietly puts the gun down, takes his hat, and walks to the door. Then he stops and the pair look at each other without a word. Then, approaching gingerly*): Listen, Mrs. Popov. Are you still mad at me? I'm in the devil of a temper myself, of course. But then, you see—what I mean is—it's this way—the fact is—(*Roaring*) Well, is it my fault, damn it, if I like you? (*Clutches the back of a chair. It breaks.*) What fragile furniture you have here. I like you. Know what I mean? I could fall in love with you.

MRS. POPOV: I hate you. Get out!

SMIRNOV: What a woman! I never saw anything like it. Oh, I'm lost, I'm done for, I'm a mouse in a trap.

MRS. POPOV: Leave this house, or I shoot!

SMIRNOV: Shoot away! What bliss to die of a shot that was fired by that little velvet hand! To die gazing into those enchanting eyes. I'm out of my mind. I know: you must decide at once. Think for one second, then decide. Because if I leave now, I'll never be back. Decide! I'm a pretty decent chap. Landed gentleman, I should say. Ten thousand a year. Good stable. Throw a kopeck up in the air, and I'll put a bullet through it. Will you marry me?

MRS. POPOV (*indignant, brandishing the gun*): We'll shoot it out! Get going! Take your pistol!

SMIRNOV: I'm out of my mind. I don't understand anything any more. (*Shouting*) You there! That vodka!

MRS. POPOV: No excuses! No delays! We'll shoot it out!

SMIRNOV: I'm out of my mind. I'm falling in love. I *have* fallen in love. (*He takes her hand vigorously; she squeals.*) I love you. (*He goes down on his knees.*) I love you as I've never loved before. I jilted twelve, and was jilted by nine others. But I didn't love a one of them as I love you. I'm full of tender emotion. I'm melting like butter. I'm weak as water. I'm on my knees like a fool, and I offer you my hand. It's a shame; it's a disgrace. I haven't been in love in five years. I took a vow against it. And now, all of a sudden, to be swept off my feet, it's a scandal. I offer you my hand, dear lady. Will you or won't you? You won't? Then don't! (*He rises and walks toward the door.*)

MRS. POPOV: I didn't say anything.

SMIRNOV (*stopping*): What?

MRS. POPOV: Oh, nothing, you can go. Well, no, just a minute. No, you can go. Go! I detest you! But, just a moment. Oh, if you knew how furious I feel! (*Throws the gun on the table.*) My fingers have gone to sleep holding that horrid thing. (*She is tearing her handkerchief to shreds.*) And what are you standing around for? Get out of here!

SMIRNOV: Good-by.

MRS. POPOV: Go, go, go! (*Shouting*) Where are you going? Wait a minute! No, no, it's all right; just go. I'm fighting mad. Don't come near me! Don't come near me!

SMIRNOV (*who is coming near her*): I'm pretty disgusted with myself—falling in love like a kid, going down on my knees like some moongazing whippersnapper. The very thought gives me gooseflesh. (*Rudely*) I love you. But it doesn't make sense. Tomorrow, I have to pay that interest, and we've already started mowing. (*He puts his arm about her waist.*) I shall never forgive myself for this.

MRS. POPOV: Take your hands off me, I hate you! Let's shoot it out!
[*A long kiss. Enter Luka with an axe, the Gardener with a rake, the Coachman with a pitchfork, Hired Men with sticks.*]

LUKA (*seeing the kiss*): Mercy on us! Holy saints above!

MRS. POPOV (*dropping her eyes*): Luka, tell them in the stable that Toby is *not* to have any oats today.

CURTAIN

Students might be interested in comparing this "battle of the sexes" with the more controlled sexual confrontation in Lawrence's "The White Stocking" (p. 208).

The Darling

Anton Chekhov

Translated by Avrahm Yarmolinsky

A pet name for "Olga"

Olenka Plemyannikova, the daughter of a retired collegiate assessor, was sitting on her porch, which gave on the courtyard, deep in thought. It was hot, the flies were persistent and annoying, and it was pleasant to think that it would soon be evening. Dark rainclouds were gathering in the east and there was a breath of moisture in the wind that occasionally blew from that direction.

Kukin, a theater manager who ran a summer garden known as The Tivoli and lodged in the wing of the house, was standing in the middle of the courtyard, staring at the sky.

"Again!" he was saying in despair. "It's going to rain again! Rain every day, every day, as if to spite me! It will be the death of me! It's ruin! Such a frightful loss every day!"

He struck his hands together and continued, turning to Olenka:

"There, Olga Semyonovna, that's our life. It's enough to make you weep! You work, you try your utmost, you wear yourself out, you lie awake nights, you rack your brains trying to make a better thing of it, and what's the upshot? In the first place, the public is ignorant, barbarous. I give them the very best operetta, an elaborate spectacle, first-rate vaudeville artists. But do you think they want that? It's all above their heads. All they want is slapstick! Give them trash! And then look at the weather! Rain almost every evening. It started raining on the tenth of May, and it has kept it up all May and June. It's simply terrible! The public doesn't come, but don't I have to pay the rent? Don't I have to pay the artists?"

"Daughter of Semyon." Less formal than the family name, "Plemyannikova." But he does not yet know her well enough to use the familiar "Olenka."

The next day toward evening the sky would again be overcast and Kukin would say, laughing hysterically:

"Well, go on, rain! Flood the garden, drown me! Bad luck to me in this world and the next! Let the artists sue me! Let them send me to prison—to Siberia—to the scaffold! Ha, ha, ha!"

The next day it was the same thing all over again.

Olenka listened to Kukin silently, gravely, and sometimes tears would come to her eyes. In the end his misfortunes moved her and she

No doubt. But Kukin's "summer garden" and the shows he puts on are hardly "The Theater." (*Vanichka* is the diminutive of *Ivan.*)

fell in love with him. He was a short, thin man with a sallow face, and wore his hair combed down over his temples. He had a thin tenor voice and when he spoke, his mouth twisted, and his face perpetually wore an expression of despair. Nevertheless he aroused a genuine, deep feeling in her. She was always enamored of someone and could not live otherwise. At first it had been her papa, who was now ill and sat in an armchair in a darkened room, breathing with difficulty. Then she had devoted her affections to her aunt, who used to come from Bryansk every other year. Still earlier, when she went to school, she had been in love with her French teacher. She was a quiet, kind, soft-hearted girl, with meek, gentle eyes, and she enjoyed very good health. At the sight of her full pink cheeks, her soft white neck with a dark birthmark on it, and the kind artless smile that came into her face when she listened to anything pleasant, men said to themselves, "Yes, not half bad," and smiled too, while the ladies present could not refrain from suddenly seizing her hand in the middle of the conversation and exclaiming delightedly, "You darling!"

The house in which she lived all her life and which was to be hers by her father's will was situated on the outskirts of the city on what was known as Gypsy Road, not far from The Tivoli. In the evening and at night she could hear the band play and the skyrockets go off, and it seemed to her that it was Kukin fighting his fate and assaulting his chief enemy, the apathetic public.

Her heart contracted sweetly, she had no desire to sleep, and when he returned home at dawn, she would tap softly at her bedroom window and, showing him only her face and one shoulder through the curtain, give him a friendly smile.

He proposed to her, and they were married. And when he had a good look at her neck and her plump firm shoulders, he struck his hands together, and exclaimed, "Darling!"

He was happy, but as it rained on their wedding day and the night that followed, the expression of despair did not leave his face.

As a married couple, they got on well together. She presided over the box office, looked after things in the summer garden, kept accounts and paid salaries; and her rosy cheeks, the radiance of her sweet artless smile showed now in the box office window, now in the wings of the theater, now at the buffet. And she was already telling her friends that the theater was the most remarkable, the most important, and the most essential thing in the world, and that it was only the theater that could give true pleasure and make you a cultivated and humane person.

"But do you suppose the public understands that?" she would ask. "What it wants is slapstick! Yesterday we gave 'Faust Inside Out,' and almost all the boxes were empty, and if Vanichka and I had put on something vulgar, I assure you the theater would have been packed. Tomorrow Vanichka and I are giving 'Orpheus in Hell.' Do come."

"Faust Inside Out"—a burlesque and probably not all that different from slapstick. "Orpheus in Hell"—probably another burlesque. (A little reflection on the inanity of these titles and, by implication, their content suggests the humor in Olga's high-toned remarks on "The Theater.")

A particularly ironic line, especially when one determines what Kukin's concept of "art" is.

And what Kukin said about artists and the theater she would repeat. Like him she despised the public for its ignorance and indifference to art; she took a hand in the rehearsals, correcting the actors, kept an eye on the musicians, and when there was an unfavorable notice in the local paper, she wept and went to see the editor about it.

The actors were fond of her and called her "the darling," and "Vanichka-and-I." She was sorry for them and would lend them small sums, and if they cheated her, she cried in private but did not complain to her husband.

The pair got on just as well together when winter came. They leased the municipal theater for the season and sublet it for short periods to a Ukrainian troupe, a magician, or a local dramatic club. Olenka was gaining weight and beamed with happiness, but Kukin was getting thinner and more sallow and complained of terrible losses, although business was fairly good during the winter. He coughed at night, and she would make him drink an infusion of raspberries and linden blossoms, rub him with eau de Cologne, and wrap him in her soft shawls.

"What a sweet thing you are!" she would say quite sincerely, smoothing his hair. "My handsome sweet!"

At Lent he left for Moscow to engage a company of actors for the summer season, and she could not sleep with him away. She sat at the window and watched the stars. It occurred to her that she had something in common with the hens: they too stayed awake all night and were disturbed when the cock was absent from the henhouse. Kukin was detained in Moscow, and wrote that he would return by Easter, and in his letters he sent instructions about The Tivoli. But on the Monday of Passion Week, late in the evening, there was a sudden ominous knock at the gate; someone was banging at the wicket as though it were a barrel—boom, boom, boom! The sleepy cook, her bare feet splashing through the puddles, ran to open the gate.

"Open, please!" someone on the other side of the gate was saying in a deep voice. "There's a telegram for you."

Olenka had received telegrams from her husband before, but this time for some reason she was numb with fright. With trembling hands she opened the telegram and read the following:

"Ivan Petrovich died suddenly today awaiting prot instructions tuneral Tuesday."

That is exactly how the telegram had it: "tuneral," and there was also the incomprehensible word "prot"; the signature was that of the director of the comic opera company.

"My precious!" Olenka sobbed. "Vanichka, my precious, my sweet! Why did we ever meet! Why did I get to know you and to love you! To whom can your poor unhappy Olenka turn?"

Kukin was buried on Tuesday in the Vagankovo Cemetery in Moscow. Olenka returned home on Wednesday, and no sooner did she enter her room than she sank onto the bed and sobbed so loudly that she could be heard in the street and in the neighboring courtyards.

"The darling!" said the neighbors, crossing themselves. "Darling Olga Semyonovna! How the poor soul takes on!"

The clearly defined time is important.

Three months later Olenka was returning from Mass one day in deep mourning and very sad. It happened that one of her neighbors, Vasily Andreich Pustovalov, the manager of Babakayev's lumberyard, who was also returning from church, was walking beside her. He was wearing a straw hat and a white waistcoat, with a gold watch-chain, and he looked more like a landowner than a businessman.

So is this detail.

That is, he looked as if he belonged to the upper class, was a gentleman. The social superiority of land to business is an old one, which has persisted long after its loss of any real meaning in the realities of social organization and economic life.

"There is order in all things, Olga Semyonovna," he was saying sedately, with a note of sympathy in his voice; "and if one of our dear ones passes on, then it means that this was the will of God, and in that case we must keep ourselves in hand and bear it submissively."

Having seen Olenka to her gate, he took leave of her and went further. All the rest of the day she heard his sedate voice, and as soon as she closed her eyes she had a vision of his dark beard. She liked him very much. And apparently she too had made an impression on him, because a little later a certain elderly lady, whom she scarcely knew, called to have coffee with her, and no sooner was she seated at table than the visitor began to talk about Pustovalov, saying that he was a fine, substantial man, and that any marriageable woman would be glad to go to the altar with him. Three days later Pustovalov himself paid her a visit. He did not stay more than ten minutes and he said little, but Olenka fell in love with him, so deeply that she stayed awake all night burning as with fever, and in the morning she sent for the elderly lady. The match was soon arranged and then came the wedding.

As a married couple Pustovalov and Olenka got on very well together. As a rule he was in the lumberyard till dinnertime, then he went out on business and was replaced by Olenka, who stayed in the office till evening, making out bills and seeing that orders were shipped.

The noon meal

"We pay twenty per cent more for lumber every year," she would say to customers and acquaintances. "Why, we used to deal in local timber, and now Vasichka has to travel to the province of Mogilev for timber regularly. And the freight rates!" she would exclaim, putting her hands to her cheeks in horror. "The freight rates!"

It seemed to her that she had been in the lumber business for ages, that lumber was the most important, the most essential thing in the world, and she found something intimate and touching in the very sound of such words as beam, log, batten, plank, box board, lath, scantling, slab . . .

As in the "theater business"?

At night she would dream of whole mountains of boards and planks, of endless caravans of carts hauling lumber out of town to distant points. She would dream that a regiment of beams, 28 feet by 8 inches, standing on end, was march-

Diminutive of "Vasily"

ing in the lumberyard, that beams, logs, and slabs were crashing against each other with the hollow sound of dry wood, that they kept tumbling down and rising again, piling themselves on each other. Olenka would scream in her sleep and Pustovalov would say to her tenderly: "Olenka, what's the matter, darling? Cross yourself!"

Whatever ideas her husband had, she adopted as her own. If he thought that the room was hot or that business was slow, she thought so too. Her husband did not care for entertainments and on holidays stayed home—so did she.

"You are always at home or in the office," her friends would say. "You ought to go to the theater, darling, or to the circus."

"Vasichka and I have no time for the theater," she would answer sedately. "We are working people, we're not interested in such foolishness. What good are these theaters?"

On Saturdays the two of them would go to evening service, on holidays they attended early Mass, and returning from the church they walked side by side, their faces wearing a softened expression. There was an agreeable aroma about them, and her silk dress rustled pleasantly. At home they had tea with shortbread, and various kinds of jam, and afterwards they ate pie. Every day at noon, in the yard and on the street just outside the gate, there was a delicious smell of *borshch* and roast lamb or duck, and on fast days there was the odor of fish, and one could not pass the Pustovalov gate without one's mouth watering.

Obviously. Compare her attitude when married to Kukin, the theater manager.

In the office the samovar was always boiling and the customers were treated to tea with doughnuts. Once a week the pair went to the baths and returned side by side, both with red faces.

"Yes, everything goes well with us, thank God," Olenka would say to her friends. "I wish everyone were as happy as Vasichka and I."

When Pustovalov went off to the provinces of Mogilev for timber, she missed him badly and lay awake nights, crying. Sometimes, in the evening, a young army veterinary, by the name of Smirnin, who rented the wing of their house, would call on her. He chatted or played cards with her and that diverted her. What interested her most was what he told her about his domestic life. He had been married and had a son, but was separated from his wife because she had been unfaithful to him, and now he hated her; he sent her forty rubles a month for the maintenance of the child. And listening to him, Olenka would sigh and shake her head; she was sorry for him.

"Well, God keep you," she would say to him as she took leave of him, going to the stairs with him, candle in hand. "Thank you for relieving my boredom, and may the Queen of Heaven give you health!"

She always expressed herself in this sedate and reasonable manner, in imitation of her husband. Just as the veterinary would be closing the door behind him, she would recall him and say:

"You know, Vladimir Platonych, you had better make up with your wife. You ought to forgive her, at least for your son's sake! I am sure the little boy understands everything."

And when Pustovalov came back, she would tell him in low tones about the veterinary and his unhappy domestic life, and both of them would sigh and shake their heads and speak of the boy, who was probably missing his father. Then by a strange association of ideas they would both turn to the icons, bow down to the ground before them and pray that the Lord would grant them children.

Thus the Pustovalovs lived in peace and quiet, in love and harmony for six years. But one winter day, right after having hot tea at the office, Vasily Andreich went out without his cap to see about shipping some lumber, caught a chill, and was taken sick. He was treated by the best doctors, but the illness had its own way with him, and he died after four months. Olenka was a widow again.

"To whom can I turn now, my darling?" she sobbed when she had buried her husband. "How can I live without you, wretched and unhappy as I am? Pity me, good people, left all alone in the world—"

She wore a black dress with white cuffs and gave up wearing hat and gloves for good. She hardly ever left the house except to go to church or to visit her husband's grave, and at home she lived like a nun. Only at the end of six months did she take off her widow's weeds and open the shutters. Sometimes in the morning she was seen with her cook going to market for provisions, but how she lived now and what went on in her house could only be guessed. People based their guesses on such facts as that they saw her having tea with the veterinary in her little garden, he reading the newspaper aloud to her, and that, meeting an acquaintance at the post office, she would say:

"There is no proper veterinary inspection in our town, and that's why there is so much illness around. So often you hear of people getting ill from the milk or catching infections from horses and cows. When you come down to it, the health of domestic animals must be as well cared for as the health of human beings."

She now repeated the veterinary's words and held the same opinions about everything that he did. It was plain that she could not live even for one year without an attachment and that she had found new happiness in the wing of her house. Another woman would have been condemned for this, but of Olenka no one could think ill: everything about her was so unequivocal. Neither she nor the veterinary mentioned to anyone the change that had occurred in their relations; indeed, they tried to conceal it, but they didn't succeed, because Olenka could not keep a secret. When he had visitors, his regimental colleagues, she, pouring the tea or serving the supper, would begin to talk of the cattle plague, of the pearl disease, of the municipal slaughterhouses. He would be terribly embarrassed and when the guests had gone, he would grasp her by the arms and hiss angrily:

Diminutive for "Vladimir"

"I've asked you before not to talk about things that you don't understand! When veterinaries speak among themselves, please don't butt in! It's really annoying!"

She would look at him amazed and alarmed and ask, "But Volodichka, what shall I talk about?"

And with tears in her eyes she would hug him and beg him not to be angry, and both of them were happy.

Yet this happiness did not last long. The veterinary left, left forever, with his regiment, which was moved to some remote place, it may have been Siberia. And Olenka remained alone.

Now she was quite alone. Her father had died long ago, and his armchair stood in the attic, covered with dust and minus one leg. She got thinner and lost her looks, and passers-by in the street did not glance at her and smile as they used to. Obviously, her best years were over, were behind her, and now a new kind of life was beginning for her, an unfamiliar kind that did not bear thinking of. In the evening Olenka sat on her porch, and heard the band play at The Tivoli and the rockets go off, but this no longer suggested anything to her mind. She looked apathetically at the empty courtyard, thought of nothing, and later, when night came, she would go to bed and dream of the empty courtyard. She ate and drank as though involuntarily.

Above all, and worst of all, she no longer had any opinions whatever. She saw objects about her and understood what was going on, but she could not form an opinion about anything and did not know what to talk about. And how terrible it is not to have any opinions! You see, for instance, a bottle, or the rain, or a peasant driving in a cart, but what is the bottle for, or the rain, or the peasant, what is the meaning of them, you can't tell, and you couldn't, even if they paid you a thousand rubles. When Kukin was about, or Pustovalov or, later, the veterinary, Olenka could explain it all and give her opinions about anything you like, but now there was the same emptiness in her head and in her heart as in her courtyard. It was weird, and she felt as bitter as if she had been eating wormwood.

Little by little the town was extending in all directions. Gypsy Road was now a regular street, and where The Tivoli had been and the lumberyards, houses had sprung up and lanes had multiplied. How swiftly time passes! Olenka's house had taken on a shabby look, the roof was rusty, the shed sloped, and the whole yard was invaded by burdock and stinging nettles. Olenka herself had aged and grown homely. In the summer she sat on the porch, feeling empty and dreary and bitter, as before; in the winter she sat by the window and stared at the snow. Sometimes at the first breath of spring or when the wind brought her the chime of church bells, memories of the past would overwhelm her, her heart would contract sweetly and her eyes would brim over with tears. But this only lasted a moment, and then there was again emptiness and once more she was possessed by a sense of the futility of life; Trot, the black kitten, rubbed against her and purred softly, but Olenka was not affected by these feline caresses. Is that what she needed? She needed an affection that would take possession of her whole being, her soul, her mind, that would give her ideas, a purpose in life, that would warm her aging blood. And she would shake the kitten off her lap, and say irritably: "Scat! Scat! Don't stick to me!"

How carefully Chekhov controls the tone!

And so it went, day after day, year after year, and no joy, no opinion! Whatever Mavra the cook would say was well enough.

One hot July day, toward evening, when the cattle were being driven home and the yard was filled with clouds of dust, suddenly someone knocked at the gate. Olenka herself went to open it and was dumbfounded at what she saw: at the gate stood Smirnin, the veterinary, already gray, and wearing civilian clothes. She suddenly recalled everything and, unable to control herself, burst into tears, silently letting her head drop on his breast. She was so agitated that she scarcely noticed how the two of them entered the house and sat down to tea.

"My dear," she murmured, trembling with joy, "Vladimir Platonych, however did you get here?"

"I have come here for good," he explained. "I have retired from the army and want to see what it's like to be on my own and live a settled life. And besides, my son is ready for high school. I have made up with my wife, you know."

"Where is she?"

"She's at the hotel with the boy, and I'm out looking for lodgings."

"Goodness, Vladimir Platonych, take my house! You don't need to look further! Good Lord, and you can have it free," exclaimed Olenka, all in a flutter and beginning to cry again. "You live here in the house, and the wing will do for me. Heavens, I'm so glad!"

The next day they began painting the roof and whitewashing the walls, and Olenka, her arms akimbo, walked about the yard, giving orders. The old smile had come back to her face, and she was lively and spry, as though she had waked from a long sleep. Presently the veterinary's wife arrived, a thin, homely lady with bobbed hair who looked as if she were given to caprices. With her was the little boy, Sasha, small for his age (he was going on ten), chubby, with clear blue eyes and dimples in his cheeks.

No sooner did he walk into the yard than he began chasing the cat, and immediately his eager, joyous laughter rang out.

"Auntie, is that your cat?" he asked Olenka. "When she has little ones, please give us a kitten. Mama is terribly afraid of mice."

Olenka chatted with him, then gave him tea, and her heart suddenly grew warm and contracted sweetly, as if this little boy were her own son. And in the evening, as he sat in the dining-room doing his homework, she looked at him with pity and tenderness and whispered:

"My darling, my pretty one, my little one! How blond you are, and so clever!"

Diminutive for "Alexander"

"An island," he was reciting from the book, "is a body of land entirely surrounded by water."

"An island is a body of land . . ." she repeated and this was the first opinion she expressed with conviction after so many years of silence and mental vacuity.

She now had opinions of her own, and at supper she had a conversation with Sasha's parents, saying that studying in high school was hard on the children, but that nevertheless the classical course was better than the scientific one because a classical education opened all careers to you: you could be either a doctor or an engineer.

Sasha started going to high school. His mother went off to Kharkov to visit her sister and did not come back; every day his father left town to inspect herds and sometimes he stayed away for three days together, and it seemed to Olenka that Sasha was wholly abandoned, that he was unwanted, that he was being starved, and she moved him into the wing with her and settled him in a little room there.

For six months now Sasha has been living in her wing. Every morning Olenka comes into his room; he is fast asleep, his hand under his cheek, breathing quietly. She is sorry to wake him.

"Sashenka," she says sadly, "get up, my sweet! It's time to go to school."

He gets up, dresses, says his prayers, and sits down to his breakfast: he drinks three glasses of tea and eats two large doughnuts and half a buttered French roll. He is hardly awake and consequently cross.

The pet name

"You haven't learned the fable, Sashenka," says Olenka, looking at him as though she were seeing him off on a long journey. "You worry me. You must do your best, darling, study. And pay attention to your teachers."

"Please leave me alone!" says Sasha.

Then he walks down the street to school, a small boy in a big cap, with his books in a rucksack. Olenka follows him noiselessly.

"Sashenka!" she calls after him. He turns around and she thrusts a date or a caramel into his hand. When they turn into the school lane, he feels ashamed at being followed by a tall stout woman; he looks round and says: "You'd better go home, Auntie; I can go alone now."

She stands still and stares after him until he disappears at the school entrance. How she loves him! Not one of her former attachments was so deep; never had her soul surrendered itself so unreservedly, so disinterestedly and with such joy as now when her maternal instinct was increasingly asserting itself. For this little boy who was not her own, for the dimples in his cheeks, for his very cap, she would have laid down her life, would have laid it down with joy, with tears of tenderness. Why? But who knows why?

See *Talks,* p. 77.

Having seen Sasha off to school, she goes quietly home, contented, tranquil, brimming over with love; her face, grown younger in the last six months, beams with happiness; people meeting her look at her with pleasure and say:

"Good morning, Olga Semyonovna, darling! How are you, darling?"

"They make the children work so hard at high school nowadays," she says, as she does her marketing. "Think of it: yesterday in the first form they had a fable to learn by heart, a Latin translation, and a problem for homework. That's entirely too much for a little fellow."

And she talks about the teachers, the lessons, the textbooks—saying just what Sasha says about them.

At three o'clock they have dinner together; in the evening they do the homework together and cry. When she puts him to bed, she takes a long time making the sign of the cross over him and whispering prayers. Then she goes to bed and thinks of the future, distant and misty, when Sasha, having finished his studies, will become a doctor or an engineer, will have a large house of his own, horses, a carriage, will marry and become a father. She falls asleep and her dreams are of the same thing, and tears flow down her cheeks from her closed eyes. The black kitten lies beside her purring: Purr-purrr-purrr.

Suddenly there is a loud knock at the gate. Olenka wakes up, breathless with fear, her heart palpitating. Half a minute passes, and there is another knock.

"That's a telegram from Kharkov," she thinks, beginning to tremble from head to foot. "Sasha's mother is sending for him from Kharkov—O Lord!"

She is in despair. Her head, her hands, her feet grow chill and it seems to her that she is the most unhappy woman in the whole world. But another minute passes, voices are heard: it's the veterinary returning from the club.

"Well, thank God!" she thinks.

Little by little the load rolls off her heart and she is again at ease; she goes back to bed and thinks of Sasha, who is fast asleep in the next room and sometimes shouts in his sleep:

"I'll give it to you! Scram! No fighting!"

Literary Sort: How tragic!

Editor: I thought it comic.

An interesting comparison: Chekhov's "Darling" with "Cool Girl" (p. 154) or "The Little Man" (p. 313)?

"Foolishness is a great deal more vital and healthy than our straining and striving after a meaningful life." So says the General and Privy Councilor . . . and turns a simple life topsy-turvy. . . .

The Privy Councilor

Anton Chekhov

Translated by Constance Garnett

At the beginning of April in 1870 my mother, Klavdia Arhipovna, the widow of a lieutenant, received from her brother Ivan, a privy councilor who lived in Petersburg, a letter in which, among other things, this passage occurred: "My liver trouble forces me to spend every summer abroad, and as I have not at the moment the money in hand for a trip to Marienbad, it is very possible, dear Sister, that I may spend this summer with you at Kochuevko. . . ."

In Germany, a health resort

On reading the letter my mother turned pale and began trembling all over; then an expression of mingled tears and laughter came into her face. She began crying and laughing. This conflict of tears and laughter always reminds me of the flickering and spluttering of a brightly burning candle when one sprinkles it with water. Having reread the letter, Mother called together all the household, and in a voice broken with emotion began explaining to us that there had been four Gundasov brothers: one Gundasov had died as a baby; another had gone into the army, and he, too, was dead; the third, without offence to him be it said, was an actor; the fourth—

"The fourth has risen far above us," my mother brought out tearfully. "My own brother, we grew up together; and I am all of a tremble, all of a tremble! . . . A privy councilor, a General! How shall I meet him, my angel brother? What can I, a foolish, uneducated woman, talk to him about? It's fifteen years since I've seen him! Andryushenka," my mother turned to me, "you must rejoice, little stupid! It's a piece of luck for you that God is sending him to us!"

After we had heard a detailed history of the Gundasovs, there followed a fuss and bustle in the place such as I had been accustomed to see only before Christmas. The sky above and the water in the river were all that escaped; everything else was subjected to a merciless cleansing, scrubbing, painting. If the sky had been lower and smaller and the river had not flowed so swiftly, they would have scoured them, too, with brick dust and rubbed them, too, with tow. Our walls were as white as snow, but they were whitewashed; the floors were bright and shining, but they were washed every day. The cat Bobtail (as a small child I had cut off a good quarter of his tail with the knife used for chopping sugar, and that was why he was called Bobtail) was carried off to the kitchen and put in care of Anisya; Fedka was told that if any of the dogs came near the front door "God would punish him." But no one was treated so roughly as the poor sofas, easy chairs, and rugs! They had never before been so violently beaten as on this occasion in preparation for our visitor. My pigeons took fright at the loud thud of the sticks, and were continually soaring into the sky.

The tailor Spiridon, the only tailor in the whole district who ventured to work for the gentry, came over from Novostroevka. He was a hard-working, capable man who did not drink and was not without a certain fancy and feeling for form, but was nevertheless an atrocious tailor. His work was ruined by hesitation. . . . The idea that his cut was not fashionable enough made him alter everything half a dozen times, walk all the way to the town simply to study the dandies, and in the end dress us in suits that even a caricaturist would have called *outré* and grotesque. We cut a dash in impossibly tight trousers and in such short jackets that we always felt quite abashed in the presence of young ladies.

This Spiridon spent a long time taking my measure. He measured me all over lengthways and crossways, as though he meant to put hoops round me like a barrel; then he spent a long time noting down my measurements with a thick pencil on a bit of paper, and ticked off all the measurements with triangular signs. When he had finished with me he set to work on my tutor, Yegor Alexeyevich Pobedimsky. My unforgettable tutor was then at the stage when young men watch the growth of their mustache and are critical of their clothes, and so you can imagine the religious awe with which Spiridon approached him! Yegor Alexeyevich had to throw back his head, straddle his legs like an inverted V, lift up his arms, let them fall. Spiridon measured him several times, walking round him during the process like a lovesick dove round its mate, going down on one knee, bending double. . . . My mother, weary, exhausted by her exertions and headachey from ironing, watched these lengthy proceedings, and said:

"Mind now, Spiridon, you will have to answer for it to God if you spoil the cloth! And you will never have any luck if the clothes don't fit!"

Mother's words threw Spiridon first into a fever, then into a perspiration, for he was convinced that the clothes wouldn't fit. He received one ruble twenty kopecks for making my suit, and for Pobedimsky's two rubles, we providing the cloth, the lining, and the buttons. The price cannot be considered excessive, as Novostroevka was about six miles from us, and the tailor came to fit us four times. When he came to try the things on and we squeezed ourselves into the tight trousers and jackets full of basting threads, mother always frowned contemptuously and expressed her surprise:

"Goodness knows what the fashions are coming to nowadays! I am positively ashamed to look at them. If brother were not used to Petersburg I would not get you fashionable clothes!"

Spiridon, relieved that the blame was thrown on the fashions and not on him, shrugged his shoulders and sighed, as though to say:

"There's no help for it; it's the spirit of the age!"

The excitement with which we awaited the arrival of our guest can only be compared to the strained suspense with which spiritualists await from minute to minute the appearance of a ghost. Mother went about with a sick headache, and was continually melting into tears. I lost my appetite, slept badly, and did not do my lessons. Even in my dreams I was haunted by an impatient longing to see a General—that is, a man with shoulder-straps and an embroidered collar sticking up to his ears, and with a naked sword in his hands, exactly like the one who hung over the sofa in our drawing room and glared with terrible black eyes at everybody who dared to look at him. Pobedimsky was the only one who felt himself in his element. He was neither terrified nor delighted, and merely from time to time, when he heard the history of the Gundasov family, said:

"Yes, it will be pleasant to have someone fresh to talk to."

My tutor was looked upon among us as an exceptional nature. He was a young man of twenty, with a pimply face, shaggy locks, a low forehead, and an unusually long nose. His nose was so big that when he wanted to look close at anything he had to put his head to one side like a bird. To our thinking, in the whole province there was not a cleverer, more cultivated, or more fashionably dressed man. He had left high school a year before he was due to graduate, and had then entered a veterinary college, from which he was expelled before the end of the first semester. The reason of his expulsion he carefully concealed, which enabled any one who wished to do so to look upon my instructor as an injured and to some extent mysterious person. He spoke little, and only on intellectual subjects; ate meat on fast days, and looked with contempt and condescension on the life around him, which did not prevent him, however, from taking presents, such as suits of clothes, from my mother, and drawing funny faces with red teeth on my kites. Mother disliked him for his "pride," but stood in awe of his brains.

Our visitor did not keep us long waiting. At the beginning of May two cart-loads of big trunks arrived from the station. These trunks looked so majestic that the drivers instinctively took off their hats as they lifted them down.

"There must be uniforms and gunpowder in those trunks," I thought.

Why gunpowder? Probably the conception of a General was closely connected in my mind with cannon and gunpowder.

When I woke up on the morning of the tenth of May, nurse told me in a whisper that "Uncle had arrived." I dressed rapidly and, washing after a fashion, flew out of my bedroom without saying my prayers. In the vestibule I came upon a tall, thick-set gentleman with fashionable whiskers and a foppish-looking overcoat. Half dead with religious awe, I went up to him and, remembering the ceremonial Mother had impressed upon me, I scraped my foot before him, made a very low bow, and craned forward to kiss his hand; but the gentleman did not allow me to kiss his hand: he informed me that he was not my uncle, but my uncle's footman, Pyotr. The appearance of this Pyotr, who was far better dressed than Pobedimsky or me, filled me with utter astonishment, which, to tell the truth, has lasted to this day. Can such dignified, respectable people with stern and intellectual faces really be footmen? And what for?

Not quite the same question as the one asked in "The Darling," (p. 365)?

Pyotr told me that my uncle was in the garden with my mother. I rushed into the garden.

Nature, ignorant of the history of the Gundasov family and of my uncle's rank, felt far more at ease and unconstrained than I. There was a clamor going on in the garden such as one only hears at fairs. Masses of starlings flitting through the air and hopping about the walks were noisily chattering as they hunted for Maybugs. There were swarms of sparrows in the lilac bushes, which thrust their tender, fragrant blossoms straight in one's face. Wherever one turned, from every direction came the note of the oriole and the shrill cry of the hoopoe and the kestrel. At any other time I should have begun chasing dragonflies or throwing stones at a crow which was sitting on a low rick under an aspen tree, with its blunt beak turned away; but at that moment I was in no mood for mischief. My heart was throbbing, and I felt a cold sinking at my stomach; I was preparing myself to confront a gentleman with shoulder-straps, a naked sword, and terrible eyes!

But imagine my disappointment! A thin, dapper little man in white silk trousers and with a white cap on his head was walking beside my mother in the garden. With his hands behind him and his head thrown back, every now and then running on ahead of mother, he looked quite young. There was so much life and movement in his whole figure that I could only detect the treachery of age when I came close up behind and saw beneath his cap a fringe of close-cropped silver hair. Instead of the staid dignity and stolidity of a General, I saw an almost school-boyish nimbleness; instead of a collar sticking up to his ears, an ordinary light blue necktie. Mother and Uncle were walking in the alley, talking. I went softly up to them from behind, and waited for one of them to look round.

Note parallel scene in which narrator mistakes General's servant (p. 370). It is the classic mistaken identity motif of comedy, here used to contrast reality and expectation.

"What a delightful place you have here, Klavdia!" said my uncle. "How charming and lovely it is! Had I known before that you had such a charming place, nothing would have induced me to go abroad all these years."

Uncle stooped down rapidly and sniffed at a tulip. Everything he saw moved him to rapture and curiosity, as though he had never been in a garden on a sunny day before. The queer man moved about as though he were on springs, and chattered incessantly, without allowing Mother to utter a single word. All of a sudden Pobedimsky came into sight from behind an elder-tree at the turn of the alley. His appearance was so unexpected that my uncle positively started and took a step backward. On this occasion my tutor was attired in his best cape with sleeves, in which, especially from the back, he looked remarkably like a windmill. He had a solemn and majestic air. Pressing his hat to his bosom in Spanish style, he took a step towards my uncle and made a bow such as a marquis makes in a melodrama, bending forward, a little to one side.

Seeing the General through the eyes of the boy helps to direct our initial response toward the comic. The boy cannot see him as anything more than odd. He cannot comment on, "Nothing would have induced me to go abroad all these years."

"I have the honor to introduce myself to your High Excellency," he said aloud: "pedagogue and tutor of your nephew, formerly a student of the veterinary institute, and a nobleman by birth, Pobedimsky!"

Such civility on the part of my tutor pleased my mother very much. She gave a smile, and waited in thrilled suspense to hear what clever thing he would say next; but my tutor, expecting his dignified address to be answered with equal dignity—that is, that my uncle would say "H'm!" like a general and hold out two fingers—was greatly embarrassed and abashed when the latter laughed genially and shook hands with him. He muttered something incoherent, cleared his throat, and walked away.

"Come! isn't that charming?" laughed my uncle. "Just look! he has put on his cape and thinks he's a very clever fellow! I do like that—I swear to God! What youthful aplomb, what life in that cape! And what boy is this?" he asked, suddenly turning and looking at me.

"That is my Andryushenka," my mother introduced me, flushing crimson. "My consolation. . . ."

Diminutive for "Andrei"

I made a scrape with my foot on the sand and dropped a low bow.

"A fine fellow . . . a fine fellow . . ." muttered my uncle, taking his hand from my lips and stroking me on the head. "So your name is Andrusha? Yes, yes. . . . H'm! . . . I swear to God! . . . Do you do your lessons?"

The ineptitude and shallowness of the question is the point here. He responds decently to neither the boy nor the tutor.

My mother, exaggerating and embellishing as all mothers do, began to describe my achievements in the sciences and the excellence of my behavior, and I walked round my uncle and, following the ceremonial laid down for me, I continued making low bows. Then my mother began throwing out hints that with my remarkable abilities it would not be amiss for me to get a government scholarship in the Corps of Cadets; but at the point when I was to have burst into tears and begged for my uncle's patronage my uncle suddenly stopped and flung up his hands in amazement.

He is caught by a pretty girl, but also he is shrewd enough to cut short the mother's petition.

"My goo-oodness! What's that?" he asked.

Tatyana Ivanovna, the wife of our steward, Fyodor Petrovna, was coming straight toward us. She was carrying a starched white skirt and a long ironing board. As she passed us she looked shyly at the visitor through her eyelashes and flushed crimson.

"Wonders will never cease . . ." my uncle filtered through his teeth, looking after her with friendly interest. "You have a fresh surprise at every step, Sister . . . I swear to God!"

"She's a beauty . . ." said Mother. "They chose her as a bride for Fyodor, though she lived over seventy miles from here. . . ."

The sophistication in this passage is somewhat out of line with the narrator's character. But this is a fairly early story. At p. 377 Chekhov includes a line that will give him a double point of view and allow for such comments. Its validity is questionable.

Not everyone would have called Tatyana a beauty. She was a plump little woman of twenty, with black eyebrows and a graceful figure, always rosy and attractive-looking, but in her face and in her whole person there was not one striking feature, not one bold line to catch the eye, as though nature had lacked inspiration and confidence when it created her. Tatyana Ivanovna was shy, bashful, and modest in her behavior; she moved softly and smoothly, said little, seldom laughed, and her whole life was as regular as her face and as flat as her sleek hair. My uncle screwed up his eyes looking after her and smiled. Mother looked intently at his smiling face and grew serious.

"And so, Brother, you've never married!" she sighed.

"No; I've not married."

"Why not?" asked Mother softly.

"How can I tell you? It just happened so. In my youth I was too hard at work, I had no time to live, and when I longed to live—I looked round—and there I had fifty years on my back already. It was too late. However, talking about it . . . is depressing."

Mother and Uncle both sighed at once and walked on, and I left them and flew off to find my tutor, that I might share my impressions with him. Pobedimsky was standing in the middle of the yard, looking majestically at the heavens.

"One can see he is a man of culture!" he said, twisting his head round. "I hope we shall get on together."

An hour later Mother came to us.

"I am in trouble, my dears!" she began, sighing. "You see, Brother has brought a valet with him, and the valet, God bless him, is not one you can put in the kitchen or in the passage; he must have a room to himself. I can't think what I am to do! I tell you what, children, couldn't you move out somewhere—to Fyodor's lodge, for instance—and give your room to the valet? What do you say?"

We gave our ready consent, for living in the lodge we would be a great deal freer than in the house, under Mother's eye.

"It's a nuisance, and that's a fact!" said Mother. "Brother says he won't have dinner in the middle of the day, but between six and seven, as they do in Petersburg. I am simply distracted with worry! By seven o'clock the dinner will be ruined. Really, men don't understand anything about housekeeping, though they have so much intellect. Oh, dear! we shall have to cook two dinners every day! You will have dinner at midday as before, children, while your poor old mother has to wait till seven, for the sake of her brother."

Then my mother heaved a deep sigh, bade me try and please my uncle, whose coming was a piece of luck for me for which we must thank God, and hurried off to the kitchen. Pobedimsky and I moved into the wing the same day. We were installed in a room between the entry and the steward's bedroom.

Contrary to my expectations, life went on just as before, drearily and monotonously, in spite of my uncle's arrival and our removal to new quarters. We were excused from lessons "on account of the visitor." Pobedimsky, who never read anything or occupied himself in any way, spent most of his time sitting on his bed, with his long nose thrust into the air, thinking. Sometimes he would get up, try on his new suit, and sit down again to relapse into contemplation and silence. Only one thing worried him, the flies, which he mercilessly swatted with his hands. After dinner he usually "rested," and his snores were a cause of annoyance to the whole household. I ran about the garden from morning to night, or sat in the room making kites.

For the first two or three weeks we did not see Uncle often. For days together he sat in his own room, working in spite of the flies and the heat. His extraordinary capacity for sitting as though glued to his table produced upon us the effect of an inexplicable conjuring trick. To us idlers, knowing nothing of systematic work, his industry seemed simply miraculous. Getting up at nine, he sat down at his desk and did not leave it till dinnertime; after dinner he set to work again and went on till late at night. Whenever I peeped through the keyhole I invariably saw the same thing: my uncle sitting at the desk, working. The work consisted in his writing with one hand while he turned over the leaves of a book with the other, and, strange to say, all of him was in constant movement—his leg swinging as though it were a pendulum, his head nodding in time to his whistling. He had an extremely careless and frivolous expression all the while, as though he were not working but playing tick-tack-toe. I always saw him wearing a smart short jacket and a jauntily tied cravat, and he always smelt, even through the keyhole, of delicate feminine perfume. He only left his room for dinner, but he ate little.

"I can't make Brother out!" Mother complained of him. "Every day we kill a turkey and squabs on purpose for him, I make a *compote* with my own hands, and he eats a plateful of broth and a bit of meat the size of a finger and gets up from the table. I begin begging him to eat; he comes back and drinks a glass of milk. And what is there in that, in a glass of milk? It's no better than dishwater! You may die of a diet like that. . . . If I try to persuade him, he laughs and makes a joke of it. . . . No; he does not care for our fare, poor dear!"

Stewed fruit in syru

We spent the evenings far more gaily than the days. As a rule, by the time the sun was setting and long shadows were lying across the yard, we—that is, Tatyana Ivanovna, Pobedimsky, and I—were sitting on the steps of the lodge. We did not talk till it grew quite dark. And, indeed, what is one to talk of when every subject has been talked over already? There was only one piece of news, my uncle's arrival, and even that subject was soon exhausted. My tutor never took his eyes off Tatyana Ivanovna's face, and frequently heaved deep sighs. . . . At the time I did not understand those sighs, and did not try to fathom their significance; now they explain a great deal to me.

When the shadows merged into one thick mass, the steward Fyodor would come in from shooting or from the fields. This Fyodor gave me the impression of being a fierce and even terrible man. The son of a Russianized gypsy from Izyum, swarthy-faced and curly-headed, with big black eyes and a matted beard, he was never called among our Kochuevko peasants by any name but "The Devil." And, indeed, there was a great deal of the gypsy about him apart from his appearance. He could not, for instance, stay at home, and went off for days together into the country or into the woods to shoot. He was gloomy, ill-humored, taciturn, was afraid of no one, and recognized no authority. He was rude to Mother, addressed me familiarly, and was contemptuous of Pobedimsky's learning. All this we forgave him, looking upon him as a hot-tempered and nervous man; Mother liked him because, in spite of his gypsy nature, he was ideally honest and industrious. He loved his Tatyana Ivanovna passionately, like a gypsy, but this love took in him a gloomy form, as though it cost him suffering. He was never affectionate to his wife in our presence, but simply rolled his eyes angrily at her and twisted his mouth.

When he came in from the fields he would noisily and angrily put down his gun, would come out to us on the steps, and sit down beside his wife. After resting a little, he would ask his wife a few questions about household matters, and then sink into silence.

"Let's sing," I would suggest.

My tutor would tune his guitar, and in a deep deacon's bass strike up "Down in the Level Valley." The singing began. My tutor took the bass, Fyodor sang in a hardly audible tenor, while I sang soprano in unison with Tatyana Ivanovna.

When the whole sky was covered with stars and the frogs had left off croaking, they would bring in our supper from the kitchen. We went into the lodge and sat down to the meal. My tutor and the gypsy ate greedily, with such a noise that it was hard to tell whether it was the bones crunching or their jaws, while Tatyana Ivanovna and I scarcely managed to eat our share. After supper the lodge was plunged in deep sleep.

One evening, it was at the end of May, we were sitting on the steps, waiting for supper. A shadow suddenly fell across us, and Uncle stood before us as though he had sprung out of the ground. He looked at us for a long time, then struck his hands together and laughed gaily.

"An idyll!" he said. "They sing and dream in the moonlight! It's charming, I swear to God! May I sit down and dream with you?"

Does this speech violate the somewhat insensitive character that has already been established for the Uncle, or does it add another dimension to his insensitivity by revealing a strain of superficial pretentiousness in his character and speech? (Note: A strong motif in late 19th Century Russian literature is "the superfluous man." Chekhov's Privy Councilor leans in that direction.)

We looked at one another and said nothing. My uncle sat down on the bottom step, yawned, and looked at the sky. A silence fell. Pobedimsky, who had for a long time now been wanting to talk to some person, was delighted at the opportunity, and was the first to break the silence. He had only one subject for intellectual conversation: epizootic diseases. It sometimes happens that after one has been in an immense crowd, only some one countenance of the thousands remains long imprinted on the memory; in the same way, of all that Pobedimsky had heard during his six months at the veterinary institute he remembered only one passage:

He has nothing to contribute.

General among animals; a delightful topic for conversation.

"Epizootics do immense damage to the national economy. It is the duty of society to work hand in hand with the government in waging war upon them."

Before saying this to Uncle, my tutor cleared his throat three times, and several times, in his excitement, wrapped himself up in his cape. On hearing about the epizootics, my uncle looked intently at my tutor and made a sound between a snort and a laugh.

"Upon my soul, that's charming!" he said, scrutinizing us as though we were lay figures. "This is actually life. . . . This is what reality is bound to be. Why are you silent, Pelageya Ivanovna?" he said, addressing Tatyana Ivanovna.

She coughed, overcome with embarrassment.

Out of character for a boy so young? (See note on page 372.)

He gets her name wrong.

The boy misinterprets. Note the Uncle's speech just preceding: "Upon my word, that's charming." It demonstrates again his failure to show earnest sympathy, as well as the superficial nature of his words and manners.

"Talk, my friends, sing . . . play! . . . Don't lose time. You know, time, the rascal, runs away and waits for no man! I swear to God, before you have time to look round, old age is upon you. . . . Then it is too late to live! That's how it is, Pelageya Ivanovna. . . . We mustn't sit still and be silent. . . ."

At that point supper was brought in from the kitchen. Uncle went into the wing with us, and to keep us company ate five curd fritters and the wing of a duck. He ate and looked at us. He was touched and delighted by us all. Whatever silly nonsense my precious tutor talked, and whatever Tatyana Ivanovna did, he thought charming and delightful. When after supper Tatyana Ivanovna sat quietly down and took up her knitting, he kept his eyes fixed on her fingers and chatted away without ceasing.

"Make all the haste you can to live, my friends . . ." he said. "God forbid you should sacrifice the present for the future! There is youth, health, fire in the present; the future is smoke and deception! As soon as you are twenty, begin to live."

Tatyana Ivanovna dropped a knitting-needle. Uncle jumped up, picked up the needle, and handed it to Tatyana Ivanovna with a bow, and for the first time in my life I learned that there were people in the world more refined than Pobedimsky.

"Yes . . ." my uncle went on, "love, marry . . . do silly things. Foolishness is a great deal more vital and healthy than our straining and striving after a meaningful life."

Uncle talked a great deal, so much that he bored us; I sat on a chest listening to him and dropping to sleep. It distressed me that he did not once all the evening pay attention to me. He left the lodge at two o'clock, when, overcome with drowsiness, I was sound asleep.

From that time forth my uncle took to coming to the lodge every evening. He sang with us, had supper with us, and always stayed on till two o'clock in the morning, chatting incessantly, always about the same subject. His evening and night work was given up, and by the end of June, when the privy councilor had learned to eat Mother's turkey and *compote,* his work by day was abandoned too. My uncle tore himself away from his desk and was drawn into "life." In the daytime he walked up and down the garden, whistled, and interfered with the men's work, making them tell him various stories. When his eye fell on Tatyana Ivanovna he ran up to her and, if she was carrying anything, offered his assistance, which embarrassed her dreadfully.

As the summer advanced, Uncle grew more and more frivolous, volatile, and abstracted. Pobedimsky was completely disappointed in him.

"He is too one-sided," he said. "There is nothing to show that he is in the very foremost ranks of the service. And he doesn't even know how to talk. At every word it's 'I swear to God!' No, I don't like him!"

From the time that my uncle began visiting the lodge there was a noticeable change both in Fyodor and my tutor. Fyodor gave up going out shooting, came home early, sat more taciturn than ever, and stared with particular ill-humor at his wife. In my uncle's presence my tutor gave up talking about epizootics, frowned, and even laughed sarcastically.

"Here comes our little bantam cock!" he growled on one occasion when Uncle was coming into the wing.

I put down this change in them both to their being offended with my uncle. My absent-minded uncle mixed up their names, and to the very day of his departure had not learned to tell my tutor from Tatyana Ivanovna's husband. Tatyana Ivanovna herself he sometimes called Nastasya, sometimes Pelageya, and sometimes Yevdokia. Touched and delighted by us, he laughed and behaved exactly as though he was in the company of small children. . . . All this, of course, might well offend young men. It was not a case of offended pride, however, but, as I realize now, of subtler feelings.

This seems to indicate that the narrator is not just a boy, but is in fact an adult looking back at himself as a boy. Yet it seems doubtful that this line can control the whole story. (Some might argue against this point by noting that Chekhov carefully and subtly shifts the point of view back and forth from past to present, from reminiscence to the person who is reminiscing; others might argue that such writing is merely sloppy.)

I remember one evening I was sitting on the chest, struggling with sleep. My eyelids felt glued together and my body, tired out by running about all day, drooped sideways. But I struggled against sleep and tried to look on. It was about midnight. Tatyana Ivanovna, rosy and meek as always, was sitting at a little table, sewing a shirt for her husband. Fyodor, sullen and gloomy, was staring at her from one corner, and in the other sat Pobedimsky, snorting angrily and retreating into the high collar of his shirt. Uncle was walking up and down the room, thinking. Silence reigned; nothing was to be heard but the rustling of the linen in Tatyana Ivanovna's hands. Suddenly my uncle stood still before Tatyana Ivanovna, and said:

"You are all so young, so fresh, so nice, you live so peacefully in this quiet place that I envy you. I have become attached to your way of life here; my heart aches when I remember I have to go away. . . . You may believe in my sincerity!"

Sleep closed my eyes and I dropped off. When some noise waked me, my uncle was standing before Tatyana Ivanovna, looking at her with a softened expression. His cheeks were flushed.

"My life has been wasted," he said. "I have not lived! Your young face makes me think of my own lost youth, and I should be ready to sit here watching you to my dying day. It would be a pleasure to me to take you with me to Petersburg."

To be taken seriously, in the light of the speaker?

Even here, the wrong name.

"What for?" Fyodor asked in a husky voice.

"I should put her under a glass case on my desk. I should admire her and show her to other people. You know, Pelageya Ivanovna, we have no women like you there. We have wealth, distinction, sometimes beauty, but we have not this true sort of life, this healthy serenity. . . ."

My uncle sat down facing Tatyana Ivanovna and took her by the hand.

"So you won't come with me to Petersburg?" he laughed. "In that case give me your little hand. . . . A charming little hand! . . . You won't give it? Come, you miser! let me kiss it, anyway. . . ."

At that moment there was the scrape of a chair. Fyodor jumped up and with heavy, measured steps went up to his wife. His face was pale gray and quivering. He brought his fist down on the table with a bang, and said in a hollow voice: "I won't allow it!"

At the same moment Pobedimsky too jumped up from his chair. Pale and angry, he went up to Tatyana Ivanovna, and he, too, struck the table with his fist.

"I . . . I won't allow it!" he said.

"What? What's the matter?" asked my uncle in surprise.

"I won't allow it!" repeated Fyodor, banging on the table.

Uncle jumped up and blinked faint-heartedly. He tried to speak, but in his amazement and alarm could not utter a word; with an embarrassed smile, he shuffled out of the lodge with the mincing step of an old man, leaving his hat behind. When, a little later, my mother ran into the lodge, Fyodor and Pobedimsky were still hammering on the table like blacksmiths and repeating, "I won't allow it!"

"What has happened here?" asked Mother. "Why has my brother been taken ill? What's the matter?"

Looking at Tatyana's pale, frightened face and at her infuriated husband, Mother probably guessed what was the matter. She sighed and shook her head.

"Come! Quit banging on the table!" she said. "Leave off, Fyodor! And why are you thumping, Yegor Alexeyevich? What have you got to do with it?"

Pobedimsky was startled and confused. Fyodor looked intently at him, then at his wife, and began walking about the room. When Mother had gone out of the lodge, I saw what for long afterwards I looked upon as a dream. I saw Fyodor seize my tutor, lift him up in the air, and thrust him out of the door.

When I woke up in the morning my tutor's bed was empty. To my question where he was, Nurse told me in a whisper that he had been taken off early in the morning to the hospital, as his arm was broken. Saddened by this news and remembering the scene of the previous evening, I went out of doors. It was a gray day. The sky was overcast and there was a wind blowing dust, bits of paper, and feathers along the ground. . . . It felt as though rain were coming. People and animals looked bored. When I went into the house I was told not to make such a noise with my feet, as Mother was in bed with a migraine. What was I to do? I went outside the gate, sat down on the little bench there, and fell to trying to discover the meaning of what I had seen and heard the day before. From our gate there was a road which, passing the forge and the pool that never dried up, led to the highway. I looked at the telegraph-posts, about which clouds of dust were whirling, and at the sleepy birds sitting on the wires, and I suddenly felt so dreary that I began to cry.

It may well be asked whether what follows is necessary to the effect of the story. Or is it merely a way to get the Uncle out of the house? (Chekhov often despaired that because of deadlines he could not artistically polish his work. Is this an example?)

A dusty bus crammed full of townspeople, probably going to visit the shrine, drove by along the highway. The bus was hardly out of sight when a light carriage drawn by a pair of horses came into view. In it was Akim Nikitich, the district police officer, standing up and holding on to the coachman's belt. To my great surprise, the carriage turned into our road and flew by me into the gate. While I was puzzling why the police inspector had come to see us, I heard a noise, and a troika came into sight on the road. In the carriage stood the chief of police, directing his coachman towards our gate.

"And why is he coming?" I thought, looking at the dusty chief of police. "Most probably Pobedimsky has complained of Fyodor to him, and they have come to take him to prison."

But the mystery was not so easily solved. The police officer and the chief of police were only forerunners, for five minutes had scarcely passed when another coach drove in at our gate. It dashed by me so swiftly that I could only get a glimpse of a red beard at the window.

Lost in conjecture and full of apprehension, I ran to the house. In the vestibule first of all I saw Mother; she was pale and looking with horror towards the door, from which came the sounds of men's voices. The visitors had taken her by surprise at the height of her migraine.

"Who has come, Mother?" I asked.

"Sister," I heard my uncle's voice, "will you send in something to eat for the Governor and me?"

"It is easy to say 'something to eat,'" whispered my mother, numb with horror. "What have I time to get ready now? I am put to shame in my old age!"

Mother clutched at her head and ran into the kitchen. The Governor's sudden visit stirred and overwhelmed the whole household. A ferocious slaughter followed. A dozen hens, five turkeys, eight ducks were killed, and in the confusion the old gander, the progenitor of our whole flock of geese and a great favorite of Mother's, was beheaded. The coachmen and the cook seemed frenzied, and slaughtered birds at random, without distinction of age or breed. For the sake of some wretched sauce a pair of valuable pigeons, as dear to me as the gander was to Mother, were sacrificed. It was a long while before I could forgive the Governor their death.

This frenzied slaughter coupled with the Uncle's anguish about "the fourth course . . . duck" (p. 380) reemphasizes the "superfluous man" motif.

In the evening, when the Governor and his suite, after a sumptuous dinner, had got into their carriages and driven away, I went into the house to look at the remains of the feast. Glancing into the drawing-room from the vestibule, I saw my uncle and my mother. My uncle, with his hands behind his back, was walking nervously up and down close to the wall, shrugging his shoulders. Mother, exhausted and looking much thinner, was sitting on the sofa and watching his movements with heavy eyes.

"Excuse me, Sister, but this won't do at all," my uncle grumbled, wrinkling up his face. "I introduced the Governor to you, and you didn't offer to shake hands. You covered him with embarrassment, poor fellow! No, that won't do. . . . Simplicity is a very good thing, but there must be limits to it, too . . . I swear to God! And then that dinner! How can one give people such food? What was that mess, for instance, that they served for the fourth course?"

See overprinted note at bottom of page 379.

"That was duck with sweet sauce . . ." Mother answered softly.

"Duck! Forgive me, Sister, but . . . but here I've got heartburn! I am ill!"

Uncle made a sour, tearful face and went on:

"It was the devil sent that Governor! As though I wanted his visit! Pff! . . . heartburn! I can't work or sleep . . . I am going to pieces. . . . And I can't understand how you can live here without anything to do . . . in this boredom! Here I've got a pain in the pit of my stomach! . . ."

My uncle frowned and strode more rapidly than ever.

"Brother," my mother inquired softly, "what does it cost to go abroad?"

"At least three thousand . . ." my uncle answered in a tearful voice. "I would go, but where am I to get the money? I haven't a kopeck. Pff! . . . heartburn!"

Uncle stopped, looked dejectedly at the gray, overcast prospect from the window, and began pacing to and fro again.

A silence followed. . . . Mother looked a long while at the icon, pondering something, then began crying, and said:

"I'll give you the three thousand, Brother. . . ."

Three days later the majestic trunks went off to the station and the privy councilor drove off after them. As he said good-by to Mother he dropped a tear, and it was a long time before he took his lips from her hands, but when he got into his carriage his face beamed with childlike pleasure. . . . Radiant and happy, he settled himself comfortably, blew a kiss to my mother, who was crying, and all at once I caught his eye. A look of the utmost astonishment came into his face.

"What boy is this?" he asked.

My mother, who had assured me that my uncle's coming was a piece of luck for which I must thank God, was bitterly mortified at this question. I was in no mood for questions. I looked at my uncle's happy face, and for some reason felt fearfully sorry for him. I could not control myself, jumped into the carriage, and hugged that frivolous man, weak as all men are. Looking into his face and wanting to say something pleasant, I asked:

"Uncle, have you ever been in a battle?"

"Ah, the dear boy . . ." Uncle laughed, kissing me. "A charming boy, I swear to God! How natural, how true to life it all is, I swear to God! . . ."

The carriage set off. . . . I looked after him, and long afterwards that farewell "I swear to God" was ringing in my ears.

Literary Sort: What a sad little story.

Editor: But have you forgotten our exchange of views after "The Darling"?

Literary Sort: Well, perhaps we can have both—

Editor: Both what?

Literary Sort: Tragedy and farce—at the same time.

Editor: Yes, I'm sure we can.

INTERLOCK WITH CLUSTER 13:
A topical link: the relationship between farce and life

TURKEY DINNER 95¢
I can't serve you, boy...
I AM A MAN

Cluster 13: pp. 382-395
A topical cluster
Focus: the personal voice

INTERLOCK WITH CLUSTER 12:
A topical link: the relationship between farce and life

13

Song for Those Who Know

Hans Magnus Enzensberger

something must be done right away
that much we know
but of course it's too soon to act
but of course it's too late in the day
oh we know

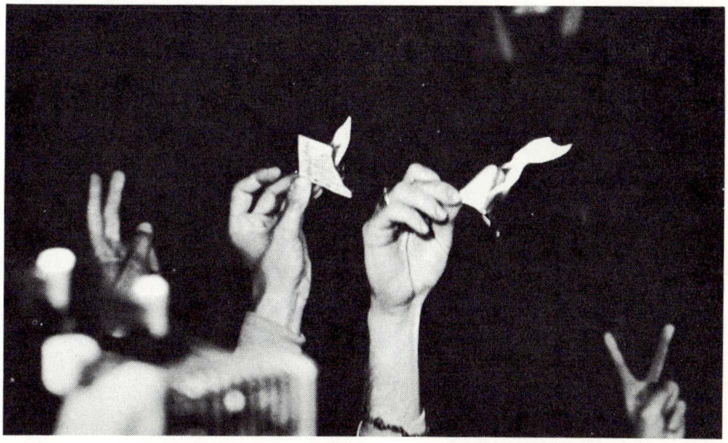

we know that we're really rather well off
and that we'll go on like this
and that it's not much use anyway
oh we know

we know that we are to blame
and that it's not our fault if we are to blame
and that we're to blame for the fact that it's not our fault
and that we're fed up with it
oh we know

and that maybe it would be a good idea to keep our mouths
  shut
and that we won't keep our mouths shut all the same
oh we know oh we know

and we also know that we can't help anybody really
and that nobody really can help us
and that we're extremely gifted and brilliant
and free to choose between nothing and naught
and that we must analyze this problem very carefully
and that we take two lumps of sugar in our tea
oh we know

we know all about oppression
and that we are very much against it
and that cigarettes have gone up again
oh we know

we know very well that the nation is heading for real
  trouble
and that our forecasts have usually been dead right
and that they are not of any use
and that all this is just talk
oh we know

that it's just not good enough to live things down
and that we are going to live them down all the same
oh we know oh we know

that there is nothing new in all this
and that life is wonderful
and that's all there is to it
oh we know all this perfectly well

and that we know all this perfectly well
oh we know that too
oh we know it
oh we know

It might be well to ask just what is it *we know,* or more important—as implied in the refrain of the song—what *we do?*

England in 1819

Percy Bysshe Shelley

An old, mad, blind, despised, and dying king,—
Princes, the dregs of their dull race, who flow
Through public scorn,—mud from a muddy spring,—
Rulers who neither see, nor feel, nor know,
But leech-like to their fainting country cling,
Till they drop, blind in blood, without a blow,—
A people starved and stabbed in the untilled field,—
An army, which liberticide and prey
Makes as a two-edged sword to all who wield,—
Golden and sanguine laws which tempt and slay;
Religion Christless, Godless—a book sealed;
A Senate,—Time's worst statute unrepealed,—
Are graves, from which a glorious Phantom may
Burst, to illumine our tempestuous day.

George III

That is, "golden" laws which help those who want to make money; "sanguine" laws under which, for example, a man might be executed for stealing a sheep.

To Toussaint L'Ouverture

Governor of Santo Domingo; he resisted Napoleon's reimposition of slavery.

William Wordsworth

Toussaint, the most unhappy man of men!
Whether the whistling Rustic tend his plough
Within thy hearing, or thy head be now
Pillowed in some deep dungeon's earless den;—
O miserable Chieftain! where and when
Wilt thou find patience! Yet die not; do thou
Wear rather in thy bonds a cheerful brow:
Though fallen thyself, never to rise again,
Live, and take comfort. Thou hast left behind
Powers that will work for thee; air, earth, and skies;
There's not a breathing of the common wind
That will forget thee; thou hast great allies;
Thy friends are exultations, agonies,
And love, and man's unconquerable mind.

That is, whether he is still free in Santo Domingo or is in prison in Paris

Of the slaves, that is.

AND YOU KNOW IT

Wesley Day

And you know it
and you know it
and yes, you know it
and you know it as well as i do
all there is to wisdom
we saw it all
and we can tell everybody about it
all there is to getting along with more than just getting
along
to fighting our way thru all the lazy things
that get in the way with getting along with
you know we saw it
a long time ago and haven't changed it
yes you know all that

yes you do you know it
and we saw it all coming
But didn't stop to change it
now all that has changed
but we really do it
and we know it
too many comfortable things softened our backs
and we knew it
they were too easy
and we knew it
before it all happened
we knew it
and didn't stop it
no.

Students might well compare this with Enzensberger's poem, pp. 383-4.

April 25, 1655—a massacre of the Waldenses, a sect of western Alpine Franco-Italian mountaineers, who had broken away from the Roman Catholic Church in the twelfth century. One year after the "massacher," the survivors were granted freedom of worship.

On the Late Massacher in Piemont

Avenge O Lord thy slaughter'd Saints, whose bones
Lie scatter'd on the Alpine mountains cold,
Ev'n them who kept thy truth so pure of old
When all our Fathers worship't Stocks and Stones,
Forget not: in thy book record their groanes
Who were thy Sheep and in their antient Fold
Slayn by the bloody *Piemontese* that roll'd
Mother with Infant down the Rocks. Their moans
The Vales redoubl'd to the Hills, and they
To Heav'n. Their martyr'd blood and ashes sow
O're all th' *Italian* fields where still doth sway
The triple Tyrant: that from these may grow
A hunder'd-fold, who having learnt thy way
Early may fly the *Babylonian* wo.

That is, from the sown "martyr'd blood and ashes"

The Pope, because of his triple tiara

—John Milton

Allusion to the Roman Catholic Church as a corrupt Babylon (see *Revelations* 17 and 18.)

Song

Areas of London, which are not "green." If it weren't for the rhyme and metric schemes, might we substitute our own home-town areas?

And when our streets are green again
When metalled roads are green
And girls walk barefoot through the weeds
Of Regent Street, Saint Martin's Lane

And children hide in factories
Where burdock blooms and vetch and rust,
And elms and oaks and chestnut trees
Are tall again, and hope is lost

When up the Strand the foxes glide
And hedgehogs sniff and wildcats yell
And golden orioles come back
To flash through Barnes and Clerkenwell

When governments and industries
Lie choked by weeds in fertile rain
For sure the few who stay alive
Will laugh and grow to love again

—John McGrath

From POETRY OF THE UNDERGROUND IN BRITAIN, edited by Michael Horovitz.
Reprinted by permission of Penguin Books Ltd.

6

Patti's Poem

Ken Macrorie

Patti Shirley came to Advanced Writing class, having missed several sessions—and without any writing to turn in. I was angry because I had told the class they would have to submit something that day, if only a page of free writing.

"I don't have it," she said.

"Then sit down right now and in the next twenty minutes fill at least a page and bring it to my office," I said. I left the room, feeling alternately justified and cruel.

A knock at the door, Patti entered and laid a yellow sheet on my desk. "I was looking out the window," she said, "at the fountain in the plaza—and I just wrote this off. It's a poem. I don't know—"

"All right," I said. "Thanks. It's a piece of writing. It will do."

She left and I couldn't resist picking up the paper right away.

PATTI'S POEM

A friend
alive last month
is
today,
I'm told,
a dead box of rocks
          en route
       from Saigon.

Outside the
smoke filmed
    window
a boy balances
    on the edge of the fountain,
    dirty blue paint & empty.

          Only
        last spring
      it was my ocean.

Surrender Speech

Chief Joseph

In 1876, when the United States government sought the enforcement of a treaty that permitted whites to invade and occupy the Nez Percé tribal lands, Chief Joseph and his people resisted—futilely—and finally were forced to flee their land. After a 1,000 mile retreat to the Canadian border they were trapped. Their only course was to surrender.

I am tired of fighting. Our chiefs are killed. Looking Glass is dead. Toohulsote is dead. The old men are all dead. It is the young men who say no and yes. He who led the young men is dead. It is cold and we have no blankets. The little children are freezing to death. My people, some of them, have run away to the hills and have no blankets, no food. No one knows where they are—perhaps they are freezing to death. I want to have time to look for my children and see how many of them I can find. Maybe I shall find them among the dead. Hear me, my chiefs, I am tired. My heart is sad and sick. From where the sun now stands I will fight no more forever.

After this honorable surrender Chief Joseph and the 400 survivors of his tribe were herded from stockade to reservation to reservation. Although about one-half of his people were allowed to return to their tribal lands, many died—including Chief Joseph's own six children—as a result of the brutal conditions of government confinement. Chief Joseph himself was never permitted to return to his land or to his people.

LET AMERICA BE AMERICA AGAIN

Let America be America again.
Let it be the dream it used to be.
Let it be the pioneer on the plain
Seeking a home where he himself is free.

(America never was America to me.)

Let America be the dream the dreamers dreamed—
Let it be that great strong land of love
Where never kings connive nor tyrants scheme
That any man be crushed by one above.

(It never was America to me.)

O, let my land be a land where Liberty
Is crowned with no false patriotic wreath,
But opportunity is real, and life is free,
Equality is in the air we breathe.

(There's never been equality for me,
Nor freedom in this "homeland of the free.")

Say who are you that mumbles in the dark?
And who are you that draws your veil across the stars?

I am the poor white, fooled and pushed apart,
I am the red man driven from the land.
I am the refugee clutching the hope I seek—
But finding only the same old stupid plan
Of dog eat dog, of mighty crush the weak.
I am the Negro, "problem" to you all.
I am the people, humble, hungry, mean—
Hungry yet today despite the dream.
Beaten yet today—O, Pioneers!
I am the man who never got ahead,
The poorest worker bartered through the years.

Yet I'm the one who dreamt our basic dream
In that Old World while still a serf of kings,
Who dreamt a dream so strong, so brave, so true,
That even yet its mighty daring sings
In every brick and stone, in every furrow turned
That's made America the land it has become.
O, I'm the man who sailed those early seas
In search of what I meant to be my home—
For I'm the one who left dark Ireland's shore,
And Poland's plain, and England's grassy lea,
And torn from Black Africa's strand I came
To build a "homeland of the free."

The free?
Who said the free? Not me?
Surely not me? The millions on relief today?
The millions who have nothing for our pay
For all the dreams we've dreamed
And all the songs we've sung
And all the hopes we've held
And all the flags we've hung,
The millions who have nothing for our pay—
Except the dream we keep alive today.

O, let America be America again—
The land that never has been yet—
And yet must be—the land where *every* man is free.
The land that's mine—the poor man's, Indian's, Negro's, ME—

Who made America,
Whose sweat and blood, whose faith and pain,
Whose hand at the foundry, whose plow in the rain,
Must bring back our mighty dream again.

O, yes,
I say it plain,
America never was America to me,
And yet I swear this oath—
America will be!

—Langston Hughes

Fear Not the Night's Darkness

Tina Morris

Fear not the night's darkness
but see beyond it the rhythms
of shapes & colors
which echo back upon
the music of your thoughts.
Follow
into the exquisite world
where thoughts are born
of Silence.

Take the hand
which reaches so gently
from the reflection of water.
It is your own
leading you beyond your Self
into the region
where there is no Self or Other.

There linger
among the flowers
of Love and Peace.

INDEX: TITLES, AUTHORS, TRANSLATORS

INDEX: TYPES OF LITERATURE

FICTION: SHORT STORIES, EXCERPTS FROM NOVELS

AUTOBIOGRAPHY AND BIOGRAPHY

ARTICLES AND ESSAYS

LETTERS

POEMS

DRAMA

CARTOONS

CREDITS

viii	William Shields
2–3	Leonard Frees—Magnum
7	Pat Foss
14–15	Lee Blacklock
22–23	VPI
26	Stock, Boston
28	Bettmann Archive
38–39	Mark Ross
52–53	Mark Ross
58–59	H. Armstrong Roberts
64	Bill Sumner
81	Michael Mathers
100	David Haas
105	Herbert Randall
112	top: George Krause
	foot: Bill Sumner
113	Bill Sumner
	insert: Philip Jon Bailey
114	Bill Sumner
115	top: David Haas
	foot: Editorial Photocolor Archives
116	William Shields
128	top: Bill Sumner
	foot: Philip Jon Bailey
142	David Haas
156	William Shields
164–165	David Haas
180	top: Stock, Boston
	left: Magnum
180	foot: David Haas
181	Charles Steiner
187	Bill Sumner
196–197	Chapin Davis
199	Every effort has been made to secure reprint rights to "Fair Cassidy." Upon receipt of information from the executors of the estate of Donagh MacDonagh, we will be happy to arrange payment of an appropriate permission fee
202	Will McBride
204–205	Bill Sumner
240	Drawing by Josefina Robirosa. Reproduced by kind permission of UNICEF, United Nations Children's Fund.
280	Leonard Frees—Magnum
297	David Haas
316–317	graveyard: Lars Speyer
	soldier: Editorial Photocolor Archives
324	Bill Sumner
333	Bill Sumner
382	top: Philip Jon Bailey
	foot left: William Ternay
	foot right: David Haas
383	David Haas
389	Bill Sumner
395	Lynn Adler

GIRLS AND BOYS YOUNG LADIES AND GENTLEMEN

Roberto Fernandez Retamos

Girls and boys, young ladies and gentlemen,
beings virtually human and decent,
I am deeply grateful for the kindliness
which has brought you to this place
with clean fingernails, well dressed and combed,
glancing discreetly at my books
and at my invincible bald spot.
But,
I have nothing to say to you:
I am the same as you, except that
the years have gone by, the years have gone by me,
and there are some people who believe that
as a consequence one is in a better situation
to say something.
I have bad news.
I too (probably a very long time ago)
cleaned my nails, parted my hair to one side, dressed neatly
and sat down before a bald head.
In vain.
Know then:
I have nothing to say to you.

Before we take leave of each other:
good luck living.

ABCDEFGH 0765432
PRINTED IN THE UNITED STATES OF AMERICA

RESPONDING: Ginn Interrelated Sequences in Literature

TALKS
WITH TEACHERS ABOUT *RESPONDING: SIX*

WALLACE W. DOUGLAS

Editorial Direction
Alan C. Purves

Advisers
Robert F. Hogan
Richard Ohmann
William E. Stafford

GINN AND COMPANY
A XEROX COMPANY

RESPONDING: Ginn Interrelated Sequences in Literature

Editorial Direction: *Alan C. Purves*

BASIC SEQUENCE

ONE: *Robert Spencer Johnson* and *James N. Britton*
TWO: *Donald G. Rutledge* and *Jerry L. Walker*
THREE: *Robert Weinberger* and *Nathan S. Blount*
FOUR: *Sister Mary Owen, S.N.D.,* and *N. Reed Mathis*
FIVE: *Philip Thompson* and *Darwin T. Turner*
SIX: *Wallace W. Douglas,* with *Albert L. Lavin*

THEME SEQUENCE

JOURNEYS: *Bruce C. Appleby*
HERO: *G. Rodney Morisset*
ME: *Delores Minor*
A GOOD LIFE: *Alan C. Purves,* with *Robert E. Palazzi*
AMERICAN DREAM: *Charles Suhor*
ARTIST: *Robert D. Robinson*

WRITER–READER SEQUENCE

THE WRITER'S VOICE: *William G. Purcell*
NARRATIVE: *Kenneth R. McElheny*
WORDS AND BEYOND: *Martin L. Parry*
THE WRITER'S VIEW: *James C. Waugh*
SHAPE: *Emanuel Raff*
READING THE WRITER: *Alan C. Purves* with *Albert L. Lavin* and *Frank Townsend*

RECORDS SEQUENCE

Charles Suhor

EVALUATION SEQUENCE

Charles R. Cooper

Advisers

William E. Stafford
Robert F. Hogan
Richard Ohmann

Home Office: Lexington, Massachusetts 02173
0–663–25052–8

CONTENTS

GENERAL INTRODUCTION

Scene:

Enter:

Twenty-five students, walking slowly, singly, and in pairs, talking, laughing, silent. You can hear such snatches as "What a test!" "Going to the movie?" "What'll we do about George?" "How do you do that problem in science?" "Hey, dumbhead!" "I'll never talk to him again." The students sort themselves out (slowly) and sit down. A teacher enters, carrying some books in one hand and a half-read letter in the other. The teacher walks to the desk, puts down the books and the letter, and, as another bell rings, straightens up and looks at the class.

Teacher: All right, class, today we're going to talk about the story I handed out yesterday. Does everyone have a copy?

(Here's the story the class is to consider:

THE SEA

Ana Maria Matute

Poor boy. He had very big ears, and when he would turn his back to the window they would become scarlet. Poor boy. He was bent over, yellow. The man who cured came by behind his glasses. "The sea," he said, "the sea, the sea." Everyone began to pack suitcases and speak of the sea. They were in a great hurry. The boy figured that the sea was like being inside a tremendous seashell full of echoes and chants and voices that would call from afar with a long echo. He thought that the sea was tall and green, but when he arrived at the sea, he stood still. His skin, how strange it was there. "Mother," he said because he felt ashamed, "I want to see how high the sea will come on me." He who thought that the sea was tall and green, saw it white like the head on a beer—tickling him, cold on the tips of his toes. "I am going to see how far the sea will come on me." And he walked, he walked, he walked, and the sea—what a strange thing!—grew and became blue, violet. It came up to his knees. Then to his waist, to his chest, to his lips, to his eyes. Then into his ears there came a long echo and the voices that call from afar. And in his eyes all the color. Ah, yes, at last the sea was true. It was one great, immense seashell. The sea truly was tall and green. But those on the shore didn't understand anything about anything. Above they began to cry and scream and were saying "What a pity, Lord, what a great pity.")

Teacher: What do you think the story is about?

Student A: Well, it's a story about a boy who drowns.

Teacher: What else?

Student B: There are some people in it who are upset.

Teacher: How many?

Student C: The mother and the father, I guess, and "the man who cured." Why is he called that?

Teacher: Let's not get off the track. No, I don't think "the man who cured" is upset. Why would a doctor go to the seashore?

Student D: He wouldn't. But there must be some others on the beach.

Teacher: Probably, but isn't there someone else in the story?

Student E: The doctor?

Student C: I don't see why they call him "the man who cured."

Teacher: We've mentioned him. But he wouldn't be there.

Student E: A lifeguard?

Teacher: Now you're guessing. It's the person who's telling the story. Now, is he sad?

The students in this class have entered the room from a variety of previous activities and are suddenly confronted with another world, that of a boy. Apparently oblivious to this variety of previous pursuits, the teacher seems to assume that the students should be like computers: feed in a question and get an answer—a response to the story. And if the students don't give the responses the teacher expects, they are wrong. Of course, the teacher might be right: "the man who cured" could be a doctor and might not go to the seashore with the family. But isn't it a mistake for this teacher to be so quick to assume that *he* (the teacher) is *not* like the students in *not* understanding anything? He seems unaware that there might well be more than one possible response to the story. He is using the recitation technique inappropriately and ineffectively.

But let's look at another way the class might go:

Teacher: Does anyone have anything to say about the story?

Student A: Uh, it's about a boy who walks into the sea and drowns. It's sad.

Student B: Yeah, but that's not all. The boy is sad and the sea is the one good thing that happens to him.

Student A: Well, yes, but it's sad that he drowns, isn't it?

Student C: No, it's stupid; it's a stupid story about a stupid kid and I don't like it.

Student D: Well, *I* do. I think it says that some of our dreams are worth pursuing even though we die for them.

Student E: Yeah, that's right.

Student C: I mean it's badly written. "The man who cured came by behind his glasses." What kind of writing is that?

Student F: When I was little, I used to think people who wore glasses had magnified eyes. Glasses make people look different.

Student G: That's just the way the kid sees the doctor. A little kid might call him "the man who cured."

Chorus: Yeah. Maybe. Uh-huh.

Student G: Anyway, I think the story is pretty good. I like the seashell parts.

(Silence)

Teacher: Why?

That wasn't a lesson in the traditional sense; it was a conversation. The teacher asked a provocative question and the students responded spontaneously. Then a second perceptive question—asked at the appropriate time—helped get the conversation going again. This teacher has recognized that there are likely to be differences of opinion and feeling among students, who might see the same thing in different ways and interpret and evaluate it differently. Instead of seeking a predetermined "right response," this teacher urges the students to respond and then to compare their responses. Perhaps the students will reach agreement on other matters besides the nature of "behind his glasses," but perhaps not.

Some might say that the students in this class haven't learned anything. But let's look again at that conversation:

Student A:	Uh, it's about a boy who walks into the sea and drowns. It's sad.	Describes the story briefly and makes a summary judgment of its effect.
Student B:	Yeah, but that's not all. The boy is sad and the sea is the one good thing that happens to him.	Does not accept this single judgment; substitutes a more abstract one.
Student A:	Well, yes, but it's sad that he drowns, isn't it?	Defends his position by repeating it.
Student C:	No, it's stupid; it's a stupid story about a stupid kid and I don't like it.	Switches the focus of the discussion from the action to the character and gives an overall response.
Student D:	Well, I do. I think it says that some of our dreams are worth pursuing even though we die for them.	Expands the interpretation and moralizes from it.
Student E:	Yeah, that's right.	Accepts the possibility of the expanded interpretation.
Student C:	I mean it's badly written. "The man who cured came by behind his glasses." What kind of writing is that?	Focuses his criticism more specifically on the author's style.
Student F:	When I was little, I used to think people who wore glasses had magnified eyes. Glasses make people look different.	Reaches into the past for something to relate to the description.
Student G:	That's just the way the kid sees the doctor. A little kid might call him "the man who cured."	Refutes the criticism and explains the connection of the image to the point of view from which the story is told.
Chorus:	Yeah. Maybe. Uh-huh.	Group accepts this explanation.
Student G:	Anyway, I think the story is pretty good. I like the seashell parts.	Moves to another aspect of the story; makes a general comment about the impact of a part of the story.
	(Silence)	Group neither accepts nor rejects the comment.
Teacher:	Why?	Asks for clarification.

In this fragment of a discussion involving classroom give-and-take, the members of the class demonstrate that they are able to

- –accept a variety of views of a work of art;
- –make a summary judgment and support it with evidence;
- –connect fictional events and images with events and images in their lives;
- –recognize that generalizations are difficult to validate;
- –see that a part of a work can support a variety of interpretations.

Furthermore, the students demonstrate these learnings by the process of sharing their thoughts and impressions about a story. These are things they have often done out of school with their friends; here they are carrying the normal processes of discourse into the classroom.

A major purpose of this volume–and the others in this series as well–is to provide students with stories, poems, plays, and essays that they can readily respond to. At times they may want simply to talk about a selection with one another. At other times they may want to articulate their responses in other ways. They may want to do some of the things *we* do with and because of our leisure reading: Sometimes we

- –read a story and want to read it out loud.
- –read a poem and want to paint or photograph a scene or make a collage.
- –read an article or essay and want to get involved in some worthy cause.
- –read a play and want to act it out or make up a dance for it.
- –read a story and think that it would make a great movie.
- –read a poem and want to warn people not to read it.
- –read a work and want to think seriously about it.

BUT. . .

Suppose the class discussion had gone this way:

Teacher: Well, what did you think of the story?
(Silence)
Student A: It was all right, I guess.
Student B: Yeah, it was O.K.
(Silence)
Teacher: Does anybody else have anything to say about it?
(Silence)
Teacher: Are you quiet because you don't like it, or what?
Student C: No, I like it; it's just that it's there and there's nothing else to say about it.
Chorus: Uh-huh. Let's not talk about it.
Teacher: That makes sense. Well, then, let's try something else. Here's another view of the sea.

THE SHELL*

James Stephens

And then I pressed the shell
Close to my ear
And listened well.
And straightway, like a bell,
Came low and clear
The slow, sad murmur of far distant seas,
Whipped by an icy breeze
Upon a shore
Wind-swept and desolate.
It was a sunless strand that never bore
The footprint of a man,
Nor felt the weight
Since time began
Of any human quality or stir,
Save what the dreary winds and waves incur.
And in the hush of waters was the sound
Of pebbles rolling round,
Forever rolling with a hollow sound.
And bubbling sea-weeds, as the waters go,
Swish to and fro
Their long, cold tentacles of slimy grey.
There was no day,
Nor ever came a night
Setting the stars alight
To wonder at the moon:
Was twilight only, and the frightened croon,
Smitten to whimpers, of the dreary wind
And waves that journeyed blind–
And then I loosed my ear–O, it was sweet
To hear a cart go jolting down the street!

Teacher: What do you think of this author's feeling about the sea?
Student D: Yeah, that's the way the sea sounds, not green.
Student E: But this is so different. He hates the sea.
Student C: Well, he's right; the sea's empty.
Student E: What do you mean?

For this particular class at this particular time, "The Sea" just wasn't the best selection for the class to consider and discuss. Yet "The Shell" was.

With "The Sea"the students did not talk because they seemed moved. But what if that weren't the case? What if the silence had come from another cause? The teacher can capitalize on such silence by exploring the reasons for it. No one expects each person to like everything he reads. Likewise, no one expects every student to like every selection in this volume. A teacher may dislike a number of selections and so not present them to the class. The editors disagreed on some selections, but they did agree that the reasons for including those works were more important than their liking or disliking them. One major reason for including a selection was the thought that it had something to say to students, that it would whet their interest, and that it would provoke response from them. And if it doesn't? Not liking, not understanding, not prizing a selection is a valid response, too. A teacher can sometimes turn distaste or apathy to advantage and stir up as exciting a conversation as would result from students' liking the work under consideration. One reason is that most people are interested in their own responses.

To turn the classroom into a workshop in which students explore literature and their responses to it, a teacher needs to work hard. He must use the kind of patience that accepts students' dislike of a work or even of the classroom. He must be able to try again and again, offering new selections, suggesting new approaches, constantly probing student responses, constantly challenging students to question themselves and their reactions. In so doing he utilizes the best sources available–paperbacks, magazines, records, photographs, the film playing at the local theater, the latest television special–as material for the class to consider and to work and play with.

A teacher must be ever ready to call on the ability to use materials and techniques in a variety of ways. The selections in this volume, for instance, have been chosen because they are what the editors think are sure to interest students and stimulate talk and activity. The selections are arranged in a series of groupings called *clusters.* Some clusters present works about the same mood or contrasting moods; some deal with works of the same genre; some consist wholly of works by the same author. The clusters are arrangements of convenience made by one group of people; obviously another group might have arranged the same works in a different way. The teacher can easily shift this arrangement to suit his class, to move out of the book to some other selection–a book perhaps, or a long play, or a film.

Every teacher has a repertory of material that he has found stimulating. Suppose that student talk about a specific selection tends toward a concern with the generation gap. Sensing this development, the teacher might well bring out a novel like *The Yearling,* or a piece like "Nights Away from Home" (text, p. 129). On the other hand, class talk might turn to idealism and to following one's dream; in that case the teacher might show the film *Citizen Kane* or read "Oh, Did I Have Dreams!" (text, p. 168).

Turning to another selection is not the only course a teacher can take. If class conversation involves the different vantage points in a story–how a young person and the adults and the narrator see things–a teacher might suggest that the class make a film that shows or interprets something from several vantage points. A teacher might also suggest that the work under consideration be enacted in an improvised drama. Afterwards might come the reading of a selection such as "A Good Man Is Hard to Find" (text, p. 282).

Teachers, then, need to be prepared to move in any one of a number of directions and to use any of a number of approaches. In a literature class, especially, predicting what will engage a particular group's interest is a risky venture. In the notes about the selections in this volume, there are suggestions about the parts of the works that the editors feel are most likely to engage students and about activities that might be particularly appropriate. These should be thought of as predictions and suggestions, not prescriptions.

This capacity–to observe students' responses to a work, quickly to analyze the situation, and then move to extend and probe those responses–is closely related to resourcefulness. We have already seen an unobservant teacher:

Teacher: How many?

Student C: The mother and father, I guess, and "the man who cured." Why is he called that?

Teacher: Let's not get off the track. No, I don't think "the man who cured" is upset. Why would a doctor go to the seashore?

This teacher did not observe that a question was being asked; or if he did, he ignored it. Instead his only concern was whether or not *C* got the "right" answer.

We have also seen an observant teacher:

Chorus: Uh-huh. Let's not talk about it.

Teacher: That makes sense. Well, then, let's try something else. Here's another view of the sea.

This teacher observed the mood of students' attention and reticence and analyzed their response coming from interest in "The Sea" but not in reacting to it. Then he moved immediately to present another work that contrasted sharply the first selection in its viewpoint and effect.

When we observe people's talk or writing about a story, poem, play, or film, we find that it deals with one–possibly a combination–of four general questions:

1. *How does it affect me?* How did I feel when I read it? What in me or in my memory did it call to mind? Is the situation one I've been in or seen? Can I believe it? What do I think of the people in it?
2. *What is it?* How is it put together? What are its parts? What class of writing does it fall into? What is its background?
3. *What does it mean?* What kinds of people are in it? What does it tell me about people and the world? What does it say about ideas? Has it any deeper meanings? What message is it seeking to get across?
4. *Is it any good?* Is it effective? Is it well made? Is it important or trivial?

Each of these four major questions has a long history, in that serious critics and scholars have been concerned with them–and people have been asking them–almost ever since there were people. Quite often when two or three students talk or write about a work, each of them is asking and/or answering a different question:

"'The Sea' is childish."	*How does it affect me?*
"No, it's just a story about a boy who drowns."	*What is it?*
"Well, I think that the story talks about the tragedy of the artist."	*What does it mean?*

Of course if the three students argue that one of those statements is better than the other two, nobody is going to go anywhere. It's somewhat like an argument that goes as follows: "The room is large." "No, it's yellow." "You're both wrong; it's ugly."

It is critical for the teacher to know what questions to ask and when to ask them. The teacher who observes student talk and who notes the kinds of questions that students ask and answer can do much to help those students (a) sharpen their own perceptions about the works they read and (b) talk intelligently about those works.

For example, under the guidance of a perceptive teacher that second dialog about "The Sea" might have gone something like this:

	Dialog	*Applicable Question*
Student G:	Anyway, I think the story is pretty good. I like the seashell part.	Is it any good? What is its effect on me?
Teacher:	Why?	(Which question is most important to *G*?)
Student G:	I dunno. I guess it makes me think of the times I've listened to a seashell.	What is its effect on me?
Teacher:	What do you mean?	What does it call to mind? (How does it affect me?)
Student G:	Well, when you listen to a seashell and you hear the noise it makes, you think of the sea and the surf; I think that's what happened to the boy. He imagined a lot from just listening.	How is it put together? (What is it?)
Student F:	Yeah, and the colors he thinks about are the colors he sees when he drowns.	
Student D:	Yes, that's what I meant when I said that the boy follows his dream.	What does it mean?
Teacher:	Then you and *G* agree about the boy's being imaginative?	(Are two questions the same?)

In asking the questions he does, the teacher not only helps the students sharpen and develop their thoughts but also acts to show them when there are similarities and divergences.

By using patience, resourcefulness, and observation, the teacher becomes a map or a compass for the students, helping them discover how much they already know, helping them explore both the worlds they enter when they read or observe and the world of their response to what they read or see or hear. The teacher does not have to tell students how to respond; he elicits their responses by talking with them, by encouraging them to act, draw, write, make films, or perform in any one of a number of activities.

The teacher helps students come to know themselves and work out of their own potential.

The teacher helps students see how they perceive or deal with or structure what they read or see. How they structure their experiences depends on who they are, what they've read, what they think, and what they believe.

These structures shift for all of us as we grow older. Children see one thing in "Humpty Dumpty" when they are little. When they are older, they may see it differently—as childish, perhaps, or as sad. A teacher who has taught "The Sea" several times may see it somewhat differently each time. In like manner a work that we read more than once changes for us each time we read it. For this reason, the editors have repeated certain selections in the several volumes that make up this literature series. Such repetition permits students to note how they have changed in their responses to the repeated selections. The change may result from their being different or from the selections being seen in a different context.

It is for this reason too that we have insisted that our notes to the student and to the teacher be somewhat spare. In this way we can best provide for the differences among students and among groups of students, and we can help them understand both the differences among people and the similarities that make them individuals who deserve our respect.

The aims of this volume, then, are these:

To provide students with a variety of stories, poems, plays, essays, and other forms of written expression.

To provide a means whereby students can articulate their responses to what is in the volume and to what is around them.

To provide a means whereby the variety of structures that students put on their experiences can be shared and explored.

To provide a set of tools so that the teacher may be a guide in this important educative process.

A.C.P.

ABOUT RESPONDING: SIX

We like to think of *RESPONDING: SIX* as a reader, maybe even a school reader. The words are old-fashioned indeed, but we like them better than "anthology." That one strikes us as perhaps a bit high-toned, a bit academic, and anyway far too static for our purposes. And "reader" seems to suggest people reading.

George Steiner has said that it may be that "we are all a little afraid of the silence and solitude of a man reading a book alone." But that—"reading a book alone"—is just what we had in mind when we were developing *RESPONDING: SIX.*

Actually a fair few people have engaged themselves in choosing the works in the volume; not just the two whose names appear on the title page, but also their editors and various friends here and there, not all of whom were in school work. So our selections represent several tastes and, no doubt, several notions of what kind of literary works high school students will like.

De gustibus. . . . We don't for a minute believe that our readers will like or even want to read every selection in *RESPONDING: SIX.* That includes teachers. We hope, though, that our selectors will have been various enough (or their tastes catholic enough, in Eliot's phrase) so that our readers will variously be able to find at least some selections that they can, each in his own way, read humanly, with pleasure. And what we very much hope, what we want very much, is that our readers should have a chance to explore *RESPONDING: SIX* for themselves, for reading of their own.

We have included in this guide some examples of fairly full formal analysis. But Dryden's "The last line is not yet sufficiently explicated" is not just now one of our favorite slogans, and *RESPONDING: SIX* not a book about in-depth critical reading. As may be suggested by the epigraphs in this guide (see especially the one for Cluster 10, page 281), we are more interested in the trans-action between a reader and a work; or rather that there should be one.

Yes. That there should be a trans-action. That is the point. And that, oddly, gives us a behavioral objective—a behavioral objective for teachers, that is. We hope that teachers will use *RESPONDING: SIX* in such ways as to make sure that students may, separately and severally, have valid human trans-actions with such works as they choose to read.

We try in the guide to suggest what we mean by "valid human trans-actions." Suffice it here to say that we are not thinking of either literary study or literary criticism, though obviously some students will be interested in one or the other, or both. We are thinking rather of what for lack of better words we can only call the experience of taking in a work. And the essence of this experience, we suspect, is the connections the reader can make between the work and his own life and interests. Or so it must be for comparatively inexperienced readers, for whom *RESPONDING: SIX* is designed.

We think that such connections, all except the most private of them, may well become the subject of conversation or the occasion for productive work of some sort.

But then we have to remember "the silence and solitude of a man reading a book alone."

And there is Wittgenstein's great sentence: "Whereof one cannot speak, thereof one must be silent."

And finally there are those desperate words, at the very end of Schoenberg's *Moses and Aaron,* when Moses cries out "Oh, word that I lack!" and falls to silence.

A note on "composition"

When I began to write this introduction, I had in mind only various versions of the first paragraph. These had been rolling around in my head for several days, along with various encouraging adjurations from an editor. But I was very conspicuously not getting anywhere with my composition. What *am* I going to say next? kept popping into my consciousness in a most worrying and daunting fashion.

Then this morning (10 April 1971, a week or so after I more or less knew that I had the introduction to do, and a full five days after the editor told me I did), I was reading an article by George Steiner in an old issue of *The Listener* (LXXXIII [26 March 1970], 400 + 402). It was called "Crisis of the Word," and it was about our doubt "whether words can do the work we want of them." That idea was interesting enough, and I was thinking about how to use it in a course I am currently teaching, but not much else. Then suddenly I came upon the quotations from Wittgenstein and Schoenberg, and Steiner's own lovely remark. With them I was off. I had an idea and the glimmering of a shape for the writing: I think I felt right away that the Wittgenstein and Schoenberg quotations were so beautiful that I had to end with them: so I would have to arrange the material in the body of the piece in such a way as to bring me to the ending that I wanted.

So here I am, something like two and a half hours later (having done a couple of chores to start with), typing the last word.

W. W. D.

SUMMARY OF CLUSTERS

Cluster 1:	topical—the writer's assimilation of his world	medium:	11 selections, 27 pages.
Cluster 2:	authorial—Anton Chekhov generic—letters	short:	9 selections, 10 pages.
Cluster 3:	generic—drama	medium:	1 selection, 26 pages.
Cluster 4:	topical—adolescence	long:	11 selections, 52 pages.
Cluster 5:	topical—life's enigmas	long:	8 selections, 40 pages.
Cluster 6:	affective—contrast, mostly humorous	medium:	6 selections, 24 pages.
Cluster 7:	generic—the ballad	medium:	8 selections, 22 pages.
Cluster 8:	topical—the importance, the universality of love	long:	12 selections, 38 pages.
Cluster 9:	topical—parent-child relationships	long:	7 selections, 40 pages.
Cluster 10:	affective—the eliciting of sorrow, frustration, or resignation	long:	9 selections, 36 pages.
Cluster 11:	topical—war and its effects	medium:	18 selections, 26 pages.
Cluster 12:	authorial: Anton Chekhov	long:	3 selections, 40 pages.
Cluster 13:	topical—the personal voice	short:	10 selections, 14 pages.

TEACHING SUGGESTIONS

School was not invented just for the little people
to become the same as big people. . . .

13 year old girl[1]

The appeal to success, prizes and prize-winning, bids fair to be the watch-word of the day. But what does this do for the majority, for the non-competing crowd who nevertheless do not politely die off and make room and cannot, through modern squeamishness, be killed off and buried? The weak are pushed into a corner and neglected, their natural tendency to shrink from labor is educated into despair by their being constantly reminded, directly or indirectly, that their labor is no good.

—Edward Thring[2]

Cluster 1: pages 1-27

The first group of selections in *RESPONDING: SIX* is mostly about art and the making of works of art.* We hope that students will find in the selections some ideas about art, some attitudes concerning it that will be new to them, or at least that will not be part of the normal baggage of their schoolroom discourse. We hope that the ideas will be interesting enough so that students will want to talk about them.

Here are some points that we saw as we read the selections in Cluster 1:

Evidently Marianne Moore and Zbigniew Herbert—in "Poetry" (text, p. 1), "Five Men" (text, p. 2), and "I Would Like to Describe" (text, p. 8)—feel that the products of their artwork (*products* and *work* should be read quite literally) are somehow suspect, or perhaps inconsequential. Some students may find this attitude surprising, especially when it comes from the mouth of the poet. For generally students will have been more familiar with a view of poetry closer to that of Keats when he praises Chapman's translation of Homer's *Iliad* and *Odyssey:*

Much have I travell'd in the realms of gold,
    And many goodly states and kingdoms seen;
    Round many western islands have I been
Which bards in fealty to Apollo hold.
Oft of one wide expanse had I been told
    That deep-brow'd Homer ruled as his demesne;
    Yet did I never breathe its pure serene
Till I heard Chapman speak out loud and bold:
Then I felt like some watcher of the skies . . .

*A paperback titled *Artist,* edited by Robert D. Robinson, is one of the volumes in the theme sequence of this literature series. The entire volume focuses on "the artist's assimilation of his world."

Here Keats sets up poetry as something fairly inhuman, something quite distant from the concerns of living, to be venerated precisely for that reason. This contrast in attitudes towards poetry is instructive, and some students may want to discuss it, especially those who are themselves interested in writing. As a matter of fact, this very conflict between the Moore and Keats schools of poetry may provide a departure point, in class discussion, for the whole problem of "relevancy" in literature. It may well be that Miss Moore's poem and Keats' poem are merely faint illustrations, mirrors, of their respective eras. One can hardly envisage Keats wearing a New York Yankee's baseball cap, munching on a mustard-laden hot dog, and screaming earthly delights at the prowess of such a retinue as Berra, Mantle, Maris, and Whitey Ford, as Miss Moore has been observed to do on occasion–and later to write a poem on the experience. Likewise, Miss Moore would hardly be the type to begin in all seriousness a poem:

"O golden tongued Romance, with serene lute!"

as Keats did in his not especially famous lyric, "On Sitting Down to Read *King Lear* Again." Perhaps that is precisely the difference between the two poets, and between the Romantic and the Modern Muses; the difference, that is, between "Sitting Down to Read *King Lear* Again" and sitting down to watch the New York Yankees. Who is to say which topic is the more "relevant," the more suitable for poetic articulation? This is precisely the concern of Zbigniew Herbert in "Five Men" (text, p. 2).

What, then, about the speaker's action in "Stopping by Woods" (text, p. 24)? What *is* the good of watching a woods fill up with snow? (Is it of any concern, by the way, that they are someone else's woods?) And what is good about making a poem out of it all?

Zbigniew Herbert's "Five Men" (text, p. 2) attempts to supply an answer to that very question by turning to what "the five [talked] of the night before the execution." Does he satisfy you, your students? Or better yet, does he satisfy himself?

Does Ted Hughes' comment (text, p. 20) that his fox is "better than an ordinary fox" and that it will live forever and "never suffer from hunger or hounds" provide a possible answer to the question of "why bother to write poetry"? (Cf. Keats' odes on the Grecian urn and the nightingale; also, Shakespeare's Sonnet 55, "Not marble nor the gilded monuments.") Obviously, Bly (text, p. 24) doesn't think he is wasting time by driving around on a snowy night. So far as that goes, he doesn't mean that he is just driving around. What, then, is it that Frost, Bly, and Hughes are doing, or saying?

In "Poetry" (text, p. 1) Marianne Moore also says that poets should be "'literalists' of the imagination," and be able to "present for inspection, imaginary gardens with real toads in them"–or words to that effect. How does that odd statement fit here with these poets and their respective poems?

Note that Orwell ("Some Thoughts on the Common Toad," text, p. 10) is being *unliterary* about one of the stock subjects for poems–spring. Hughes is taking a more or less unlikely subject for a poem and showing how, in the course of time, it found its way into his creative consciousness. Chekhov's letter (text, p. 25) suggests how wide-ranging an artist's attention is, how many things interest him. And certainly the Meschery and the Schechner poems (text, pp. 22-23) celebrate a subject (two basketball players) that Keats would have been hard pressed to immortalize à la Chapman's Homer on *his* Grecian urn.

Some students will be amused by the following poems; others may be interested to see them brought into the class business.

The Maker*

So he said then: I will make the poem,
I will make it now. He took pencil,
The mind's cartridge, and blank paper,
And drilled his thoughts to the slow beat.

Of the blood's drum; and there it formed
On the white surface and went marching
Onward through time, while the spent cities
And dry hearts smoked in its wake.

—R. S. Thomas[3]

What Curious Dresses All Men Wear†

What curious dresses all men wear!
The walker you met in a brown study,
The President smug in rotogravure,
The mannequin, the bathing beauty,

The bubble dancer, the deep-sea diver,
The bureaucrat, the adulterer,
Hide private parts which I disclose
To those who know what the poem knows.

—Delmore Schwartz[4]

Do these poems have anything to do with Marianne Moore's statement about the need for poets to "present for inspection, imaginary gardens with real toads in them"?

Regarding this art-and-reality theme, your students might like to take a look at the quotation from Fowles (text, p. 117), and consider, too, Alison Lurie's comment from her novel *Real People:*

> Fiction is condensed reality; and that's why its flavor is more intense, like bouillon or frozen orange juice.[5]

Miss Lurie's "frozen orange juice" statement comes right back to the heart of poetry and to Hughes' "better than an ordinary fox," not to mention his stalking "Pike."

But those are only the points that we saw in the selections, and it is not necessary that students should see the same ones. The fact of the matter is, though, that in their

*This poem appears on page 161 of *Artist,* one of the volumes in the theme sequence of this literature series. "The Maker" from TARES by R. S. Thomas. Reprinted by permission of Rupert Hart-Davis, publisher.

†"What Curious Dresses All Men Wear" by Delmore Schwartz. Every effort has been made to secure reprint rights. Upon receipt of information from The Schwartz Estate, we will be happy to arrange payment of an appropriate permission fee.

own way, using their own language, at least some students will already have started to tackle these problems of art and reality in connection with the arts (and crafts) they are interested in. The selections may provide some new formulations, new words, new examples that they can use as needed—which will not necessarily be in the schoolroom.

The Classroom (of all places!) and Art (of all things!)

1. There, in the classroom, a possible first move in the direction of student experience with their own art might be based on Schechner's "Elgin Baylor" (text, p. 23) or Meschery's "To Bill Russell" (text, p. 22) and Frost's "Stopping by Woods" (text, p. 24) or (since it's simpler) Bly's "Driving to Town" (text, p. 24). What do students do or watch with the kind of high pleasure described in those poems?
2. Another beginning might be found in making some artistic structure with more or less inartistic materials. All schools have barren walls that can be used as ground for a mural of the sort made for a new incinerator in London. When the architect's department found that it would cost £5000 to have a "prominent artist" do a "real" sculpture for the building, ". . . they switched to do-it-yourself. The staff . . . gathered bits of rubbish—holed saucepans, bedsprings, bicycle bits, tools—and, *with due attention to form and space,* built, as it happens, a very enjoyable mural.[6]

   Such a project would involve

   cooperative work—organization and division of jobs
   observation—in choosing site and objects
   planning—"with due attention to form and space"
   talk—to carry on the activities
   writing—for permission, advice, assessment
   reading

   Note: These six points, necessary changes being made, constitute a kind of paradigm for planning English-activities or work.

3. Collage-construction makes for an excellent creative exercise in which individual students or groups of students might attempt to express an artistic assimilation of world/life/reality . . . .

Notes on the Making of a Collage

One of the most effective ways of helping students order their personal experiences and their reactions to literature is to involve them in making collages. For the student who is characteristically reluctant to talk or write in the classroom, making a collage can be an invaluable activity for helping him move from nonverbal to verbal expression. Often such a student finds it much easier to talk about what he has done in developing a collage than to grapple directly with abstractions.

Historically, a collage was photographic in nature; that is, it was made up of pictures assembled from other pictures. But a collage need not be so restrictive. Nonesthetic materials have served many a sculptor or painter. (Picasso, for example, fashioned a snorting Taurus from the mundane construct of bicycle seat and handlebars.) Glass fragments, bottle caps, peanut butter, coat hangers, sea shells, buttons, beads, and the like have all had their place in artistic expression on canvas, in sculpture, in mobile or stabile. What we are primarily concerned with here, however, is the picture collage. But other materials should certainly be kept in mind and introduced at any effective point in the construction of the collage.

In preparing for collage-making, you might well show models of collages—if any are available—emphasizing that "artistic talent" in the usual sense of the term is unimportant in making a worthwhile collage. Stress, too, that a collage does not necessarily show a "scene" from a literary work. Instead it conveys a theme or a mood or reveals various relationships among characters or ideas through a variety of visual devices. Encourage students to feel free to focus their collages on anything—from a topic as general as *war* or *love* to the feelings they experience from something as specific as toothpaste. Bundles and bundles of magazines, newspapers, postcards, stamps, product labels, book dust jackets, matchbook covers, leaflets, and the like may well be good things to have on hand as a reservoir of materials.

In making a collage the student needs to consider several questions:

1. Is he more interested in having the viewer see each separate component? Or is he more interested in the viewer's deriving an overall impression of the total collage?
2. Is he intending to create an impression of unity or of diversity?
3. Is he intending to use only photos, or will he consider other materials such as wire, string, bottlecaps, shells, and the like?

To have the viewer come away with a general impression, the collage-maker should place the small parts close to each other.

To have the reader come away with a sense of parts, the collage-maker should make the parts distinctive by increasing the size of the individual components or by increasing space between components.

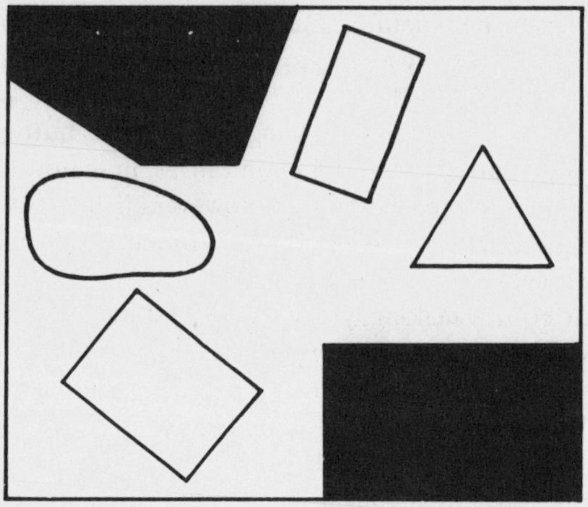

Having made that first decision, the collage-maker should pick his subject, and select, and cut the pieces that he wants to use.

Next, in arranging the parts, the collage-maker should *not* think like a writer—that is, in terms of moving from left to right and from top to bottom—but like an artist in T-22 terms of the whole visual space on whatever surface he is using. He should block that space into some large pattern like one of the following:

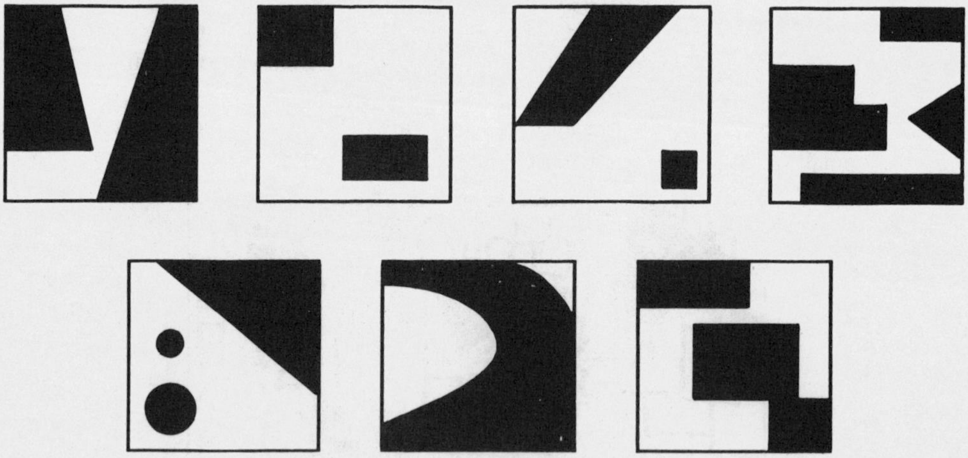

The shaded portions represent those parts of the collage that would contrast in color, lightness, type or clarity of picture, or the like. Each pattern leads the eye in a different way, into the center of the space or away from it in a sweep, or in a progression, in a sense of balance, or one of precariousness.

The students might experiment with various patterns—placing the pictures or other materials in several patterns until they have achieved a pattern that they find suits their ends in making the collage. Once they have chosen the pattern, they can proceed to affixing the materials to the sheet.

There is no need to make the collage on a rectangular flat surface: successful collages have been applied to beach balls, made in a triangular form, applied to cut-out figures, applied to the insides of boxes with peep-holes cut in various places on the sides. Each of these forms of the collage creates a special effect, one which uses the total space symbolically.

If the students decide that they are less concerned with the total impression than with individual parts, they are creating a picture essay. In this case, the layout of the pictures and the words should be such that there is some of the background space around each of the pictures, thus separating the parts from each other. Despite this difference from the collage, the picture essay should be so arranged on the total space as to make a pattern that will lead the eye from picture to picture in the order that the creator wants.

An alternative to the picture collage is the sound collage. Suppose, for example, that students choose to make a sound collage about the school. The best way for them to do so is to use two tape recorders. With the first one students would go around the school for several days, gathering typical sounds—noises of classes, class changes, lunch periods, guidance interviews, the custodians cleaning the building, sports events, and the like. Then they would play these random sounds onto a second tape, putting sounds together or taping one sound over another, in any order they find effective.

After students have made their picture collages and/or sound collages, let them present their work to the rest of the class. The class might well then comment on or discuss the effect of the finished products.

4. Another classroom activity would be one that is grounded in conversation about problems or interests that members of the class (including teacher) have met when making photographs, acting, playing musical instruments, composing, or doing various kinds of arts and crafts.

   However, it should be noted that classes devoted to abstract conversation on the technical problems of and techniques employed in creating certain art forms can be abtruse and boring stuff. (It's like teaching point-of-view by lecture and definition, without giving the student a chance to experience the technique concretely in his own efforts at writing.) Therefore, concrete demonstrations might be in order. Perhaps a student exhibit would open the classroom.

   [Example: A student-made film (or for that matter, a collage, a painting, a drama, a poem, or even a leather belt or beads) followed by a question-and-answer, dialog, give-and-take seminar among *students*—with the teacher—as one member of the class—seated as inconspicuously as possible.]

5. Another beginning might be to have students list "things I remember about" whatever strikes their individual fancies, perhaps after they have heard the lines from "How It Strikes a Contemporary" given below.

How It Strikes a Contemporary
Robert Browning

He stood and watched the cobbler at his trade,
The man who slices lemons into drink,
The coffee-roaster's brazier, and the boys
That volunteer to help him turn its winch.
He glanced o'er books on stalls with half an eye,
And fly-leaf ballads on the vendor's string,
And broad-edge bold-print posters by the wall.
He took such cognizance of men and things,
If any beat a horse, you felt he saw;
If any cursed a woman, he took note;
Yet stared at nobody,—you stared at him,
And found, less to your pleasure than surprise,
He seemed to know you and expect as much.

Then the question could be raised of what would have to be done with the lists to make them worth reading by someone who doesn't know or care anything about the author as a person; that is, make them worth reading in the way any piece of literature is. (Rupert Brooke's "The Great Lover" might be a help to some students; it's about the objects and places he remembers with love, and is little more than a list.)

That project may turn out to be harder than it sounds, for the sensibilities of many young people today are rather flattened out, if not corrupted by, the stereotypes of mass art and advertising; and many do not know how to listen or look. They might profit intellectually from trying, though.

Some day some students may be interested in trying to make a poem out of the following list of best sellers and the comments on them.

BEST SELLERS*

FICTION

1. **LOVE STORY,** by Erich Segal (Harper & Row, $4.95). A film script passing as a novel about tragic young love.
2. **THE CRYSTAL CAVE,** by Mary Stewart (Morrow, $7.95). An English romantic novel.
3. **GREAT LION OF GOD,** by Taylor Caldwell (Doubleday, $7.95). Back near the top again.
4. **THE FRENCH LIEUTENANT'S WOMAN,** by John Fowles (Little, Brown, $7.95). A "Victorian" novel of contemporary insights.
5. **CALICO PALACE,** by Gwen Bristow (Crowell, $7.95). Solid historical fare.

NONFICTION

1. **EVERYTHING YOU ALWAYS WANTED TO KNOW ABOUT SEX,** by Dr. David Reuben (McKay, $6.95). And then some.
2. **THE SENSUOUS WOMAN,** by "J" (Stuart, $6). Another sexcess.
3. **ZELDA: A BIOGRAPHY,** by Nancy Milford (Harper & Row, $10). The sad life of Mrs. Scott Fitzgerald.
4. **HARD TIMES,** by Studs Terkel (Pantheon, $8.95). Back in the running.
5. **BALL FOUR,** by Jim Bouton and Leonard Shecter (World, $6.95). A wry, literate look inside Big League baseball.

*Book List from the *Chicago Daily News.* Reprinted with permission of the *Chicago Daily News.*

—teachers of English should be writers first and readers second: and the most important question training colleges and departments of education can put to the would-be teacher of English is "What do you write?," not "What do you read?"

—A. W. Rowe[7]

Cluster 2: pages 28-37

This selection of Chekhov letters is not sufficient to support generalizations even about Chekhov himself, let alone about The Writer. And it will not be sufficient even if the letters should be supplemented with other Chekhov material or related selections from *RESPONDING: SIX.* So anything done with these letters—or by means of them—had better be in some sense impressionistic. To put it another way, even if the letters are assigned as a block, it will *not* be necessary subsequently to try to discover how many facts about Chekhov the students remember, or what order of generalization they have been able to derive from the particulars in the letters. The students need not be expected to come up with statements that are easily tested and validated because they are based on details plain to all. One danger in "teaching" a cluster of a writer's personal letters is the obvious one—to be avoided at all costs: Don't beat the letters to death! These letters have been selected and arranged to present Chekhov as a human being, all faults and foibles intact, and to send a class out on a symbol-image-philosophy-hunting expedition, so that they might discover the little kernels of truth in this Great Master's writings, is to destroy the very object of the cluster. Such an exercise would merely add to the formaldehyde in which many English teachers have preserved poor Chekhov. If students are left to themselves with the letters, it might prove a humanizing experience for all involved, including Chekhov.

The way should rather be opened to idiosyncratic responses, even those of a sort that may not be very easily communicated. After all, though students may not find enough material here to let them do "research" papers on Chekhov, it is hard to believe that they can read the letters without getting some kind of feeling about him. If students are permitted to express themselves freely, the range of their response may surprise everyone concerned.

But the problem is how to arrange classrooms so that responses can be free and personal. Best do it, perhaps, by trying to arrange for artistic expression of the responses.

The assignment, if there is to be one, can be made very loosely: On the basis of these letters (and whatever else we can find to use), we are going to make some things—poems, stories, whatever. "We" means everyone in the class, but it is unlikely that all students will really want to participate. Why should they? (Read "class" to include "teacher." Read "make" in its old artistic sense of "compose.")

Perhaps it will be useful to bring in the Ted Hughes essay in Cluster 1 (text, p. 14), especially because of what he has to say there about the way the fox stayed in his mind, surfacing after years and giving him material for a poem.

> I have said that poetry is the spontaneous overflow of powerful feelings: it takes its origin from emotion recollected in tranquillity: the emotion is contemplated till, by a species of re-action, the tranquillity gradually disappears, and an emotion, kindred to that which was before the subject of contemplation, is gradually produced, and does itself actually exist in the mind. In this mood successful composition generally begins. . . .
>
> —William Wordsworth

[Note: for a more modern version of this Wordsworthian idea see Samuel Beckett's quotation on p. T-63 of this guide.]

A display of writers' notebooks should be a help. Some may be on hand in the school library, but probably the local public library will be a better source.

If comment about the notebooks seems in order, some of the following points can be made:

1. Authors are evidently interested in quite specific material, concrete observations. Presumably the things they see are vehicles of or signs for the emotions that Wordsworth was drawing attention to.
2. What is noted down often seems to us (and perhaps did to the writer) quite random or inexplicable items.
3. Like squirrels, writers seem to amass material and ideas for the sake of doing it, rather than from any conscious notion of what it will be used for.
4. Writers don't seem to know when a detail will surface in their consciousness; but sometimes they seem to act as if trying to promote the return of something.

There is some interesting material on this last point in Dorothy Wordsworth's Grasmere Journal for October 1800, when her brother was working on "Michael."

On the 11th Dorothy noted, "William composing," and she added a line or so later, "After dinner we walked up Greenhead Hill in search of a sheepfold." Still later: "The sheepfold is falling away. It is built in the form of a heart unequally divided."

The "in search of" suggests that finding a sheepfold was somehow important to the composing Wordsworth had been doing before dinner. And of course a sheepfold is an important detail in "Michael."

On the 15th Dorothy Wordsworth recorded, "Wm. again composed at the sheepfold after dinner." On the 18th: "William worked all the morning at the sheepfold, but in vain." He was back there on the 20th, the 21st, and the 22nd, being unsuccessful on the second two days. He was working there again on the 9th and 11th of November, though with what results his sister doesn't say.

Of course one can't be sure that these matters will be interesting to students. Given their conditioning to formal assignments, they are likely to find talk about writers' habits aimless and unproductive. And someone among the best students will, like as not, interrupt by saying, "This is all silly. We're not getting anywhere. And besides where can we find time for the kind of playing around that writers seem to do? We've got a job to do, haven't we? What about exams?"

To which there is only one answer possible: No deadline has been set for creating a "thing" (i.e., *a real toad in an imaginary garden*) that will express their response to Chekhov's letters. The problem, in effect, is theirs. What can they come up with?

That move opens the way for another kind of talk, this time about organizing the class and, as a subsidiary to that, about various individual or small group ways of meeting the assignment.

Now there will be a setting in which the students will be able to work alone or in self-organized groups and on creative tasks of their own choice. That is no unimportant thing to have accomplished; and there is no reason for discouragement if students don't know how to enjoy and use the freedom. After all, when else have they had such an experience?

I think about sculpture all the time. I work at it for ten or twelve hours a day. I even dream about it. If, as a result, I was only to produce something that everyone immediately understood, I wouldn't have been thinking very profoundly.

—Henry Moore[8]

Cluster 3: pages 38-63

Because it was written for radio, *Albert's Bridge* does not require staging, and so it is particularly well suited for classroom presentation by reading aloud. Of course it may also be taped, with sound effects and music. Students interested in either mode of presentation will have similar but not identical problems. For example, voice differentiation will be more important in a taped version than in one where the readers can be seen; hence students doing a tape will need to be more careful in casting.

Readers in front of a class can, of course, pantomime painting. Do they feel they need to?

How can the sound of painting be suggested on the tape? What music will create the impressions called for in the script? Ask your students what other technical problems they must consider when working on either a tape or a reading.

In thinking about *Albert's Bridge,* students may get some help from the following comment by Henry Moore:

> The *King and Queen* is rather strange. Like many of my sculptures, I can't explain exactly how it evolved. Anything can start me off on a sculpture idea, and in this case it was playing with a small piece of modelling wax. Whilst manipulating a piece of this wax, it began to look like a horned Pan-like, bearded head. Then it grew a crown and I recognized it immediately as the head of a king. I continued and gave it a body. Then I added a second figure to it and it became a King and Queen.[9]

Some words and phrases in the above passage are very much worth noting:

evolved: suggests that the conception of the statue and the statue itself developed from simple to complex.

Anything can start me off: suggestion of the accidental in the genesis of a work of art; what is meant by "inspiration" probably.

sculpture idea: not just an idea, an abstraction; but an idea of a particular sort: one of or for a sculpture; suggests a visual content to the idea.

playing with: again starting without a plan, waiting for an inspiration to come.

piece of modelling wax: unformed material.

began to look like: chance development into something recognizable by or in the conscious mind.

it grew: things that grow have their own internal principles of motion or change, they grow because they are alive; Moore's language suggests that in the unformed wax there was some such principle at work. It's a figure of course, but a very interesting one.

I recognized it: the conscious mind or imagination takes over.

I . . . gave it a body: now the development is planned, under the control of the artist's regnant mental functions. What happens from now on will be more or less intentional, the results can be analyzed.

I added a second figure: presumably to complete the composition he now had in his mind, his idea for a sculpture.

What Stoppard has done in *Albert's Bridge,* it seems fair to say, is play with ("explore" is perhaps too strong a word) a certain number of general ideas and dramatic conventions:

1. The accountant/cybernetic/efficiency approach in business and government
2. The romance of work, alienation of labor
3. The little man with dreams
4. The intellectual in the "real" world
5. Practical father, other-worldly son; dithering mother; young master and maid servant
6. Conflict of class values

Stoppard's chief problem: What kind of plot can I make that will hold together (1) a fable about business efficiency and (2) a middle-class boy who marries a servant he has got pregnant? (Note, by the way, that Stoppard makes no attempt to explain why Albert marries Kate, instead of just paying her off; no motivation is provided, and is needed, really.) Or to put it another way, it is as if he asked himself, "If I have a start with (1) and (2), how can I develop an end?"

Or that is what one sees as his chief problem, since there is now a completed work to look at. At a guess, however, where Stoppard probably started (his "small piece of modelling wax") was with the wonderful final scene; wonderful, that is, in the potentiality of its sound effects on radio. Having "recognized" what he had there, then he may have begun to plan how he could get to it. At which point he would have been ready to ask some questions about plot and story.

All this may be rather presumptuous of us; that is, Stoppard may just as easily have started his play with the mere idea of a man painting a bridge, and then he may have asked himself: "Who is this man?" "Where does he come from?" and "What is he doing with an inane job like that?" Ask your students where *they* think Stoppard began to build his bridge? Their answers may be infinitely more interesting than and surely as valid as ours.

Your students may also be interested in another of Stoppard's plays, *Rosencrantz and Guildenstern Are Dead.* It is a somewhat hilarious play, if one is acquainted with Shakespeare's *Hamlet,* that no doubt began in Stoppard's mind with the question: What were Rosencrantz and Guildenstern doing backstage during all those lengthy soliloquies by the princely young Hamlet? *Where* were they during the action (the plot)?

Some of your students might enjoy applying *that* technique to *Albert's Bridge.* The logical choice for a Rosencrantz and Guildenstern focus would be Fraser. Why is he in the play? As it happens, that is an interesting question. *Where* is Fraser until the near ending of the play? Why does he pop up so suddenly? It really doesn't make much sense, or is it meant to? Any answer as to "why" Fraser is in the play may have more to do with what he has been doing *outside* of the realm of the play's plot. And that is an area which only your students and yourself can imaginatively speculate on. Perhaps, then, the class will enjoy a project of creating a play about the shadowy Fraser. A possible title: *Fraser, Fraser, Where Were You When Albert Began to Paint.* (*Note:* If such a project is undertaken, the action of the play could shift between certain actual scenes from *Albert's Bridge* and other scenes depicting Fraser's activities outside the reality of Stoppard's plot. Fraser might well be courting or married to Kate's sister.)

Other students may not appreciate such a peripheral analysis of *Albert's Bridge* and will want to get right to the *heart* of the matter by talking about what they see as the content or meaning of the play. And probably a debate or argument will result, because they will want to propose reductive answers, making the play be "about" one thing or another. For some it will be a satire on business, progress, or statistical/"scientific" solutions to all kinds of problems. Others will insist that Albert's obsession is the central "point" of the play. Others will be caught by the confrontation between Albert, the self-styled "philosopher," and the comic, inept Fitch, the statistician-efficiency expert; and they will want to work the play out as a justification of the former and his way of life. That's a hard job, of course, considering the play as a whole, but students may well be up to it.

These questions could lead further, to a discussion of the worth of the play, and its "relevance." Obviously its thematic materials—business, obsession, parents and children, population, and the relationship between the mathematical and the muddled human view of life—are all of continuing concern.

But some shrewd students may wonder whether the play is anything more than a clever put-on. With luck, there may even be a student or two who will want to know why it has to be anything more than that. Of course the real question is not whether it's a put-on, but whether it's a good one. The difficulty here is in deciding what is meant by "good." Certainly the play does not conform to the Aristotelian guidelines that most teachers will have been taught (and perhaps will be anxious to teach), mainly because Aristotle would have little to do with tragedies that were put-ons. So, it's best to turn to your students, and if the play works, perhaps it is then good. And as the Beatles said: "Let It Be."

I had an idea that a Man might pass a very pleasant life in this manner—let him on a certain day read a certain Page of full Poesy or distilled Prose, and let him wander with it, and muse upon it, and reflect upon it, and bring home to it, and prophesy upon it, and dream upon it, until it becomes stale—but when will it do so? Never.

—John Keats to J. H. Reynolds,
19 February 1818

Cluster 4: pages 64-115

The selections in Cluster 4 contain material on or concerning the following themes:

—art and reality
—ambitions, ideals, dreams
—convention and revolt
—minority experience (including that of children)
—growing up

But the fact that such labels are available does not mean that the selections should be mined for evidence of their thematic accuracy, or that students should be tested on their ability to excavate. On the other hand, knowledge of the existence of such material may come in handy when classroom conversation is being planned for.

It is useful to remember A. N. Whitehead's remark, "A merely well-informed man is the most useless bore on God's earth."

One gambit to use with Cluster 4 might be to let students read around silently, as they choose. (Note the epigraph above, from Keats.) Eventually some of them may want to respond—to talk, perhaps, or write something of their own, or maybe just think or dream. . . . Whether intervention is possible will, of course, depend on how public the response seems to be. Obviously a student who is dreaming ought not to be interfered with; the same probably goes for students who want to talk to one another, even if the subject of their talk doesn't seem to be any one of the themes mentioned. The ideal situation is one in which a teacher can make some contribution to the talk; or, perhaps even better, is asked to.

If no evidence of response is forthcoming, no evidence at all, not even to the close observation of a teacher familiar with the individuals in the class—well, that in itself says something about something. It should be remembered, though, that going on with reading is a response.

(By the way, this device will fail if the reading time is used as a chance to catch up on "records.")

Another opening might be to read or to have read one or two of the poems in Cluster 4, as a cue for talk, either with the class as a whole or with groups and individuals in it.

PENNYCANDYSTORE • page 66

–How do you fall in love with unreality? What is unreality anyway?
–Have you ever heard leaves cry "Too soon! too soon!"? (On that question, note the girl's feelings about death in "Cheerleader," page 105 of the text.)

THE CAROUSEL • page 100

–What is the author's purpose in saying "And then an elephant rolls slowly round"? Is there no one on the elephant? Why?
–It seems likely that the carousel is supposed to stand for something like life, or perhaps a quality of life. In that respect, what–if anything–does the poem have to do with Ferlinghetti's "unreality"?

BUT HE WAS COOL • page 108
WE REAL COOL • page 109
BLACK JACKETS • page 110

–What would "Cheerleader" (text, p. 105) do if she had to meet the people in these poems?

BLACK JACKETS • page 110

(What one would like here is a full understanding of Gunn's view of the "red-haired boy." Maybe the way to get it is to talk about the scene. It's a pub of a certain kind, probably outside a city (why?). In addition to the Boy and the Boys in "Black Jackets," there's one other actor present–the Speaker. Barman, barmaid, and various other drinkers are to be assumed, but they don't get into the act.)

–What kind of person is the speaker? (See lines 14 and 24, and the relationship between the Boy and the Speaker.)
–The Boy sees the jacket as "no more than leather." Why? Is it to be inferred that once it meant more? What?
–If the Boy stays with the present (line 24), are we to conclude that he is different from the others, who are "concocting selves" (line 14)?

(These questions on "Black Jackets" are not testing questions. They are merely some inquiries about problems that occurred to us as we were talking about the poem. And we are not sure about the answers; as a matter of fact, maybe they don't have any good answers. Do loose ends keep a poem from being "good"? The literature on *Hamlet* may possibly answer that.)

TRAIN WHISTLE GUITAR • page 67

Probably Murray meant readers of "Train Whistle Guitar" to remember chiefly the confrontation scene between Luzana Cholly and the two runaways (text, p. 80), in which the assimilationist line* is set forth about as exactly as can be:

> Then he was talking about going to school and learning to use your head like the smart white folks. You had to be rawhide but you had to be patent leather too, then you would really be nimble, then you would really be not only a man but a big man. . . .
>
> And then he was talking about Negroes and white folks again, and he said the young generation of Negroes were supposed to be like Negroes and be like white folks too and still be Negroes. . . .

"Train Whistle Guitar" was first published in 1953: Murray was then a member of the English Department at Tuskegee Institute. It should be interesting to see how students now respond to Luzanna Cholly's (and Murray's and the story's) message. The first part of the above quotation (about going to school) is one of the central doctrines in the mythology of the United States. It was applied first of all in the case of the Catholic Irish in the 1840's and 1850's, then even more vigorously (by the Irish among others) to the immigrants from southern and eastern Europe between, say, 1880 and 1925. Now, of course, it is being told to Black Americans, Chicanos, and Puerto Ricans–by the children and grandchildren of earlier generations of immigrants. (Black Americans can be called immigrants in respect to their entrance into northern cities. The treatment of Chinese and Japanese is a special phenomenon, as is that of American Indians.)

Do the students still believe Luzanna Cholly? That is, do they still believe that schooling will assure their entrance into the mainstream of society, as it is called?

Do they still believe *in* his message? That is, do they still want to get in? What do they think of his "then you would really be not only a man but a big man"? Do they value being a "big man" in the sense that Luzanna Cholly uses the words? Note his line in the next-to-last paragraph: "Make old Luze glad to take his hat off to you some of these days."

The fact of the matter is that any number of students may find "old Luze" and his advice both quite preposterous or at least sentimental; and some of them may even see the implications of the name he calls himself: "old Luze." Some rather vigorous expressions of disapproval and disagreement may be expected.

On the whole we rather think such responses should be tolerated if not in fact sought. At least we cannot insist too strongly that we didn't put the story in to push Luzanna Cholly's get-ahead ethic.

*On that same topic (assimilation) see the overprinted remark concerning Gwendolyn Brooks' "We Real Cool" on text page 109.

To any students who say that the boys see through Luzanna Cholly, it may be pointed out that they don't really. They discover that he has had a hard life, like everyone else, that he hasn't really been able to defy white society, that he isn't quite the heroic figure legend had made him. But they are not given any action or reflection which would say that they see through his last advice.

By way of counterpoint: One of the arguments against the above political-social analysis of "Train Whistle Guitar" is that the story goes beyond the mere abstract of whether it is or is not of an assimilationist line. (And in this respect, it is well to remember that our own great white whale, Moby Dick, in spite of a century's critical symbol-spearing of him, has in the end managed to retain the flesh and blood of an actual whale!) If a student does not emphasize this view, perhaps the teacher should make a point of it. The argument, if we may take the liberty with Old Luze's consciousness, might go something like this:

> Folks think I'm crazy, but that's OK with me. Better to be crazy and alone than to be a Negro that's supposed to be like a Negro and yet like white folks too and yet still be a Negro. Then I don't want no kids on my *train* no more than I don't want no medals 'cause if I'm goin' to be invisible, it'll be on my own terms. Sure, Old Luze don't know nothing from nothing; Old Luze ain't been nowhere, but where he has been and what he does know ain't about to be felt by the new generation of Negroes, the ones that's supposed to be like Negroes and yet be like white folks too and still be Negroes.

The point here is that maybe Old Luze himself *doesn't* believe in the get-ahead-in-the-mainstream ethic (the assimilationist line). The fact that Luze chooses a life of continual trains and self-pronounced invisibility (cf. Ralph Elison's novel, *The Invisible Man*), a life beyond people (note his disposition for front-line foxholes), leads a reader to believe that Murray may have written something here that goes beyond his own political and social message. The assimilationist "message" of the story may just be consumed by the grace, the rhythm, and the beauty of the imitation-Blues writing. And thus the integrity of Old Luze's life style may appeal to more high school students of the 1970's than it did to the security-oriented, mainstream-participating students of the 1950's. The latter may have regarded Old Luze as a loser and a fool, whereas the students of today may identify more honestly with Old Luze's plight—indeed he *is* a loser (from the Establishment point of view), but is he not also beautiful? *Beautiful* in that he has come to terms with himself at the expense of no one else but himself? (To the young, "doing your own thing without hurting anyone else" is an absolute good in ethical relationships.)

Today, there may be a great deal of irony in that line, "the new generation of Negroes, the ones that's supposed to be like Negroes and yet be like white folks too and still be Negroes." And this irony may not have been Murray's intention in the 1950's; however, a new generation of students, attuned to a life style not remote from Old Luze's, may provide for a provocative re-interpretation of "Train Whistle Guitar."

SIMPLE ARITHMETIC • page 82

IN EXILE • page 96

THE LONELY DAY • page 101

CHEERLEADER • page 105

These four selections (and one might well include "Train Whistle Guitar" text, p. 67) may be approached (in class discussion) by struggling to sense an understanding of the value systems implicit in each selection. In a way, each selection is concerned with a type of *exile* that stems from a relationship between either two people or between a person and an institution (or a person representing an institution). There is indeed a "growing-up" process—an "essential" education—in all five selections. The following passage may speak right to the heart of our concern.

> Of all the forms of impoverishment that can be seen or felt in America, loss of self—a sort of death-in-life—is surely the most devastating. . . . Beginning with school, if not before, an individual is systematically stripped of his imagination, his creativity, his heritage, his dreams, and his personal uniqueness, in order to fit him to be a productive [and consuming] unit in a mass technological society. Instinct, feeling, and spontaneity are suppressed by overwhelming forces. As the individual is drawn into the meritocracy, his working life is split from his home life, and both suffer from lack of wholeness. In the end, people virtually *become* their occupations and their other roles, and are strangers to themselves.
>
> —Charles A. Reich, "The Greening of America."[10]

We suggest that this passage be read by/to students to provoke responses (from *both* students and teacher) that will lead to the *feeling* of the explicit and implicit pathos and tragedy in these selections. Let us call this cluster the group-sensitivity exercise. (More specific questions and points will be found in the overprinting in the Teacher's Annotated Edition of the text, pages 64-111.)

A Note on the Strong Dream Motif Running Through Cluster 4

In each of the selections in Cluster 4 dreams constitute a very real presence, whether they be in actuality (as in the narrator's hero worship of Luzanna Cholly in "Train Whistle Guitar") or in the rhythm and movement of the writing (as in "The Pennycandystore" or "Train Whistle Guitar"). It might also be observed that many of the dreams come up against some of the harsh realities of existence, and to some extent they are defeated, or are "tattered" by reality (the young woman in "The Lonely Day," provides a good example). This does not mean that the various writers are moralizing on the advantages of "facing up to reality"; after all, the passage from girl to woman and from boy to man constitutes a certain kind of "death" of innocence and of dreams.

It is hoped, however, that this "death" does not come in the form of what Mr. Reich terms "loss of self." As teachers, we can aid the student in his struggle to preserve "his imagination, his creativity, his dreams, and his personal uniqueness. . . ." Thus follows our argument for an open and a free classroom, an environment in which it is possible to begin to answer Herman Hesse's Siddhartha (see text, p. 65) by liberating students from the mere pursuit of facts and instead communicating with them in the spirit of a *mutual feeling toward wisdom.*

> Did W[ordsworth]. ever tell you that the accident of his being given a manuscript book was the first *occasion* (I do not say *cause*) of his writing poetry? He thought it a pity, after filling up a few pages, to leave the remainder "white and unwritten still," and so got into the habit of reducing to shape the thoughts which had before been vaguely haunting his brain. . . .
>
> —Aubrey De Vere to W. R. Hamilton, January 1843

Cluster 5: pages 116-155

THE BOY OF WINANDER • page 118

The first version of this poem was written in Goslar, in Germany, in 1798. Wordsworth had gone there to learn German. Adding that language to the French he already had would, he seems to have supposed (egged on by Coleridge), give him more chance to make money by translating. But he didn't have much success with the project. The winter was long and cold, and he and his sister Dorothy were never quite accepted by the respectable folk of Goslar, who, according to Coleridge, thought "sister" was a euphemism for "mistress."

We, of course, see W. in 1798 as the young (he was but twenty-eight) man who gave us *Lyrical Ballads* (published in the late summer of 1798). So we tend to think of him as already a poet. But we have to realize that for any cultivated reader or established literary figure such things as "lyrical ballads" would not have been "poetry" at all, but only a kind of magazine verse. That *we* think of W.'s experimental poems as "poetry" is a result of a great transvaluation in taste that occurred during the nineteenth century, which has made it possible for the permitted stock of poetic material to include certain sorts of working and lower class characters, more or less realistically presented. Wordsworth himself was partly responsible for this change in taste.

In the winter of 1798, however, W. was only a very minor writer of topographical verse—except perhaps in the view of young college students (cf. Bob Dylan). W. could have seen himself only as something of a failure (in a family of rather successful businessmen and speculators), unable to get on with something practical, like a scholarship, and having no success at all at the far more difficult task of making a name for himself as a poet. In his discouragement, he turned back to his earliest memories of happiness and began working them into poetic form, perhaps less for the benefit of cultivated readers, who could hardly have been much interested in such reminiscences, than out of concern for his peace of mind.

The results of W.'s excursion into his past were these lines on "The Boy of Winander," versions of the Lucy poems, a portion of "Nutting," the skating and boat stealing episodes that were later worked into the first book of *The Prelude,* and various other sketches in which W. seems to have been working out the details of that relationship between himself and "Nature" that became a great central theme of *The Prelude.*

The information in that note is not intended for dissemination to a class, but it might come in handy sometime, if a student should raise questions (even very rudimentary ones) about the uses of poetry, literature, or reading.

The information may be useful, too, in talking about reality and art, especially in connection with the autobiographical pieces in Cluster 4 and the interviews in Cluster 6. (Also see the John Fowles' quotation on text page 117 and Anton Chekhov's letter of May 30, 1888 on text page 25.)

If no one ever wants to talk about such questions (which seems very unlikely, though recognizing the interest may be hard), well, no great harm is done, ever, by a little information, and this is a rather out of the way place anyway.

At least, though, the poems associated with "The Boy of Winander" might be called to students' attention. And so far as the poem itself is concerned, it should be interesting to see whether any student-readers sense the utter and very impressive aloneness of the boy. Where do children reared in suburb or city find a place for such an experience? For that matter, exactly what is going on in the original poem (lines 1-23 of this version)?

TIMOTHY WINTERS • page 119

A good poem for just reading, perhaps even to the class as a group. Comment doesn't seem to be required. But a student who has just read "The Boy of Winander" may feel a need to say something about "Timothy Winters." After all, they are two poems about boys, one right after the other—

The two are probably not comparable as poems, but there is a point at which the minds of the authors impinge on each other in such a way as to allow comparison. That point may be stated in this figure:

$$\text{Nature: Boy}_1 = \text{Welfare Worker: Boy}_2$$

Perhaps the whole of modern history is encapsulated in that difference between the one boy's relations to nature and the other's relations to the welfare worker. The oddly winning, however uninteresting, personality of "Cheerleader" (text, p. 105) is a kind of point of reference; and so, for that matter, is the vacuous personality of "Cool Girl" (text, p. 154). Is there a benefit (to students and teacher) to be derived from considering these four selections as a composite: (1) "Cool Girl" (text, p. 154); (2) "Timothy Winters" (text, p. 119); (3) "Cheerleader" (text, p. 105); and (4) "The Boy of Winander" (text, p. 118)?

EARLY SORROW • page 120

Discussion of the "problem" in "Early Sorrow" hardly seems necessary, and this story might possibly provide an occasion for improvisation and for whole group activity.

What happens after the fight is the obvious object of attention, though a case might be made for using the scene at the Boer farm. With an experienced class, it may be enough to give a summary of the story up to whichever scene is used. With an inexperienced class, probably it will be better to read the actual text. The class should do the casting. Volunteers or teacher-picked actors are a mistake. They prevent discussion by the class, and in the second case at least, introduce an unpleasant suggestion of superior adult knowledge, which here is no doubt false anyway.

What happens after casting ought to be left to the actors, who may, of course, want to consult with the class, but need not be expected to do so.

NIGHTS AWAY FROM HOME • page 129

Ideally one would like the use of this selection to depend upon a choice of topics or upon areas of interest that a class or a class-group has made while planning work for some agreed-upon period of the school term. If, that is, they have proposed to center their work on something like adolescence, or the ways in which young people learn to be adult, or alienation or revolt, then "Nights Away From Home" may be drawn upon to support or add to the material they bring to the discussion. There are other selections in *RESPONDING: SIX* which can be used for this purpose; for example, "Early Sorrow" (text p. 120) or "Train Whistle Guitar" (text, p. 67), or "Albert's Bridge" (text, p. 39).

But if a leading question is necessary, a possible one might be this: *Have you ever been on your own and had to get help from an adult*?

Conroy gives himself-as-a-child a fairly neutral camera-eye. (Is Murray's narrator's "eye" in "Train Whistle Guitar" (text, p. 67) different from Conroy's?) Conroy doesn't speculate about the feelings, thoughts, or motives of the adults he meets. They come into his view, do thus and so, and he reports it. That's about all. Is there a chance for exploring character by role-playing the adults Conroy reports about? One possibility would be a series of dramatic monologs (cf. "My Last Duchess," text. p. 206), in which the characters speak of their view of the boy, or recall the parts of their past that he suggested to them.

"Nights Away From Home" is in part a collection of anecdotes. These may be used for models of narrative writing.

HOW WE FALL IN LOVE • page 145

A pretty powerful story that does rather more than touch the school experience. The feelings that run beneath its surface—and not very far beneath at that—will be familiar to most high school seniors. If they are made the subject of public discussion, by way of a class assignment, the result is likely to be a certain amount of maneuvering: giggles, somewhat suggestive smirks and remarks, a certain amount of thrashing about, possibly some real misbehavior—anything that will prevent public exposure of the feelings engendered by the story. Hence tact, tactics, concern for discipline, and above all, regard for the feelings of young people, especially their need for privacy, all suggest that this story may best be left to individual discovery.

After all, the title is likely to be enticing enough.

However, if the class wants to discuss "How We Fall in Love," would they be interested in the following quotation as an avenue into the story?

> . . . It is really a complex movement taking place, of which we are mere parts. We represent historical forces and it is really these forces that are coalescing and moving toward each other. And it is not a fraud, forced out of desperation. We live in a disoriented, deranged social structure, and we have transcended its barriers in our own ways and have stepped psychologically outside its madness and repressions. It is lonely out here. We recognize each other. And, having recognized each other, is it any wonder that our souls hold hands and cling together even while our minds equivocate, hesitate, vacillate, and tremble?
>
> Peace. Don't panic, and don't wake up.
> Dream on. I am
> Yours,
>
> Eldridge[11]

The famous third chapter of D. H. Lawrence's *Women in Love* and also the thirteenth chapter of Lawrence's *The Rainbow* may be suggested to anyone whose interest has been caught by "How We Fall in Love." Chapters Ten and Twelve of *The Rainbow* also have material on school.

COOL GIRL • page 154

This piece may hit some value systems hard, an effect which is perhaps emphasized by the questions that follow it in the text on page 155. But note that the girl is a type that many students now find somewhat off-putting, if not downright pathological.

There are other interviews in *RESPONDING: SIX:* "What Counts Is Knowledge. And Feeling" (text, p. 157), "Oh, Did I Have Dreams!" (text, p. 168), and "Cheerleader" (text, p. 105). Some students may want to study them and then go interview someone—principal, coach, teacher, someone in the neighborhood. If the subject will allow it, taping the interview will be interesting.

> [Youth] culture is very new. I think it began around 1964, probably along with the Beatles, and all young people of today are affected by it, whether they're with it or not. The youth culture is something. The culture that this country supposedly has is nothing, at least nothing alive. The main attraction of the youth culture is that it is a culture of some sort. I think a lot of kids are attracted to it because it's something to belong to. You've got to have something to belong to. You've got to have people who believe the same things you do basically. It's a group of your own kind of people.
>
> —A high school girl, age seventeen.[12]

Cluster 6: pages 156-179

One of the most conspicuous characteristics of American middle-class culture, especially of the academic variety, is the very high value put on the humorous disengagement represented by the selections from Thurber and Auden in this cluster. And some students may well (and not without some justification) reject them as beneath their interest, or they may even attack the life style that nourishes such work. Either position is a tenable one, and should not be criticized, even if the students go so far as to question the intention of the cluster itself.

It should be interesting to note how many students are willing and able to respond to the jokes, if they even see them as such, in the Thurber and the Auden selections.

WHAT COUNTS IS KNOWLEDGE. AND FEELING • page 157

OH, DID I HAVE DREAMS! • page 168

But it will be even more interesting (and socially more important) to see how students respond to Lucy Jefferson and Jesus Lopez. Can they *see* them, or do they simply notice them? For the teacher, the main job must be to discover tactics that will elicit a valuable response from students reading these interviews. Or, to be fairer to students, the job is to see that nothing inhibits such response. By a valuable response we mean simply one that implicates the students' feelings. A question about the Literary Sort's view of Lucy Jefferson (text, p. 163) may be a right start.

Another beginning might be to expand by improvisation the scenes (in "What Counts Is Knowledge. And Feeling") between Lucy Jefferson and Miss Pruner, and the scenes in the hospital.

What is the full meaning of Lopez' speech (in "Oh, Did I Have Dreams!" at the top of page 171) about being "just what is called an overpaid laborer"? What does it say about him, about American society? Who calls him that?

Social studies or history teachers should be able to provide additional documents to go with these interviews.

The effect of "What Counts Is Knowledge. And Feeling" and "Oh, Did I Have Dreams!" seems powerful enough to us, so that we think it ought to be possible simply to call the interviews to the attention of the students who seem right for them, for whom they seem right, and then sit back and wait for results. We reckon there ought to be some place in an English class for that sort of free behavior.

Any one of the following poems suggests a topic that students might discuss before reading the interview with Jesus Lopez.

Ameinias*

Of Ameinias nothing more is known for sure
Except: he was most worthy, though quite poor.
Which may explain why he remains obscure.
John Simon[13]

Youth°

A young Apollo, golden-haired,
Stands dreaming on the verge of strife,
Magnificently unprepared
For the long littleness of life.
Frances Cornford[14]

Here Dead Lie We Because We Did Not Choose†

Here dead lie we because we did not choose
To live and shame the land from which we sprung.
Life, to be sure, is nothing much to lose;
But young men think it is, and we were young.
A. E. Housman[15]

Along the same line, Edgar Lee Masters' *Spoon River Anthology* is a collection of poetic monologs which has both appeal to students as well as direct applicability to the Terkel interviews.

SNAPSHOT OF A DOG • page 164

THE DOG THAT BIT PEOPLE • page 173

But, of course, we would be somewhat unfair, if we just let the Thurber pieces go by without pointing out the greater *seriousness* of the first one. "Snapshot of a Dog" is based on the dog-lover's sentimental phrase, "Really, he's almost human, don't you think?" "So," says Thurber, "how can I write up the behavior of Rex so as to make him *almost human*?" The working out of that technical problem is cause for admiration. And the imagination capable of remembering (and perhaps elaborating) that final scene of Rex's death is not to be underestimated. Especially since one can imagine Thurber himself gagging at the dog stories of Albert Payson Terhune, and their pale descendant, the Lassie TV show. How does he keep things in control?

"The Dog That Bit People," however, is simply an extravaganza on its first sentence–which is, incidentally, a real example of the thesis sentence that the composition books are always asking children to produce. Some students may get a little fun out of pursuing the rest of Thurber's organizing devices, in the light of the rules, that is. How many of the composition-grammar books provide for learning about, or would even allow to be used, that slick "But the Airedale, as I have said," with which Thurber gets back on his track in the second paragraph? It's enough to make you think, perhaps–just perhaps–there's some writing going on, somewhere, in spite of all the helpful advice of grammar-composition texts.

MISS GEE: A BALLAD • page 177

Miss Gee can, of course, be compared to Corrine in "How We Fall in Love" (text, p. 145). Or would it be fairer to compare her with "Cool Girl" (text, p. 154)? Or perhaps "Cheerleader" (text, p. 105)? Or is puritanical Miss Gee, as the Literary Sort seems to believe (text, p. 179), really the object of Mr. Auden's ire? Is it not possible that the technologos spirit of efficiency (see Albert's Bridge" on text pages 43-44), as seen in the surgeon and his merry band of Oxford Groupers, is the subject of the poet's ridicule? In any event, Auden's distance from his material (in many of his other poems as well as in "Miss Gee") is rather chilling in itself. This is indeed grim, black humor.

Certainly, I must confess my own barbarousness, I never heard the old song of Percy and Douglas that I found not my heart moved more than with a trumpet; and yet is it sung but by some blind crowder [or fiddler], with no rougher verse than rude style; which, being so evil appareled in the dust and cobwebs of that uncivil age, what would it work, trimmed in gorgeous eloquence of Pindar?

—Sir Philip Sidney

Cluster 7: pages 180-201

*A Note on Ballads**

Sidney's somewhat snobbish comment on "the old song of Percy and Douglas" is typical of cultivated literary opinion of ballads; it suggests, by the way, why Wordsworth was somewhat ill-advised in calling his experimental poems "lyrical ballads" (see *Talks,* page T-38). What Sidney means is that, in spite of himself, he is moved by the "old song"; and he wonders how much more he would be if it were done in the literary manner, by a real poet, for example, Pindar.

In these times, some students may be interested (amused?) by the explanations that scholars have given of the origin of ballads. On the whole, the scholars seem to have wanted to de-emphasize the connection of ballads and the oral culture; perhaps they have wanted even more to "disconnect" the ballads from any possibility of original composition by a folk singer like Sidney's "blind crowder." (Note, by the way, the tie there to allegedly blind "Homer.") In the nineteenth century the German balladists argued for communal or group composition, holding that the ballads were not made *for* the people but rather *by* the people *as a whole.* Group composition, especially by *das Volk,* is surely not a very likely hypothesis. So it is probably safe to think that the chief value of that theory was that it separated the origin of the ballads from the kind of unlettered, uncultivated individuals who were to be found singing them.

The scholars referred to in the introduction to this cluster (text, p. 181), who treated the ballads as "literary debris" of the Middle Ages, were taking a contrary route to the *das Volk* theory, and were trying to connect the ballads pretty directly to the literary culture. They made them abridgements of the medieval romances, which were, of course, *true* poems, with *real* authors, just like Pindar. Presumably such abridgements would have been made by folk entertainers (amateurs?) for the benefit of the common people who could not take time from work to listen to a minstrel's performance, and who wouldn't have appreciated his sort of art anyway. The bareness or, in some views, the

*Also see text page 181.

refinement of ballad narration would be explained by the bad memories of the many folk singers who passed on the abridgements.

The Early Ballads • pages 183-197

Perhaps the best way to "do" the early ballads is to let them be the occasion for collecting some modern works that touch on the same sort of material: political loyalty–class interests–control of the executive power in "A Song of the Duke of Buckingham" (text, p. 183); social disorganization–"disorder in the streets"–violation of property rights in "Johnny of Cockley's Well" (text, p. 187); generation gap–destruction of the young–convention-bound adults in "Graeme and Bewick" (text, p. 198); and the human condition in "Come on Good Fellowe, Make an End" (text, p. 195). From such work, some students may come to hear in their bones the voices of the unknown singers who made these poems, expressing in them their feelings of the troubles of their times. Those students who do so may want to explain their discoveries to the class or write them up.

"A Song of the Duke of Buckingham" (text, page 183) is essentially historical, and it may be compared with the accounts in standard histories and encyclopedias. See especially Dickens' version in *A Child's History of England,* Chapter XXV; it is a good example of what the French call *haute vulgarisation* (i.e., popularization of knowledge that has a certain estimable quality to it).

The king is Richard III, Buckingham is Henry Stafford, a member of one of the great ducal families in 15th-century England. He had helped Richard take the throne from his nephew Edward V (a boy of thirteen when his father, Edward IV, died). Buckingham had turned against Richard after the murder of Edward V and his brother in the Tower. Shakespeare covers the murders of the Princes in *Richard III,* Act III, scene iv, and the circumstances leading to Buckingham's execution in Act IV, scene iv.

The revolt and death of Buckingham were among the final episodes in that long period of gang warfare (cf. *Romeo and Juliet* and *West Side Story*) that romantic historians have chosen to call the Wars of the Roses. Buckingham and various other of the great territorial magnates, having had enough of Richard III, had hopes to substitute for him Henry Tudor, Earl of Richmond. In the popular accounts of the time, the rebels were defeated by an accident: a storm kept Henry from getting across the Channel from his exile in France. A year or so later, at Bosworth, Henry did defeat Richard, take the throne, and begin to give the merchants of London, Bristol, and the other great trading cities the kind of government they needed. Buckingham, it should be noted, was on good terms with the city people, and it was Richard's policies in economics and governing, as much as the murder of the princes, that made Buckingham break with the King.

Buckingham's execution speech in *Richard III* (Act V, scene i) suggests some of the turmoil, the deaths and disorder, that had been brought to England by the quarreling among the great baronial families–Percy, Neville, Beauchamp, Mowbray, Howard, Stafford, and others–to say nothing of the squabbling over the throne among the descendants of Edward III and his brothers, Edmund of Langley, Duke of York, and John of Gaunt [Ghent], Duke of Lancaster.

Gaunt's prophecy speech (*Richard II,* Act II, scene i) may be compared to Buckingham's execution speech (*Richard III* Act V, scene i), since it was, after all, the deposition of Richard II by a Lancastrian, Henry Bolingbroke (Henry IV), in which all the trouble began. The troubles didn't start, of course, until the death of Henry V (Shakespeare's Prince Hal) in 1422 and the long minority of Henry VI (an infant at the time of his father's death), to which was added, in his maturity, some sort of mental disability. The barons took those opportunities to enrich themselves from the Royal Treasury and with the lands and goods of their fellows and members of the lesser nobility and gentry.

The prophecy of much blood and disorder is the first part of Gaunt's famous death speech: "This blessed plot, this earth, this realm, this England." Gaunt's subsequent speeches in the scene give Shakespeare's view of the causes of that century of disorder in England. And it is surely permitted to suppose that Shakespeare was quite aware that Bolingbroke was Gaunt's son. Maybe he was even aware of the execution of the son of the ballad's Duke of Buckingham in 1521, by Henry VIII.

In one version, the "song" begins with these two lines:

> You Barons bold, mar[r] ke and behold
> the things that I will [w] rite.

Some students may be interested in discussing just how many warnings the composer intended to send to the "barons bold." Line 10, for example, suggests the intense concern for descent of property through the familial line that is characteristic of feudal organization of social relations. When the Duke married his man to a rich woman, he was violating another social bond. So in a way the poem may be "about" Buckingham's rash ignoring of class interests as well as Bannister's treachery. It may also be "about" the rise to power of various "new men." Even the Howards, the current holders of the Dukedom of Norfolk, were hardly from the old baronial class.

As we have said before, we don't intend information of the sort we have just given to be transferred to students in a bolus of lecture material. But history has its fascinations (its "cunning passages, contrived corridors"), and from time to time there may be students who can be set off by a hint or two about the historical content of a selection like "A Song of the Duke of Buckingham." And of course having such information at hand will prove useful in dealing with students who already are fascinated by history, and who perhaps may know something about one or another of the Dukes of Buckingham. And, in that respect, students might very well be aware of the implicit relationship between the body-politic and the ballad. Certainly the assassinations of Robert Kennedy, Martin Luther King, and John Kennedy have occasioned emotional and lyrical responses from both noted and unnoted modern folk singers. And most assuredly, students are aware of the social significance, the "involvement" via Consciousness III, evident in the works of Tom Rush, Joan Baez, Pete Seeger, Bob Dylan, Julius Lester, and Joni Mitchell. Certainly it would be advantageous to use the multi-media when the class reads and works with this ballad cluster, and most likely there is at least one budding guitar-strumming balladeer in your classroom—whose talents should be encouraged and sought. We wonder how some of the "ancient" (but certainly not irrelevant) ballads might sound set to the nasal twangs of an undiscovered Dylan, Rush, or Mitchell.

With the modern or so-called "art" ballads, one might work back to the ballads of the sixteenth and seventeenth centuries. "The Quarry" (text, p. 182), "Ode to Billy Joe" (text, p. 198), and "Fair Cassidy" (text, p. 199) are typical of the kind of ballad that students will likely have met in literature anthologies. That is, they are poems about fated and hopeless passions, with their emotional content fairly close to the surface. A rather literary exercise (but still a fairly plausible one) might be to suggest a comparison of the narrative styles of these and the older ballads. Ballads for comparison may be found in almost any anthology of British literature and in some anthologies of American. But more substantial sources are easy to come by: B. J. Whiting has edited a collection of British ballads for Crofts Classics; Robert Graves has done one of English and Scottish ballads; collections of American folk songs are also available.

Some exploration of the story in "all in green my love went riding" (text, p. 200) may seem necessary, but at this stage of "reading skills development" perhaps just listening to the wonderful sounds in the poem is enough and perhaps all that can be expected. And, speaking of listening, Joan Baez has recorded this Cummings ballad in her album, *Baptism,* an album in which she sets various poems and prose pieces to music or to musical accompaniment. (*Baptism,* by the way, has been used with great success in high school English classes. If you feel that this type of presentation is beneficial to your class, then we also recommend the Vanilla Fudge's album, *The Beat Goes On;* it is in its rock way—a ballad, and one which students will perhaps rediscover via the English class.)

What might be the consequences were we to change our emphasis in an attempt to give fresh meaning to [students'] literary experiences; were we to encourage them to become active participants as well as spectators in their reading of imaginative literature; were we, instead of imposing a structure into which they must accommodate their experience, to accommodate our structure to their needs and experience?

—Caroline Shrodes[16]

Cluster 8: pages 202-239

LOVE IS • page 203

"Love Is" is a concrete poem. Jakov Lind—a modern German dramatist—in his autobiography, *Counting My Steps,* recounts his early elementary school experience with writing, which—according to his teacher—"had to be neat and correct":

> With a certain strength of character I defended myself against writing for a long time. I hated to write because I hated the rules against spilling of ink. Spots, dots and lines, doodles and drawings, everything done with black ink on white paper was writing to me. My parents were on Hartl's side; they agreed with this old Nazi that lines and dots are permitted only if made to look like words. Yet words looked to me like unimaginative drawings. . . .[17]

Perhaps the concrete poem is an answer to Lind's charge against the unimaginative physical appearance of words. When students discover, or better yet are *allowed* to discover, that words do *not* have to appear as a phalanx of lifeless letters, marching flush-left to flush-right, in a *neat* and *correct* sequence, then perhaps language is liberated for students to have pleasure with.

—Debi Ducote[18]

Concrete poem by Debi Ducote. First published in *Vieux Carre Courier,* New Orleans.

The above is a student's concrete poem. Books that both you and your students might be interested in are the following:

Concrete Poetry, Edited by S. Bonn, Dufour.
Concrete Poetry: A World View, M. Solt, Indiana University Press.
Anthology of Concrete Poetry, Edited by Emmett Williams, New Directions.

THE SICK ROSE • page 206

The worm in the rose: a conventional symbol/metaphor of death and beauty: mutability; all things are subject to decay. *Et ego in Arcadia:* I [Death] have been in Arcadia too.

In this poem Blake may once again be manifesting his obsessive preoccupation with (as he saw it) the over-valuation of the intellect at the expense of the feelings and imagination. But the images are very powerful, very highly charged; and it is probable that any such simple reductive explanations will simply dissatisfy students. They may not know how to express their dissatisfaction, of course, except by refusing to understand the poem, calling it queer or dredging up some memory of Blake's "madness" (as Blake's wife is said to have remarked: "I have very little of Mr. Blake's company. He is always in Paradise.") and protesting that the poem is mad, too. So this may be the kind of work that deserves a wordless response, or one in another medium. Would your students be interested in making concrete poems out of "The Sick Rose"?

MY LAST DUCHESS • page 206

Unless they have been very strictly conditioned to paying attention to the poem only–the text and nothing but the text–students are likely to think about the off-stage action: the scene between the Duchess and the Painter, the Duchess at sunset (where is the Duke?), the Duchess and the "officious fool," the Duchess and the Duke, the Count and his daughter, the Count with his ambassador on the latter's return. The fact is that there is probably enough "in" the poem to sustain a good deal of such imaginative playing around. There are chances, then, for writing, acting, improvising in pantomime, and so forth. (As a matter of fact, Tom Stoppard's *Rosencrantz and Guildenstern Are Dead* (see *Talks*, page T-31) is a take-off on precisely this idea: Where are Rosencrantz and Guildenstern when Hamlet is ranting about on-stage? What are *they* doing there in the off-stage wings?)

Students might discuss the thoughts of the Count's emissary as he listens to the Duke's explanations. Will he be disturbed by what he is hearing? What of the Count's daughter, if the marriage contract should be arranged?

THE WHITE STOCKING • page 208

In Lawrence's view, "The White Stocking" was, very likely, a study of sexual jealousy, which dramatized some of his notions about the balance (or imbalance) of forces and powers in male-female relations. (What Lawrence would have had to say about Women's Lib is not to be thought.) By no means so powerful as some other of Lawrence's treatments of these matters, "The White Stocking" is all the same suggestive enough so that the control offered by "close analysis" may be useful.

To follow the Lawrentian argument, note:

Page 208: Elsie Whiston is "a pretty little thing," whom her husband watches "appreciatively," but evidently a little distantly, since he doesn't (after two years of marriage) realize that Valentine's Day alone would be enough to "rouse" her. Nevertheless when she goes out of the room "all his light and warmth" go with her. Presumably he is bound to her by feelings, physical attraction, but lacks some sort of intellectual comprehension; the distinction is typical not only of Lawrence but of his time.

Lawrence seems to be at some pains to establish the girl's "slovenliness and untidiness," by stage business as well as direct comment: she "roughly scrambled together her profuse little mane of hair," she quickly washes cups left over from supper, wears an old and torn jacket, rips a torn piece of lace from the hem of her petticoat, and tosses it on her dressing table.

These actions seem familiar and attractive to her husband; presumably he doesn't take her seriously.

Page 209: The scene with the postman (cf. "My Last Duchess" on text pages 206-207). Also see the passage of commentary at the end of the first section of the story on text page 212.

Pages 209-210: The behavior with the earrings suggests not only her all too simple pleasure in things, to say nothing of her flirtatiousness, her enjoyment of its danger, but also some sort of social pretentiousness: she is behaving above herself, imitating what she takes to be the manners of a fashionable person. Lawrence saves her for us by making her laugh at herself.

Page 210: In the scene beginning "Whiston had made the fire burn, so he came to look for her," Lawrence demonstrates a masterly handling of characterization and action:

1. The simplest kind of story-telling suspense: Will Whiston see the earrings? He has two chances, by the way. But of course he won't see them; he doesn't notice her enough. Her "intent blue eyes" probably express her desire to *force* his attention.
2. The paragraph beginning "He did not see much" (text, p. 210) is an important cue to the reader, helping to establish his feelings toward Whiston. (cf. text, p. 208: "He was a shapely young fellow," etc.) Lawrence is establishing Whiston's goodness, simplicity, *naturalness* (the last as opposed to his wife and Adams)–details that are necessary to control our response to his brutal rage in the last scene of the story.
3. Whiston's real lack of suspicion until, at breakfast, Elsie tries to provoke him in her silly way: "She was not satisfied. He ought to be more moved." Even then Lawrence emphasizes his "steady strength of fondness" and his knowledge of her weakness for foolish lying. His anger comes gradually and with some cause. But we are to realize that in this part of the scene Lawrence is expressing what he

considers to be a lack or failure in their relationship; the wife *is* silly, but the fact is that the husband *ought* to be more moved, more aware of her as a person with emotional as well as sensuous needs. He ought to have noticed her when she became serious.

4. Note again the lift in the narrative or dramatic tension that comes with Whiston's comment on the verse (text, p. 211). Also, how easily she turns him aside by her remark on the stocking sent the year before, telling the lesser delinquency or transgression to distract attention from the greater. Whiston's simplicity has an important effect on the feelings with which we come up to the final scene.
5. Note the theatricality of Elsie's behavior (text, p. 212, the stage directions and comments on the speeches) when she "reveals" her "assignation" with Adams. But notice also Whiston's stupid and cruel response when (in a rare moment of naturalness) she explains why she went with Adams.
6. "Queer how he drew away from her, cut her off from him" (text, p. 212) is Lawrence's own comment on the situation, telling his reader what to notice and how to take it.
7. Note the distinction in their responses to the quarrel (text, p. 212): she forgets being "aggrieved" by wearing the earrings and being "self-conscious, and quite brilliantly winsome" to the baker and other tradespeople, too, no doubt. But Whiston went all day with "his heart all the while anxious for her, yearning for surety, and kept tense by not getting it."

An analysis of that sort, which shows Lawrence's command of his medium, might well be continued through the whole of "The White Stocking." Indeed, perhaps it ought to be; a sense of "story" is not at all a bad thing for students to take away from an English class.

However, it may be fairer to Lawrence and to his spirit to build class activity around, or let it rise from, the analytical or commentary passages that are strung through the narrative. The most important of these are the following:

1. Text, p. 211: the paragraph beginning "Presently he rose, and went to wash himself. . . ."
   a. The details of his body, some of which echo those in the scene (text, p. 210) where Whiston is seen "crouched before the fire blowing the coals."
   b. The implied comparison of Elsie to a bird in a hunter's hand.
   c. The mixture of feelings aroused in Elsie just by the sight of her husband's neck.
2. Text, pages 214, 215, 216, 218: The descriptions of Elsie dancing with Sam Adams, especially the last two. The passages constitute an extraordinary sexual fantasy or a fantasy on a sexual theme. (Maybe

the second act prelude of *Tristan und Isolde* should be played.) The opposition between Elsie-Adams and Elsie-Whiston is evident enough, but what exactly does it amount to? On that question, note details of this sort:

a. Text, p. 215: In Elsie's heart is "a little tightness, like conscience."

b. Text, p. 216: She goes for the second dance "almost helplessly, carried along with him, unwilling yet delighted."

c. Text, p. 216: "She was not aware of what she was doing, only a little grain of resistant trouble was in her."

d. Text, pp. 216 and 217: Elsie's feelings about Whiston: "his slim young man's figure real and enduring before her," "something shapely about him as he sat, about his knees and his distinct figure, that she clung to," his "enduring form."

If Whiston is better for Elsie than Adams is—and everything in the story says that he is—the question is why. Compare the curious a-sexuality of the walk home, and the scene in the fields (text, p. 219).

3. In the light of this material, it seems plausible to say that the plot of "The White Stocking" rises from Lawrence's conviction that there is some inadequacy in the marriage of Elsie and Whiston. This is perhaps explained in the passage (text, p. 211) on their handling of the white stocking (that is, of Elsie's needs) and on her getting used to her husband and relaxing in the liberty she found in marriage. The plot, then, is the events which in fact do resolve the matter of the white stocking. The plot is also all that material that controls our responses to the story and the characters so that, in spite of everything, we are prepared to take a sympathetic view of Elsie and Whiston and their plight.

The resolution of the consequences of the white stocking is accomplished by the scene (beginning text, p. 221), in which Elsie is finally brought or driven to assert *her* self. What, exactly, are they fighting over?

a. Text, p. 223: "And his lust to see her bleed, to break her and destroy her, rose from an old source against her. It carried him. It wanted satisfaction."

b. Text, p. 224: "She felt that now nothing would prevent him if he rose to kill her. She could not pretend to him any more. She was yielded up to him. They both trembled in the balance, unconscious."

But note again the relationship suggested in the very last view of Elsie that we are given (text, p. 224): "tear-stained, swollen face and . . . eyes all forlorn and pathetic . . . she sobbed aloud: 'I never meant—'" And note also Whiston's appearance, especially his *outward* expression of compassion and anguish for Elsie: "My love—my little love—" There appear to have taken place some changes; certainly the tension has dissipated, and emotions are no longer sub-surface. Lawrence has exploded his tense, emotional conflict, and seems masterfully, in this final scene, to be letting the emotion subside—gradually, slowly, and almost sexually. There appears to have taken place with both Whiston and Elsie an emergence of character and a mergence of characters. To be sure, in the most elemental and emotional forces, a love story has taken place. And in its elemental passage we are given a good example of Lawrence's control and of the raw beauty and the erotic charm of Lawrence's writing.

LEDA AND THE SWAN • page 226

PEOPLE DO GOSSIP • page 227

The first poem is a sonnet with two quatrains in the Shakespearian mode and a Petrarchan sestet.

The long dialog (text, p. 226) is intended to amuse, not to inform—or at least to suggest that the informative need not be solemn. Similarly the little poem by Sappho is intended to counter Yeats' somewhat heady romantic classicism.

The two quatrains give a very human and rather violent handling of the myth, against which Yeats plays the sestet with its formal recall of the literary tradition and then the great open question: Did she [Leda] suffer with the knowledge of all that was to happen because of the great god's whim?

I KNEW A WOMAN • page 228

For fullest enjoyment of this lovely poem, the reader may need some familiarity with the great seventeenth-century love and devotional lyrics. But to track down all the allusions to them runs the danger of turning an immediate sensuous experience into a literary one. (Of course, the same might be said of Lawrence's "The White Stocking," or, for that matter, all literature.)

The poem cries to be accompanied by dance or pantomime. But we must not scandalize the unwary. Perhaps a musical accompaniment might be sought.

At any rate, no one should overlook the bravado of lines 22-24:

> Let seed be grass, and grass turn into hay:
> I'm martyr to a motion not my own;
> What's freedom for? To know eternity.

The defiance of time is a convention of the genre. Compare Andrew Marvell, "To His Coy Mistress," line 33 to the end:

Now therefore, while the youthful hue
Sits on thy skin like morning dew,
And while thy willing soul transpires
At every pore with instant fires,
Now let us sport us while we may.
And now like amorous birds of prey,
Rather at once our time devour
Than languish in his slow-chapped power.
Let us roll all our strength and all
Our sweetness up into one ball,
And tear our pleasures with rough strife
Through the iron gates of life;
Thus, though we cannot make our sun
Stand still, yet we will make him run.

LOVE IS MORE THICKER THAN FORGET • page 229

The first and third stanzas consist of simple comparisons built around paired opposites (thick-thin, forget-recall, seldom-frequent, always-never, big-little), at least some of which are associated with the diction of conventional love poems.

The first stanza is based on "more"; the third stanza on "less."

The second and fourth stanzas are also built around a similar comparative-contrast "exercise." Note that "mad and moonly" (line 5, stanza 2) is a rather conventional love association that provokes "sun and sunly" (line 13, stanza 4). The rest of the contrast is a rather obvious juxtaposition between the images of "sea" (stanza 2) and "sky" (stanza 4).

All this information may help to unlock some of the "meaning" in Cummings' word play. Is he simply defining the undefinable, Love?

Some students may be interested in Cummings' unusual syntactical arrangement. Does it add anything to the poem? The ordinary structure of the sentences in lines 6-8 and 13-15 is as follows:

> And love, which is the only thing we know that is deeper than the sea, shall, no less than the sea, always exist.

> And love, which is the only thing we know that is higher than the sky, shall no more die than the sky.

It may well be argued that the compression in the original lines is too great for readers to cope with. On the other hand, for those with a literary turn of ear, there may be some pleasure in working out the puzzle.

But the poem is largely incantatory and should perhaps be left so.

If there are realists in the class, they may find something to say about the following little poem, allegedly composed by Richard Burton in answer to an interview question, "How would you describe Elizabeth?"

"Elizabeth is heather at dawn, the Lady in the Lake, passion and fire, a kitten lost, at times terribly, terribly vulnerable, yet a bead of mercury. Cleopatra, never. Aphrodite, yes! Elizabeth is a down pillow . . . a woman."
There's just a breath of a pause before he whispers, "And I happen to love her . . . very much."

All of that could be taken as a "found" poem, though perhaps not a very good one. A found poem is a collection of words or statements, generally set as prose (though simple lists have also been used), in which a discerning eye can detect some one or more of the physical attributes of poems (rhythm, sometimes even meter, lineation, half-developed figures, evocative details). In this case, the beginnings of a poem might be made simply by setting Burton's phrases one to a line. Might anything else be done to strengthen the appearance of a poem?

UPON JULIA'S CLOTHES • page 229

One of the seventeenth-century lyrics that Roethke is recalling in "I Knew a Woman."

The thing is to make sure that the effect of "Next" in line 4 is not missed, and that "brave Vibration" is fully understood.

Again a nice chance for acting out, and perhaps a less disturbing one than "I Knew a Woman."

MY OEDIPUS COMPLEX • page 230

It's a joke, but a clinically accurate one. It is as if O'Connor asked himself, "Can I invent a story that will dramatize the flow of feelings in the Oedipal situation without drifting into psychopathology?" Once that is seen to be the problem of the story, the given in which it originates, the "improbability" of some of the events is accounted for. But it is still an interesting question how seniors in high school will be able to take the joke and the improbable events.

The story seems to be hilarious for its success–that is, the success of *telling* the joke. The point of view–from the young child's eyes (or tongue, as it were)–paves the way for the credibility of the joke. Would the story have been as interesting or as funny as it is had it been told from the father's or the mother's–or for that matter from Sonny's line of vision? As a matter of fact, why not use these probabilities as departure points for composition experiments? Some students may want to try their hand at this type of writing, and such an activity should certainly help them relate to and understand more intimately the problems of point of view than would a class discussion or lecture on techniques. (See the note preceding the comments for Cluster 2, *Talks,* page T-26.)

Notes on Critical Writing

> He [Ezra Pound] was a marvelous critic because he didn't try to turn you into an imitation of himself. He tried to see what you were trying to do.
>
> —T. S. Eliot

> Never trust the artist, trust the tale. The proper function of the critic is to save the tale from the artist who created it.
>
> —D. H. Lawrence

If we take the Eliot and Lawrence quotations as the touchstones of a critical writing program, a general procedure suggests itself, one that perhaps obliges us to modify traditional ideas of critical writing. Pound grants that a world exists outside himself and sets out to explore it while preserving its integrity. Lawrence warns that critics may be trapped into thinking that artistic integrity lies in the artist's intentions: The "tale," he cautions, is the only basis of criticism. True criticism, which lies in trying to see not only what an artist is trying to do but also how well he does it, demands a very personal commitment between critic and work. There is little merit, then, at the high school level in asking students to model their critical writing on the works of professional critics—not, at least, until students have sharpened their own critical sensibilities and are reasonably articulate.

It is a basic tenet of this series that meaningful reading can take place only when a reader responds actively to the work he is reading. The same must also be said of meaningful writing, and especially of what is generally called "critical writing." We take "critical writing" to mean the setting down of one's response to a work in such a way as to make manifest to another person precisely what that response is. Critical writing attempts to convey a perception of a work and to articulate the inferences drawn from it. Above all, it attempts to understand someone else's writing. This is perhaps its only real difference from what is loosely called "creative writing," or writing that comes from the student's own experiences and perceptions.

The basic problem facing the teacher of critical writing lies in Eliot's assessment of Pound's critical genius. Pound avoids the mistake of seeing others merely as an imitation of himself: The implication is that student-critics must also be able to see beyond themselves—to recognize what is unique in others. This statement implies getting involved in another's creative process. In teaching critical writing skills, then, it might be best first to talk of critical "responses," and to allow student responses to manifest themselves in any number of ways, verbal and nonverbal: in drama, dance, sculpture, and music, in the making of films and collages, and in translating one genre into another. At all points in these activities you might well encourage discussion by asking questions that bring students back to the works themselves. One useful line of questioning appears in the dialog in the General Introduction (*Talks,* pages T-6–T-12). Specific lines of questioning for each activity suggested above appear in the individual paradigms, such as collage-making (*Talks,* page T-20).

Once the student has developed patterns of response, he moves quite easily into writing down his responses. But unless he reacts readily, he cannot be expected to enjoy the relatively systematic ordering of ideas demanded by critical writing.

Perhaps the most common form of critical writing is the critical essay. This need not be a rigid form; it may be highly analytic or highly personal, formal or informal. (Compare the political writings of Alsop and Buchwald or the essays of Henry James and D. H. Lawrence.) There is ample room for a personal style. With beginning writers, it is perhaps best to assign topics only after a good deal of general discussion and only after each student has had the chance to select and narrow his own topic. As a rule, critical writing in which two works are compared seems the easiest to do. Comparison invites all sorts of critical possibilities and lays the foundation for later intensive examination of a single work or of a single concept in several works.

To be successful, criticism must be rooted in strong convictions. Thus it seems best to start with questions that ask the student to respond emotionally to a work or to related works. From the very beginning of the assignment, stress the importance of a variety of questions–that is, point out that each set of works evokes its own peculiar set of questions.

One good way to start is for the student to ask himself: "How does this work affect me?" As he goes through the work, he should be encouraged to think aloud to himself and let certain words trigger associations, both from within the work and from his own personal experience. If he jots down his musings, he'll find that he has an inventory of ideas that can be pruned and shaped into a unified essay.

If the student sees more points of contrast than comparison, he should say so and receive your support. Whatever his position, he should be aware that he is trying to convince someone of the validity of his interpretation.

The point of such patterns of self-questioning is not to make literary critics out of the student, but to make each one more aware of the critical powers he is already using. Students use the same lines of questioning when they compare movies, television shows, and hit songs. Once they realize that fact, working with the written word in the classroom becomes less formidable.

A book must be an ice-axe to break the sea frozen inside us.

—Franz Kafka[19]

Cluster 9: pages 240-279

FROST AT MIDNIGHT • page 241

This is a reflective and meditative poem, a feeling poem. And if it is used for a whole class, the best approach may be to read it aloud, slowly and carefully, giving plenty of time for taking in the sentences as they come.

The structure of the poem is associational: the fluttering fire on the grate reminds Coleridge of his feelings as a schoolboy at Christ's Hospital, and these lead him to consider, in human sympathy, what he expects or hopes for his own child, then nearly a year and a half old. It may be worth noting that the loneliness of school seems to have remained with Coleridge a long time. He was sent to Christ's Hospital after the death of his father, in 1782, when he was ten; and he didn't see his home again until he was eighteen.

"Frost at Midnight" is a powerful poem. As E. M. Forster said of *The Rime of the Ancient Mariner,* it "speaks to the heart of a reader, and it was to the heart that it was written, and otherwise it would not have been written." "Frost at Midnight" speaks *from* the heart too, from the poor, torn, and—in so many ways—empty heart of Coleridge; though indeed students need not know anything at all about him, however much they may feel his despair.

Because of the poem's charged emotion and the poet's sentiment, it may be useful to anticipate the "ice-axe's" cutting too deep with some students and provoking a defensive response—rejection, mockery, a refusal to "understand" the poem. Whether we say such students are more vulnerable or more sensitive, we must acknowledge the human validity of their plight and flight, even while we hope and try to control the anxiety it may produce in us. For other students—those who are either able to deal with the feelings stimulated by the poem or who are less open to its attack—a whole range of individual activities may be admitted, some of which, by the way, may have to be largely private.

Some students may be interested in investigating Coleridge's circumstances when he was writing the poem (February, 1798). On February 19, 1798, for instance, Coleridge was finishing his autobiographical letters to Thomas Poole, with one describing life at Christ's Hospital. And generally speaking, the letters from, say, December through March have interesting evidence of what it meant to be Coleridge. The standard edition of the letters is that edited by Earl Leslie Griggs, *The Collected Letters of Samuel Taylor Coleridge* (4 volumes, Oxford, 1956-1959). The edition done by Ernest Hartley Coleridge (2 volumes, Oxford, 1895) is incomplete but can be used. The standard biographies are those of E. K. Chambers (Oxford, 1938) and J. D. Campbell (London and New York, 1894).

Wordsworth's "Tintern Abbey," which was composed in April, 1798, seems to have some tonal and even verbal reminiscences of "Frost at Midnight." Some students may be interested in working them out.

Students with less developed literary curiosities may be able to find something to do or say in response to or as an extension of Coleridge's expression of homesickness, of paternal dreams, of an extremely high valuation of Nature, which is not quite identical with the natural world. Concerning homesickness and paternal dreams, students might compare this selection with Willie Morris' "Leaving" (text, p. 265), Frank Conroy's "Nights Away from Home" (text, p. 129), and Philip Roth's "In Exile" (text, p. 96).

At the manifest and rational center of "Frost at Midnight" is the question: Why civilization and its discontents? And if a general class discussion is possible, that is a great place to begin it.

MY PAPA'S WALTZ • page 243

Most students today will be able to say what it is the man sees himself-as-boy clinging to, besides his father's shirt. So a good reaching move might be to ask what this comment by Norman O. Brown has to do with the poem:

> America then and now symbolizes to me a climate, spiritual and cultural, in which it is possible to think about what it would mean to bring an end to that nightmare which is history.[20]

"Then" refers to Brown's "flight from England to the United States in 1936," about which he says:

> I left my motherland and my mother and father and did not see them again for more than 25 years. There was no quarrel or rupture but there was a deep and permanent separation.[21]

As a matter of fact, the quotations from Brown might be put on the board as a cue for discussion, into which the poem could be drawn. Note that the quotations might be said to apply to "Frost at Midnight," too.

THE SKY IS GRAY • page 244

Obviously the question following the story (text, p. 264) emphasizes its political content, which is massive enough, though perhaps not exactly defined. *Just what does Mama mean by "man"?* In the altercation between the Young Student and the Preacher in Section VII (text, p. 251), the reader's support (though perhaps not all his sympathy) no doubt goes to the Student. The Preacher loses his temper; the Student follows principles of non-violence. Questioning, such as the Student indulges himself with, is regarded as an absolute Good in contemporary cultures that derive from the eighteenth-century Enlightenment and nineteenth-century philosophical scepticism. The Student speaks for emancipation and the intellect and for action; the Preacher, for superstition, conformity, and the narrowing attitudes of the small town—the rural stasis.

But note that there are two groups who may reject the Young Student. One is the Activists, who will say that questioning is not enough. (It should be noted that the Student leans at least verbally in the direction of the Activist: "Words mean nothing. Action is the only thing. Doing. That's the only thing" (text, p. 255). Few hardcore activists, however, would have reacted passively to the Preacher's slap.) The other is the Silent Majority, who will say, simply, that the Student is getting out of line, that he probably is paying too much attention to books ("theory") and forgetting the way things are in reality, and that he lacks respect for authority.

Both positions are probably outside the terms of the story. That does not make any less probable their occurrence among its effects. And if the story is used, there seems to be neither reason nor way to stop the arguments it may cause. They may be tempered, however, by offering Section IX, the episode with the old white couple, as an attempted resolution, or if not that, at least as a scene that balances the one in Section VII. Some students will give the story a totally contemporary reading and see an irony in the balance between the two scenes. To see the old white couple's actions toward Mama and her son as a mixture of condescension and fear is perhaps an interpretation that results from the grim course of events since the confrontation at the bridge in Selma in 1965.

The political issues in the story may, perhaps, be clarified by discussing the following passage in connection with them. It is about the Freedom Farm Cooperative, founded by Mrs. Fannie Lou Hamer of Ruleville, Mississippi.

> The cooperative has purchased and now cultivates 40 acres of greens, peanuts, okra, corn and squash. It has an option on 640 additional acres, and hopes to raise the money for them by January. In the meantime, it has bought, renovated and rented three houses to poor families.
>
> The cooperative also administers a "pig bank." As Mrs. Hamer describes the bank: "Every person who receives a pig has to sign a pig agreement—not to sell him or trade him off, but to keep that pig, and from each litter, give two back to the bank. . . . And you know," she goes on, "for the first time, we are giving to whites, poor whites."[22]

Of course Lucy Jefferson (text, p. 157) and Jesus Lopez (text, p. 168) are also relevant to "The Sky Is Gray," and "Cheerleader" (text, p. 105) is perhaps not irrelevant. And what about Gwendolyn Brooks' "We Real Cool" (text, p. 109) and Don Lee's "But He Was Cool" (text, p. 108) and "Hero" (text, p. 320)?

"The Sky Is Gray" can also be viewed psychologically and sociologically as a particularly forceful illustration of Moynihan's thesis about the matriarchal organization of the black family in the United States: the absent father (here, away in the army), the mother as the central bearer of standards and the reality principle, other females in an extended family as supporters of the mother. For this theme, note especially Section IV (text, pp. 247-248), the narrator's summary of the contest with the mother over his pet birds, which she needs to use for food. The opening paragraph of the section is an obvious attempt to make the memory credible. But how necessary is it to the story as a story?

Incidentally, the black family is not the only one in the U. S. that has a matriarchal structure. Another one is suggested by the vaudeville and nightclub jokes about the Jewish Mom, to say nothing of Philip Roth's *Portnoy's Complaint,* from which we have printed an excerpt (see text, p. 96). Roth's book may be the culmination of all such jokes. In earlier folklore and fiction (cf. James T. Farrell's novels about Studs Lonigan and, especially, Danny O'Neill), the Irish family had the same structure and served the same mythic purpose that Moynihan has now given the black family. And the *sociological* literature—at least that of a popular sort—is not empty of references to the absent white suburban father and his absorption by his job in the city. Inevitably, any discussion of matriarchy will lead to the NOW! movement—i.e., Woman's Lib. Of course, in light of Woman's Lib, Mama's final statement to her son—"You a man"—might take on some new and rather interesting interpretations.

LEAVING • page 265

Leaving home—the sense of lost roots—is an important, persistent theme in American literature. After all, we are all—excepting the American Indians—descendants of people who left or were taken from their native lands. "Leaving" can, therefore, speak to some deep-seated feelings and memories in all of us. (Cf. Thomas Wolfe's novel, *You Can't Go Home Again.*)

Morris' leaving is more than a geographical movement. Looking back, he realizes that when he got on the bus in Vicksburg to go to Austin, he was beginning a process of emancipation from the culture and society of his people. (It is the culture and society whose dark underside is represented in "The Sky Is Gray"; see text page 244.) The central expression of this fact is in the paragraph beginning, "Yet more than being desperately in love . . ." and the one following (text, p. 266). Read aloud to seniors, these paragraphs might well stimulate some writing. A panel discussion of their import is another possibility. The mobility of the school population should be kept in mind.

MY FATHER MOVED THROUGH DOOMS OF LOVE • page 269

This passage may aid in thinking about the poem:

> The peculiarities of emotional arousal explain the role of emotions in artistic creativity as well as the hazard of excessive rationality in the artist's work. Cold reasoning invariably produces predictable associations. Emotional excitation mobilizes remote memories and increases the chance of producing original associations.
>
> —Pavel V. Simonov[23]

And that passage may be a reminder of Wordsworth's famous view (which is perhaps less than a definition) of "all good poetry" as "the spontaneous overflow of powerful feelings"; "it takes its origin from emotion recollected in tranquility: the emotion is contemplated till, by a species of re-action, the tranquility gradually disappears, and an emotion, kindred to that which was before the subject of contemplation, is gradually produced, and does itself actually exist in the mind."

Although it may be argued that Wordsworth's statement has easily stood the test of time and is indeed applicable to "all good poetry," we should also be aware of a *modern* sentiment concerning the poet's creative process: Samuel Beckett's Molloy, in something of a parody of Wordsworth, said, "It is in the tranquility of decomposition that I remember the long confused emotion which was my life."[24] Does this statement speak to anything other than to its own tongue-in-cheek? Does it speak to our "Age," especially the post-World-War-II view of the Age, the multi-media global-village view? Does it speak to your students? Jules Feiffer once claimed that he couldn't contemplate and write in tranquility, that in order to create he needed to be within an arm's reach of life's paranoia. So he lives in N. Y. City.

Cummings' poems often are products of a very agile mind's play with language. They are by no means playful, however, nor should they be treated as tricks, done in attention-getting style.

Since the minds of young people are generally plastic and inventive, the best thing may be to let students alone with the poem, to make of it what they will and can. Note that many of their own songs reflect the experiments with language that Joyce, Stein, Cummings, Woolf, and other writers were interested in forty and fifty years ago; so they may get along better with Cummings than we expect. Perhaps your students won't come to know Cummings intellectually, but most likely they will *feel* him. And what they feel, they like.

Students will surely sense that "my father moved through dooms of love" is about a child's sense of his father, not so much what the poet knows he feels about his father, as the words that come to him when he is feeling his father's presence. If some obscure passages elude them, no matter—or not much. What is important is that Cummings' language and the imaginations of students be allowed to work together freely, even loosely. "Dooms of love," for example, "depths of height," "griefs of joy," and the other paradoxical phrases (in technical terminology, most of them are oxymorons) have extraordinary evocative force, the effect of which may well be weakened by attempts at explication or glossing. On the other hand, the effect of "dooms" may, for some, be increased by consulting a dictionary.

DO NOT GO GENTLE INTO THAT GOOD NIGHT • page 271

This may be a hard poem for seniors to deal with, not so much because of its meaning as because of its motive. A complaint about the speaker's lack of feeling is predictable, and maybe not unjustified. There is also the more literary question: Why not "go gentle" into death, if it can be equated with "that good night"? The question may be especially troublesome to students acquainted with hymnal tradition or familiar (for whatever reason) with burial services.

Very likely the talk on this problem will go on quite a while. At some point, though, perhaps as soon as arguments and attitudes begin to be repeated, Donne's "Death

Be Not Proud" can be added to the material of discussion. For "Do not go gentle" is really quite a literary poem; in a way—a very moving way—it is a commentary on the meek acceptability of the whole churchly response to dying, in all its wide range from, for example, "Unveil thy bosom, faithful tomb" to "Nearer my God to thee" to Donne's great and witty sonnet. Thomas is speaking as a modern man, who finds it quite impossible to say, and not on poetic grounds alone:

> Death was full urgent with thee, Sister dear,
> And startling was his speed;—
> Brief pain, then languor till thy end came near—
> Such was the path decreed,
> The hurried road
> To lead thy soul from earth to thine own God's abode.

The above verses are from Newman's "Consolations in Bereavement," and of course it is the like of them that may make it hard for students to handle the feeling contained in Thomas' poem.

Then, too, the contemporaneity of Thomas' sentiment, "Rage, rage against the dying of the light," is likely to appeal to many students. In that case, a good composite of attitudes to study might be the following: Bontemps' "A Summer Tragedy" (text, p. 301), Tennyson's "Ulysses" (text, p. 310), Auden's "The Unknown Citizen" (text, p. 315), and this poem. Such a discussion may even lead tangentially to "The Sky Is Gray" (text, p. 244) and to its conflict between the Student, who should be most inclined to "rage," and the Preacher, who it appears should have "gently" accepted the "dying light."

I STAND HERE IRONING • page 272

No modern high school student will have any trouble identifying the speaker in the second paragraph, who cues the mother's soliloquy. But they may well feel somewhat uneasy, wondering what this nineteen-year-old girl (with the perhaps somewhat excessively forlorn childhood) could have done to bring her to the attention of a college counselor. She is sometimes uncommunicative, and she has (in counselor language) overreacted to the atom bomb, using it as an excuse to avoid meeting the responsibility of taking examinations. But one gathers from the mother's account, which of course may be self-serving—like the Duke's in "My Last Duchess" (text, p. 206)—that the girl is finding satisfaction (the beginnings of a successful neurotic pattern?) with her peers and in her life style. What are we to infer about the daughter and her "satisfaction" from the one time we see her in action? Note the mother's last plea to the counselor, the representative of social norms:

> Let her be. So all that is in her will not bloom—but in how many does it? There is still enough left to live by. Only help her to know—help make it so there is cause for her to know that she is more than this dress on the ironing-board, helpless before the iron.

Certainly, the anguish and honesty of this mother's plea is enough to make one wonder—in these days of efficiency, in-put, out-put, etc. (See "Albert's Bridge," pages 47-48 of the text; just think of Fitch as the counselor!)—but who *needs* the counseling, the student or the counselor? But that's an old query that runs along this line: "Why are the mad placed behind bars? To protect us from them or to protect them from us?" (For more on that same tangent, see Donald Barthelme's "Game" on page 336 of the text, and the Birdbrains cartoon immediately following it on page 341 of the text.)

Imagining and then dramatizing the scene that led up to the counselor's phone call may help students work through the implications and feelings in the story.

We can satiate ourselves with food. But repeated contacts with works of art strengthen our enjoyment of these creations of human genius instead of weakening it. To become satiated with such creations signifies that one does not have a genuine interest in art but only a primitive need for distraction, that one does not have a thirst to unravel nature's enigmas but only a Philistine curiosity and, to push the observation further, that one does not seek love in the human sense but only sexual excitation for which a toad's nerve centers are sufficient.

—Pavel V. Simonov[25]

Cluster 10: pages 280-315

A GOOD MAN IS HARD TO FIND • page 282

One hesitates to kill the effect of a story or poem by premature or overmuch analysis. But "A Good Man Is Hard to Find" is a powerful story and ought to be able to survive a good deal. Students may well be able to enjoy its effects (their sensations) even in the face of discussion of its elements.

The names of the children in "A Good Man" (John Wesley, for the Methodist reformer; June Star, for Hollywood) constitute a nice shorthand way of suggesting the cultural limits of the characters. Then there is the unpleasant behavior of the children. And we must also remember their mother in her silence, her slacks, and her kerchief, the sad little gentilities of the grandmother, the awful conversation in the car, the grim scene in the country restaurant. Flannery O'Connor is unrelenting in the destruction of her characters, who have been dead—she seems to want us to feel—long before they meet the Misfit. (This may be a dangerous line to pursue very far, since Miss O'Connor, who is securely hidden in her distance from the material, does not overtly suggest that her characters are in any way *unusual.* A good question to ask might be as follows: Is this the average, normal, and healthy all-American family out for its usual ride in the country? Answers to that question might prove interesting.)

Where is the true horror of "A Good Man Is Hard to Find"? Where but in the way Flannery O'Connor herself, in her story that so strictly controls our feelings, prevents or stifles our response to what the Misfit is doing to the family? Even in the terrible moment when Bailey is being led off to the woods to be shot (for his shirt, we will discover) and at "the dark edge" turns and "supporting himself against a gray naked pine trunk" shouts, "I'll be back in a minute, Momma, wait on me!"—even then we are not allowed to do much more than record the intense pathos of the speech. The terror or horror is almost all dissolved in his mother's speech, "Come back this instant"—as to a child. Her speech is as dreadful as her son's, but since she has been so lovingly portrayed as silly and foolish, and therefore the cause of all their disaster, all we really hear in the speech is its ludicrous inappropriateness. She calls to her son "in a tragic voice," but again our response is cut off as we are hurried on to her terribly inadequate speech to the Misfit, "I just know you're a good man. . . . You're not a bit common."

Perhaps the best way to make sure that Flannery O'Connor's intention is caught by everyone is to imagine a staging of the last scene of the short story. Particular attention must be paid to the stage business: for example, the grandmother straightens her poor hat and the brim comes off, which is close to a vaudeville effect. What are the mother and June Star doing?

The Misfit is, among other things, a religious maniac, a product of the dark Augustinian-Calvinist sense of sin that so fascinated Flannery O'Connor. It is unlikely that high school seniors will see him that way, nor is there any reason they should. But if they talk about his "up-tightness" (or whatever word is current), they will be getting what is essential in him for the story.

A Note on the Final Scene

Some critics-teachers-scholars have made a case out of that final episode–after the Grandmother is shot and the Misfit cleans his glasses, his eyes "red-rimmed and pale and defenseless-looking" (has he shed a tear or two?)–and have gone on record to say that the Misfit's final actions show (symbolize?) *hope,* as seen in his *compassionate* rebuke to Bobby Lee, "Shut up, Bobby Lee. . . . It's no real pleasure in life" (text, p. 294).

Whether this final scene is actually symbolic of a Beckettian sense of illusionary but necessary hope, or whether it is mere irony, it should be considered in the light of the Misfit's pose. After all, he hasn't changed *that* much (if at all) in the end; he remains a fanatic, out to convert a series of Grandmothers. And one of the horrible visions of that final scene may be in our own response to the Misfit's final estimate of Grandmother: "She would of been a good woman . . . if it had been somebody there to shoot her every minute of her life." The horror here is perhaps not so much in the speech itself as it is in the affirmative way several of us will catch ourselves nodding our heads! Surely there will be students in every class who might react similarly and who might agree that Grandmother certainly deserved what she got. What does this say of Miss O'Connor's control of our emotions? Of the story's humor? And of ourselves? Is there any hope in all this? Or is it all, including our response, futile and absurd?

Student Film-Making

Film-making gives students an opportunity to be creative in a medium that is more familiar to them than any other; after all, they have been television-watchers and moviegoers for most of their lives.

Students frequently film their productions with 8-millimeter or super-8 home movie outfits. Some schools own their own equipment; others may be fortunate enough to have closed-circuit TV and taping machines. No matter what your resources, you'll find that student film-making can be unusually rewarding—pedagogically speaking. Even if your students never get around to the actual filming of their scenario, they are almost sure to feel that the preparation for filming—the writing of a script, the planning of lighting effects, the designing of costumes, blocking out of scenes, and rehearsing the several scenes themselves—is a worthwhile, meaningful exercise. If nothing else, film-making will help make students more discriminating movie-goers.

The following publications may prove helpful for teachers who wish to provide opportunities for students to produce their own films:

Audiovisual Instruction. Published by the Department of Audiovisual Instruction, N.E.A. (See especially the issues of February, 1969, and January, 1970.)

Broadbeck, Emile, *Handbook of Basic Motion-Picture Techniques.* Chilton, 1966.

Manoogian, Haig P., *Film-Maker's Art.* Basic Books, 1966.

Media and Methods. Media and Methods Institute, Inc., Philadelphia, Pennsylvania.

Stephenson, Ralph and Debrix, J. R., *The Cinema as Art.* Penguin, Pelican, 1965.

WILLIAM AND EMILY • page 295

AFTER LONG SILENCE • page 296

Students are probably going to "like" the Masters poem more than the Yeats. After all, being young, they are not likely to grasp all that Yeats has compressed into "the supreme theme of Art and Song," or, that is, into the last two lines of the poem. Nor perhaps should they, or be asked to. (By the way, how would your students read those lines?)

Why not just read the two poems aloud some time, at the end of a period, for example? The reader doesn't particularly have to be one of the "good" sort, just a person who seems likely to get a little of Yeats' feeling. "William and Emily" shouldn't offer any problem, except in maintaining the breath through the long second sentence.

THE BLACK AND WHITE • page 298

The play is short enough to put on in a class reading. Students should do the casting and directing. If the audience should be another grade, would the reading differ?

A SUMMER TRAGEDY • page 301

This story can go with "The Little Man" (text, p. 313) and "The Unknown Citizen" (text, p. 315). Used that way, it might be especially valuable for students who want to make the poems, especially the second one, part of an attack on the welfare state or big government.

And again, this story may best be used to enrich a topic or unit in social studies.

You Have Seen Their Faces, with text by Erskine Caldwell and photographs by Margaret Bourke-White, is a famous book about the society and countryside that are the cause of the events in Bontemps' story. It was originally published by Viking in 1937. An even more famous book of the same sort is *Let Us Now Praise Famous Men,* with text by James Agee and photographs by Walker Evans, published in 1941, reprinted in 1960.

NOBODY LOSES ALL THE TIME • page 309

THE LITTLE MAN • page 313

THE UNKNOWN CITIZEN • page 315

"The Little Man" and "The Unknown Citizen" might be read together if or when topics like modern man, the industrial state, or contemporary individualism are being discussed in history or social studies classes.

There is a chance that some students may be interested in extending the list of appropriate bourgeois activities or in acting out those that are given.

The original title of Parra's poem "The Little Man" is *El Pequeno Burgués,* which makes one think that the translation misses a very important implication in the title: "Little man" is "bourgeois," and it is in that concern for material appearances and respectability that he is mediocre or "little."

Note that in "The Unknown Citizen" the reference to "his employers Fudge Motors Inc." makes it clear that the poem is not a criticism of "authoritarian socialism/communism."

"Was he free? Was he happy?" The answer may not be so clear as Auden (and folk brought up on Orwell) may think, and the questions make us think of Jesus Lopez in "Oh, Did I Have Dreams!" (text, p. 168). There may be some students who will want to argue that case in writing, in a panel discussion, maybe even in debate. If the class doesn't want to hear them out (which would not be surprising), they might put their argument on tape for use later, when circumstances are favorable to them, or to be listened to alone by different students when they become interested.

A monolog by JS/07/M/378 might be made by students for use with Tennyson's "Ulysses" (text, p. 310).

The last three chapters (XI-XIII) of Orwell's *The Road to Wigan* have material and ideas that are related to or comment on the apparent theme of Auden's poem.

"nobody loses all the time" could very well serve as a final comment on the anonymity of Auden's "Citizen" and Parra's "The Little Man."

The Durrenmatt statement (text, p. 310) fits well here, especially in any discussion of the Cummings poem and the Bontemps short story, "A Summer Tragedy" (text, p. 301), and Auden's "The Unknown Citizen" (text, p. 315). All three pieces deal with a common topic, Death. However, the tone in the Cummings' and Auden's poems is certainly less solemn and tragic (although it may be as serious) than Bontemp's treatment of death. Does *distance,* as Durrenmatt contends, have anything to do with the tragic or comic effect of a selection? If we understand that question, then perhaps we can also better understand Flannery O'Connor's control of our responses to "A Good Man Is Hard to Find" (text, p. 282).

ULYSSES • page 310

The first five lines of the poem make an unusual speech for god-like Odysseus, sacker of cities. Odysseus of the nimble wits he was in Helen's eyes, and master of intrigue and stratagem. Zeus called him admirable, the wisest man alive, and so he was to Athene too. Surely that Odysseus of Homer would be sensible enough to admit that he too is aged, that the "unequal laws" he complains of are of his own making, and that "these barren crags" are the very ones he was always weeping for on remote Ozygia, after Calypso of the lovely locks had ceased to please him, and his beloved Ithaca and wise Penelope filled all his longing thoughts. Tennyson's peevish and dissatisfied Ulysses is not much like the resourceful and cunning Odysseus of the classic tradition, whose caution and wariness, whose civilized intelligence provoked the admiration of even bright-eyed Athene.

So far as that goes, Tennyson's Ulysses, when he gets going about following knowledge ". . . like a sinking star / Beyond the utmost bound of human thought," is nothing like Homer's Odysseus. In Tennyson he is close to Faust or at least to a Victorian scientific optimist. The changes in the myth that are made in the heroic part of the poem, to convert it to Tennyson's personal use, admittedly reflect his feelings after the death of his friend Arthur Hallam, especially his "need of going forward and braving the struggle of life." The view of Ithaca and its people may be a kind of unconscious representation of the view a cultivated Victorian intellectual took of the men who were building industrial England.

The sketch of Ulysses in the first seventeen lines of the poem is worth discussing. Looked at coldly, the details give us a Ulysses who is discontented, hedonistic, and honor-seeking in a rather vulgar and boastful way. Given the present climate of opinion among students, a conversation between Telemachus and Penelope might point up Tennyson's achievement. In Book I of the *Odyssey* Zeus and Athene discuss the plight of Ulysses, whom they both respect and admire. What would they think, listening to *this* speech?

In the past, the final section of the poem—Ulysses' philosophy, it might be called—has been much admired as an expression of the high romance of the questing intellectual adventure. What do contemporary students think of it? How many of them can stand the last two or three lines?

Can any students catch the playing fields of Eton, the imperialist ethic, in Ulysses' dream of himself and his men, off all alone following knowledge to the farthest bounds of Empire? Of course, students might easily Americanize and contemporize this speech by putting it into the mouths of a few well-known politicians.

Those questions suggest our present attitude toward "Ulysses"; the wary reader may suspect that such attitudes are as they are because we now don't much like what we have been used to doing with the poem. And as we look at the questions, we wonder if they really are right for our purposes. It is not the attitude toward the poem that we distrust, but rather the form of the questions, which are rather directive, rather insistent, as if we were out to chivvy everyone around to our view.

Something can be saved of our intention, perhaps, if it is clearly accepted—in a felt way—that what is set forth here, in this guide, is but one understanding among several, out of whose interplay the classroom finally is composed. The others are the writer's, the teacher's, and the students', the latter, of course, being various, though not unorganizable. It is vital that the last, the students' interests and understanding, be at the center of things, and at the beginning too. The students must talk to one another, not to the teacher or to one another through the teacher, and they must talk about what is of interest to them.

Leavis speaks of the "felt life" of the book, a phrase which calls attention to the dynamic, living tissue of responses that reading creates. The master question for us teachers is always how we can enter that system, enter it in all its living intransigence, not as an intruder but as a participator. With "Ulysses," for example, some students may respond immediately and most strongly to the image of Ulysses' circumstances that is suggested in the first lines; others will be caught by the peculiarity of the phrase "matched with an aged wife"; some may simply lose themselves in the sound and image of "Far on the ringing plains of windy Troy." Others may not feel the poem until they come to the famous lines about knowledge. Others may be captured by Ulysses' somewhat dismissive, and not a little proprietary, attitude toward Telemachus—of which they may know something in their own lives. Others may remember the great opening lines of the sestet of "Leda and the Swan" (text, p. 226) and then simply luxuriate in the Trojan story. Or finally, others may begin to feel the poem only in its last paragraph, which, when they have divested it of its Victorian content, will make them dream of voyages to the far places of the earth.

But of course even that list of possible responses is overly schematic, too orderly for reality. In a real classroom those responses may appear in combination or partially or not at all. Yet it is with them and their like that we must do our work, trying to arrange things so that, out of the interplay among those students who have found some interest in a work, there will develop (be developed?) an increase in awareness of what they know, an increase in control of what they know.

In the case of "Ulysses," then, a beginning may be found in nothing more substantial than a teacher's report of his response to the poem, not how he read it, but what he felt as he was reading it. Of course that opening will work only if the report is real, if it is, in fact, the teacher's own response, not what he regards as the correct literary one.

> Ultimately the person, even the child, must choose for himself. Nobody can choose for him too often, for this itself enfeebles him, cutting his self-trust, and confusing his *ability* to perceive his own internal delight in the experience, his own impulses, judgments, and feelings, and to differentiate them from the interiorized standards of others.
>
> —Abraham Maslow[26]

> We conceived of an English class as the place in school where one could come closest to learning what it is to be human. We thought that there students and teachers could attend most closely to and be most open about the very texture of their lives. . . . In the English class one [can step] back just far enough to be able to examine his life and the life of those around him insofar as it [is] embodied in the language community in which he [lives] and in the literary contributions that continually [enable] him to see his situation from slightly different perspectives.
>
> —R. C. Townsend[27]

Cluster 11: pages 316-341

If war is too important to be left to the generals, perhaps poems about war are too important for teaching. At any rate, it is hard to know how to intrude on these poems—if, indeed, one should. The ideal, we all know, would be for students to come to these pieces quite on their own; as a matter of fact, we wonder if the make-up of the section may not catch some as (or if) they leaf through the book. Or perhaps some students will choose some point about war for a paper. Or a history class may be doing one or another of the world wars, or the Victorian collapse, or the rise of the United States as an imperial power, or some similar topic. Or some student reading "Ulysses" (text, p. 310) may respond "critically" to the lines:

> And drunk delight of battle with my peers
> Far on the ringing plains of windy Troy.

In any such circumstances, there may be a chance to call attention to the poems in this section.

A connection between the lines from "Ulysses" and Yeats' "An Irish Airman Foresees His Death" (text, p. 331) is obvious, and both are a comment on the high Victorian spirit, as is Bernard Fall's "An End of Empire" (text, p. 321). Here is another passage to consider:*

> On July 1, 1916, thirteen divisions of British infantry, knowing nothing but how to stay shoulder to shoulder and not to flinch, almost every man a volunteer, went over the top. The first wave was mowed down; the second wave lapped a little further and seethed to a stop;

the third passed through that writhing debris and was itself lashed from the German trenches; the fourth trod on bodies all the way across no man's land. By nightfall sixty thousand men lay in that small compass, one in every three of them stone dead. It was the greatest day's blood-letting any army anywhere had ever suffered, or ever would. General [Sir Douglas] Haig, however, was not convinced that one more push would not do it.

On July 14, by a kind of accident, a night attack succeeded where the battering had failed, and a gap was torn in the German line. This was the very thing the British army had been created for–this was the moment to realize the dream. This was the moment to loose the cavalry! After some difficulty in picking their way over the riven ground, three divisions of cavalry launched themselves with bugles chanting and lances glancing in the sunlight into the cornfields behind the German trenches. It was the summation of all the best thinking, the culmination, the martial orgasm. They were cut down by machine guns slashing through the corn–the horse flesh and the men–before they had gone from the gallop to the charge. On September 15 General Haig reluctantly tried tanks. They failed and proved his point [about tanks]. The last attack on the Somme came on November 13. In four months General Haig had advanced, at the maximum point, five miles. For this he had spent four hundred and twenty thousand men; the French, fighting rather incidentally on his right at the same time, had lost two hundred thousand men. . . .

–John Lord, *Duty, Honor, Empire*[28]

"Western Wind" (text, p. 317), "Thinking of My Brothers" (text, p. 318), "Pity for Prisoners" (text, p. 318), and "Ten Days Leave" (text, p. 330) are all poems about homesickness or the loneliness of soldiers. "Mother, the wardrobe is full of infantrymen" (text, p. 319), "Hero" (text, p. 320), and the Cummings sequence (text, pp. 325-329) touch on fear, disillusion, despair, and rejection of the heroic line.

"An Irish Airman Foresees His Death" (text, p. 331) is a mad and romantic expression of the heroic spirit that every other selection in this cluster is speaking against. The poem was written for Major Robert Gregory, the son of Yeats' good friend Lady Gregory, wife of Sir William Gregory, an Anglo-Irish landowner. Major Gregory was killed over Italy in January, 1918. "In Memory of Major Robert Gregory" gives quite a different impression of the man; and it may be supposed that in "An Irish Airman," especially in lines 3-6, Yeats was expressing some of his own yearning toward aristocratic *noblesse.* In spite of the poem's stance, in spite of what is being said, this is certainly the most complex work in the section, far more so even than the Barker sonnets (text, pp. 332-333), for all their syntactical trickiness. And in its impure way, Yeats' poem is probably also the most beautiful.

In *The Right Response,* Sidney Bolt quotes one of his students, who said of the "Airman": "Nobody in that frame of mind should be allowed within a mile of an expensive aircraft." Is that an appropriate or acceptable response?

The three sonnets by George Barker (text, pp. 332-333) are about "War and the pity of War," as Wilfred Owen said of his own work in the famous preface to the collection of poems he wrote during his time in the British Expeditionary Force, between October 22, 1915, and November 4, 1918, when he was killed at the Sambre Canal.

In Appollinaire's "Cornflower" (text, p. 334) those students who have grown callous from watching this "best-covered of all wars" on TV may catch some of the absolute horror and shock that the slaughter in World War I caused in the civilized world. "Worried" (text, p. 335) can be taken as a comment on present tendencies to accept if not defend, the slaughter of our own times; although it should be noted that this poem was written in the 16th century.

Donald Barthelme's "Game" (text, p. 336) is the story of two "military" souls lost (?) in the belly of a missile silo. If some students reject the story as being "insane" and its author likewise, let them consider the following incident from the Vietnam war, against which should be juxtaposed the "insanity" of "Game":

Scene: A deserted but well-secured (i.e., captured) village of empty thatch huts somewhere in South Vietnam.

Characters:

A commissioned officer.
A special wind-resistant Zippo lighter.
A T.V. interviewer.

Dialog:

T. V. Interviewer (holding the mike in the face of the officer; worried about the lighting):

What are you doing now, Sir?

Officer (holding his Zippo lighter to the roof of a hut; calmly, logically, coolly):

Son, we must destroy this village in order to save it!

(He winks.)

Fade Out

That bit of reality was extracted from a late 1960's live and in-color TV news vignette. It might well serve if "Game" is charged as "insane" or "unreal."

Would "Game" be an interesting vehicle for a student pantomime? If so, suggest using three characters (Narrator, Shotwell, and the Missile) with tapes as background (either music or the actual text). Also, now that Barthelme has presented the narrator's point of view, what about Shotwell's? Or the missile's?

Again, the story might be a launching pad for interesting, creative writing. (See *Talks,* page T-57.)

Students might like to consider the following quotation in the light of both the narrator and his friend, Shotwell:

> I was classified a fighting man after completing basic training in October of 1965. The biggest change in my makeup was that I could hold more beer.
>
> —Larry Hughes, *You Can See a Lot Standing Under a Flare in the Republic of Vietnam.*[29]

Barthelme's "Game" affords an opportunity for students to engage in improvisational drama. The following references may prove helpful:

Barnfield, Gabriel, *Creative Drama in the Schools.* Hart Publishing Company, 1969.

Spolin, Viola, *Improvisation for the Theatre.* Northwestern University Press, 1963.

Somewhat in spite of what was said earlier about not intruding on the students' experience of the works in this cluster, we can see possibilities for productive, constructive work growing out of this collection. It might well make a script for presentation with film, slides, music. Or a book could be made that would include additional poems and appropriate supporting pictures. In both cases considerable planning for visual effect would be necessary, and of course there would have to be discussion to get as close as possible to accurate perceptions of the intentions of the works.

The two prose pieces may have to be treated separately, though it would be desirable if the multi-media presentation could include vignettes of their essential scenes. Certainly they might be acted out independently. But trying to include them would involve some rather complex planning. And it cannot be stated too often that the value of projects such as these lies less in the product than in the conversation and discussion that students must engage in because of their working together.

> It is important in discussion of students' writing to keep emphasizing that the main point is not the finished work, the poem or whatever, but rather how the experience helps the student.
>
> —Joseph Featherstone[30]

Cluster 12: pages 342-381

THE BRUTE • page 344

Forgetting what they watch every night on television, students who read this lively sketch may complain that it is not "real" or that it is "exaggerated." They can be reminded of whatever series Lucille Ball is doing, some of the old Honeymooners sketches, "Hogan's Heroes," or even things like "Beverly Hillbillies" and "Green Acres." The point here, by the way, would not be to take lofty glances at television and the mass media, but simply to raise a question about "living" characters, "lifelike" situations, and the other staples of textbook judicial criticism, which students have been conditioned to think meaningful.

As a matter of fact, if taste-building is what is wanted, a nice exercise can be built around casting the play with known performers from television or the movies, perhaps even with fellow students who are said to be good at acting. To take Madame Popov as an example, the choice of actress depends to some extent on whether the play is seen as low comedy, close to slapstick, or as a farcical sort of work.

A director who views the play as low comedy would probably have his mind fixed on the great duel scene (beginning on text page 354), and he would want an actress who could milk that episode for everything in it and more. On the other hand, the director who feels the play to be essentially farce, though pretty broad, would have his attention all on Smirnov's long speech about women (text, pp. 350-351), which he would want to have taken with some seriousness. In that speech, Smirnov says, "Present company excepted" and then goes on to give a pretty fair description of Madame Popov, at least as she has appeared up to then. Should it be said straight or sarcastically? Note that the whole speech starts the change in Madame Popov's behavior (not her "character") that motivates Smirnov's "What a woman!" The fact should not be lost sight of that both the duel and the speech on women are in the *same* play, presumably without violating the unity of its effect.

Students may want to experiment with the staging and reading of the very opening of the play and the speeches down to the ringing of the bell (text, p. 345). Here are some questions or problems worth class consideration:

> In how many ways can Madame Popov hold the photograph and stare at it? What is Luka doing before his first line?
>
> How should Luka say the sentences, in his first speech, about the cook and the cat? In practice, this is a problem of pointing "to catch

berries" and "with the birds" so that there will be a joke (a *double entendre*), but Luka shouldn't be aware of it.

What is the pitch of Madame Popov's voice in her first speech? How can the speech be kept more or less sincere, yet at the same time suggest that, by the end of the play, she will have returned to the world? What is she doing with the photograph as she talks?

How can Madame Popov react to the various items that Luka mentions in his second speech?

What is the use of the pause indicated before "raiment of death"? What is Luka doing to motivate Madama Popov's "Are you listening, Luka?" And note the later stage direction, "Suddenly a titter breaks through her tears." Note the conclusion of her speech.

THE DARLING • page 357

It is (perhaps unfortunately) easy to feel that Chekhov, playing the detached, Olympian observer (with some social superiority?), finds the Darling interesting simply because she knows so little, has so little understanding. We feel in his stance perhaps a little too much of the city man being amused by the behavior of provincial folk. And no doubt Olga's simple pretension to "opinions" about art, business, and science are amusing, since as she herself sees, in a delicious insight, that she is really a hen wanting the cock (text, p. 359). In the end, though, Chekhov won't allow us amusement only; he makes us reject the distance that he has created. For too much of our own lives is contained in the Darling's. If we have any doubts about that, Chekhov's questions (text, p. 365) "Why? But who knows why?" are there to settle them. In answers (if any) to those questions is contained the seriousness of all great comedy.

How else does Chekhov control our understanding of the Darling so that, however, much we may laugh at her, we always take her seriously?

De Maupassant's "A Simple Heart" treats the same sort of character but with more sentiment, with no leaven of humor. Some students may be interested in comparing their feelings as they read the two stories.

THE PRIVY COUNCILLOR • page 367

Chekhov once said, or is supposed to have said, that after a writer has finished a work he should go back and cut it by a half or so, and then he should cut the remainder by a good deal. How much can be cut from "The Privy Councillor"? What must be kept?

If it is somewhat difficult to see the comedy in the sadness or mournfulness of "The Darling," it may be next to impossible to catch the various tragedies (or anyway half-tragedies) that occur or are suggested in "The Privy Councillor." For, as acting out its scenes will make clear, the basic mode of the story is close to the unrelieved farce of *The Brute.* And the choice of a boy as a narrator makes the author's "rhetorical" problem a rather tricky one. (See discussion of Frank O'Connor's rhetorical stance in "My Oedipus Complex" on page T-56 of *Talks.*) The same experiment with point of view might well apply here: What would a student do with the Uncle as narrator?)

The Boy's behavior in the final departure scene with his Uncle (text, pp. 380-381) is not unlike the summary account of Olga's relationship with Sasha at the end of "The Darling" (text, pp. 365-366). And both scenes may suffice to illustrate the intent of the dialog on text, p. 381, in which both the Editor and the Literary Sort can finally meet on a point: "Tragedy and farce–at the same time."

T-78

Is life divided up into sections? No, I say
Then why have subjects at school?
Teach living at school,
And living means understanding,
And understanding is all.

Therefore I say throw out your timetables,
Throw away your rulers and bring in teachers
Comprehensives* without rules and [tracks] and exams (one way),
Comprehensives with laughter and learning and communication
(two way).
That's what I want, man,
But it costs bread and that's needed for our next nuclear
submarine.

The key to life is flexibility
Then you can breathe
Not suffocate and die.

Don't get panarchy
I don't want anarchy
Just sympathy
For the pimply.

–17-year-old student[31]

*Comprehensives: high schools, not examinations

Cluster 13: pages 382-395

The epigraph on page T-78 was submitted in a competition sponsored by *The Observer* (London) in December, 1967. Children were asked to describe "The school that I'd like." The response amounted to some half-million words, innumerable charts, collages, architectural or pseudo-architectural drawings.

The Observer is a generally Tory newspaper, and one would expect the children among its "readership" to be not merely middle-class but also well-conditioned or acclimated to the school-culture, the kind of children who go into a school as of right, so to speak, feeling comfortable that they belong to it and, more important, that it belongs to them. It is surprising, then, to read Edward Blishen's summary impression of the pieces submitted in the competition:

> . . . An enormous, remarkably good-humored, earnest, frequently passionate and, at best, highly intelligent plea for a new order in our schools. No one who read through all those words could have believed for one moment that here were children seizing an opportunity to cock a snook at the *status quo,* for the sake of the snook. Juvenile irresponsibility was awfully hard to find. The radical note that was so pervasive was astonishingly steady, reasonable and supported by instances. I have never read so much that was so full of complaints and criticisms, of schemes for imaginative innovation, and yet that was, as a whole, so very sober.

A selection of the submissions is gathered in *The School That I'd Like* (Penguin Books, 1969), with an introduction by Edward Blishen.*

Like the pieces in Cluster 10 (text, pp. 280-316), these in Cluster 13 had also better be left to make their own way. A possible, as well as interesting route, however, would be to develop a book for which they might be a beginning. The first concern on such a project would be to decide just what it is that is common to them all, and whether there are significant sub-groups to make sections. A second concern would be to decide for whom the book is planned—that is, what readers. A third concern might be whether editorial comment is needed, not in the abstract, but quite concretely: Are there comments or explanations that must (considering the audience or the compilers' feelings) be made? A fourth concern would involve design and publication. Obviously this is not an assignment that will be done over a weekend or even "two weeks from today." It had better be thought of as quite a long-term job, which will be done sporadically, and indeed may never be finished.

*Excerpts from *The School That I'd Like* appear in the paperback volume "A Good Life," edited by Alan C. Purves. *A Good Life* is one of the volumes in the theme sequence of this literature series.

FINDING OUT ABOUT YOUR STUDENTS

"Start where they are!" You have read and heard that injunction many times. But . . . where are they?

One thing is sure: Where they are is not in the reading test scores, guidance office records, teachers' grade books, or teachers' lounge gossip. To find out where your particular students are, you will probably need to do the locating yourself. And what better help than a map—a map made up of these coordinates:

- —your students' interests
- —the preconceptions of literature they hold
- —what they like to read
- —the readiness with which they become involved in what they read
- —their habitual approach to a book, particularly a literature book

To aid you in drawing your map, we offer here five questionnaires for you to adapt, duplicate, and use as you see fit.* However, a word of caution: None of the questionnaires has any right or wrong answers; none of the questionnaires functions legitimately as an instrument for marking or grading students. Each is intended solely to help you find out *who* your students are and *where* they are.

Each is also intended to help *them* find out who *you* are. Thus, it might be useful for you, too, to respond to the questions on each questionnaire. We strongly urge you to share your findings with the class. We realize however, that to do so all at one session might be unwise.

One caution: It would be better *not* to use these questionnaires at all, than to use them—or have students regard them—as inquisitorial forms.

Interest Measure

The aim of this first questionnaire is to help you ascertain your students' interests, their likes and dislikes.

*The measurement package for this literature series provides still other ways of helping find out where your students are—what their attitudes are, how adept they are at interpreting what they read, how able they are to reason about their interpretations. Also in that package are instruments to measure such specific capabilities as the ability to recognize different voices, tones, and moods; the ability to understand metaphor; the ability to discern and understand a story line. And in the administrative manual included in the measurement package is an indepth discussion about assigning and evaluating student writing.

INTERESTS QUESTIONNAIRE

Please answer the following questions as fully and as honestly as you can. There are no right or wrong answers.

1. What are your favorite television programs?____________________

2. What kinds of television programs do you dislike?____________________

3. What kinds of books do you dislike?____________________

4. What kinds of books do you especially like?____________________

5. What books have you read a second time?____________________

6. What do you like to do in your spare time?____________________

7. What kinds of movies do you make a special effort to see?____________________

8. What hobbies and/or special interests do you have?____________________

9. Do you enjoy athletics?____________________
   a. Principally as a participant?____________________
   b. Principally as a spectator?____________________
   c. What sports do you like best?____________________

10. What kind of work do you hope to do after you leave high school or college?____________________

If you wish, you might ask *why* after most of the questions in the INTERESTS QUESTIONNAIRE, for students' justification of their interests and tastes are as important to know about as are the interests and tastes themselves. On the other hand, you may feel that to ask *why* at this point would unduly intimidate the students. If so, you can pursue such inquiry as all share the results. They must be shared to be of value.

Preconception Measure

This questionnaire seeks to help ascertain what sorts of preconceptions people hold about what they read and what they see on television and in the movies. Again, to be of optimum value, the findings must be shared. What are *your* preconceptions? Students should know.

QUESTIONNAIRE

In general, what do you think about stories, poems, plays, television programs, and movies? Please answer the following questions briefly but honestly.

1. a. What do you think plays should be about? ________________

   ____

   b. Is there *any* subject that you think plays should not deal with?

   ____

2. a. Do you think that some words are more poetic than others? ____

   ____

   b. If you answered *yes* to item 2a, please give one or two examples of what you consider poetic words. ________________

3. a. Do you think that certain kinds of scenes (those showing brutality, for instance) should be removed before a motion picture is released for public viewing? ________________

   b. If you answered *yes* to item 3a, what kinds of scenes would you rule out? ________________

   ____

4. Do you think it a waste of time for a person to write about places he has visited and things he has done? ________________

   ____

5. Do you agree with those who say that writers are different—they look different and behave differently—from other people? ________

   ____

6. Does any one line in the following pairs of lines seem to you to be better for use in a poem? You may choose only one in each pair. Or you may choose both. Or you may choose neither line. Put an X in the appropriate space(s) provided.

   _____ a. When golden day is done
   _____ b. Two potted plants at the windowledge
   _____ c. Neither of the lines above

   . . .

   _____ d. Barricades hammered into place
   _____ e. Home, no more home to me, whither must I wander?
   _____ f. Neither of the lines above

   . . .

   _____ g. One scene as I bow to pour her coffee
   _____ h. Earth has not anything to show more fair
   _____ i. Neither of the lines above

7. Do you think it a waste of time for a person to write about the ideas and opinions he holds and the principles he stands for? ______

____

8. Do you think that writing about two men in a secret missile base would make a more interesting or a less interesting story than writing about a young person on a first date? ______________

____

9. In general, do you think stories and plays should have a message, a deeper meaning? ______________________________

____

10. Should the performers on television and in the movies be handsomer or more beautiful than people in real life? ______________

____

11. Do you think that there is any subject that poems should NOT be written about? ______________________________

____

12. Do you think that writers and actors and other artists have looser morals than other people? ______________________

____

13. Which of the following do you consider a *trustworthy* source of knowledge and information? (You may *X* more than one item.)

_____ a. Books	_____ e. Radio
_____ b. TV	_____ f. Newspapers
_____ c. Motion pictures	_____ g. Billboards
_____ d. Magazines	_____ h. Other people

The items making up this preconception measure—intentionally put in random order—get at the degrees to which your students have indulged in stereotyping kinds of literature, other kinds of communications media, and the persons involved in them. Generally speaking, a positive response to the yes-no items (1b, 2a, 3a, 4, 5, 7, 9, 10, 11, 12) indicate some degree of prejudice and stereotypical thinking. Most of such prejudice, however, would seem to be relatively harmless, for it is out of such kinds of prejudice that taste evolves.

On the other hand, a student who responds negatively to all of the yes-no items is perhaps just as biased as one who answers all of them positively.

In examining individual responses to the questions, you can discover why certain poems, plays, essays, and stories might well draw negative responses from students and why others might well draw decidedly positive responses.

As far as item 6 is concerned, students who reject items b, d, and g (all are from poems) may balk at reading contemporary poetry. You might well explore such bias with those students. Similarly, you will do well to examine responses to items 1a, 2b, 3b, 8, and 13, to identify instances of overly stereotyped reactions, and perhaps to devise ways of broadening students' outlook.

Finally, students who set writers, actors, and other artists apart might think that literature itself is not—and is not to be regarded as—related to real life. Here, too, is a stereotype worthy of exploration with your students.

Reading Interests Measure

The following questionnaire is much more limited in scope than the *Interests Measure.* This one seeks to identify students' reading interests.

READING INTERESTS QUESTIONNAIRE

A. Imagine that a motion picture studio has offered to make a movie about anything and starring anyone. Your class can order any kind of movie it wants. As spokesman for the class, all you have to do is to fill out this form:

1. What should the film be about?____________________
____
2. What part of the world should the film concern?__________
____
3. What sort of people should the film be about?____________
____
4. What actors would you want in the film?________________
____
5. What sort of story should the film tell?________________
____

B. Imagine that the following conditions exist: A publisher has offered to produce a book just for your class. It is a book that any writer of the class's choice would write and one that would be about anything the class wanted. As spokesman for the class, all you have to do, is to fill in the following blanks:

1. Is there any particular writer you would like to have write the book? (You can choose any writer, living or dead.)____________
____
2. What sort of book would it be (novel, a volume of short stories, a full-length play, a volume of one-act plays, a comic book, a book of poems, a book of songs, other?)________________
____
3. Should the book be about real or fictitious people?__________
____
4. If the book is a story or a play, where would you have it take place?____________________________
____
When? ____________________________

5. What sort of things would happen (funny, sad, exciting, mysterious, ordinary)? ____________________

____

____

____

To analyze students' responses to the items on this questionnaire is not difficult. A quick reading of student replies and a noting of students' special interests and aversions can result in your gaining a clear sense of what sorts of things you can confidently ask students–individuals, as well as the class as a whole–to do later. With this information you know whom to ask to do what on a class project and whom not to ask to do creative or routine jobs.

Making a group profile can become a useful project for both you and your students. Simply count the number of students responding positively to each item, and calculate what percentage of the whole that number represents. Accompanying this report might be a sample of the types of work liked and disliked. With this information, you and the class might be able to talk out whatever infatuations, aversions, strong prejudices all of you have: why they seem to prefer one kind of movie to another, for example, or why so few want to read love stories, or why so many watch (or go to) Westerns that star one particular actor. In addition, information obtained from this questionnaire can help you develop materials, and devise projects and other class activities that are likely to be more successful than might otherwise be the case. Knowing that most of your students say they dislike poetry, for example, provides some hints about (1) the sorts of value questions to raise about class reading and (2) what poems to suggest for individual reading and responding.

Involvement Measure

The following questionnaire represents one effective way of finding out (1) how readily your students become involved in what they read and (2) what capacities they have for reading various kinds of literary works.

QUESTIONNAIRE

There are no right or wrong answers to the questions below. Your answers should be thoughtful and honest.

1. While reading a short story or a novel, have you ever thought of yourself as one of the characters?
   If so, give an example. That is, give the character's name and/or the title of the book or story. ____________________

   ____

2. Have you ever met someone, only to feel that he/she was like a character in a play or movie that you had seen or in a story you had read? ____________________

   ____

3. a. When you read—particularly when you read a story or a play—do you ever make a mental picture of the setting? ________________
____
____
____

b. If so, is that mental picture like some actual place you have seen? Often? ________ Sometimes? ________ Seldom? ________ Never? ________

4. a. In doing something or going somewhere, have you ever felt that you have had the experience before, only to realize that that first experience occurred in something you had seen in the movies or on TV or read about? ________________

b. If so, give an example. ________________
____
____

5. When reading a story, do you ever imagine that the characters in it look like people you know? ________________
Often? ________ Sometimes? ________ Seldom? ________
Never? ________

6. Do you ever feel that people you see in TV dramas or in the movies are real people and not actors playing their roles? ________________
Often? ________ Sometimes? ________ Seldom? ________
Never? ________

7. When reading, have you ever said to yourself, "Something like this happened to me"? ________________
Often? ________ Sometimes? ________ Seldom? ________
Never? ________

Each of the seven questions asks the student to indicate how he usually relates to the books and stories he has read and the movies and television shows he has seen. Some students will no doubt indicate their general lack of involvement; many, on the other hand, will answer some of the questions positively. Neither response, of course, is wrong or right. Yet if you see from a student's responses that he gets overly involved in what he reads, you and the student might explore his many connections. On the other hand, if you find a student who remains aloof, you might want to build on that aloofness toward developing in the student a sense of critical distance. Both are established critical approaches, and discussion of responses to the questionnaire can prove fascinating.

Critical Approach Measure

The following questionnaire seeks to identify the characteristic ways in which students approach the reading of poems, plays, stories, and essays. Some students might consistently look for a message; others might seem constantly to ask how the works relate to their own personal experience. Still others might feel it vitally important to know why and under what conditions a writer developed the works under consideration.

To administer this critical approach measure, use a selection that students have probably not read. Ask students to read the work and then to turn to the questionnaire. You should fill it out too.

QUESTIONNAIRE

After reading a story, poem, play, essay, or whatever, people often ask themselves certain questions they consider important to their understanding of what they've read. Which questions do you think are important to ask about the selection you've just read? Follow these steps:

A: Below are twenty questions that might well be asked about the selection. Choose the FIVE questions that you think are the most important ones to ask, and put an *X* in the space provided in front of each one. (YOU ARE NOT EXPECTED TO ANSWER THOSE QUESTIONS.)

B: From the FIVE questions you have *X'd*, choose the ONE that you consider MOST IMPORTANT to ask, and write the figure *5* in front of the *X*.

C: Put the figure *4* in front of the *X'd* question you consider second in importance. Put a *3* in front of the *X'd* question that is third in importance, a *2* in front of the *X'd* question that you consider fourth in importance and a *1* in front of the question you consider least important to ask.

(REMEMBER: YOU ARE NOT EXPECTED TO ANSWER THE QUESTIONS THEMSELVES.)

_____ 1. Is there any one part of the selection that explains the whole selection?
_____ 2. What does the selection tell me about people I know?
_____ 3. What metaphors (or comparisons) or other figurative devices are in this selection?
_____ 4. Is there anything in the selection that has a hidden meaning?
_____ 5. How is the way the selection is written related to what it's about?
_____ 6. Is the selection well written?
_____ 7. What kind of piece of writing is this selection? Is it like any other piece of writing I know?
_____ 8. Are any of the people in the selection like people I know? Are any of the situations like situations I've been in?
_____ 9. What happens in this selection?
_____ 10. Is this selection about important things? Is it worth my time?
_____ 11. Does the selection tell me anything about people or the world in general?

______ 12. Does the writer use words or sentences differently from the way people usually use them

______ 13. How can we explain the way the people behave in this selection?

______ 14. How is the selection organized?

______ 15. Is there a lesson to be learned from this selection?

______ 16. Is this a proper thing for people to write about?

______ 17. When was the selection written? Should I know something about the writer?

______ 18. Does the selection succeed in getting me involved or is it just so-so?

______ 19. What emotions does the selection arouse in me?

______ 20. What does the writer think about what he is writing about? What is his attitude?

To analyze and interpret the information this questionnaire gives is not a difficult task. First try to ascertain whether there is a class trend. On an unused questionnaire, simply put down the numerical total each question receives. The question with the highest number will, then, be the one that is most significant for the class. There will probably be four or five that many will choose and an equal number that almost nobody will choose. It may be, for instance, that questions of feeling (items 18 and 19) are most popular, and that questions of form (items 3, 12, 14) are least frequently chosen. Other patterns among the questions might emerge—patterns like these:

Questions of personal involvement: 8, 16, 19
Questions of description: 3, 5, 7, 9, 12, 14, 17, 20
Questions of meaning and interpretation: 1, 2, 4, 11, 13, 15
Questions of value: 6, 10, 18
Questions of form and technique: 1, 3, 5, 6, 7, 12, 14
Questions of character and action: 2, 8, 9, 11, 13
Personal responses: 2, 8, 10, 15, 16, 18, 19
Interest in background: 7, 17, 20
Interest in theme: 4, 10, 11, 13, 15

This critical approach measure can provide both the starting point and focus for encouraging students to explore their responses and for encouraging students to broaden their outlooks. That is, you first ask students to consider this question: "Why do you ask that?" Second, you ask students to consider this question: "What if you asked this?" The first question asks the student to amplify his response; it leads him to a more precise statement of his response. The second question encourages the student to take an imaginative leap into another way of looking at things. Both promote learning and knowing.

If the questionnaire responses of the class as a whole reveal a preferred set of questions, you might first ask the "why" question and then the "what if" question.

If responses seem divided between two sets of questions, you might divide the class into groups according to the similarity of responses. In each group, present the "why" and "what if" questions and let students explore their responses. Then bring the two groups together for a class dialog.

If no discernable pattern appears in the questionnaire responses, you might well note the preferences of individual students and then encourage a variety of dialogs. If, for example, one student who is habitually silent had indicated that he considered the question about a moral (item 15) most important–and if the rest of the class are talking primarily about how a work makes them feel (item 19)–you might get that reticent student involved by asking him a question like this: "What do you think the writer wants you to think about what happened?"

Finally, a fourth effective way to use the information obtained from student responses to this critical approach questionnaire is to talk over each of the questions with the class. Invite students to explain why they chose or rejected each question. Explain why you prefer the questions you prefer. Why did you reject some? Was it the selection? your training? your interest?

NOTES

[1]Edward Blishen, Ed., *The School That I'd Like* (Harmondsworth, Middlesex: Penguin Books, Ltd., 1969), p. 7.

[2]Quoted in Sir Alec Clegg, "The Education of John Robinson," *The Listener,* LXXXIV (August 13, 1970).

[3]William Cole, Ed., *Eight Lines and Under* (New York: Macmillan, 1967), p. 35.

[4]*Ibid.,* p. 38.

[5]Alison Lurie, *Real People* (New York: Random House, 1969), pp. 178-179.

[6]*New Society,* XVI (August 13, 1970), p. 216, emphasis added.

[7]A. W. Rowe, "Writing Prose and Verse," *English versus Examinations,* Brian Jackson, Ed. (London: Chatto and Windus, 1965), p. 99.

[8]*Daily Telegraph Magazine* (London), (July 26, 1968), p. 29.

[9]*Ibid.,* (July 12, 1968), p. 16.

[10]Charles A. Reich, "The Greening of America," *The New Yorker,* (September 26, 1970), p. 43.

[11]Excerpt from Eldridge Cleaver's letter of September 15, 1965 (Folsom Prison) to Mrs. Beverly Axelrod, a lawyer who gave him legal assistance, (from *Soul On Ice,* Eldridge Cleaver, New York: Dell, 1968), pp. 150-151.

[12]Jane Thompson, "Turn On, Lay Down, and. . . ," *The High School Revolutionaries,* Marc Libarle and Tom Seligson, Eds. (New York: Random House, 1970), pp. 104-105.

[13]Cole, *op. cit.,* p. 53.

[14]*Ibid.,* p. 128.

[15]*Ibid.,* p. 67.

[16]Caroline Shrodes, "The Scholars and the Anti-Self," *ADE Bulletin,* No. 26 (September, 1970), p. 7.

[17]Jakov Lind, *Counting My Steps* (New York: Macmillan Co., 1969), p. 17.

[18]Debi Ducote, poem in "Focus: Concrete Poetry," *Vieux Carre Courier* (New Orleans), January 29, 1971, p. 6.

[19]Franz Kafka, from a letter to Oskar Pollak.

[20]Norman O. Brown, "Norman O. Brown's Body," *Psychology Today,* IV (August, 1970), p. 45.

[21]*Ibid.*

[22]*New York Times Magazine,* October 11, 1970.

[23]Pavel V. Simonov, "Emotions and Creativity," *Psychology Today,* IV (August, 1970), p. 53.

[24]Samuel Beckett, *Malloy* (New York: Grove Press, 1965).

[25]Simonov, *op. cit.,* p. 54.

[26]Abraham Maslow, *Toward a Psychology of Being* (2nd ed. New York: Litton Educational Publishing Co., 1968), pp. 49-50.

[27]R. C. Townsend, "Training Teachers for an Open Classroom," *College English,* XXI (April, 1970), p. 718.

[28] John Lord, *Duty, Honor, Empire* (New York: Random House, 1970), pp. 317-318.

[29] Larry Hughes, *You Can See a Lot Standing under a Flare in the Republic of Vietnam: My Year at War* (New York: William H. Morrow & Co., 1970), p. 12.

[30] Joseph Featherstone, "Teaching Writing," *The New Republic,* (July 11, 1970), p. 14.

[31] Blishen, *op. cit.,* pp. 19-20.

TEACHER'S NOTES

TEACHER'S NOTES

TEACHER'S NOTES

TEACHER'S NOTES